PRODIGAL CHRIST

PRODIGAL CHRIST

A Parabolic Theology

KENDALL WALSER COX

BAYLOR UNIVERSITY PRESS

Unless otherwise stated, Scripture quotations are from the New Revised Standard Version Bible, copyright 1989, Division of Christian Education of the National Council of the Churches of Christ in the United States of America. Used by permission. All rights reserved.

Cover and book design by Kasey McBeath
Cover image by Bruce Herman, left panel of triptych, "Eucharist," 2003 (oil on wood with gold and silver leaf, 72″ × 144″)

Portions of this material are taken from Kendall Cox, "Parabolic Retelling and Christological Discourse: Julian of Norwich and Karl Barth on the Parable of the Lost Son," in *Reading the Gospels with Karl Barth*, ed. Daniel L. Migliore (Grand Rapids: Eerdmans, 2017), and are used by permission from Wm. B. Eerdmans Publishing Co. Portions of chapter 4 appeared in "The Parable of God: Karl Barth's Christological Interpretation of Luke 15:11–32," *Journal of Reformed Theology* 13 (2019): 215–37, and are used by permission from Brill Academic Publishers.

The Library of Congress has cataloged this book under hardcover ISBN
    978-1-4813-1312-4.
Library of Congress Control Number: 2022940711

For Phinizy,
who taught me the love that says,
"If I might suffer more, I would suffer more."[1]

[1]   These are Jesus' words to Julian. In one passage she recounts, "For the paine was a noble, precious, and wurshipfulle dede done in a time by the working of love. And love was without beginning, is, and shall be without ende. For which love he saide fulle sweetely this word: 'If I might suffer more, I wolde suffer more.' He saide not, 'if it were nedfulle to suffer more' but, 'if I might suffere more.' For though it were not nedfulle, and he might suffer more he wolde" (LT 22.38–43; cf. 22.21–23, ST 12.20).

". . . and a voice said, 'There is one who is good.
There is one who can see all without hating.'"[2]

—Tomas Tranströmer

"But the mother raised her face,
And her face like sunlight shone,
What matters whether evil or good,
Since you have returned, my son."[3]

—Lea Goldberg

"But if I look up and fix my eyes on the aid of the divine mercy,
this happy vision of God soon tempers the bitter vision of
myself. . . . This vision of God is not a little thing. It reveals him
to us. . . . His very nature is to be good, to show mercy always
and to spare."[4]

—Bernard of Clairvaux

[2] Tomas Tranströmer, "In the Nile Delta," in *The Great Enigma: New Collected Poems*, trans. Robin Fulton (New York: New Directions, 2006), 62.

[3] Stanza 14 from Lea Goldberg's poem "The Prodigal Son."

[4] Bernard of Clairvaux, sermon 36 in *On the Song of Songs II*, vol. 3 of *The Works of Bernard of Clairvaux*, trans. Kilian Walsh, O.C.S.O. (Kalamazoo, Mich.: Cistercian, 1983), 179.

CONTENTS

ACKNOWLEDGMENTS

There are many colleagues, friends, loved ones, professors, and mentors without whom this body of work would not be. It began many years ago in the form of doctoral research in the Department of Religious Studies at the University of Virginia (UVA), where I subsequently taught for several years. I am profoundly grateful for my extended time there in an excellent community of scholars who sharpened and supported me.

I am particularly indebted to my advisor, Kevin Hart, for his guidance as I discerned my approach to this topic and for his thorough and charitable feedback all along the way. Kevin was writing his phenomenology of parable as I began my research back in 2011. One of the things I most appreciated about his oversight was his magnanimity in making space for me to explore similar questions differently, from the premises of another theological tradition. The rest of my committee was also invaluable to the process. I am grateful to Larry Bouchard for his perspicacity and compassion. He always had an open door to speak about everything from interpretation theory to my studio art practice to the granular upheaval of life. Larry deepened my understanding of Ricoeur and narrative, and he stretched my reading of New Testament parable. Paul Dafydd Jones assisted my study of Karl Barth in particular, and, without his expansive knowledge of *Church Dogmatics*, setting Barth alongside another major figure would have seemed too daunting a task for me. Tony Spearing was a generous and delightful outside reader. Not being a medievalist myself, I was reliant upon his expertise with respect to Julian and the genre of homiletic *exempla*. I am also indebted in a small but significant way to Tony's wife, Elizabeth, who is one of Julian's translators. Carol Troxell introduced us when I was working for her at New Dominion Bookshop. It was Elizabeth who first confirmed the premise of my interpretation of Julian, which no one had written about at length at the time. That incidental conversation gave me the confidence to venture a more robust thesis.

It was in large part because of Charles Marsh that I found myself at UVA in the first place. We met through his wife, Karen Wright Marsh, and her work with Theological Horizons. The warmth and hospitality of their open home has been a gift to me and many others in the community over the years. I became Charles' research assistant for the Project on Lived Theology and worked for him on Bonhoeffer, among other things. His example and the connections forged through the Project helped keep my academic pursuits grounded in their practical import for a life of faith and action. During and after my degree, I was a fellow in the Institute for Practical Ethics and Public Life, under Jim Childress. Few people have been as steadfast, kind, and materially supportive as Jim as I navigated postgrad work and the job market. Without him, I have no doubt I would not be where I am now. Marcia Day Childress also became a beloved teaching mentor who blessed the messy interdisciplinarity of my interests. I am thankful for the way she opened me up to the wonderful world of the Medical Humanities. Others at UVA to whom I owe special thanks include Jamie Ferreira and Chuck Mathewes. It was an immense privilege to study with them, and they have each been formative in particular ways for my understanding of modern philosophy, theology, and ethics.

The shepherding of my earlier teachers warrants mention as well. Jay Ford and Steve Boyd, my undergraduate Religion professors at Wake Forest University, endured a barrage of earnest questioning during countless office hours and were the first to encourage me to pursue an academic path. Elizabeth DeGaynor, once my high school English teacher and now a theology professor, awoke my awareness of the existential and ethical importance of literature and remains a pedagogical exemplar for me. My childhood pastor, Skip Ryan, engaged my nascent theological mind with a seriousness I took for granted at the time but later realized is rare and admirable.

For their affectionate and vitalizing company along the way, I must thank my brilliant *Doktorschwesters*, namely, Emily Filler, Emily Gravett, Shelli Poe, and Gillian Breckenridge. It was Kait Dugan soliciting a paper on this topic for the Barth Conference in 2015 that made me return to the research in a meaningful way. I still well up with appreciation for that push and for the intervening years of invaluable friendship in which Kait has challenged, sharpened, and encouraged me. Adam Neder is another dear colleague whose care and insight has left its mark on this work as well as my life. I am also grateful to Daniel Migliore, Faye Bodley-Dangelo, Bruce McCormack, and Eric Gregory for being interlocutors around Barth, constructively engaging portions of my research, and producing work that has expanded the trajectory of Barth scholarship. Of the many academic friends and intellectual companions who have made writing, teaching, and conferencing livelier and more bearable during this period, I think especially of Brendan Sammon, Daniel McClain, Christian Amondson, Joshua Ralston, Ken Oakes, Brandy Daniels, Robert Hand, Christy and Chris Yates, and Kathryn and Justin Mutter. Brian Williams, my tireless dean in the Templeton Honors College, has been a gracious supervisor and true friend in carving out time for me to complete what I began so long ago. My colleague and quintessential good neighbor, Kathryn Smith, saw me to the finish line by helping with indexing.

Then there are those outside the academy without whom I could not have undertaken much writing at all given the life transitions that coincided with the start of my postdoctoral fellowship at UVA: my parents, Brenda and Frank Cox, as well as Jennifer Seidel, Eva Avalos, and Mandy Benedict.

I must add a special word of thanks for artist Bruce Herman, whose evocative painting is featured on the cover. These figures form a portion of the left panel of his triptych, "Eucharist." When I met Bruce at an arts conference many years ago, one of the first things we discussed was Karl Barth's fondness for Matthias Grünewald's *Isenheim Altarpiece*, so it is fitting to feature his own work here. Ever since, he has been a guiding presence in my teaching on art and aesthetics. It is an honor to have his stunning figurative painting embody the central image of this book: God's visceral maternal embrace of humankind in Christ.

Finally, the exceptional editorial staff at Baylor University Press has been charitable and accommodating in light of the conditions under which I brought the book to completion, during a pandemic, having moved to a new state, with little childcare, while teaching and administrating. Carey Newman compelled me to radically reimagine the structure of the work at the start. It was like dismantling a patchwork quilt and trying to put it back together otherwise. His editorial wisdom and passion for making a good book inspired me to take this initial risk. Cade Jarrell patiently kept me on course to the end. Jenny Hunt, Kasey McBeath, and everyone else I have encountered at the press have been supportive and indispensable to the project. I am delighted to be wrapping up under Dave Nelson's direction.

My debt of gratitude to these individuals, as well as many who must go unnamed here, reminds me of the extent to which any constructive offering in the world is little more than a mosaic of gifts received, and sometimes scavenged, from others.

Kendall Cox
December 2021
Director of Academic Affairs
Templeton Honors College
Eastern University
St. David's, Pa.

Introduction

"Narrative . . . is really an enlarged act of *naming* that answers
the question, 'Who?'"[1]

—Larry Bouchard

". . . theology should be . . . the telling of a story."[2]

—Karl Barth

Jesus Christ is the prodigal son. This startling claim stands at the heart of Karl
Barth's reading of Luke 15:11–32 in his *Doctrine of Reconciliation*.[3] "After all," he
explains, "the main character in the story is the younger son who leaves his father
and is lost, but returns and is found again" (VI/2, 23). In his "going out and coming in . . . we have a most illuminating parallel to the way trodden by Jesus Christ
in the work of atonement." Barth's christological interpretation of the parable has
been regarded as singularly innovative, more indicative of Barth's general modus
operandi than the meaning of the text itself. But might it make a difference for
our sense of the genuine hermeneutical possibilities of the passage if Barth is
not the only reader who detects a parallel between Christ and the younger son?
There is an obscure yet illuminating precedent for a christological interpretation

---

[1]   Larry Bouchard, *Theater and Integrity: Emptying Selves in Drama, Ethics, and
Religion* (Evanston, Ill.: Northwestern University Press, 2011), 32.
[2]   Letter to Berkouwer, December 10, 1954; see Eberhard Busch, *Karl Barth:
His Life from Letters and Autobiographical Texts*, trans. John Bowden (Philadelphia:
Fortress, 1976), 381, n. 205.
[3]   Barth's christological reading of the parable is located in §64.2 of *Church
Dogmatics IV: The Doctrine of Reconciliation*, 22–23. All in-text citations of Barth
are from Karl Barth, *Church Dogmatics*, ed. and trans. Geoffrey William Bromiley
and Thomas F. Torrance (Edinburgh: T&T Clark, 1956–1975). Henceforth it will
be abbreviated *CD*, referred to by volume title (e.g., *The Doctrine of Reconciliation*),
and/or by volume/part, page (e.g., IV/2, 21).

1

of the parable embedded in the fourteenth-century English anchorite Julian of Norwich's Example of the Lord and Servant in her *Revelations of Divine Love*.[4] Julian's example is an oblique gloss on the Lukan narrative that recasts the figures of the father and son as a "courteous" lord and "ready" servant.[5] She offers her scriptural retelling according to the fourfold of spiritual interpretation and, like Barth, concludes that the fallen servant/son figure is Jesus Christ.[6] Julian's example prefigures his exegesis in remarkable ways, generating surprisingly similar theological claims and highlighting an otherwise overlooked hermeneutical trajectory belonging to the text itself.

The significance of this discovery exceeds an incidental correspondence with Barth; rather, uncovering a precedent in Julian's example indicates that his exegesis may not be indicative of an arbitrary or artificial Christologizing of the story. The literary cogency of the association they draw between Jesus and the prodigal son is apparent when the passage is appropriately contextualized in its encompassing narrative and its structure is coordinated with the referential nexus of Scripture upon which both Julian and Barth draw. The first chapter, "Prodigal Reading," lays some groundwork for an understanding of parable and its interpretation appropriate to Julian's and Barth's capacious theological retellings. Their readings of the parable lead them to claim that, in Julian's words, "God never began to love humankind," because, as Barth maintains, "from all

---

[4]   Julian's two sets of writings go by several names, *Revelations of Divine Love* being one of the most common in English. Sometimes I will use this to reference them taken together. However, most of the citations I use are from Nicholas Watson and Jacqueline Jenkins, eds., *The Writings of Julian of Norwich: "A Vision Showed to a Devout Woman" and "A Revelation of Love"* (University Park: Pennsylvania State University Press, 2006). Following Watson and Jenkins, when referenced separately, the two texts will be called *A Vision* or the Short Text (ST), cited by section (e.g., sec. 12), and *A Revelation* or the Long Text (LT), cited by chapter (e.g., ch. 52) or chapter and line (e.g., 52.1–2). Where no text is indicated, citations are from the Long Text.

[5]   The textual evidence for the claim that the Example of the Lord and Servant is an interpretation of the Parable of the Prodigal Son is fairly submerged. My analysis in chs. 2 and 3 will bring the connection to the surface. I initially commenced the comparison between Julian and Barth strictly on the basis of the structural and thematic similarities between her example and his exegesis. But I became increasingly convinced that, as Denys Turner argues, Julian's example "is clearly intended to be a gloss" on Luke 15:11–32. See Turner, *Julian of Norwich, Theologian* (New Haven: Yale University Press, 2011), 4, 126. Julian's translator Elizabeth Spearing has likewise confirmed in conversation that she reads the passage this way. Her husband Tony Spearing's observation that the example "resembles a New Testament parable" is also suggestive. See A. C. Spearing, introduction to *Revelations of Divine Love*, trans. Elizabeth Spearing (New York: Penguin, 1998), xxviii.

[6]   I will say more about spiritual interpretation in the first chapter and about Julian's interpretation in the third.

eternity" God makes "the being of this other [God's] own being" (*A Revelation* 53.1; *CD* II/2, 121). In light of the prominent role the parable plays in guiding them to such a radical conclusion, I think we are invited to consider parable as an exemplary and enduring theological genre. The story is so theologically fecund for them not simply because of its content. Their creative renderings of it draw attention to the fittingness of the form of parable for christological discourse. They are not merely interpreting a particular parable in an unusual way. They are doing Christology in the mode of parable, or what I will address in the conclusion as "parabolic theology."[7]

Julian and Barth in Conversation

Julian and Barth are admittedly an uncommon pairing. Only a handful of times have I encountered their names alongside one another in the same sentence, and for good reason. They work within markedly different religious milieus, ecclesial traditions, and theological genres. Julian (ca. 1342–ca. 1416) is best known for producing the first extant works written by a woman in the English vernacular.[8] She spent the better portion of her life enclosed in a small anchorage or cell attached to the side of a church in the bustling port city of Norwich, where she became a sought-after spiritual advisor. A contemporary of Chaucer, her writings were hidden, lost, or suppressed for centuries. Once rediscovered, she was primarily studied by contemplatives and medievalists. Only in recent years has Julian received appropriate recognition as a systematic and biblical theologian in her own right.[9] Her rich but extremely compact writings arise from many years of reflection on a series of visions she experienced while meditating on the crucifix during a life-threatening illness for which she had prayed.[10] This has led many to treat her primarily as a mystic or devotional

---

[7]   What I mean by this is explained in ch. 5.

[8]   In her autobiography, *The Book of Margery Kempe*, Margery mentions her visit in 1415 to "an anchoress . . . who was called Dame Julian" (Spearing, introduction to *Revelations of Divine Love*, xi). See *The Book of Margery Kempe*, trans. B. A. Windeatt (Harmondsworth, U.K.: Penguin, 1985), 77. On the nature of the anchoritic life, see Grace Jantzen, *Julian of Norwich: Mystic and Theologian* (New York: Paulist, 2000), 28–33, 48–49.

[9]   See, for example, Denise Baker, *Julian of Norwich's Showings: From Vision to Book* (Princeton: Princeton University Press, 1994); Jantzen, *Julian of Norwich*; Joan Nuth, *Wisdom's Daughter: The Theology of Julian of Norwich* (New York: Crossroad, 1991); and Gillian T. W. Ahlgren, "Julian of Norwich's Theology of *Eros*," *Spiritus: A Journal of Christian Spirituality* 5, no. 1 (2005): 37–53.

[10]   Julian's writing is prompted by a severe illness she undergoes on May 8, 1373, when she is "thirty and a half years old." On what is thought to be her deathbed, as a priest holds up the crucifix for her to meditate upon, all else fades away and the passion

writer. However, Denys Turner rightly regards Julian's Long Text as "one of the great works of medieval theology in any language by an author of either gender," insisting that she should be set among her "medieval peers—Anselm, Bernard of Clairvaux, Bonaventure, Thomas Aquinas."[11]

The Swiss theologian Karl Barth (1886–1968), born more than five centuries after Julian, is widely acknowledged as "the greatest dogmatic theologian since Schleiermacher."[12] A prolific writer, his incomplete, multivolume *Church Dogmatics* alone spans around nine thousand pages. As a post-Enlightenment Reformed thinker, he is skeptical of mysticism and "religious experience"— even if he told his son that he "saw" the plan for his Christology, namely the organization of *CD* IV where we find his interpretation of the parable, in a "dream."[13] There is no reason to believe Barth read a female visionary writer who was little known at the time or could have been influenced by her interaction with the parable.

As the voluminous body of research accruing to each attests, there is an unwieldy amount to be said about them as individual theologians, which makes a substantial introduction to either or a comprehensive comparison between the two impractical. As I will be focusing on their interaction with a well-known

---

of Christ comes to life before Julian's eyes. She beholds what she calls "a revelation of love . . . made in sixteen shewings," which she records in two texts (ST, sec. 1).

[11]   Turner, *Julian of Norwich*, x. Here he is echoing Thomas Merton, who claimed of Julian: "She is one of the greatest English theologians. . . . Actually, in Julian of Norwich, we find an admirable synthesis of mystical experience and theological reflection. . . . In a word, Julian of Norwich gives a coherent and indeed systematically constructed corpus of doctrine, which has only recently begun to be studied as it deserves." Merton, "The English Mystics," in *Mystics and Zen Masters* (New York: Dell, 1961), 140–41.

[12]   Bruce L. McCormack, *Orthodox and Modern: Studies in the Theology of Karl Barth* (Grand Rapids: Baker, 2008), 89.

[13]   Modern and Reformed, Barth appeals more openly to Scripture and reason/ faith than tradition and experience/vision as sources for theological reflection. But, of course, these are false dichotomies. Barth's whole theology is a dialogue with a historical tradition and is, in many ways, supremely occasional. The point is, however, that he does not regard the ecclesial tradition as having the same authoritative status as it would have had for Julian (and tends to have among Catholic theologians), nor would he admit private revelation as a source for doctrine. Interestingly, however, in a letter to his son Christopher (June 2, 1951), Barth tells him he "saw" the plan for his Christology (and the organization of *CD* IV) in a "dream." See Eberhard Busch, *Karl Barth: His Life from Letters and Autobiographical Texts*, trans. John Bowden (Philadelphia: Fortress, 1976), 377. Busch calls the result an "artistic arrangement." This fact—along with Barth's assertion, "God may speak to us through Russian Communism, a flute concerto, a blossoming shrub or a dead dog" (I/1, 55)—thwarts an easy polarization of Julian and Barth with respect to their range of theological resources.

parable, the point of contact between their texts should be accessible and fruitful even without an extensive background in their thought. However, a prefatory word about their writings as well as some of the language I will be using may be helpful, particularly for those who are new to one or both figures. First, it is worth clarifying why I am grouping their interpretations under the category *retelling*. Second, I should account for my approach to Julian as a *visionary* theologian and the decision to downplay the language of "mysticism" otherwise so frequently used to describe her. Third, although he is undeniably a great systematician, in what follows, I will be adopting what has been called a *literary-narratological* approach to Barth's theology, and this warrants explanation.

Retellings

The consonance between Julian's and Barth's interpretations can be difficult to see. While the differences between them will stand out in subsequent chapters, understanding their texts as retellings brings under a common rubric a variety of forms of interaction with the parable, from Julian's loose recasting of the characters in a medieval homiletic tale to Barth's modern critical mode of exegesis as well as his use of the parable as the governing narrative of his Christology.

Despite obvious points of dissimilarity, Julian and Barth have in common that they are both profoundly recursive thinkers who advance their Christologies by retelling a particular parable. The texts under consideration arise from imaginations that are deeply rooted in the repetitive figural narratives and imagery of the Bible. They likewise progress through allusive reiteration. Julian's thought has a "distinctly spiral" shape. In Turner's words, it "moves forward, as one does along a straight line. It constantly returns to the same point, as one does around a circle. The repetition therefore is never identical, for it has always moved on . . . into higher reaches or greater depth."[14] Similarly, George Hunsinger says of Barth's method, "What first appears like repetition turns out on closer inspection to function rather like repetition in sonata form." This is Barth's way of "alluding to themes previously developed while constantly enriching the score with new ideas." As a result, "the more one reads Barth, the more one senses that his use of repetition is never pointless. Rather, it serves as a principle of organization and development within an ever forward spiraling theological whole."[15]

---

[14]   Turner, *Julian of Norwich*, 4.

[15]   George Hunsinger, *How to Read Karl Barth: The Shape of His Theology* (New York: Oxford University Press, 1991), 28. While Barth's theology is systematic or dogmatic, as William Thompson points out, it also has a "meditative form." In fact,

Janet Soskice observes that this generatively repetitive quality is a way of recruiting readers into a movement of thought. Julian's prose attempts to enclose us as humanity is enclosed in Christ, "'folding' the reader into its purposes in a manner that anticipates the fugal treatment of the Trinity in Karl Barth's *Church Dogmatics*."[16] Although neither overtly acknowledges as much, both achieve this participatory force through a multilayered retelling of a particular scriptural narrative, interweaving evocative intertexts along the way, enriching trajectories of meaning with each repetition. In this, they each mirror the parabolic form in different ways.

The narrative form is more apparent in Julian's work, as she rewrites the biblical story in her own terms, reimagining and expanding the drama and dialogue. In her case what needs to be seen is not so much that her example is a literary retelling but that it is also an instance of biblical commentary and constructive theology. Barth's engagement with parable, though it is more explicitly exegetical, is properly considered a kind of retelling as well for a couple of reasons. First, he makes multiple passes over the biblical passage in which he recounts the whole narrative again in light of different intertextual identities. Second, his discrete excursus in §64.2 is only part of the story. Barth also employs the language and structure of the parable pervasively to narrate his Christology and, to a certain extent, his doctrine of the Trinity. Animating the doctrines of justification and sanctification narratively in mirrored terms, "the Lord as Servant" and "the Servant as Lord," Barth recasts the figures in the parable similarly to Julian. Both theologians "reparabolize" the original biblical narrative, bringing it to life again in their own distinctively parabolic or polyvalent discourses.

There are other phrases that might be used for the phenomena of retelling, for example, *Nachleben* ("afterlife"), Reception History, renarration, rewriting, Midrash, or simply allusion, among others. It would be particularly appropriate to regard Julian's and Barth's interpretations as "*biblical* retellings" because they recount a story from the Bible. However, this is a phrase used in the field of Religion and Literature in reference to a specific type of contemporary literary narrative.[17] I am employing "retelling" here in a broader way to indicate any repetition of a biblical story in which that story serves as both form and content. It is

---

he thinks *Church Dogmatics* is "like a continual Transfiguration." See Thompson, *Struggle for Theology's Soul: Contesting Scripture in Christology* (New York: Crossroad Herder, 1996), 103.

[16]   Janet Martin Soskice, *The Kindness of God: Metaphor, Gender, and Religious Language* (Oxford: Oxford University Press, 2007), 131.

[17]   On other ways of describing biblical retellings in fiction, see Emily Olmstead Gravett, *The Literary Phenomenon of Narrative Biblical Retellings* (PhD diss., University of Virginia, 2013). Rarely I will use "renarration" interchangeably with "retelling." The

true, as Barth says, that "it is rare in life to be able to separate form and content," but to speak of Julian's example and Barth's exegesis as "retellings" is to stress that these texts, though interpretive, retain the narrative shape of the parable and generate new meaning.[18] By virtue of reanimating the parabolic form, a "retelling" is inherently constructive and not merely explanatory or illustrative.

Where I specify "*theological* retelling," I am highlighting the way a scriptural narrative is deployed in theologically assertive or systematic ways, according to a "rule of faith," with certain doctrinal commitments already at work, and with a view to the way any given passage corresponds to a larger understanding of the revelation of God in Christ. To "read theologically" is, inherently, to read intertextually and, for Julian and Barth, canonically.[19] When "retelling" appears alongside related terms, such as "interpretation," "reading," "excursus," "exegesis," or "account," this does not suggest they are interchangeable but only highlights that the texts to which they apply function on different levels. Interaction with the parable has a number of distinct though interrelated dimensions—for example, the strictly exegetical (attending to what the text says), the hermeneutical (attempting to explain what it means, then and now), and the theologically constructive (generating claims about God by situating the parable in its comprehensive literary and historical context). In an ordinary sense, all such dimensions count as a kind of retelling. However, my use of this language is specifically meant to bring out that quality of Julian's and Barth's texts by which they are not merely discourses *about* the meaning of the parable but rather, in recounting the parable itself, retain the divalence of the parabolic form, repeating both its form and its content in a nonidentical way.

Visionary Example, Exemplary Vision

Julian describes her Example of the Lord and Servant as a "shewing" or "showing," sometimes translated "vision" or "revelation," and this raises important questions about how to approach her writing. "Shewing" is Julian's language not only for the visions she has on what was thought to be her deathbed but also for the teachings and insights she receives over a period of years by various other

---

downside here is that "renarrate" bears the negative connotation in common parlance of unreliably narrating the truth for particular ends.

[18]   See Karl Barth, *Dogmatics in Outline*, trans. G. T. Thompson (New York: Harper & Row, 1959), 96. Cf. *CD* I/2, 493.

[19]   Despite the modern divide between exegesis and theology, I take for granted, as Julian and Barth evidently do, that, in William Thompson's words, "genuine Christian theology is always biblical, and genuine biblical study is always theological" (*Struggle for Theology's Soul*, ix). I will say more about the language of intertextuality in the first chapter.

modes—namely, words spoken to her by the Lord and what she calls "mystly" (spiritual or mystical) understanding.[20] Her more concise record of what she sees while meditating on the cross is known as the Short Text, written a decade or more after her illness.[21] After many years of prayerful contemplation, Julian reworks and expands her original insights into the more theologically reflective and sophisticated Long Text.[22] Julian tells us the interval about the Lord and Servant does not appear in the Short Text because the "full understanding of this mervelouse example was not geven" at the time.[23] Eventually she "had teching inwardly," which helped her recognize and distinguish "all the pointes and the propertes that were shewed in the same time."[24] It is this additional "teaching"

[20]   Turner, *Julian of Norwich*, xi.

[21]   The Short Text is thought to have been written between the mid-1370s and the mid-1380s.

[22]   Watson and Jenkins, whose modernized Middle English edition I will be employing in what follows, refer to the Short Text as *A Vision* and the Long Text as *A Revelation*. Many readers refer to Julian's texts together using some variation of *Revelation(s) of (Divine) Love*. But Watson and Jenkins reserve *A Revelation of Love* for the Long Text. Textual criticism is an important topic that I am skipping over here. For a description of the manuscripts of Julian's two texts and their histories, see Edmund Colledge and James Walsh, S.J., eds., *A Book of Showings to the Anchoress Julian of Norwich*, 2 vols. (Toronto: Pontifical Institute of Medieval Studies, 1978), 1–33; Colledge and Walsh, "Editing Julian of Norwich's *Revelations*: A Progress Report," *Medieval Studies* 38 (1976): 404–27; Watson and Jenkins, *Writings of Julian of Norwich*, 24–43. For a short summary of these issues, see Denise Baker, *The Showings of Julian of Norwich* (New York: W. W. Norton, 2005), xx–xxi.

[23]   Watson and Jenkins, *Writings of Julian of Norwich*, 277. The decision to rely on this version of Julian's texts is largely a practical one but admittedly imperfect. Theirs is a "synthetic edition" that takes into consideration the differences between manuscripts. Watson and Jenkins make a compelling case for a hybrid approach that blends the more original dialectic of Julian's Middle English with the analytic clarity that marks the two primary manuscripts (Sloane and Paris) (39–40). Further, their modernized spelling as well as the textual notes and critical commentary are a help to those who are not already students of Middle English. For an explanation of the decision to combine manuscripts, and other orthographic issues, see 43–49.

[24]   There is disagreement about the revision process and timeline. Colledge and Walsh believe revisions began after 1388 and ended after Julian's writing of the Example of the Lord and Servant. Watson and Jenkins think 1394 is the earliest Julian could have begun reworking her earlier text, and they suggest that the revision process lasted until the early fifteenth century, just before her death around 1416. I will refer to the revised version either as the Long Text (abbreviated LT) or *A Revelation of Love* (abbreviated *A Revelation*). According to Baker and Salih, two later "understandings" specifically prompt Julian to revise her Short Text, in 1388 ("love was his meaning") and in 1393 (the Example of the Lord and Servant). See Denise Baker and Sarah Salih, introduction to *Julian of Norwich's Legacy: Medieval Mysticism and Post-Medieval Reception*, ed. Denise Baker and Sarah Salih (New York: Palgrave Macmillan, 2009), 3.

that occupies her imagination for the interim years between the writing of her two texts and produces her extensive revision of the whole experience.[25] The example is later presented as the key to unlocking the whole.

Julian is often referred to as a "mystic," which can overshadow other meaningful dimensions of her thought and writing. Her work is certainly consonant with "mystical theology," as Bernard McGinn describes it.[26] But a modern Jamesian understanding of mysticism in terms of "ineffable experience" of "union with God" does not correspond to Julian's own account of what she is doing.[27] For example, she does not regard her showings as incommunicable, nor are they incongruous with ordinary sensory experience or mere transcriptions of passive experiences meant for private devotion.[28] Kevin McGill argues it is more accurate to regard Julian as a "visionary writer."[29] While it may be anachronistic to

---

[25]   On the relationship between the ST and LT, see B. A. Windeatt, "Julian's Second Thoughts: The Long Text Tradition," in *A Companion to Julian of Norwich*, ed. Liz Herbert McAvoy (Cambridge: D. S. Brewer, 2008), 101–15.

[26]   Bernard McGinn argues that the opposition between experience and theory or reflection is a distinctly modern one. But in "mystical theology"—a phrase that predates "the coining of the term 'mysticism' by over a millennium"—the "interactions between conscious acts and their symbolic and theoretical thematizations are much more complex" than commonly recognized. Reflection or interpretation is not merely derivative or "something added on to mystical experience," but rather "mystical theory in most cases precedes and guides the mystic's whole way of life." Mystical experience is already theologically informed. See McGinn, *The Presence of God: A History of Western Christian Mysticism*, vol. 1 of *The Foundations of Mysticism* (New York: Crossroad, 1991), xiv.

[27]   See William James, *The Varieties of Religious Experience: A Study in Human Nature* (London: Longmans, Green, 1902). According to popular modern definitions informed by the work of William James, "a mystic is someone who reports experiences that can be clearly distinguished from normal conscious experience." It is assumed that what defines "mystical experiences" is that they "cannot be adequately described in language, yield knowledge that cannot be achieved by discursive means and . . . are free from obstructive sensory input" (Kevin McGill, *Julian of Norwich: Mystic or Visionary?* [New York: Routledge, 2006], 2). For a critique of James' categories, see Grace Jantzen, "Mysticism and Experience," *Religious Studies* 25 (1989): 295–315.

[28]   As Janet Soskice says, "Neither version is raw reportage" (*Kindness of God*, 127). This is because of, in McGinn's words, "the textually and theologically mediated nature of all Christian mysticism" (*Presence of God*, xv).

[29]   Kevin McGill develops this category at length. "Mystical theology" properly understood conveys nearly the same meaning as "visionary theology" in McGill's use. While Julian, along with her key English contemporaries, is commonly called a "mystic," this classification, as well as the definition of mysticism upon which it depends, has been problematized in more recent scholarship. For example, Nicholas Watson points out that the academic study of mysticism is a modern rather than a medieval reality (Watson and Jenkins, *Writings of Julian of Norwich*, 7). Writing

overstate the distinction between the mystical and the visionary on account of modern misunderstandings, there are good reasons for shifting our focus away from her status as "a mystic."[30] It can obscure Julian's insightful scriptural commentary and theological creativity. The content of the example in particular calls for an examination of her interaction with Scripture and the tradition rather than her devotional pattern, spiritual practice, or "state of consciousness" alone.

Although Julian's use of "showing" and "beholding" suggests "seeing" in a visual sense, it can also mean "contemplating" or even "reading."[31] The way Julian meditates upon the story and offers it as a multilayered lesson demonstrates that she is "thoroughly acquainted with" and "adept in the practice of 'medieval exegesis'" or "spiritual interpretation."[32] Turner argues that "Julian's compendious use of the word 'see' is best understood" in light of "the medieval practice of scriptural hermeneutics."[33] Julian uses "see" not only to mean "behold" (visually) but also to encompass the whole range of human perception, sensation, and knowledge. In her text, "I saw" often means: "I heard," "I understood," "I realized," or simply "I thought." The relation Julian sets up between her visions and their interpretation parallels the relation within "standard medieval practices of biblical exegesis" between text and hermeneutic.[34] She deliberately approaches her example according to the traditional distich of medieval "spiritual" exegesis, and her meditation upon it serves as a form of *lectio divina*.[35] This is unsurprising in light of the close relationship between

---

on the English mystical tradition in the late fourteenth and early fifteenth centuries, Watson is not sure Hilton, Rolle, *Cloud*-author, Margery Kempe, and Julian should be treated as mystics and groups them, instead, under the rubric "vernacular theology." See Watson, "The Middle English Mystics," in *The Cambridge History of Middle English Literature*, ed. David Wallace (Cambridge: Cambridge University Press, 1999), 544. He connects them with other "socially and politically motivated users of English" such as Chaucer, Langland, and the Lollards.

[30] Denys Turner says making a sharp distinction between the mystical and the visionary "on the strength of a Jamesian account of the mystical is to concede too much to that Jamesian account" (*Julian of Norwich*, 29).

[31] Colledge and Walsh modernize "behold," rendering it "contemplate" (*Book of Showings*, 132).

[32] Colledge and Walsh, *Book of Showings*, 132. "Spiritual interpretation" will be addressed in the first chapter.

[33] Turner, *Julian of Norwich*, 80.

[34] See Oliver Davies, "Transformational Processes in the Work of Julian of Norwich and Mechtild of Magdeburg," in *The Medieval Mystical Tradition in England* (Cambridge: D. S. Brewer, 1992), 39–52.

[35] Watson and Jenkins, *Writings of Julian of Norwich*, 272. Colledge and Walsh likewise think Julian is consciously working in this tradition and would have been familiar with Cassian's distich (*Book of Showings*, 134–39). They say, "Her book is

"reading, interpreting, and praying the Bible" and "Christian mysticism," which from its inception has had "a distinctively exegetical character."[36] In short, it is important to understand that the example bears for Julian the status of Scripture. This offers an important clue that it is a retelling of a biblical passage.

Another indication that Julian is retelling a biblical story is that the showing is presented in the form of a masterfully crafted homiletic *exemplum*.[37] An *exemplum* is a characteristic element in late medieval sermons, consisting of a "parable" or "similitude," a short metaphorized narrative that enacts a moral or theological point, often by glossing a scriptural narrative or theme.[38] According to Larry Scanlon, "this narrative form dominated later medieval culture, particularly in England" and was popularized in the vernacular by Julian's contemporary, Chaucer. The "sermon *exemplum*," in particular, "appears in nearly every form of serious medieval discourse" and is "employed by clerics to persuade lay audiences."[39] It becomes so important to the developing lay vernacular tradition because of its "rhetorical status"

---

a great monument to the Western monastic traditions of *lectio divina* of which she was heiress; and the learning she had inherited began and continued in the loving, prayerful study and memorization of sacred scripture" (45). Julian's language of "mystly" can be coordinated with what is known in the tradition as the "*mysticus ordo*" or "*mystica interpretatio*" (134). I will say more about medieval "spiritual interpretation" in the first chapter.

[36]   McGinn, *Presence of God*, 3. McGinn goes on to explain, "Christian modes of preparing for the direct experience of the presence of God were tied to particular ascetical practices, sacramental rituals, and forms of prayer; but they were also based on the spiritual values, patterns of life, and paradigmatic figures revealed in the scripture and explained by the fathers. The incorporated experience and inherited language that guided the believer toward the divine encounter were fundamentally scriptural."

[37]   The form of the example is already signaled in ch. 50 when she asks for a "low" and "common" thing. On medieval *exempla*, see Larry Scanlon, *Narrative, Authority, and Power: The Medieval Exemplum and the Chaucerian Tradition* (Cambridge: Cambridge University Press, 2007). On Julian's use of the form, see Colledge and Walsh, *Book of Showings*, 129, 133. Colledge and Walsh call it a "preacher's *exemplum*" (133). It is to be distinguished from the "public *exemplum*" not in its form or ability to establish "cultural authority" but in its content. Public examples tend to address matters of "lay authority" (i.e., in the realm of princes and politics) while homiletic examples are more concerned with church ritual as well as sin and virtue (Scanlon, *Narrative*, 70, 81).

[38]   Watson and Jenkins, *Writings of Julian of Norwich*, 272.

[39]   Scanlon, *Narrative*, 3, 57. As Scanlon notes, Chaucer's many affirmations of the narrative form within specific episodes of *Canterbury Tales* demonstrate his awareness that "narrative can produce authority from within its own discursive logic; that is, fictively" (243). Because of their accessibility and memorability, *exempla* garnered the "power doctrine often lacked" (31).

as a way of appropriating "the textual authority the form had reserved to the clergy."[40] Simple and vivid, an *exemplum* is inherently "didactic." Collections of *exempla* are often called "alphabets" (e.g., the *Alphabetum narrationum*). Julian refers to her own example as "the beginning of an A.B.C." for her "evencristen."[41] As a form of teaching, an example is also *performative*.[42] It "illustrates a moral" but only insofar as "what it recounts is the enactment of that moral" and "the moral does not simply gloss the narrative."[43] In much the same way as parable, its content can be grasped adequately only through its retelling in narrative form.

What is most salient about this, for the purposes of approaching Julian, is it tells us her use of the genre is implicitly a matter of theological and moral authority. The narrative fiction, as well as its presentation as a "vision," enables her to shroud her exegesis of a biblical parable while also reflecting constructively upon it and querying prevailing teachings on everything from sin to atonement to the triune life of God. The nature of *exempla* as narrative enactments helps her enfold the imaginations of her readers into her theological vision without explicitly resorting to those modes of writing and teaching prohibited of her. Julian is keenly aware of the dangers of writing in the vernacular as a laywoman. For the most part, she adopts literary forms that lead to her usual classification as a mystic rather than an exegete or theologian. As Denise Baker explains, "Like the Continental women mystics, Julian initially authorizes herself as an intermediary between the sovereign teacher, Jesus, and her fellow Christians; as a woman, she can minister to them only because she is the medium for a divine lesson"—that is, because there is supposedly nothing of herself in the teaching.[44] By foregrounding "contemplation, rather than authorial strategy" and shrewdly characterizing herself as "unlettered," Julian creates "the screen she needed to explore alternatives" to established teaching.[45]

---

[40] Scanlon, *Narrative*, 4, 138.
[41] Collections of sermonic or theological stories used by preachers were called an "A.B.C." An "A.B.C." is also a grammar text, which would have been used for literacy. In such cases, the letters were often connected with biblical stories in order to aid memory as well as to facilitate moral education. Julian's example is a homiletic parable with vivid mnemonic features.
[42] McGill, *Julian of Norwich*, 81.
[43] Scanlon, *Narrative*, 30, 33.
[44] Baker, *From Vision to Book*, 7.
[45] For an example of Julian's self-deprecating presentation of herself, see ST, sec. 6. Lynn Staley, "Julian of Norwich and the Later Fourteenth-Century Crisis of Authority," in *The Powers of the Holy: Religion, Politics, and Gender in Late Medieval English Culture*, ed. David Aers and Lynn Staley (University Park: Pennsylvania State University Press, 1996), 107–78, 109.

At the same time, the longing to suffer in solidarity with Christ, common to late-medieval affective piety and contemplative prayer, does indeed form a significant basis for Julian's visionary experience as well as her record of them.[46] But her meditative practice involves "an imaginative participation in the events of Jesus' life," which Ewert Cousins has termed a "mysticism of the historical event."[47] This "is more than mere recalling, for it makes us present to the event and the event present to us."[48] Here the lines between vision and text, present and past, immediate and mediated are blurred. *A Revelation* reads as gloss after gloss on the Gospel narrative, and throughout Julian paraphrases and interprets the whole breadth of Scripture.[49] Her "showings" reanimate the historical passion of Christ, in particular, which is known to her through a variety of oral and visual avenues, including preaching, reading, "popular pious verse," and sacred art.[50] Her "imaginative awareness" of Christ's suffering is undoubtedly shaped by the Franciscan devotional art-objects readily encountered in the churches of Norwich.[51] The visionary episodes she describes especially mirror the "silent preaching" of late fourteenth-century wall paintings.[52] Julian contemplates her showings like they are images, with

[46] See ST, sec. 1. Baker, *From Vision to Book*, 34f. For a brief summary of the context of the religious devotion that gives rise to Julian's prayer for "three gifts from God: imaginative identification with Christ's sufferings on the cross, bodily sickness in youth to the verge of death, and three 'wounds' of contrition, compassion and longing for God," see Spearing, introduction to *Revelations of Divine Love*, xiii–xv.

[47] Baker, *From Vision to Book*, 44, 47.

[48] Ewert Cousins, "Francis of Assisi: Christian Mysticism at the Crossroads," in *Mysticism and Religious Traditions*, ed. Steven T. Katz (Oxford: Oxford University Press, 1983), 163–90, 166–67.

[49] Colledge and Walsh note the manifold references to the Vulgate embedded in Julian's text and recommend treating her as "Scripture scholar, Latinist, rhetorician and theologian" (*Book of Showings*, 132).

[50] Colledge and Walsh, *Book of Showings*, 85, 87. McGill notes, "The devotional practice of the later medieval period was dominated by the image of Christ's human suffering. Such images proliferated the medieval world of the late fourteenth and fifteenth centuries in stained glass, statuary, paintings, Psalters, Books of Hours and medieval theatre" (*Julian of Norwich*, 67). This forms an important backdrop for what Julian is doing both in her own visualization and in her representation of it for her readers. He says, "Julian seeks to share her vision through its resonance in the common, accessible and didactic imagery" (74).

[51] Colledge and Walsh, *Book of Showings*, 52–53. They note, in particular, the vernicle and "medieval crucifixion iconography" with which the churches of Norwich were "richly furnished" (55). See also Peter Lasko and Nigel J. Morgan, eds., *Medieval Art in East Anglia 1300–1520* (Norwich, U.K.: Jarrold and Sons, 1973).

[52] McGill, *Julian of Norwich*, 50, 73. McGill notes that Julian's image of Christ's bloody face is connected to a devotional woman owning the Karlsruhe Psalter (after

all "the dramatic and spectacular effects of a motion picture."[53] But they also function as "a 'text' for meditation."[54] In the late Middle Ages, visual media served as a form of "communal reading" and "re-reading."[55] Her mode of presentation reflects a continuum between verbal and visual instruction in which the narrative retelling is intensified through visual imagination.[56]

The important point here is that the visionary quality of her writing is bound up with Julian's role as a "teacher." Her "showings" are "didactic images" or "readable pictures" that bring the "book" of Jesus' body to life.[57] In a culture practiced in "visual participation," her revelation of love is anything but private and incommunicable. It is implicitly crafted for others, which calls for a broadening of what counts as "teaching," an activity traditionally prohibited for anchorites and especially for women.[58] So although Julian initially presents herself and her experience in terms of "the dominant commonplace of late medieval devotion," David Aers observes that "her distinctive rhetorical strategies actually resist it, unravel it, estrange us from it and, gradually but decisively, supersede it."[59] Julian's writings do "not fit comfortably within standard taxonomies of theological genre in her own times," or in ours, "insofar as those taxonomies are limited to categories of monastic styles of biblical theology, scholastic styles of systematic theology,

1234) and images from Psalm 26 (59). See Jeffrey Hamburger, *The Visual and the Visionary: Art and Female Spirituality in Late Medieval Germany* (Princeton: Princeton University Press, 1998).

[53]   McGill, *Julian of Norwich*, 16. Julian appeals to "the imagery of the Passion and Incarnation that was commonplace to the visual arts and devotional practices of the late Middle Ages." This gives her visions "greater immediacy for her audience" because "there is a commonality between what Julian was shown and imagery that was accessible and familiar to those who had never had a vision" (14).

[54]   Baker, *From Vision to Book*, 49, 51.

[55]   Michael Camille, "Seeing and Reading: Some Visual Implications of Medieval Literacy and Illiteracy," *Art History* 8, no. 1 (1985): 26–49, 32. The medieval viewer would have read what was seen and attempt "to see what was written" (McGill, *Julian of Norwich*, 86).

[56]   See, for example, Walter Ong, *Orality and Literacy: The Technologizing of the Word* (London: Routledge, 1982). The relationship between visuality, literacy (or illiteracy), and "communal reading" in Julian's time differs dramatically from our individual or private modern reading habits in text-based society.

[57]   McGill says, "It is worth remembering that Julian is not shown a vision of God . . . but a revelation of God's love in the Passion of Christ" (*Julian of Norwich*, 11). "A.B.C." examples often represented "the book of Christ's body" as "a source of learning available for everyone to see" (83). See 75, 26.

[58]   McGill, *Julian of Norwich*, 35.

[59]   David Aers, "The Humanity of Christ: Reflections on Julian of Norwich's *Revelation of Love*," in Aers and Staley, *Powers of the Holy*, 81.

and otherwise to the 'mystical.'"[60] While her work participates in all of these genres, it is itself unprecedented, eclectic, singular.[61] But what is overwhelmingly clear is that Julian's vision is methodical and cohesive and that her Example of the Lord and Servant is a constructive instance of scriptural interpretation that follows the criteria of spiritual interpretation and homiletic *exempla*.[62] The details of her example are engaged at length in the second half of chapter 2, "Prodigal Christ," and in chapter 3, "Prodigal Mother."

Narrative Exegesis of the Name

The narrative form is more readily apparent in Julian given her genre, and, for the same reason, her constructive and interpretive moves are submerged. By contrast, it is the narratival creativity of Barth's constructive christological interpretation that warrants drawing out here, in light of his otherwise modern critical mode of biblical exegesis. In his case, what needs to be explained is the literary quality of the subsequent approach to his vast oeuvre. It is beyond the scope of what follows to provide a comprehensive account of Barth's Christology or rehash the many longstanding debates among Barth scholars over his doctrinal development and divine ontology. Instead, I have largely constrained myself to engaging the exposition of the parable found in §64.2 in light of his doctrine of election (§32–33) and the first aspect of reconciliation (§59). These are not arbitrary selections, but they are admittedly limited. Attention to other portions of *Church Dogmatics* would undoubtedly shed more light on Barth's exegesis of the Parable of the Prodigal Son with respect to his Christology, soteriology, theology of Scripture, and doctrine of God.

Despite my particular focus, because Barth's application of the structure and language of the Parable of the Prodigal Son ranges over his doctrines of election, reconciliation, and atonement, I must make a number of assumptions concerning the content of these doctrines. Most significantly, I do not dispute that, for Barth, "the union of the Son with the man Jesus is pressed back into the divine

---

[60]   Turner, *Julian of Norwich*, x.

[61]   Turner says, "It generates no successors. . . . It neither belongs to nor creates any theological genre" (*Julian of Norwich*, 16).

[62]   As A. C. Spearing points out, Julian's initial audience is men and women who want to lead the contemplative life (see ST, sec. 4); by her Long Text, "she drops this limitation and seems to envisage a broader public of devout laypeople" (introduction to *Revelations of Divine Love*, viii). This point is easily obscured by the sheer extraordinariness of her visions as well as her occasional self-effacement with respect to the authority of her voice and reasoning. It seems likely that Julian would hide her biblical interpretation for the same reason she hides her theological reasoning. As a laywoman, she must present herself as medium, as *mater-ial*, rather than origin or creator.

life."[63] His excursion on Luke 15:11–32 supports such an understanding of his Christology; in fact, Barth's interpretation of the parable is almost unintelligible apart from it. Barth's multilayered theological deployment of the parable calls into question the tendency to put distance, whether epistemological or ontological, between the historical atonement and the being of God. It therefore reinforces those interpretations of Barth that emphasize the humanity of Christ and a strong identity between the eternal Son and the human Jesus.[64]

While there is surely ontological import to Barth's christological identification of the prodigal son, a more narratival approach is warranted by the primary texts under consideration.[65] Barth does not shy away from scholastic distinctions and definitions. However, the prominence of "the name" in his Christology draws attention to another mode of thought—one in which what is philosophically conceived as "being" or "essence" is accessed and described through the literary or narratival categories of "character" and "identity."[66]

[63]   Paul Dafydd Jones, *The Humanity of Christ: Christology in Karl Barth's "Church Dogmatics"* (London: T&T Clark, 2008), 129.

[64]   See, for example, Eberhard Jüngel, *God's Being Is in Becoming: The Trinitarian Being of God in the Theology of Karl Barth; A Paraphrase*, trans. John Webster (London: T&T Clark, 2001); McCormack, *Orthodox and Modern*; Kevin Hector, "God's Triunity and Self-Determination: A Conversation with Karl Barth, Bruce McCormack and Paul Molnar," *International Journal of Systematic Theology* 7, no. 3 (2005): 246–61; and Jones, *Humanity of Christ*.

[65]   By "narratival," I mean: having a storylike form (including style, plot, character development, linearity, climax, etc.). By "literary" I mean: employing the devices and figures of speech common to the art of literature (fiction, drama, poetry). In Robert Alter's words, "literary analysis" includes "the manifold varieties of minutely discriminating attention to the artful use of language, to the shifting lay of ideas, conventions, tone, sound, imagery, syntax, narrative viewpoint, compositional units, and much else" (*The Art of Biblical Narrative* [New York: Basic Books, 1981], 12–13). Bruce McCormack has pointed out that the "narrative" mode of theology has specifically become associated with "post-liberalism," particularly among Anglo-American Barthians. So I must clarify that, in approaching Barth as I do, I am not intentionally working within (or against) this particular school of theology. While I refer at points to Hans Frei's work with respect to narrative identity, in emphasizing the category of "narrative" as well as the "literary" quality of Barth's scriptural interpretation I am simply following Barth's own "literary-*narratological*" (Hunsinger) method of engaging the biblical text. I am not thereby making coded epistemological claims concerning "(anti)foundationalism" or suggesting the "suspension" of "reality-references." That is another matter altogether. See McCormack's essay "Beyond Nonfoundational and Postmodern Readings of Barth: Critically Realistic Dialectical Theology," in *Orthodox and Modern*, 109–65, esp. 113–38.

[66]   I will be using "identity" in a narratival rather than analytical sense. Larry Bouchard's clarification is helpful: "*Identity* is from the Latin for 'the same,' *idem*, as in 'this is identical to that.' But it is more helpful to define it in terms of what a person

After all, according to Barth "this Subject [God] is disclosed only in the name of Jesus Christ. . . . It is wholly and entirely enclosed in Him" (II/2, 5). In a letter to G. C. Berkouwer, Barth remarks on what this means for his method:

> My intention . . . has been that all my systematic theology should be as exact a development as possible of the significance of this "name" (in the biblical sense of the term) and to that extent should be the telling of a story which develops through individual events.[67]

"Systematic theology" must be "the telling of a story" because a name can only be narrated. David Ford insists on the "priority of narrative" in the task of theology, saying "systematic work" is always "in the service of . . . re-reading" the scriptural story, for "the essence of the matter, however reconstructed, can never be expressed without narrative."[68] In other words, the basic narrativity of the name cannot be substituted for an essence or set of attributes. In Barth's retelling of the name of Jesus Christ, all the major doctrinal loci—from creation to covenant to election to reconciliation—converge and refract as nonidentical repetitions of the same story. Even "grace," he says, is only "the paraphrase of the name of Jesus" (II/2, 173). This understanding of the essentially "storied" nature of the theological enterprise guides my approach to Barth's retelling of the parable as a retelling of the person and work of Jesus Christ.

Although the focus is on Barth's exegesis of the parable, it may be useful to make a few preliminary comments on his handling of Scripture. This is another complicated and substantial topic in its own right, which cannot be addressed in full.[69] I primarily want to note how integral Barth's scriptural interpretation is to his theological method.[70] One commentator says, "From

---

identifies with or that by which one is *named*. Such identifiers usually persist over time, meaning that identity is a mode of continuity-in-change. . . . Identity as *identifying-with* refers to how the self is organized in relation to extrinsic yet internalized matters. . . . Identity is part of how the self persists by being situated with meanings and relations that allow it to transcend itself. Naming symbolizes and helps to establish this persistence" (*Theater and Integrity*, 23).

   [67]   Letter to Berkouwer, December 10, 1954; see Busch, *Karl Barth*, 381, n. 205.

   [68]   David Ford, "Narrative in Theology," *British Journal of Religious Education* 4, no. 3 (1982): 117.

   [69]   See Francis Watson, "The Bible," in *The Cambridge Companion to Karl Barth*, ed. John Webster (Cambridge: Cambridge University Press, 2000), 57–71, as well as authors cited below.

   [70]   There is much to say on this topic. Most importantly: Barth disregards the stark modern division between exegesis and dogmatics. As Paul McGlasson says, "At least part of Barth's reason for doing extended biblical exegesis in the content of Christian

beginning to end, Barth's *Church Dogmatics* is nothing other than a sustained meditation on the text of Holy Scripture."[71] Here again, the centrality of the "name" is of the utmost importance.

"Christocentrism" is a word frequently used to describe his theological method, but Barth himself says, "Sometimes I don't like the word Christology very much. It's not a matter of Christology, nor even of christocentricity and a christological orientation, but of *Christ himself.*"[72] This is manifested hermeneutically, as Hunsinger notes, in Barth's expectation "that Jesus Christ is attested, directly or indirectly, by virtually any biblical passage, whether in the Old Testament or the New. He therefore reads all of Scripture from a center in Jesus Christ."[73] In this sense, Barth's "theological exegesis" of the Parable of the Prodigal Son is not uncharacteristic for him.[74] We encounter a similar pattern of reading in his excurses on, for example, Jonah (II/1), Leviticus 14 and 16 (II/2), Isaiah 7–8 (IV/1), the Parable of the Good Samaritan (I/2), and so on.[75] In such cases, "Barth ingeniously discerned parallels in Scripture—both literary

theology was to wage a direct assault on the bifurcation of scholarly work into two such separated disciplines. Theology, for Barth, should again be biblical in a technical, disciplined sense, and likewise should the study of the Bible be disciplined by confessional theological concerns." See McGlasson, *Jesus and Judas: Biblical Exegesis in Barth*, American Academy of Religion Series (Atlanta: Scholars Press, 1991), 4.

[71]   Watson, "The Bible," 57.

[72]   In McCormack's words, for Barth, "Christocentrism" "refers to the attempt . . . to understand every doctrine from a center in God's Self-revelation in Jesus Christ. . . . 'Christocentrism,' for him, was a methodological rule—not an a priori principle, but a rule which is learned through encounter with the God who reveals Himself in Christ—in accordance with which one presupposes a particular understanding of God's self-revelation in reflecting upon each and every other doctrinal topic, and seeks to interpret those topics in the light of what is already known about Jesus Christ." Bruce L. McCormack, *Karl Barth's Critically Realistic Dialectical Theology: Its Genesis and Development 1909–1936* (New York: Oxford University Press, 1995), 454. Busch, *Karl Barth*, 411; see n. 16.

[73]   George Hunsinger, introduction to *Thy Word Is Truth: Barth on Scripture*, ed. George Hunsinger (Grand Rapids: Eerdmans, 2012), xi.

[74]   Phrases such as "theological exegesis" and "reading the bible theologically" are used by multiple commentators in reference to "the organic relationship between exegesis and the theological enterprise" in Barth's *Church Dogmatics* (Mark Gignilliat, *Karl Barth and the Fifth Gospel: Barth's Theological Exegesis of Isaiah* [New York: Fordham, 2009], 3). See also Richard Burnett, *Karl Barth's Theological Exegesis: The Hermeneutical Principles of the Römerbrief Period* (Tübingen: Mohr [Siebeck], 2001); and Mary Kathleen Cunningham, *What Is Theological Exegesis? Interpretation and Use of Scripture in Barth's Doctrine of Election* (Harrisburg, Pa.: Trinity Press International, 1995).

[75]   Consider, too, Barth's treatment of figures such as Moses, Joseph, Job, and David—all of whom become "a pointer or type that was somehow reconfigured, restored, and surpassed in Christ" (Hunsinger, introduction to *Thy Word*, xii).

and theological—to the narrative of [the] saving history" of Christ's incarnation, death, and resurrection.[76] Hunsinger observes that this pattern is marked by "a deep structure" of "affirmation," "negation," and "negation of the negation."[77] As I will show in subsequent chapters, this basic narrative shape is key to both Julian's and Barth's intertextual readings of the parable. It is worth highlighting that this forms an important point of rapprochement between Julian's medieval, precritical or "pre-modern," manner of reading and what Rudolf Smend calls Barth's "postcritical scriptural interpretation."[78]

Despite the fact that Barth is a distinctively "modern" theologian, his exegetical method does not represent a complete breach with the "pre-modern" tradition represented in Julian's interpretation of the parable.[79] According to

[76]   Hunsinger explains, "Insofar as [other biblical] stories displayed some elements of the same pattern, they could be read as pointing to Christ at the center. They could be taken as attesting to the uniqueness of Christ without losing their essential distinction from him" (introduction to *Thy Word*, xi).

[77]   While this clearly echoes Hegel—and Barth admits, "I myself have a certain weakness for Hegel and am always fond of doing a bit of 'Hegeling'" (see Busch, *Karl Barth*, 387)—it is important to remember that Hegel was interpreting (and ontologizing) the narrative structure of Jesus' life attested in the Gospels. This same pattern (of a positive followed by a negative and its overcoming) is also discerned in strictly structuralist accounts of narrative. The concept of "story" itself depends upon mischief and negation (see ch. 1). This is there in the text itself; it is a fundamentally christological pattern; and Julian discerns it as well.

[78]   See Rudolf Smend, "Nachkritische Schriftauslegung," in *Parrhesia: Karl Barth zum 80. Geburtstag am 10. Mai 1966*, ed. Eberhard Busch, Jürgen Fangmeier, and Maz Geiger (Zurich: EVA, 1966), 215–37; and George Hunsinger's essay on Smend's reading of Barth, "Postcritical Interpretation: Rudolf Smend on Karl Barth," in Hunsinger, *Thy Word*, 29–48.

[79]   For an extensive explanation of what it means to regard Barth as a "modern" theologian, see McCormack, *Karl Barth's Critically Realistic Dialectical Theology* and *Orthodox and Modern*. Above all, McCormack says, the meaning of "modernity" in Christian theology concerns the rise of "historical consciousness" (*Orthodox and Modern*, 10). He goes on to add, "Beyond the historicizing tendencies unleashed by the rise of historical consciousness, any truly 'modern' theology will also include the following: an acceptance, in principle at the [very] least, of critical methods for studying the Bible; a recognition of the loss of respect among philosophers for classical metaphysics in all their (Greek) forms; the recognition of the breakdown of the old Aristotelian-biblical cosmology in the course of the seventeenth century; and the acceptance of the necessity of constructing doctrines of creation and providence which find their ground in more modern theological and/or philosophical resources" (11). He highlights among Barth's modern traits his antimetaphysical stance concerning theological epistemology, his neo-Kantianism, his embrace of the critical study of Scripture, his opposition to natural theology and foundationalism, his indifference to evolutionary theory, and the "historicizing" evident in Barth's later divine ontology and Christology. McCormack sees his "own contribution to the European discussion of Barth's relation

Henri de Lubac, "the exegesis of a Karl Barth" is "reminiscent in many ways of the exegesis of the early Fathers."[80] This is apparent not only in the specific execution of his reading of the Parable of the Prodigal Son in §64.2 and his appeal therein to the indirect interpretive methods of patristic, medieval, and early Reformation theologians (which he uses to chasten the strictly historical-critical approaches of late nineteenth-century and early twentieth-century Protestantism), but also in his more extensive practice of "christological" or "typological" exegesis. Referring to this, Kathryn Greene-McCreight identifies "two of the most theologically fruitful aspects" of the exegetical portions in *Church Dogmatics*: (1) Barth's "reading of the Old and New Testaments as a canonically interconnected whole," and (2) his "postcritical qualification of modern criticism."[81] Greene-McCreight explains that Barth reads the Bible as a "single," "theologically interdependent" text "which bears the communication of the Holy One." What Barth shares in common with interpreters and theologians "from the earliest Christian tradition up until the dawning of the Enlightenment," she says, is "a reading of Scripture that attends to a canonical Rule, or the Rule of Faith."[82] For him, the unity of Scripture grounded in Jesus Christ, regarded in faith as the Word of God, "is a theological reality to be confessed, not a historical judgment to be tested in the fires of criticism."[83]

At the same time, Barth clearly "embraces the fruit of the biblical criticism of the modern period."[84] In fact, Barth did not appreciate the term "post-

----

to modernity" as demonstrating "the extent to which Kant and the later Marburg neo-Kantianism influenced not only his earliest 'liberal' theology (prior to 1915) but also decisively stamped his dialectical theology" (see 11–13).

[80]   Henri de Lubac, *Scripture in the Tradition*, trans. Luke O'Neill (New York: Crossroad, 2000), 77.

[81]   Kathryn Greene-McCreight, "'The Type of the One to Come': Leviticus 14 and 16 in Barth's *Church Dogmatics*," in Hunsinger, *Thy Word*, 67–68.

[82]   Greene-McCreight, "Type," 68. By this, Greene-McCreight most basically means that Barth, like the church fathers, construes the Bible as a drama or narrative unified by the identity of God in Christ. We see this, for example, in Barth's assertion that "name" governs all scriptural interpretation. See above.

[83]   Greene-McCreight, "Type," 67. This attitude has resulted in accusations of "biblicism." However, Barth is clearly "no fundamentalist," evident in the fact that (1) "he gives ample recognition to error within the biblical text" (see, for example, his comments on the problem of infallibility in I/2, 529f.) and (2) "he is no enemy whatever of higher criticism, from which, indeed, he profits all through the exegetical portions of the *Dogmatics*." See Robert McAfee Brown, "Scripture and Tradition in the Theology of Karl Barth," in Hunsinger, *Thy Word*, 5.

[84]   Greene-McCreight, "Type," 69. As Barth writes in *CD* §19, "Scripture as a Witness to Divine Revelation," "The demand that the Bible should be read and understood and expounded historically is, therefore, obviously justified and can never be taken too seriously. The Bible itself posits this demand: even where it appeals expressly to divine

critical" and saw himself as a thoroughly "critical theologian."[85] His assertion is, rather, that "the critical historian needs to be more critical."[86] Greene-McCreight explains, "In order to deal with the Bible responsibly on its own terms, Barth argued, historical criticism was indispensable but not enough."[87] The reason a historical-critical approach to the study of Scripture is not enough is that it cannot attend to "the actual subject matter common to both [the biblical writer] and the reader"—the revelation of God in Christ to which the biblical texts testify.[88] Barth affirms the "concrete humanity" of the Bible (I/2, 464). Yet he wants to "ferret out the revelation of God from the word of the past" in a way that will "speak to present-day life" and distinguish it from "all the historical, theological, and cultural in which it is clothed."[89] While he does not follow the patristic and medieval notion of different "senses" of Scripture, he believes that the "figurative and prophetic reference" to Christ "is not added on or read into, but ingredient in the verbal sense 'by reason of the fact that the Bible gives us God's own witness to Himself' and 'its word in all words is this Word.'"[90] We see this clearly in his reading of the Parable of

---

commissionings and promptings, in its actual composition it is everywhere a human word, and this human word is obviously intended to be taken seriously and read and understood and expounded as such. . . . The demand for a 'historical' understanding of the Bible necessarily means, in content, that we have to take it for what it undoubtedly is and is meant to be: the human speech uttered by specific men at specific times in a specific situation, in a specific language and with a specific intention" (I/2, 464).

[85]   Eberhard Jüngel, *Karl Barth: A Theological Legacy*, trans. Garrett E. Paul (Philadelphia: Westminster, 1986), 73–74. Jüngel suggests "metacritical" as a better descriptor. As Hunsinger notes, Smend later modifies "his terminology (though not his point) by suggesting that Barth's views" combined "critical," "postcritical," and "anti-critical" elements (Hunsinger, "Postcritical Interpretation," 30).

[86]   This famous remark comes from Barth's second edition of his *Epistle to the Romans* (8). Barth's reading can be compared to the later "canonical criticism" of Brevard Childs. Childs writes, "I would suggest that it was Karl Barth who has captured the true insights of the Reformers when, in response to Bultmann and his legacy, he argued for a far more radical position regarding the nature of the Bible, namely to be more critical than the critics!" See Childs, *Biblical Theology of the Old and New Testaments: Theological Reflection on the Christian Bible* (Minneapolis: Fortress, 1993), 215.

[87]   Greene-McCreight, "Type," 68.

[88]   See George Hunsinger's translation of Rudolf Smend's comments ("Postcritical Interpretation," 30; citing from "Nachkritische Schriftauslegung," 216).

[89]   From a letter to Edward Thurneysen, cited by Walter Lindemann, *Karl Barth und die Kritische Schriftauslegung* (Hamburg-Bergstedt: Herbert Reich Evangelischer Verlag, 1973), 11. In a sense, then, Barth engages in his own project of demythologization.

[90]   Kathryn Greene-McCreight, *Ad Litteram: How Augustine, Calvin and Barth Read the "Plain Sense" of Genesis 1–3* (New York: Lang, 1999), 175. In other words, it is "within the plain sense reading" that "the figurative and prophetic reference to Christ" is to be found.

the Prodigal Son. Although the christological referent appears tangential at first, Barth finally shows that it is "invited by the text itself" (IV/2, 25). This is a matter not of being closed to historical-critical insights but of being open to "the way the words go" (*circumstantia litterae*, Aquinas).[91] As a result, Barth's approach to Scripture is, in Hunsinger's words, "indeed 'naïve,'" but "in a different, more sophisticated way." His "postcritical," or *more* critical, theological exegesis constitutes a kind of "second naïveté" (Ricoeur).[92] As Barth says, "Proper exegesis finally presses beyond the many questions to the one basic question by which they are all embraced"—that is, to the question of the identity of the bearer of the Name.[93]

This orientation of the biblical texts to their proper subject matter and attentiveness to "their actual words and sentences" engenders manifold intertextual resonances and narrative figurations to which Barth, like Julian, is keenly attuned.[94] The resulting "literary-*theological*" or "literary-*narratological*" quality of Barth's writing—which I will draw out in connection with Ricoeur's theory of intertextuality—forms the hermeneutical assumption of my comparison of it to Julian's pre-historical-critical retelling of the parable.[95] While

[91]   As Barth says, "Strict observation obviously requires that the force of a picture meeting us in a text shall exercise its due effect in accordance with its intrinsic character, that it shall itself decide what real facts are appropriate to it, that absolutely no prejudgments shall be made" (I/2, 725). Similarly: "The ill-advised hunt for a historical truth *supra scripturam* [prior to Scripture] is called off in favor of an open investigation of the *veritas scripturae ipsius* [truth of Scripture itself]" (I/2, 494).

[92]   Hunsinger, "Postcritical Interpretation," 32.

[93]   See Karl Barth, *The Word of God and the Word of Man*, trans. Douglas Horton (New York: Harper, 1957), 53. This is Hunsinger's translation ("Postcritical Interpretation," 31).

[94]   Barth says, "Revelation stands, no it happens, in the Scriptures and not behind them. It happens. There is no way around this in the biblical texts—in their actual words and sentences—given what the prophets and the apostles, as witnesses to revelation wanted to say and have said." From Karl Barth, *Christliche Dogmatik* (München: Chr. Kaiser, 1927), 344; see Hunsinger's English translation, "Postcritical Interpretation," 42.

[95]   This is George Hunsinger's terminology. He revises Smend's description of Barth's postcritical scriptural interpretation as "literary-historical," playing up the narratival and theological dimensions of Barth's "historical" focus. He points out that Barth's understanding of "history" is "more complex" than "the one commonly presupposed by modern exegetes." Barth could employ the category of "history" while also "making room for God." We see this, for example, in Barth's ongoing use of the "older more naïve significant" of the concept "history," which he retranslates as "saga" (see, for example, III/1, 80–82; IV/2, 478). Hunsinger compares Barth's insights to those of the literary critic Frank Kermode, saying both pay "close attention to the direct wording and literary structure of the texts" ("Postcritical Interpretation," 33).

there is much more to be said about Barth's approach to Scripture, I hope this helps show that the philosophical and methodological span between Barth's modern exegesis and Julian's medieval interpretation is not as gaping as one might expect. Their focus on the identity of the storyteller with his storytelling enables them to produce rare and wonderfully resonant theological retellings of the biblical parable. They will be laid out alongside one another in chapter 2, "Prodigal Christ," and Barth's theological elaboration of the parable is addressed further in chapter 4, "Prodigal Son of God."

1

Prodigal Reading

"Beyond the desert of criticism, we wish to be
called again."[1]

—Paul Ricoeur

The Parable of the Prodigal or Lost Son is among the most renowned and celebrated stories in Scripture.[2] Lauded as "the gospel within the gospel," "the greatest of all Jesus' parables," and "the greatest short story ever told," it is found only
in Luke 15:11–32 and is closely related to the preceding parables of the Lost
Sheep (vv. 1–7) and Lost Coin (vv. 8–10).[3] It tells of filial waywardness and paternal compassion. A spendthrift shirks his duties, wanders off, and, when he falls
on hard times and heads home, finds his father's love steadfast, even heightened.
He is welcomed back with deep affection and a feast fit for a wedding.

Situated within "the travel narrative" of Luke (9:51–19:27), the broader
narrative context of the parable is Jesus' departure from Galilee for Jerusalem,

---

[1]   Paul Ricoeur, *The Symbolism of Evil* (New York: Harper & Row, 1969), 349.
[2]   This well-known parable is found only in Luke. I will usually refer to this passage as "the Parable of the Prodigal Son" because the story is best known in English
by this name. However, the epithet is absent from the Greek and pushes the story in a
certain direction. The German title *Der verlorene Sohn* ("the Lost Son") more clearly
relates to the other two parables in Luke 15 (of the Lost Sheep and Lost Coin).
[3]   Jill Robbins, *Prodigal Son / Elder Brother: Interpretation and Alterity in Augustine, Petrarch, Kafka, Levinas* (Chicago: University of Chicago Press, 1991), 10. See
J. E. Compton, "The Prodigal's Brother," and F. Sommer, *The World's Greatest Short
Story*, respectively; cited by John Donahue, S.J., *The Gospel in Narrative: Metaphor,
Narrative, and Theology in the Synoptic Gospels* (Philadelphia: Fortress, 1988), 151.

where he makes his "triumphant entry" and is later crucified. Along the way, the "tax collectors and sinners," who are "stock-in-trade for the despised," come to hear Jesus' teaching.[4] "The Pharisees and scribes" take issue with this, saying, "This fellow welcomes sinners and eats with them" (15:1–2). In response to that accusation, Jesus tells the three parables of Luke 15, culminating with the story of a son who was lost and found:

[11]Then Jesus said, "There was a man who had two sons. [12]The younger of them said to his father, 'Father, give me the share of the property that will belong to me.' So he divided his property between them. [13]A few days later the younger son gathered all he had and travelled to a distant country, and there he squandered his property in dissolute living. [14]When he had spent everything, a severe famine took place throughout that country, and he began to be in need. [15]So he went and hired himself out to one of the citizens of that country, who sent him to his fields to feed the pigs. [16]He would gladly have filled himself with the pods that the pigs were eating; and no one gave him anything. [17]But when he came to himself he said, 'How many of my father's hired hands have bread enough and to spare, but here I am dying of hunger! [18]I will get up and go to my father, and I will say to him, "Father, I have sinned against heaven and before you; [19]I am no longer worthy to be called your son; treat me like one of your hired hands."' [20]So he set off and went to his father. But while he was still far off, his father saw him and was filled with compassion; he ran and put his arms around him and kissed him. [21]Then the son said to him, 'Father, I have sinned against heaven and before you; I am no longer worthy to be called your son.' [22]But the father said to his slaves, 'Quickly, bring out a robe—the best one—and put it on him; put a ring on his finger and sandals on his feet. [23]And get the fatted calf and kill it, and let us eat and celebrate; [24]for this son of mine was dead and is alive again; he was lost and is found!' And they began to celebrate.

[25]"Now his elder son was in the field; and when he came and approached the house, he heard music and dancing. [26]He called one of the slaves and asked what was going on. [27]He replied, 'Your brother has come, and your father has killed the fatted calf, because he has got him back safe and sound.' [28]Then he became angry and refused to go in. His father came out and began to plead with him. [29]But he answered his father, 'Listen! For all these years I have been working like a slave for you, and I have never disobeyed your command; yet you have never given me even a young goat so that I might celebrate with my friends. [30]But when this son of yours came back, who has devoured your property with prostitutes, you killed the fatted calf for him!' [31]Then the father said to him, 'Son, you are always with

---

[4]   Arland A. Hultgren, *The Parables of Jesus: A Commentary* (Grand Rapids: Eerdmans, 2000), 468.

me, and all that is mine is yours. [32]But we had to celebrate and rejoice, because this brother of yours was dead and has come to life; he was lost and has been found."[5]

Few if any narratives figure as powerfully or pervasively in Western art and literature. Deeply embedded in our cultural imagination, diverse interpretations, retellings, and representations abound.[6] Even the least biblically literate know the meaning of the saying "the prodigal returns." The first sustained retelling of the parable is found in Augustine's spiritual autobiography *Confessions*, in which he identifies himself with the younger son, taking the prodigal's narrative as the template for his own conversion.[7] Bernard of Clairvaux later crafts a moral and spiritual allegory modeled on the Lukan story about "a king's son" who is lost and found.[8] It served as one of the most popular subjects of theater and visual art in late medieval and early modern Europe. In the fifteenth and sixteenth centuries, the Prodigal Son Play was its own subgenre of the English drama.[9] Rembrandt, like so many Protestant artists of his time, produced a number of engravings and paintings based on the parable, including one of his most famous works, *The Return of the Prodigal Son*.[10] Henri Nouwen offers a devotional reflection on this painting, identifying in turns with each of the parabolic characters, in *The Return of the Prodigal Son: A*

[5]   New Revised Standard Version (NRSV). Unless otherwise indicated, all scriptural citations that are not embedded in quoted passages are taken from the NRSV.

[6]   Of course, elements of this story transcend a specifically Western heritage. Compare to the later Buddhist story of the young man who "left his father and ran away," in the *Lotus* (or *Saddharma-pundarika*) *Sutra*.

[7]   See, for example, *Confessions* I.18 (where we see Augustine's interiorization of the prodigal's departure and return), II.4 (about stealing pears and the *regio egestatis/* wasteland), III.6 (which compares philosophical texts to husks of swine), and VII.10 (concerning the *regio dissimilitudinis*).

[8]   Bernard of Clairvaux, "The Story of the King's Son," in *"The Parables" & "The Sentences,"* trans. Michael Casey, O.C.S.O., and Francis Swietek, Cistercian Father's Series 55 (Kalamazoo, Mich.: Cistercian, 2000).

[9]   See Hardin Craig, "Morality Plays and Elizabethan Drama," *Shakespeare Quarterly* 1, no. 2 (1950): 64–72. Craig notes, for example, the court drama *The Rare Triumphs of Love and Fortune*, a morality play called *The Disobedient Child*, and the most famous sixteenth-century Prodigal Son Play, *Acolastus*, among others (71).

[10]   Among other examples in fifteenth- to sixteenth-century visual art, see Rembrandt's self-portrait *The Prodigal Son in the Tavern* (1635–1636); Albrecht Dürer's famous engraving of *The Prodigal Son among the Pigs* (1496–1497); Cornelis Anthonisz' *The Prodigal Son Welcomed into the Church* and other woodcuts from the series *The Allegory of the Prodigal Son* (1540s); and Hieronymus Wierix's print (after Maarten de Vos) *The Four Enemies of Righteousness and the Theological Virtues* (ca. 1580), which combines the Parables of the Lost Sheep and the Lost Son. See Roland E. Fleischer and Susan C. Scott, eds., *Rembrandts, Rubens, and the Art of Their Time: Recent Perspectives* (University Park: Pennsylvania State University Press, 1997).

Story of Homecoming. More recent stage performance include the remarkable 1929 ballet choreographed by George Balanchine to Sergei Prokofiev's score and Hugo Alfvén's ballet suite *The Prodigal Son* (1957). Allusive works are also common in modern literature, including short stories by Herman Broch and André Gide and poems by Williams Wordsworth, Rainer Maria Rilke, Rudyard Kipling, Leah Goldberg, Angelina Muñiz-Huberman, Wendell Berry, and Elizabeth Bishop, among many others. Among recent retellings in novel form are Norman Maclean's autobiographical *A River Runs through It* about two Presbyterian fly-fishing brothers, Ron Hansen's novel *Atticus* that resets the narrative in the American West and Mexico in the late twentieth century, Marilynne Robinson's theologically abundant *Gilead* series, and Toni Morrison's novella *Home* about race, war, kinship, and place in midcentury Georgia. One could go on. Distinctive as these creative construals are, artists and authors tend to identify or sympathize with the younger son, to put themselves and the audience in his place. It is as if they are answering the parable's call to "come on, stand here on our side, on the side of human beings."[11]

Theological and exegetical engagement with Luke 15 is at least as profuse and varied. There is debate at every point—over the parameters of the text, its title, its referents and message, whether it constitutes one parable or two. Not a few scholars object that the phrase "the Prodigal Son" captures the wrong idea about the parable's content. The epithet is absent from Greek manuscripts. It derives, rather, from the mention in verse 13 of the son wasting or spending himself in ζῶν ἀσώτως, variously translated "riotous," "foolish," "wasteful," "loose," or "prodigal living."[12] The English word "prodigal" bears the negative connotations of "reckless," "wasteful," "wayward," and "imprudent," especially in its connection with the New Testament parable. Yet, from the Latin *prodigus*, it also means "lavish," "extravagant," or "bountiful." The German caption *Der verlorene Sohn*[13]

---

[11]   Barbara Brown Taylor, "The Parable of the Prodigal Son," Lenten Noon Day Preaching Series, Calvary Episcopal Church, Memphis, Tenn., March 5, 1999. This is Taylor's paraphrase of Gregory of Nazianzus' interpretation of the parable.

[12]   This nomenclature may also be rooted in the judgment of the elder son on his brother when he reminds his father that the younger son "wasted" or "devoured" his living or inheritance (Luke 15:30). As David Holgate's study shows, "the prodigal son" is a common "topos" of Greco-Roman literature, which may be why the title is applied to this parable early on. See Holgate, *Prodigality, Liberality, and Meanness in the Parable of the Prodigal Son* (Sheffield, U.K.: Sheffield Academic Press, 1999).

[13]   This immediately enables readers to see the son as "lost and found," like the sheep and the coin, rather than first of all licentious and profligate. Further, it has the effect of shifting the emphasis from the "conversion" of the younger son to his

appeals more clearly to the language and context of the parable (in vv. 24, 32). By stressing the word "lost," it underlines the thematic continuity between the three consecutive parables in Luke 15 and helps us see the sheep, the coin, and the son as analogous figures.

The passage has been renamed a number of times. Some appellations stress the lostness of *both* sons—"The Prodigal Sons" or "The Parable of the Rebellious Son(s)."[14] Others assert the primacy of the father's character with titles such as "The Parable of the Pursuing Father," "The Parable of the Father's Love," "The Parable of the Good Father," "The Parable of the Waiting Father," "The Powerless Almighty Father," "The Parable of the Gracious Father," "The Parable of the Prodigal Father," "The Father of Two Lost Sons," and "The Manifestation of the Father."[15] At least one reader gets right to the theological point and simply calls it "A Parable of the Atonement."[16]

This history of renaming begs the question: What is the "main point" of the parable? Is it to vindicate Jesus' message and actions,[17] to show the loving character of God,[18] to proclaim the good news,[19] to illustrate double predestination,[20] to declare the "in-gathering" of the outsiders and pen-

---

"being found" by God. Both points indicate obvious trajectories when it comes to differences in theological reflection on the text.

[14]   David Wyatt, *Prodigal Sons: A Study in Authorship and Authority* (Baltimore: Johns Hopkins University Press, 1980); and Colin Brown, "Parable of the Rebellious Son(s)," *Scottish Journal of Theology* 51, no. 4 (1998): 391–405.

[15]   Kenneth Bailey ("the Pursing Father"), Joachim Jeremias and Paul Ricoeur ("the Father's Love"), J. G. Lees ("the Good Father"), Helmut Thielicke ("the Waiting Father"), Eduard Schweizer ("the Powerless Almighty Father"), Robert Stein ("the Gracious Father"), Bruce McLeod and N. T. Wright ("the Prodigal Father"), Brad Young ("the Father of Two Lost Sons"), Kevin Hart ("the Manifestation of the Father"), and so on.

[16]   Robert G. Crawford, "A Parable of the Atonement," *The Evangelical Quarterly* 50, no. 1 (1978): 2–7.

[17]   Joachim Jeremias, *The Parables of Jesus* (New York: Charles Scribner's Sons, 1963), 131.

[18]   Anders Nygren, *Agape and Eros* (Philadelphia: Westminster, 1953), 81–84.

[19]   Adolf Jülicher, *The Parables of Jesus*, trans. S. H. Hooke (London: SCM Press, 1972).

[20]   In her *Gilead* series, Marilynne Robinson links the story to the doctrine. She notes that it is surprising Calvin does not do so in his commentaries. See her interview with Rebecca Painter in "Further Thoughts on a Prodigal Son Who Cannot Come Home, on Loneliness and Grace: An Interview with Marilynne Robinson," *Christianity and Literature* 58, no. 3 (2009): 487–89. Raised in a Calvinist tradition, I heard the elder brother interpreted as the figure of reprobation and linked with other rejected firstborns.

itents,[21] to exemplify conversion or repentance,[22] to depict the joy of God over the restoration of the lost,[23] or to display or incite the "polar reversal" of first and last in the Kingdom of God?[24] The answers are manifold. Attending differences over the parable's central focus are disagreements over how to parse out specific features of the narrative. The two sons, for example, have been taken as illustrations of different ethical, ethnic, religious, and spiritual dualities. While Augustine, and many following him, associates the elder son with Jews and the younger son with Christians or gentiles, Tertullian inverts the association, pairing up Christians ("safe and sound") with the elder and Jews and "heathens" (who "perish") with the younger. As an image of salvation, the older and the younger sons have been interpreted as portraying, respectively, the righteous and sinners, the self-righteous and the humble, the unrepentant and the repentant, and the letter of the law and the spirit of the law (Luther). For Calvin, as for Ambrose, the elder son does not represent Jews per se but is a fluid figure for those who are "cruel" and take "offense at the kindness of Christ" being extended to others.[25] Similarly, the elder son is often aligned with Jesus' "critics" and those who "protest" the good news.[26]

[21]   Eta Linnemann, *Parables of Jesus: Introduction and Exposition* (London: SPCK, 1966), 80.

[22]   A conversion and/or penitential reading is common throughout the early Christian commentaries (e.g., Ambrose, Augustine, John Cassian, Bonaventure, Nicholas of Lyra, Calvin, and others) up through the present; the younger son is taken as a figure of *repentance*. This runs contrary to the approach we find in Julian and Barth as well as in my own reading.

[23]   Donahue, *Gospel in Narrative*, 151. "These parables [in Luke 15] do not simply provide a defense of Jesus' fellowship with outcasts; they speak more of the joy of finding and of being found." Alluding to the same parables, Augustine similarly observes, "God and man rejoice more in the conversion of a great sinner than in uninterrupted piety" (*Confessions* VIII.3).

[24]   John Dominic Crossan, *In Parables: The Challenge of the Historical Jesus* (New York: Harper & Row, 1973), 73f.

[25]   John Calvin, *Commentary on a Harmony of the Evangelists, Matthew, Mark, and Luke*, vol. 1, in vol. 16 of *Calvin's Commentaries* (Grand Rapids: Baker, 2003), 350.

[26]   Jeremias, *Parables of Jesus*, 130–31. I have encountered the quite opposite reading of the elder son in conversation with a friend, who suggested (on the basis of the christological resonances of "all that is mine is yours," v. 31) that the elder son is an imperfect figure for Jesus Christ. Christ is the true elder son who resolves the problem of the younger son's restoration in the household of God by willfully sharing the "inheritance" (a central Pauline metaphor for salvation) belonging to him alone. This makes for an interesting comparison with Anselm's soteriology, in which Jesus receives a reward/ransom that he chooses to pass on.

Given the historical and literary context of the passage, later scholars move away from the anachronistic idea that either of the brothers refer to Christians and maintain instead that they represent different kinds of Jewishness or different stages in Israel's history. For example, the elder brother is sometimes associated with law-observing Jews, and the younger with Jews who have fallen away from religious observance.[27] The prodigal son can likewise be seen as an image of Israel in exile.[28] Others have emphasized the philosophical Greco-Roman context as well, pointing to the correspondence between the parable and similar stories illustrating "the golden mean" of virtue. Where the younger son embodies prodigality or wasteful recklessness, the older son embodies the opposite vice: meanness or miserliness.[29] The father is an image of perfect liberality or openhandedness.[30]

Still other readings set aside differences between the sons and emphasize the grace of God toward all kinds of sinners. But even among those readers who polarize the sons, most do so under the unifying element of the father's love for both. It is almost universally taken for granted that the gracious father figure represents God.[31] A structuralist analysis, however, warns against the easy identification of God with authoritative figures in Jesus' parables (e.g., the father, master, judge, etc.). In Luke 15:11–32, the younger son is the pivotal character, or what might be called the "determiner" in the story, making both the father and the older brother contrasting "respondents" with whom hearers are prompted to align themselves.[32] The parable turns on the prodigal and initiates a crisis for its recipients: Will your lived response extend grace like the loving father or withhold it like the begrudging brother? Will we be good soil for the parable-seed? Despite this structural feature, the interpretive possibility that follows from it is almost entirely overlooked in the history of its reception—excepting Julian and Barth.

---

[27]   See J. Duncan M. Derrett, *Law in the New Testament* (Eugene, Ore.: Wipf & Stock, 2005).

[28]   N. T. Wright, *Jesus and the Victory of God* (Minneapolis: Fortress, 1996), 126.

[29]   See Aquinas, *ST* II-II, q. 119, a. 1.

[30]   There is a twist, as there always is with parables. The father's perfect liberality mirrors the younger son's prodigality, suggesting grace exceeds any human conception of virtue.

[31]   E.g., Origen, Tertullian, Augustine, Bernard, Calvin, etc., and, more recently, Jeremias, Young, Donahue, Hultgren, Holgate, and others. Cf. Rabbinic *mašalîm*.

[32]   Robert Funk, *Parables and Presence: Forms of the New Testament Tradition* (Philadelphia: Fortress, 1982), 62f. Such a position justifies Julian and Barth's focus on the younger son, without necessarily denying the original unity of vv. 11–32 as some other interpreters do.

Wandering in the Wilderness, Reading the Parables

Bound up with divergent claims about the message of the Parable of the Prodigal Son are underlying questions concerning how to read—how to read the Bible and, more specifically, how to read the parables of Jesus.[33] Method and meaning are mutually informing. Accounts of the parable's message are informed not only by exegetical considerations and theological commitments but also by assumptions about the form and function of the literary genre of narrative-parable. Larger historical and hermeneutical forces are at play as well, including debates pertaining to the Bible as literature and/or sacred scripture, the classification of biblical genres, the connection between New Testament and rabbinic parables (*meshalim*), the relationship of early Christianity to first-century Judaism, and the rise of various criticisms. While they cannot be addressed at length here, a few major epochal developments in the interpretation of Jesus' parables are worth observing in connection with the enduring question of what parable is and how it works on us as well as the more specific problem of how to assess christological readings of this Lukan passage.[34] Tracing this circuitous path up to the present and back through the parable leads us to a distinct vista onto the loving-kindness of God.

In the "spiritual interpretation" of patristic theologians, the Parable of the Prodigal Son often figures as a broad paradigm for repentance and conversion. We see this in Irenaeus, Tertullian, Clement of Alexandria, Origen, Ambrose, and Augustine, among others. However, sometimes ancient and medieval commentary also moved well beyond main characters and themes, extrapolating creatively from the details of the narrative. The polyvalence of the text and the interior application of its meaning are taken for granted. Nicholas of Lyra, following John Cassian, famously distinguishes four levels of scriptural meaning:

---

[33]   For a survey of the history of parable interpretation, see, among others, Norman Perrin's *Jesus and the Language of the Kingdom: Symbol and Metaphor in New Testament Interpretation* (Philadelphia: Fortress, 1976); and Warren Kissinger's comprehensive work *The Parables of Jesus: A History of Interpretation and Bibliography* (Metuchen, N.J.: Scarecrow, 1979).

[34]   It is admittedly somewhat specious to organize these methods chronologically as I do because, on the one hand, there has always been opposition to *allegoresis* (from the patristic period through the Middle Ages) and spiritual interpretation does not disappear on account of the rise of historical criticism. However, even while various approaches might cut across the ages or have historical analogues, there is a loose progression in terms of the prevalence of an overall approach at a particular point in time. The phases of parable interpretation can be separated and grouped in any number of other ways. My version roughly aligns with the breakdown offered by Kissinger (see *Parables of Jesus*, xiii–xiv).

Littera gesta docet | The letter teaches facts or events

quid credas allegoria | allegory what you are to believe

quid agas tropologia | tropology what you are to do

quo tendas anagogia | anagogy where you should aim,
                             or what to hope for.[35]

This fourfold formula is distilled further in the distich:

> The outer Scripture is the literal sense, which is more obvious, since it is sig-
> nified immediately through the words; the inner Scripture is the mystic or
> spiritual sense, which is more hidden, since it is designated through the things
> signified by those words.[36]

Henri de Lubac calls the first sense more "noetic" and the other more "pneu-
matic." As Origen describes it, the broad and varied "mystical" or "spiritual"
meaning is simply that which is not "grasped" with "textual immediacy."[37] It covers any interpretive engagement that is not strictly literal, historical, plain, or
direct in the modern exegetical sense.[38] Although contested from the beginning,
this mode of reading flourishes up through the Middle Ages.

[35]   The poem is credited to Cassian at the beginning of Nicholas of Lyra's *Postilla*
on the Letter to the Galatians. Quoted by Christopher Ocker, "Scholastic Interpre-
tation of the Bible," in *The Medieval through the Reformation Periods*, vol. 2 of *A
History of Biblical Interpretation*, ed. Alan J. Hauser and Duane F. Watson (Grand
Rapids: Eerdmans, 2009), 265. See *In Gal.* 4, 3 (Bible de Douai, 6, Anvers, 1634), 506.
The senses of Scripture are articulated in a variety of ways in patristic and medieval
Christian thought. They generally include (1) historical or literal (which refers to the
original sense or the meaning of "the letter"), (2) allegorical or spiritual (involving
the typological or christological as well), (3) moral or tropological (which has to do
with the personal application or interiorization of the text in one's own life), and (4)
eschatological or anagogical (which concerns future or soteriological significance).
So, to borrow an example from John Cassian, the fourfold scriptural significance of
Jerusalem would be as the city in Palestine (literal), as the church (allegorical), as the
soul (tropological), and as heaven (anagogical).
[36]   Quoted by Henri de Lubac in *Medieval Exegesis: The Four Senses of Scripture*, vol. 2, trans. Mark Sebanc (Grand Rapids: Eerdmans, 2000), 34. See Nicholas
of Lyra, *Postilla in Cantia Canticorum* (PL 113, 29a); and John Cassian, *Collationes*
14.8 (PL 49, 964a).
[37]   Denys Turner, *Julian of Norwich, Theologian* (New Haven: Yale University
Press, 2011), 81.
[38]   Henri de Lubac, *Scripture in the Tradition*, trans. Luke O'Neill (New York:
Crossroad, 2000), 2, 34. Henry Chadwick, *Early Christian Thought and the Classical Tradition: Studies in Justin, Clement, and Origen* (Oxford: Oxford University
Press, 1966). Notably, there were early detractors of such a mode of reading. Cyril of

Augustine's comments on Luke 15:11–32 in *Quaestionum evangeliorum* are indicative of later characterizations of spiritual interpretation in general and *allegoresis* in particular.[39] On his reading, the character of the prodigal son is not simply a general example of metanoia. More specifically, for Augustine, he embodies the overreaching desires of the soul. Likewise, the distant region into which he wanders is not merely sin but, namely, our human "forgetfulness of God." The hunger he experiences shows he lacks "heavenly bread" (i.e., the Word), and the pigs he tends in his lowest moment are "unclean spirits," or the devil. After the boy "comes to himself" and returns home, the father's going out to meet him is like the incarnation, and his right arm, with which he embraces the son, is Jesus Christ. Like Irenaeus and Origen, Augustine sees "the Lord Himself" figured in the fatted calf sacrificed upon the son's restoration, while "the best robe," the father's own garment, represents "the dignity that Adam lost."[40]

This approach to Scripture is later deemed "eisegesis," where tangential spiritualizing or Christologizing can make the play of sound ring true. It is seen as an arbitrary reading *into* the text that overlooks the obvious, to be distinguished from "exegesis," or reading out *from* the text.[41] Parting sharply with the long and varied tradition of spiritual interpretation, the post-Enlightenment consensus following Adolf Jülicher is that parables make "a single point of comparison" and have "the broadest possible application."[42] Concomitantly, a

---

Alexandria, for example, challenged not only the tenuous connection between the fatted calf and the savior but even the identification of the elder son with Israel. See Cyril, *Commentarum in Lucum* (PG 72, 802–10).

[39]   Augustine, *Quaestionum evangeliorum II* (PL 35, 1344–48).

[40]   Chrysostom, Ambrose, and many other patristic writers interpret this parable similarly. Although Tertullian inverts the identities of the brothers (equating the elder with Christians and the younger with Jews) and lands on a different main point (that it is a story about Christ's relationship to sinful heathens), his interpretation of the parable is remarkably similar to Augustine's in the details (see *On Modesty*, ch. 9). For him, the father also refers to God, the son's wasted property to the knowledge of God, swine to demons, the father's robe to the condition from which Adam fell, the fatted calf to the Eucharist, etc. See M. F. Wiles, "Early Exegesis of the Parables," *Scottish Journal of Theology* 11, no. 3 (1958): 294; and Tertullian, *Liber de pudicitia VIII–IX* (PL 2, 994–99).

[41]   Robert Stein, *The Method and Message of Jesus' Teaching* (Louisville, Ky.: Westminster John Knox, 1994), 47. Discussing the interpretation of the parables, Stein says, "Origin and Augustine . . . therefore read into the text (eisegesis) rather than read out of the text (exegesis). They make the parable say something other than what Jesus and Luke intended."

[42]   This shift is marked by the seminal work of Adolf Jülicher, *Parables of Jesus*; original German version: *Die Gleichnisreden Jesu*, 2 vols. (Tübingen: Mohr [Siebeck],

clear line is drawn between "parable" and "allegory." Centuries of commentary are dismissed on the view that

> the parables of Jesus were treated as allegories . . . deliberately mysterious pictures or stories, every feature of which referred to something other than itself. In order to interpret an allegory, one needed the key to identifying the various elements. The insider, possessing the key, could identify the elements and hence grasp and express the meaning of the allegory in non-allegorical language. The outsider, on the other hand, did not possess the key, and hence for him the allegory remained forever a mystery.[43]

Instead of encrypting its message, on the modern-critical understanding, parable is meant to straightforwardly "illustrate" (*veranschaulichen*). A parable is defined as a similitude or "a vivid and simple picture or story the meaning of which was *self-evident* to the hearer or reader."[44] Like a simile, it draws a straightforward analogy by establishing a *tertium comparationis* or "ratio" between the *Sache* (subject)—the "real concern" of the parable—and the *Bild* (picture), to which the matter is compared.[45] The latter serves to illuminate the former, after which it becomes dispensable. The details of the parable receive attention only as they pertain to the primary point of comparison, which is typically a general (ethical) principle that is fairly transparent and universally recognizable.[46] This means "a parable is essentially instructional in nature" and "the pictorial element in the parable is not intended to be *interpreted* but to be *applied*."[47]

1888–1899). However, allegorical reading had already come under scrutiny during the Reformation and particularly in Protestant Scholasticism. See Calvin, *Commentary on a Harmony*, 345.

[43] Perrin paraphrasing Jülicher's view, in *Jesus and the Language of the Kingdom* (92).

[44] Perrin, *Jesus and the Language of the Kingdom*, 93 (emphasis added).

[45] Perrin, *Jesus and the Language of the Kingdom*, 94.

[46] Paul Ricoeur, "Biblical Hermeneutics," *Semeia* 4 (1975): 29–148, 92. According to Ricoeur, allegory, metaphor, and interpretation all suffer the same fate in Jülicher's work on parable. Jülicher works with three categories of parable: (1) simile (*Gleichnis*), (2) narrative-parables (*Gleichniserzählungen*) (i.e., expanded similes), and (3) example stories (of which there may be only one, the Parable of the Good Samaritan). Notably, Jülicher eschews "metaphor" in preference for "simile" because, working with a "substitution" theory of metaphor, he sees metaphor as an opaque trope of language intimately linked to the genre of allegory.

[47] Jülicher depends upon Aristotle's account of figurative language in his *Rhetoric*, rather than *Poetics*. He defines parable in terms of simile, not metaphor. Perrin's translation (*Jesus and the Language of the Kingdom*, 93–94) is from Jülicher, *Die Gleichnisreden Jesu*, 1:83 (emphasis added).

This nineteenth-century German Liberal approach is soon critiqued for disregarding "the ethnicity of parable lore."[48] While Jesus' parables have a dual Jewish and Greco-Roman context, they are closer to rabbinic *meshalim* than Greek figures in terms of proximity, chronology, form, and function.[49] Later exegetes give greater consideration to the particularity of Jesus' Jewish *Sitz-im-Leben*.[50] The Greek παραβολή (*parabolē*) is used in the Septuagint and the Synoptic Gospels in place of the Hebrew מָשָׁל (*māšāl*), which is not a fixed literary form. This leads historically minded readers, such as Joachim Jeremias, to set aside form-critical classifications as "a fruitless labor" because "to force the parables of Jesus into the categories of Greek rhetoric is to impose upon them an alien law."[51] At the same time, the one-point-of-comparison approach prevails, and parable continues to be contrasted with allegory in particular because it is feared to obscure the simplicity of parable's overarching message.

As readers begin to give more attention to issues such as composition, redaction, tradition history (*Traditiongeschichte*), and so on, the eschatological context of Jesus' preaching comes to the fore.[52] By the mid-twentieth century, the symbol "Kingdom of God" becomes determinative for interpreting the parables of Jesus.[53] This is one of the primary ways New Testament parables have

---

[48]   It is specifically Paul Fiebig and Christian Bugge who challenge Jülicher on this point. Brad Young, *The Parables: Jewish Tradition and Christian Interpretation* (Peabody, Mass.: Hendrickson, 1998), 21. See Paul Fiebig, *The Parables of Jesus in Light of the Rabbinic Parables of the New Testament Period* (Tübingen: Mohr, 1912).

[49]   On the relationship between patristic interpretation and the allegorical associations of Jewish midrashic literature, compare J. Duncan M. Derrett, "The Parable of the Prodigal Son: Patristic Allegories and Jewish Midrashim," *Studia Patristica* 10 (1970): 219–24; and Yves Tissot, "Patristic Allegories of the Lukan Parable of the Two Sons," in *Exegesis: Problems of Method and Exercises in Reading*, ed. François Bovon and Grégoire Rouiller, trans. Donald G. Miller (Pittsburgh: Pickwick, 1978), 362–409. While Derrett thinks the meaning of Jesus' parables are closer to the allegories of the Midrashic tradition than to "patristic allegories," Tissot rejects the dichotomy implied in Derrett's position between early "Palestinian" and later "Hellenistic" Christianity.

[50]   See especially Jeremias, *Parables of Jesus*; and Charles Dodd, *The Parables of the Kingdom* (New York: Scribner, 1961).

[51]   Jeremias, *Parables of Jesus*, 20. *Mašal* encompasses proverbs, riddles, taunt songs, short and long comparisons, wisdom sayings, narrative parables, as well as allegories.

[52]   See Norman Perrin, *What Is Redaction Criticism?* (Philadelphia: Fortress, 1969).

[53]   The *illustrand* (what is illustrated), in New Testament parable, is said to be the kingdom rather than Scripture or ethics, as in rabbinical parables. Notably, for Ricoeur, the Kingdom of God is not the "ultimate referent" of the parables but a "qualifier" that parables share in common with other modes of biblical discourse

been distinguished from rabbinical parables. The consensus is that Jesus' parables (1) are not only *about* the kingdom but also (2) enact what they describe. "Kingdom" is to be understood not as *place* but as *act*. Evident here is another major development in parable interpretation, shaped by a post-Heideggerian, post-Bultmannian interpretive movement known as *Hermeneutik* or the New Hermeneutic, which draws attention to the fundamental role of language in the work of understanding.[54] A central insight of existential-hermeneutical approaches is that language does not just express thought and being; it *constitutes* them.[55] The radical linguisticality of human existence and the performativity of language become common themes in parable theory. Parabolic speech is conceived as a "language-event" (*Sprachereignis*) or "word-event" (*Wortgeschehen*) in which "something decisive happens through what is said."[56] According to Eberhard Jüngel, what happens is nothing less than the kingdom itself. He says, "The parables of Jesus bring the Kingdom of God into language [*zur Sprache*] as parable."[57] Breaking with the "historicizing" comparison view, the parables are no longer understood as pedagogical tools to impart instruction or information; rather they are meant "to confront us with ultimacy" (Jüngel), to generate a crisis moment and elicit an existential decision.

This new focus on the nature of language itself spawns greater interest in the literary form of the parables. Particularly within American scholarship, the trend in late twentieth-century parable theory is away from "historical, moralistic, and theological concerns."[58] Perrin says the weakness of the "historical-eschatological" emphasis is the lack of attention to the "parables as texts with

that tells us it is pointing to something else. The ultimate referent of the parables is, according to Ricoeur, human existence ("Biblical Hermeneutics," 34).

[54]   It is introduced by Ernst Fuchs, Gerhard Ebeling, Eta Linnemann, and other students of Rudolf Bultmann. See for example James M. Robinson and John B. Cobb Jr., eds., *The New Hermeneutic*, vol. 2 (New York: Harper & Row, 1964).

[55]   Language is seen as an "expression of life." This reflects Bultmann's reliance upon a Dilthean hermeneutical model. See Wilhelm Dilthey, *Dilthey: Selected Writings*, ed. H. P. Rickman (Cambridge: Cambridge University Press, 1986), 9, 219f.

[56]   Linnemann, *Parables of Jesus*, 32. The main philosophical influence of the New Hermeneutic, as well as "literary-existentialist" interpretation, is Heidegger, viz. his work on the disclosure of being in language. See also Perrin, *Jesus and the Language of the Kingdom*, 108; Ernst Fuchs, *Marburger Hermeneutik* (Tübingen: Mohr [Siebeck], 1968), 243–45. Cf. Fuchs, "The New Testament and the Hermeneutical Problem," in Robinson and Cobb, *New Hermeneutic*; and Gerhard Ebeling, *Wort und Glaube* (Tübingen: Mohr [Siebeck], 1975); ET: *Word and Faith*, trans. James Leitch (Philadelphia: Fortress, 1963), 325–32.

[57]   This is Perrin's translation of Jüngel, in *Jesus and the Language of the Kingdom* (117–18). See Jüngel, *Paulus und Jesus* (Tübingen: Mohr [Siebeck], 1962), 135–37.

[58]   Kissinger, *Parables of Jesus*, xiv.

an integrity of their own" because it is preoccupied with "the message of Jesus as a whole."[59] So a more literary-existentialist analysis emerges in which the parables are treated as independent "aesthetic objects," in Dan O. Via's words.[60] Borrowing from structuralism and poststructuralism, the story is read "as a story," focusing on its "internal dynamics" and "formal meaning."[61] This marks a transition from a rhetorical to a poetic understanding of the parables, in which they are handled not as illustrations but as "poetic metaphors." Freed from the strictures of comparison and instruction, the parables of Jesus are undomesticated and riddling, "almost impossible to live with."[62] Franz Kafka's stories are taken as paradigmatic of this new understanding of the form. In "On Parables," Kafka "thematizes the open, irresolute nature of parabolic discourse," noting the way the genre conveys the incomprehensible as incomprehensible.[63] Parable thus becomes integrally linked with paradox and incommunicability. Its meaning derives from its impact.

Other-Speaking: The Known and the New in Parabolic Language

Divergent assessments of Jesus' storytelling, and subsequently the meaning of a given parable, reflect a basic problem of definition. "Parable"—from παρα, "alongside of," and βάλλειν, "to throw"—does indeed imply "comparison." Hence Midrashic and Gospel discourses that begin with the question, "To what shall the matter be compared?" or the statement "The Kingdom of Heaven is like . . ." are called, almost synonymously, "parables" and "similitudes." This basic sense of the term is not lost. However, throughout the Bible, and especially in the Synoptic Gospels, παραβολή can refer to not only "parable" but also "similitude, allegory, fable, proverb, apocalyptic revelation, riddle, symbol, pseudonym, fictitious person, example, theme, argument, apology, refutation, jest."[64] Though the

---

[59]   Perrin, *Jesus and the Language of the Kingdom*, 105.

[60]   "Literary-existentialist" is Dan O. Via's term, picked up by Ricoeur and others. Exemplified by Dan O. Via, Amos Wilder, John Dominic Crossan, and Robert Funk, among others. Via, *The Parables: Their Literary and Existential Dimension* (Philadelphia: Fortress, 1967), 151.

[61]   Via, *Parables*, 153.

[62]   Perrin, *Jesus and the Language of the Kingdom*, 200.

[63]   Richard T. Gray, *A Franz Kafka Encyclopedia* (Westport, Conn.: Greenwood, 2005), 215. Franz Kafka, "On Parables," in *The Complete Stories* (New York: Schocken, 1971), 457.

[64]   In its New Testament usage, parable "has not only the meaning 'parable,' but also 'comparison' (Luke 5:36, Mark 3:23) and 'symbol' (Heb. 9:9; 11:19; cf. Mark 13:28); in Luke 4:23 it should be rendered 'proverb' or 'commonplace,' in 6:39 'proverb'; in Mark 7:17 it means 'riddle' and in Luke 14:7 simply 'rule'" (Jeremias, *Parables of Jesus*, 20).

word παραβολή is notably absent from the Gospel of John, παροιμία is used (e.g., 10:6; 16:25, 29) with a similar range of translations: parable, figure of speech, proverb, byword, symbolic discourse—or allegory. "Figure" is here contrasted with speaking "openly" or "plainly" (παρρησία: without concealment, figuration, or comparison). This is informative. Like parable, παραβολή, παροιμία encompasses almost any kind of figurative form of speech.

Despite the fluidity of its application, three corresponding terms of comparison predominate in modern definitions of parable: (1) *simile* or similitude (the prevailing nineteenth-century German Liberal "comparison" view), (2) *allegory* (mainly by contrast, in reference to premodern or other purportedly outmoded readings), and (3) *metaphor* (evoked from the mid-twentieth century on, especially in literary-existentialist theories). Simile will be left aside here.[65] However, allegory and metaphor are worth addressing at length in light of the way they shape fundamentally different approaches to parable and its figurative possibilities.

Allegory and parable are both forms of "other-speaking" (from ἄλλος, "other," and αγορευειν, "to speak in public").[66] In the same way that allegory entails, in de Lubac's words, "a meaning *other* than the letter, or auxiliary to it," according to Ricoeur, "to call a certain narrative a parable is to say that the story *refers to* something *other than* what is told; it 'stands for . . .' something else."[67] Despite their root similarity, a stark definitional contrast between allegory and parable continues to hold sway, even among post-historical-critical theorists who otherwise welcome points of rapprochement with premodern interpretation. In fact, one of the defining features of modern and contemporary parable scholarship is

[65]   Quite a few biblical scholars, including Jülicher, draw a sharp line between metaphor and simile in order to elevate the conceptual productivity of the former and relegate mere comparison to the latter. But, as Aristotle explains, the main difference between metaphor and simile is grammatical, not functional—except in the case of *catachresis*, or the use of metaphor to "name that which has no name" (*Poetics*, 1457b, 25–26). A simile may serve the same purpose and have the same effect as metaphor. Likewise, sometimes a metaphor is nothing more than a simile without the "like" or "as."

[66]   See Northrop Frye's lucid account of the continuum of allegory, from the transparently representative (e.g., sociopolitical satires) to the opaquely paradoxical (e.g., the modern parables of Kafka and Borges). Frye, *Anatomy of Criticism* (Princeton: Princeton University Press, 1957), 91. If there is a definitional distinction to be made, it is slight: allegory is a mode of composition that involves "saying something other than it means," while parable, like metaphor, says what it means by speaking of another thing at the same time (Linnemann, *Parables of Jesus*, 6).

[67]   De Lubac, *Scripture in the Tradition*, 12; Ricoeur, "Biblical Hermeneutics," 30 (emphasis added).

a widespread distaste for allegory as well as *allegoresis*—and, very often, a failure to distinguish between the two. It is not uncommon to find scholars accusing one another of "allegorizing" and competing to be less allegorical than their predecessors.[68] It seems "allegory" has practically assumed the status of a slur.

Allegories are summarily dismissed as "mystifications," "veiled revelations," or "cryptograms" that have "to be de-coded term by term."[69] Merely encrypted similitudes, "overdone" and "fanciful," they can be rendered "without essential loss, in discursive, non-figurative language."[70] So, at best, allegory is dispensable. It "can always be *translated* into a text that can be understood by itself," and "once this better text has been made out, the allegory falls away like a useless garment."[71] At worst, it amounts to textual abuse, such that many modern scholars suppose "the moment the interpreter crosses the line from parable to allegory, the interpretation has become invalid . . . because it does violence to the integrity of the text as a text."[72] These are not neutral descriptions.

On closer examination, it appears allegory is caught in the crosshairs of an argument better aimed elsewhere. It is telling that, for some, "allegorizing" is synonymous with "Christologizing" (reading the parables in light of Jesus' life) and "spiritualizing" or "theologizing" (making claims pertaining to God, doctrine, truth, or transcendence), while for others it extends to "moralizing" (drawing practical lessons from parabolic discourses).[73] Scriptural allusions

---

[68]   E.g., Robert Funk says, "Jülicher's legacy is a trap because he was never able to escape from the allegory he so fervently rejected. For him and his successors parable interpretation is a form of reduced allegory; instead of many points corresponding to a variety of details, there is only one point corresponding to one, or a pair of details." See Funk, "Sauntering through the Parables," in *Funk on Parables: Collected Essays*, ed. Bernard Brandon Scott (Santa Rosa, Calif.: Polebridge, 2006), 93–142, 98.

[69]   Dodd, *Parables of the Kingdom*, 1, 4, 100, n. 33.

[70]   Dodd, *Parables of the Kingdom*, 3; Funk, *Parables and Presence*, 30.

[71]   Ricoeur, *Symbolism of Evil*, 163. Cf. Crossan, *In Parables*, 11. In his later work, John Dominic Crossan revises his earlier assessment, praising allegory as a form of "polyvalent narration" (*Cliffs of Fall: Paradox and Polyvalence in the Parables of Jesus* [New York: Seabury, 1980], 97).

[72]   Norman Perrin, "Historical Criticism, Literary Criticism, and Hermeneutics: The Interpretation of the Parables of Jesus and the Gospel of Mark Today," *Journal of Religion* 52 (1972): 367.

[73]   Those who resist spiritualizing the parables promote ethical emphases (Jülicher), while those who oppose moral readings point to their eschatological significance (Dodd, Jeremias). But Donahue calls Luke's eschatological presentation of the Parable of the Great Supper, as well as his christological reading of the Good Samaritan, "allegorical" (*Gospel in Narrative*, 133). Crossan takes soteriological readings as a form of allegorizing (*In Parables*, 64). Funk associates theologizing with allegorizing. See Robert Funk, *Language, Hermeneutic, and the Word of God: The Problem of Language in the New Testament and Contemporary*

themselves are treated as symptomatic of "allegorizing tendencies."[74] It seems that by "allegorizing," what is often meant is drawing the wrong reference or point of comparison. Even historical criticism fails to escape accusation:

> The once dominant historico-critical reading . . . may be regarded as in some sense allegorical in that it enabled the domestication of ancient texts to modern apologetic needs. . . . Every critical reading shares something with allegory; every attempt at entering the world of the text, or seeing the text as mirroring our world and reflecting it back to us, involves some kind of allegory.[75]

In other words, any association that implies an outside—an extratextual or even intertextual point of comparison or contact—might ensnare us in "allegory."

Yet if there is one thing to say about the genre of parable, and its analogues among the tropes, it is that—as *figurative* speech—we must ask, "Figure for what?" Or must we? Finally, evident in much late twentieth-century talk about "the kingdom in parable," there is a negation of this "for" itself. Insofar as the kingdom is said to come to speech in language *as* language, the figure is not of or for or in reference to anything. If it is said to be—that is "allegorizing," an embarrassing precritical regression.

Curiously, those who most readily slap the "allegorical" label on older, more theological, interpretations of the parables also appeal most consistently to "metaphor" for understanding the form. But how does metaphor help? The influential twentieth-century New Testament scholar Charles Dodd offers an

---

Theology (New York: Harper & Row, 1966), 152. That this is really a dispute over referents is evident early on. Dodd and Jeremias break with Jülicher because, in the pursuit of "progress" and "moral precepts," the parables get "stripped of their eschatological import" (Jeremias, *Parables of Jesus*, 70). They are as much concerned about "the *content* Jülicher assigned to the parabolic teaching as they are with the nature of the parable" (Funk, "The Parable as Metaphor," in *Language*, 148). But they simply replace Jülicher's moral application with an eschatological or historical application—which, in the end, is deemed a kind of "historicizing" by Jüngel, who sets aside any "thematic" approach to the Kingdom in parables (Perrin, *Jesus and the Language of the Kingdom*, 117; in reference to Jüngel, *Paulus und Jesus*).

[74] Robert Funk, "The Old Testament in Parable: A Study of Luke 10:25–37," *Encounter* 26 (1965): 252. Funk practically conflates "allegory" and "biblical allusion" here (254). He rejects the view that "parables make use of a repertory of Old Testament images and motifs in a quasi-allegorical way" because of "the consequence that the parables of Jesus are not really intelligible to someone not immersed in Old Testament lore."

[75] See Frances Young, "Allegory and the Ethics of Reading," in *The Open Text: New Directions for Biblical Studies?* ed. Francis Watson (London: SCM Press, 1993), 116–17.

account of parable in terms of metaphor that has achieved broad reception and longevity. As he defines it,

> (1) the parable is a metaphor or simile which may (a) remain simple, (b) be elaborated into a picture, or (c) be expanded into a story; (2) the metaphor or simile is draw from nature or common life; (3) the metaphor arrests the hearer by its vividness or strangeness; and (4) the application is left imprecise in order to tease the hearer into [their] own application.[76]

Oft evoked as it is, this definition leaves us with a bridge to build between *form* (points 1–2) and *function* (points 3–4).

One immediate challenge with the claim "parable is a metaphor" is that a narrative, such as the Parable of the Prodigal Son, being longer and more complex than a trope or similitude, is not, strictly speaking, "a metaphor."[77] But a more fundamental problem must be addressed first, concerning the understanding of metaphor at play here. There are two particularly common pitfalls, both of which are prevalent in accounts of parabolic discourse and create problems for its interpretation. The first arises when metaphor is reduced to a *rhetorical* procedure of comparison and exchange, in which the form or figure becomes dispensable. The second concerns the *poetic* power of metaphor, or its affective or nonreferential impact. These approaches to metaphor are mirrored in two pervasive but problematic conceptions of parable: on the one hand, that it is merely a vehicle for abstract principles and, on the other hand, that it poetically "breaks open worldviews" without delivering theological content.[78] The first is much more common in the history of parable interpretation as well as ordinary encounters with the parables of Jesus. The second, however, poses a larger theoretical hurdle in that it intuits something important about the performativity of parable but, in overstating this, endangers its own insights. As Janet Soskice observes, neither adequately accounts for the cognitive significance of metaphorical language or, more specifically, its capacity to alter per-

---

[76] See Dodd, *Parables of the Kingdom*, 5. This numeration was added by Funk (*Language*, 133) for the sake of clarity.

[77] Throughout, I am following Janet Martin Soskice, *Metaphor and Religious Language* (Oxford: Clarendon, 1987), though I am having to condense and gloss over a great deal. Soskice defines metaphor as a trope of language and is critical of the tendency in New Testament scholarship to conflate metaphor with the narrative genre of parable.

[78] Wright, *Jesus and the Victory of God*, 176. Wright is specifically critiquing Perrin in using this phrase. He says treating the parables as noncognitive interruptions "is explicitly a dehistoricized, deJudaized, existential reading, like that of Bultmann" (see n. 122).

ception and generate new insight—something readers consistently experience and assert nonetheless.[79]

In *substitution* and *comparison* theories of metaphor, which prevail in the discipline of rhetoric from Aristotle to the early twentieth century, the metaphor-statement is simply "another way of saying what can be said literally" or "plainly."[80] Metaphor-as-substitution involves deviant word use. Either (1) an improper or unfamiliar word (vehicle) is substituted for a proper or ordinary one (tenor) or (2) the meaning of a combination of words diverges from their lexicalized senses. In both cases, the assumption is that metaphor imparts no special *content*.[81] It clothes the concept, makes it more palatable, accessible, or imaginable. Because of this Thomas Aquinas, among others, heralds it as an invaluable pedagogical device, while for the same reason, early modern philosophers tend to insist that "plain" speech is preferable.[82] In John Locke's assessment, for example, figurative language simply obscures what can otherwise be said more clearly and thus ultimately leads the mind astray.[83]

In a reductive understanding of metaphor, the vehicle (the speech) is simply decorative, while the tenor (the message) is considered accessible "regardless of

[79]   Soskice, *Metaphor and Religious Language*, 57–58.

[80]   Soskice, *Metaphor and Religious Language*, 24. This is also called an "ornamentalist" theory. The exception is catachrestic metaphors, which, Aristotle notes, fill a lexical gap, supplying a term where there was none.

[81]   Comparison theory differs somewhat from a basic substitution theory in that it does not treat metaphor as a simple substitution of one term for another but emphasizes the perception of similarities (Aristotle, *Poetics*, 1459a, 8).

[82]   Of course, metaphors can be effective didactic tools. However, it is widely acknowledged that some kinds of figurative speech resist reduction to propositional content, which Ricoeur speaks of in terms of living, rather than dead, metaphors. Paul Ricoeur, *The Rule of Metaphor: Multi-disciplinary Studies of the Creation of Meaning in Language*, trans. Robert Czerny, Kathleen McLaughlin, and John Costello, S.J. (London: Routledge & Kegan Paul, 1978), 7. C. S. Lewis similarly distinguishes between "the teacher's metaphor" (which is a dispensable pedagogical illustration employed for the sake of the student) and "the pupil's metaphor" (in which the use of language and discovery of reality take place simultaneously, such that the metaphor is inseparable from the concept). Our interest is in the latter. See Lewis, "Bluspels and Flalansferes: A Semantic Nightmare," in *The Importance of Language*, ed. Max Black (Englewood Cliffs, N.J.: Prentice Hall, 1963), 36–50.

[83]   John Locke says, "All the artificial and figurative application of words eloquence hath invented, are for nothing else but to insinuate wrong ideas, move the passions, and thereby mislead the judgment; and so indeed are perfect cheats." See Locke, *Essay concerning Human Understanding* (London: William Tegg, 1849), III.X, 34, 370. According to Soskice, Locke, like Hobbes and other seventeenth-century empiricists, misrepresents Aristotle as crudely substitutionist (Soskice, *Metaphor and Religious Language*, 25).

the figures."[84] This is a problem because, as Soskice argues, "'regardless of the figures,' one does not have the same meaning at all."[85] Her explanation is worth engaging at length:

> The difficulty with the position of those, like Hobbes, who suggest that we should replace our metaphors with "words proper" is that words proper do not say what we wish to say. . . . Relational irreducibility characterizes other forms of figurative speech common to religious writings and is especially noteworthy in the case of parable. *Rather than irreducibility being a flaw, it is one of the marks of the particular conceptual utility of metaphor.* . . . There is no particular virtue in literal language for literal language's sake; we may need to use metaphor to say what we mean and particularly . . . when we are seeking terminology to deal with abstract states of affairs, entities, and relations.[86]

The peculiar power of metaphor activates precisely when what is being communicated cannot easily be said otherwise.

A strict substitution, comparison, or decorative view lives on a questionable dichotomy between literal and metaphorical, logical and poetic, or plain and figurative.[87] But even where a sharp distinction between metaphorical and non-metaphorical language might be conceivable, in many cases, the substitution of "plain" language for "figures" is senseless, for metaphorical "significance is not reducible to a single atomistic predicate."[88] This complicates the modern one-to-one approach to parable interpretation. If metaphor can be reduced without loss, then Jesus could simply substitute, "When you give alms, do not blow your trumpet," for its propositional content, "Beneficence should not be ostentatious" (Matt 6:2).[89] More expressive and accessible in metaphor, in this case, the claim can indeed be stated openly without it. But what about parable? As Sallie McFague observes, while we might paraphrase the Parable of the Prodigal Son

---

[84]   I. A. Richards, *The Philosophy of Rhetoric* (Oxford: Oxford University Press, 1936), 100.

[85]   Soskice, *Metaphor and Religious Language*, 48.

[86]   Soskice, *Metaphor and Religious Language*, 95 (emphasis added).

[87]   Arguably all language is metaphorical at root, as Derrida argues in his essay "White Mythology: Metaphor in the Text of Philosophy," *New Literary History* 6, no. 1 (1974): 5–74, translated from "La mythologie blanche," *Poetique* 5 (1971): 1–52. Consider, for example, the metaphor in *metaphora*—to transfer or carryover. Even so, it is helpful to be able to speak in a *qualified* way of a difference between literal and nonliteral uses of language, or between what are sometimes called static steno-symbols and plastic tensive-symbols, between the language of predication and the language of poetry (Heidegger), between lexicalized and novel word usage, etc.

[88]   Soskice, *Metaphor and Religious Language*, 95.

[89]   Dodd, *Parables of the Kingdom*, 5.

with something like "the theological assertion 'God's love knows no bounds,'" doing so would obviously detract from "what the parable can do for our insight into such love." She says, "What *counts* here is not extricating an abstract concept but . . . letting the metaphor do its job."[90] It cannot be "boiled down."[91]

Nevertheless, a rhetorical definition of metaphor is residual in much parable scholarship, even that which simultaneously draws on more contemporary theories of language.[92] A peculiar inconsistency appears in many late twentieth-century applications of metaphor to parable. They assume a reductive single-point-of-comparison account of metaphor and parable while also asserting that "what is pointed to by the metaphorical predication is ultimately beyond the power of language to express" and "cannot be translated into discursive language."[93] Theories of parable are beset by this sort of contradiction due to the difficulty of aligning the well-trodden rhetorical *definition* of metaphor with apt intuitions of its poetic or catachrestic *function*. To use Phillip Wheelright's distinction, the *epiphor* (the "carrying over" or transference of meaning) in metaphor involves more than a this-for-that exchange in its *diaphoric* (or semantically productive) function. This gets at the heart of a recurring debate over how to interpret the parables of Jesus.[94] It is a question of the

---

[90]   Sallie McFague, *Speaking in Parables: A Study in Metaphor and Theology* (Philadelphia: Fortress, 1975), 15.

[91]   It is worth adding to this point; a sharp plain vs. figurative distinction in scriptural interpretation is further troubled by the fact that often the literal or intended meaning is metaphorical. According to Aquinas, "the literal sense (*sensus literalis*) of Scripture is its intended sense," and its intended sense may be figurative (*ST* Ia, q. 1, a. 10). Similarly, for Denys the Carthusian, the literal meaning is *not* "that which is first signified by the literal words" but "what is signified through those things" (Denys, *Opera omnia*, 42 vols. [Tournai: Pratis, 1896–1935]; see 1:444 and 4:362–63). Kissinger describes "Antiochene" exegesis, over against "Alexandrian," saying "the Antiochenes did not look for hidden meanings in the biblical text but sought to set forth the literal sense intended by the author" (*Parables of Jesus*, 27). But as Hans Frei has pointed out, literal sense as intended sense is not the only *sensus literalis* of Scripture. For the three uses of "literal," see Frei, *Theology and Narrative: Selected Essays*, ed. George Hunsinger and William C. Placher (Oxford: Oxford University Press, 1993), 102–4.

[92]   As Donahue puts it, "Metaphor brings together two discrete elements that are united by a point of comparison" (*Gospel in Narrative*, 7). Hultgren likewise defines a parable as "a figure of speech in which a comparison is made between God's kingdom, actions, or expectations and something in this world, real or imagined" (*Parables of Jesus*, 3).

[93]   Donahue, *Gospel in Narrative*, 9.

[94]   Philip Wheelwright distinguishes two poles of metaphorical language: (1) *epiphor*, which is "operative when there is an intrinsic, recognizable similarity between the referents of the terms of a nonliteral comparison or identification," for

dispensability of the narrative-picture to the content it "transports." Are New Testament similitudes and narrative-parables temporary stand-ins for certain moral, eschatological, or theological principles? Are they merely illustrative of a concept? Can the parable-form be discarded after its content is extracted? Some contemporary biblical scholars still proffer a flat "yes" here, such that Parable of the Prodigal Son merely "drives home" the overall message of the Bible: God is like a loving father/master who is ready to forgive the penitent.[95] But, more often, New Testament scholars relegate such a simple comparative function to "the rabbinical figures"—treating them as primarily "didactic" and confined to teaching settings "associated with a very specific text of Scripture or with a very particular problem in ethical living"—in order to distinguish the mysterious force of Jesus' parables by contrast.[96] In John Crossan's words, the parables of Jesus "articulate a referent so new or so alien to consciousness that this referent can only be grasped within the metaphor itself."[97] In this case, *what* parabolic speech imparts is inseparable from *how* it imparts it.

---

example, Shakespeare's "All the world's a stage," and (2) *diaphor*, where "there is a suggestive juxtapositioning and synthesis of seemingly unrelated and incongruous semantic elements the referents of which can indeed be perceived as belonging together, but primarily by virtue of their having been metaphorically linked," for example, Gertrude Stein's "Toasted Suzie is my ice-cream." Wheelwright, *The Burning Fountain: A Study in the Language of Symbolism* (Bloomington: Indiana University Press, 1968), 71–72. See also Frank Burch Brown, *Transfiguration: Poetic Metaphor and the Languages of Religious Belief* (Chapel Hill: University of North Carolina Press, 1983), 27.

[95]   Brad Young's explanation demonstrates the extent to which the disagreement over the illustrative role of parable is interwoven with another disagreement, over whether Jesus' parables are unique or generic. Young rightly treats Jesus' parables in light of the broader tradition of Jewish haggadah, situating them within rabbinic *mašal* and explicating them through parallel stories. But, in Young's view, the purpose of Jesus' parables, as well as the rabbinical parables of Second Temple Judaism, is straightforwardly to "instruct" and "drive home a point." They impart a lesson or concept that can be articulated after the story without the story (Young, *Parables*, 7, 33, 72).

[96]   Crossan, *In Parables*, 19. Similarly, Hultgren says rabbinic parables are "primarily exegetical; their purpose is to interpret, clarify, and apply the scriptural tradition" (*Parables of Jesus*, 8). Cf. Günther Bornkamm, *Jesus of Nazareth* (New York: Harper & Brothers, 1960), 69; David Stern, "Jesus' Parables from the Perspective of Rabbinic Literature: The Example of the Wicked Husbandmen," in *Parable and Story in Judaism and Christianity*, ed. Clemens Thoma and Michael Wyschodgrod (New York: Paulist, 1989), 58. Against this reduction of the rabbinical tradition, see Daniel Boyarin, *Intertextuality and the Reading of Midrash* (Bloomington: Indiana University Press, 1990).

[97]   Crossan, *In Parables*, 13. Crossan relies on Jacob Neusner's work on Pharisaic tradition before 70 C.E. Rabbinical parables that parallel Jesus' in content originate at a later date and are of synchronic but not diachronic use. Crossan cites Neusner (against Bultmann): "Paradox is not a dominant characteristic of the Pharisaic-rabbinic sayings

Over against a strictly illustrative or instructional view of parable, one way of ensuring the indispensability of Jesus' word-pictures or metaphorical narratives is by highlighting their irreplaceable affective impact. At the same time, this introduces a second major misunderstanding that is characteristic of *emotive* or *noncognitive* theories of metaphor. This set of approaches shares with substitution theories the view that the purpose of metaphor is not to communicate new content for thought. However, in this case, it is because the import of metaphor is strictly affective.[98] In its association with logical positivism, such a conclusion has been reason enough to deny metaphor any conceptual worth. But for others, the nonreferential impact of metaphor is precisely what lends it performative power and ensures its formal unsubstitutability. On this view, the significance of metaphor is more akin to "a picture or a bump on the head" than a proposition.[99] It is, in Soskice's words, "a form of speech act theory in which metaphor is a phenomenon of the speech situation."[100] What is thought to distinguish metaphor here "is not meaning but use . . . for a metaphor *says* only what shows on its face—usually a patent falsehood or an absurd truth" if taken according to its literal sense.[101] The problem is that no attempt is made here to explain how a metaphor, through a strategy of absurdity, might thereby produce an "increment to meaning."[102]

It is not difficult to see the affinities with certain literary-existentialist approaches to parable that associate it with paradox and crisis.[103] The work of

---

and does not occur in stories as the primary vehicle for narrative." See Neusner, "Types and Forms in Ancient Jewish Literature: Some Comparisons," *History of Religions* 11, no. 4 (1972): 354–90, 376. But perhaps the more important difference is that the *illustrand* in Jesus' case is the tensive-symbol "Kingdom of God." The rabbinical "to what shall the matter be compared" usually leads to a concrete illustration of a text or ethical principle, while Jesus is attempting to express the ineffable "Kingdom of God," which exceeds thought (Crossan, *In Parables*, 17–19). This, of course, has to do with a certain interpretation of the kingdom, as *act*, not *place*, which heightens the point that one's theology and one's philosophy of language are mutually informing.

[98]   For examples, see Monroe Beardsley, *Aesthetics: Problems in the Philosophy of Criticism* (New York: Harcourt, Brace, 1958), 134–35.

[99]   Donald Davidson, "What Metaphors Mean," in *On Metaphor*, ed. Sheldon Sacks (Chicago: University of Chicago Press, 1979), 44.

[100]   Soskice, *Metaphor and Religious Language*, 28.

[101]   Davidson, "What Metaphors Mean," 30–31.

[102]   Soskice, *Metaphor and Religious Language*, 29. Cf. Ricoeur, who integrates the absurdity into the meaning-making process.

[103]   This is true namely of those later American theorists influenced by the New Hermeneutic, who "see the narrative unit . . . as a 'language' or 'speech event' and see its importance, *qua* event, in the impact it has on the reader; in its ability to shock, to shatter, and to reshape the 'world' in which the reader lives. . . . The imagery is not

Crossan, for example, emphasizes the way parable interrupts "everydayness," brackets "world," and reverses expectation.[104] In his later writing, Crossan goes further, sloughing off his earlier attention to referentiality itself, calling it "romanticist."[105] He argues that Jesus is "the paradox of God," that Jesus' parables proclaim the Kingdom of God in and as paradox, "turning the aniconicity of Israel's God onto language itself."[106] In his reading of the Parable of the Good Samaritan, for example, Crossan argues against the historical-critical consensus, claiming it is not an example story at all.[107] Rather, in forcing the connection between two opposites—"neighbor" and "Samaritan" (i.e., "enemy")—the "metaphorical point is that *just so* does the Kingdom of God break abruptly into human consciousness and demand the overturn of prior values, closed options, set judgments, and established conclusions."[108] Likewise, he treats the Parable of the Prodigal Son as a story of "polar reversal" or "a variation on the banquet theme," where the invited are absent and the uninvited present. It depicts an amoral—or, in actual practice, immoral—situation that defies the enclosure of human expectation, value, thought, and even language.[109]

Evidently inspired by Jacques Derrida's philosophical inflection of Saussurean linguistics, Crossan undercuts the notion that the parables "mean" at all when he says, "He who finds the meaning loses it, and he who loses it finds it."[110] "Finding," in this case, is experiencing the full weight of absence and indeterminacy. In struggling with tensions such as good–enemy or wayward–favored, "the inbreaking of the Kingdom" is experienced—but not comprehended.[111] This strain of parable theory understandably leads one biblical scholar to object: "The impression arises that . . . salvation comes from metaphor alone!"[112]

---

only misunderstood if taken as reality depicting, but becomes totally misleading, for . . . 'reality is the world we create in and by our language'" (Soskice, *Metaphor and Religious Language*, 109). She is quoting from John Dominic Crossan, *The Dark Interval: Towards a Theology of Story* (Salem, Ore.: Polebridge, 1994), 40, 45.

[104]   Crossan, *In Parables*, passim.

[105]   See especially John Dominic Crossan, *Raid on the Articulate: Comic Eschatology in Jesus and Borges* (New York: Harper & Row, 1976); as well as *Cliffs of Fall*, 67.

[106]   Crossan, *In Parables*, 78; *Cliffs of Fall*, 20. He is saying Jesus rejects representation in language in the same way that the prophets before him rejected images of God and idols.

[107]   Crossan, *In Parables*, 57.

[108]   Crossan, *In Parables*, 65.

[109]   Crossan, *In Parables*, 73f.

[110]   See Derrida's lecture "Structure, Sign, and Play in the Discourse of the Human Sciences," in *Writing and Difference*, trans. Alan Bass (Chicago: University of Chicago Press, 1978). Crossan, *Cliffs of Fall*, 101.

[111]   Derrida, "Structure, Sign, and Play," 66.

[112]   Donahue, *Gospel in Narrative*, 11.

Resorting to what you might call a "shock and awe" account of figurative language in order to explain its mysterious "extra import," the emphasis on the power of parable's nonreferentiality is reminiscent of emotive theories of metaphor. This can play into a false dichotomy: either figures of speech are straightforwardly explanatory or they simply jolt and incite. For certain modern and contemporary New Testament scholars, recourse to metaphor and parable allows them to demythologize the truth claims of the text without disposing of the narratives altogether.[113] They deem Jesus' sayings "striking in *manner* but not especially in *matter*."[114] This sentiment depends upon the view that, in Robert Funk's words, "the language of poetry is centripetal and hence not assertive: it does not affirm anything directly about the external or sensory world."[115] Where "the classical mind says, that's only a story . . . the [post-] modern mind says, there's only story."[116] The poetic function of metaphor thus outpaces its rhetorical definition, leaving readers in the lurch.

The How Much More of Metaphor

In light of Dodd's influential definition of parable in terms of metaphor, we need a clearer account of both. The first thing to be said is that metaphor is a *semantic* phenomenon. In Janet Soskice's crystalline definition, metaphor is "speaking about one thing in terms which are seen to be suggestive of another."[117] It occurs at the level of the sentence rather than between isolated terms (as in a classical comparative definition) or longer units of discourse (like narrative-parables).[118] So it is not quite accurate to call a parable "*a* metaphor or simile," as Dodd and many after him do, for the meaning is not produced merely through the interaction of terms in a discrete statement.

---

[113] Soskice, *Metaphor and Religious Language*, 106f.

[114] E. P. Sanders, *Jesus and Judaism* (Philadelphia: Fortress, 1985), 7 (emphasis added). Wright (referring to Perrin) quotes Sanders (referring to B. B. Breech and James Scott) (see Wright, *Jesus and the Victory of God*, 176, n. 122).

[115] Funk, *Parable and Presence*, 117. On the "assertorial" function of metaphor, see Brown, *Transfiguration*, 24.

[116] Soskice, *Metaphor and Religious Language*, 109. Quoting from Crossan, *Dark Interval*, 40, 45.

[117] Sockice's definition (*Metaphor and Religious Language*, 49).

[118] This is a debated point. Soskice sharply distinguishes metaphor from parable and does not discuss the extension of metaphors into longer units of discourse. Ricoeur argues that "metaphor can occur not only between words but between whole sequences of sentences," and sometimes refers to a parable as a "story-metaphor." He eventually develops a more sophisticated application of metaphor to parable, as a process of metaphorization, introduced below (Ricoeur, *Figuring the Sacred*, 161).

Second, there is a broad set of theories that walk the line between the polar pitfalls of strictly illustrative and strictly emotive accounts. These might be loosely grouped together as *tensive* theories of metaphor.[119] While the function of tension in the work of reference is accounted for in different ways, in each case, significance is said to happen *between* elements—between referents, meanings, or spheres of association, between speech and world and/or text and interpreter.[120] Regardless of how this is explained, metaphorical meaning is seen as inherently participatory; it involves an encounter with language that is lived through. It requires interpretation and therefore fundamentally plays on a world of understanding "outside" or "in front of" the text.[121] What is most salient about tensive accounts, for the purpose of

[119] I am using "tensive" to group together a range of theories that bear fine nuances that cannot be teased out here (see the subsequent note). As a compilation of views, what follows is in a real sense nobody's position, but only indicates the general contours of a third way between reductively comparative and noncognitive or emotive accounts of metaphor. My description of metaphor modifies Soskice's (*Metaphor and Religious Language*, 24f.), combining it somewhat with Ricoeur's in *Rule of Metaphor* (4f.). Soskice's survey resists brief summarization and is worth consulting at length. She uses "tensive" in a narrower sense than I am here, specifically to describe Ricoeur's account, in which the metaphorical process consists of three predicative stages: (1) naïve (*this is that*), (2) deconstructive (*this is not that*), and (3) tensional (*this is and is not that*). The metaphorical achievement takes place only at the end but is elicited by the discordance between terms and by the impotence of a literal meaning. The tensive quality of metaphor is likewise threefold, occurring (1) between terms (subject and modifier), (2) between interpretations (literal and metaphorical), and (3) between the metaphorical statement and reality/life (or between description and redescription). See Ricoeur, *Rule of Metaphor* (247–56).

[120] I am thinking of, viz., Beardsley's account of *controversion* (where the tension is located between "two meanings"), Max Black's *interactive* approach (where the tension is between "two subjects"), I. A. Richards' and Ricoeur's *tensive* view (in which there are two referents or a "split reference"), and Soskice's own *interanimative* theory (where there is an association between two sets of terms). See Black, *In Models and Metaphors: Studies in Language and Philosophy* (Ithaca, N.Y.: Cornell University Press, 1962), 38–39. For Soskice, metaphor is not *speaking of this and meaning that* (substitution); nor is it *speaking of this and referring to nothing* (emotive); nor is it even necessarily *speaking of this* and *that* at the same time (interactive) or *speaking of it* and *also not speaking of it* (the narrower Ricoeurian sense of "tensive"). Metaphor is "a form of language use with a unity of subject-matter" that "draws upon two (or more) sets of associations" (Soskice, *Metaphor and Religious Language*, 45). It is a matter of speaking of one thing *through* a suggestive network of associations borrowed from something else. However, Soskice still views tension as an essential feature of metaphor; the question is only where to locate it.

[121] A noteworthy difference between Soskice and Ricoeur is that she emphasizes the *intention* of the metaphor-maker whereas Ricoeur assumes that "the text is mute" and traces the work of *interpretation* in making the text speak anew. This

parable, is that they manage to hold together (1) the irreducibility of (some) metaphors as well as (2) their intelligibility and power to genuinely communicate new content. On the one hand, certain metaphors are semantically and conceptually *innovative* and are therefore genuinely untranslatable and unsubstitutable; on the other hand, metaphor, although fictive, is still *referential*, and its referentiality can involve both reality-depiction (scientific) and reality-redescription (poetic).[122] Metaphor does more than register similarities, as Aristotle says in *Poetics*; it can constitute or produce new similarities, new relationships, new ways of seeing. In Frank Burch Brown's words, metaphor involves "not only a transformation of the ordinary meanings of the terms employed but also . . . *a transformation of ordinary thought, an innovation in meaning* that could only have been *achieved through the specific expression employed.*"[123]

This leads to a third observation common to theorists who emphasize tension. If metaphors seem *extendable* narratively, it is because they are based on

---

is one of the reasons Soskice construes Ricoeur's tensive theory of metaphor as "speaking of this *and* that." But Ricoeur's "is"/"is not" is not so much a matter not of authorial intent but of finding another path of reception for an enigmatic text in lieu of its author's ability to clarify referential intent. Frank Burch Brown agrees with Soskice that "Ricoeur places too much emphasis on literal falsity and the negative precondition for the metaphoric transformation of meanings" (*Transfiguration*, 172). He perhaps overstates our ability to make mistakes in following the direction of the metaphorical statement. And, admittedly, Ricoeur's use of Gottlob Frege's distinction between "sense" and "reference" is not always clear (he often uses "meaning" interchangeably with both). However, I think Soskice's and Ricoeur's understandings can be reconciled somewhat if we keep in mind that she is defining the metaphor-statement as a *linguistic* phenomenon in which communication happens almost automatically (e.g., in humor), while he stresses the participatory dimension of *reception*. His point is that interpreters may have to pass through two distinguishable stages of understanding if and when we stumble over a first/literal sense's failure to produce meaning.

[122] Ricoeur proposes that we understand this "fiction-redescription" pairing in much the same way as Aristotle's account of *mythos* and *mimesis*. The productivity of metaphor and parable can be accounted for in terms of *poïesis* or "a *mimesis* of serious action by means of a *mythos* invented by the poet." The act of *mimesis* is never strictly replicative in that (1) it is itself an act of interpretation (and therefore implicitly novel) and (2) it can and does produce new vistas onto reality. Ricoeur, *Rule of Metaphor*, 244. He says, "Metaphor is the rhetorical process by which discourse unleashes the power that certain fictions have to redescribe reality" (7).

[123] Brown, *Transfiguration*, 27 (emphasis added). There is a continuum between more *epiphoric* and more *diaphoric* metaphors, between those that describe or intuit similarity and those that redescribe or constitute similarity—for example, simply saying "God is a loving father" or narrating God as "the one who goes into the far country."

models.[124] This is one of the reasons metaphor is sometimes conflated with parable, as in Dodd's definition. But, as Soskice clarifies, in models we *regard* one thing or set of things in terms of another, while in metaphor we *speak* about one thing or set of things in terms of another.[125] Metaphors (linguistic) are rooted in models (usually visual or relational).[126] So it is inaccurate to say, for example, "'Father' is a 'metaphor' for God." Rather, fathers, paternity, and parenthood in general comprise *a model for seeing* God and God's relationship to humanity in a certain way. The metaphor occurs when we put the image to words and pray, "Our Father who art in heaven . . ." The models underlying and fueling metaphorical language are what give metaphor its inherent expandability and suggestiveness and safeguard against the dispensability of the figure. Good models, for example, the parenthood of God, (1) enable elaboration of the metaphorical statement itself and (2) suggest previously unrecognized possibilities for "seeing as."[127] As Ricoeur says of the perception of resemblances, this "seeing" is also a "construction."[128] Metaphor communicates what "words proper" cannot because it relies on models as heuristic fictions that not only factually describe and imaginatively redescribe but also "disclose for the first time," allowing us to draw new and complex references.[129] Metaphorical reference is thus "possible prior to

---

[124] This list is a summary and revision of the primary traits of metaphor found in the accounts of Ricoeur and Soskice.

[125] Soskice, *Metaphor and Religious Language*, 50–51.

[126] See the groundbreaking work of philosopher of science Mary Hesse: *Models and Analogies in Science* (Notre Dame, Ind.: University of Notre Dame Press, 1966) and *The Structure of Scientific Inference* (Berkeley: University of California Press, 1974). Soskice dismantles the notion that metaphors and, more specifically, metaphorical religious language are not referential or reality-depicting by engaging the history and philosophy of metaphor in science (*Metaphor and Religious Language*, ch. 6).

[127] Soskice, *Metaphor and Religious Language*, 51. This is the *diaphoric* pole of metaphor.

[128] Ricoeur, "Biblical Hermeneutics," 79.

[129] Ricoeur, "Biblical Hermeneutics," 89. Mary Hesse states, "The use of models . . . is not motivated by the ability of these models to empirically describe a pure reality. The strength of scientific models lies instead in their ability to break away from a descriptive discourse and provide a possibility to *see 'something' as 'something else.'* Since the purpose of using models in science is to explore reality by establishing new relations in it, the scientific model has a heuristic function in producing new hypotheses and so *discovers new dimensions of reality.*" See Berth Danermark, Mats Ekström, Lisselotte Jakobsen, and Jan Ch. Karlsson, *Explaining Society: Critical Realism in the Social Sciences* (New York: Routledge, 2006), 94. Translated from Bengt Kristensson Uggla, *Kommunikation på bristningsgränsen* (Stockholm: Symposion, 1994), 400. The authors of *Explaining Society* correlate Hesse's theory of models with

definitive knowledge," challenging the assumption that referentiality is necessarily direct, simple, reducible, or empirically verifiable.[130]

Finally, parable is likewise not simply a realistic narrative proving a pre-known principle or reflecting ordinary life but, in Ricoeur's definition, "a *mythos* (a heuristic fiction) which has the mimetic power of 'redescribing' human existence."[131] In this sense, parables actually come to function as models. So, while Soskice is correct about metaphors being *based on* models, Ricoeur, in sometimes referring to a metaphor *as* a model, intuits something important.[132] As evidenced by the extraordinary artistic output in response to the Parable of the Prodigal Son, a metaphorical story can in turn become a symbol for the imagination, eliciting further elaboration, redoubling the generativity of the root metaphor. It is not simply the case, then, that metaphor is *speech* that elaborates on the model; metaphors and metaphorical narratives may also become models for thought that alter our regard. And this is precisely what Ricoeur is interested in—how a "symbol *of*" becomes a "symbol *for*" (Clifford Geertz), how we make the transition from image or text to life.[133]

Parable as the Metaphorization of Metaphor

A simple definition of parable as "extended metaphor" persists in parable scholarship today, but it leaves open the relationship between a "theory of 'genres,' which rules the narrative form" and a "theory of 'tropes.'"[134] What designates the meaning vector of a particular parable? This has everything to do with the location of meaning within a story.

Parable is better understood as a mode of discourse in which there is a confluence of (1) *a narrative form* and (2) *a metaphorical process*. Ricoeur defines a parable as *a metaphorized narrative*.[135] Parable is a story that has undergone a

---

C. S. Peirce's notion of "abduction" (a mode of inference that is neither deductive nor inductive, that is more redescriptive than explanatory).

[130] Soskice (*Metaphor and Religious Language*, 124, n. 16) references Richard Boyd. See Boyd, "Metaphor and Theory Change: What Is 'Metaphor' a Metaphor For?" in *Metaphor and Thought*, 2nd ed., ed. Andrew Ortony (Cambridge: Cambridge University Press, 1993), 481–532.

[131] Ricoeur, "Biblical Hermeneutics," 32. A much-abused concept, "*Mimesis* . . . stops causing trouble and embarrassment when it is understood no longer in terms of 'copy' but of redescription" (*Rule of Metaphor*, 245).

[132] Ricoeur, "Biblical Hermeneutics," 31, 95.

[133] Ricoeur, *Figuring the Sacred*, 147. On the difference between metaphor and symbol (as well as analogy, image, etc.), see Soskice, *Metaphor and Religious Language*, 55.

[134] Ricoeur, "Biblical Hermeneutics," 89.

[135] Ricoeur, "Biblical Hermeneutics," 30, 88–89, 118. This is Ricoeur's most condensed definition.

transfer of meaning (*metapherein*) from one interpretive site to another through "an intersection between texts."[136] The meaning of parables is localized in structure or plot, rather than in one-to-one connections between discrete elements.[137] The metaphorical import occurs at the level of the whole narrative taken as "scenic." As Ricoeur explains this, "fictional narratives seem to constitute a distinctive class of metaphorical processes" because "the bearers of the metaphor are not the individual sentences of the narratives," or isolated elements, "but the whole structure, the narratives as a whole."[138] This is particularly significant for theological interpretation of the parables, for example, a christological interpretation of the Parable of the Prodigal Son.

Ricoeur reminds us here of the enduring insights of structuralist analysis, beginning with the methodological decision "to treat the parable as an autonomous aesthetic object, presenting an organic unity."[139] This involves a commitment to the *last text*, the canonical text. That is just what historical criticism cannot give us: a literary whole regarded as a world of its own. Without undercutting its gains, Ricoeur contests the way historical criticism disconnects the parables from one another and from the Gospel in order to examine

---

[136]   Ricoeur often employs the language of "transfer," which has led some to wonder whether he falls back on a substitution or comparative account of metaphor. However, he describes this transfer as reciprocally impactful for both texts involved, bringing his use closer to "interanimation"—though on the plane of discourses rather than short utterances. He speaks of "not just the collision between two semantic fields in a sentence," saying we must "extend the process of metaphorization to the widespread semantic conflicts" that occur among longer discourses in narrative-parables (*Figuring the Sacred*, 161).

[137]   Ricoeur, *Figuring the Sacred*, 125, 198.

[138]   Ricoeur, "Biblical Hermeneutics," 94. Ricoeur borrows the term "scenic" from Alfred Lorenzer's work in psychoanalysis. See Jürgen Habermas, "Hermeneutics and the Social Sciences," in *The Hermeneutics Reader: Texts of the German Tradition from the Enlightenment to the Present*, ed. Kurt Mueller-Vollmer (New York: Continuum, 2002), 293–319.

[139]   Ricoeur, "Biblical Hermeneutics," 37. The work of formalists and French structuralists, such as Vladimir Propp, Algirdas Greimas, and Roland Barthes—as well as the "historico-literary criticism" of Dan O. Via—bequeaths us a set of tools helpful for exploring the *narrative form* of the parables. These include, for example, analyses of the component parts of narrative: plot, characters, types, actions, actantiel roles, functions, dialogue, etc.; distinctions between "mimetic modes" (e.g., realistic, epic, etc.); typologies of scenes and narrative sequences (e.g., tragic or comic); the contrast between isotopies (stable elements) and isomorphisms (changing elements); and, perhaps most importantly, the distinction between "surface structures" (chronology of the individual drama) and "deep structures" (achronical structure based on relations between functions). Ricoeur borrows the term "historico-literary" from Via ("Biblical Hermeneutics," 37f.).

them in a purified form as isolated texts.[140] By contrast, the presuppositions of a structuralist or semiotic approach are more akin to later literary analysis than exegesis in its modern sense because "the incorporation of the narrative and its interpretive commentary into one text is an irrecusable textual fact."[141] The whole notion of "*a parable*" is an artifact of modern criticism, severing the "original kernel" of the supposed "*ipsissima verba* of Jesus" from its context.[142] What it actually leaves us is merely a narrative, unrecognizable as a parable as such, for a parable can be grasped as a parable only when it is seen in its literary context as a *symbolic* narrative. The parables are thus taken as a "corpus," situated within Gospel, with all the late accretions of written composition including interpretation, retelling, reframing—in short: artistry.[143] The goal of analysis is to uncover the changing elements (or isomorphisms) between the story and its interpretation, reading the parables "both *with the help of and against the distortions* provided by this ultimate context."[144]

What structuralism shows us about the form of stories is that "appearances are abundant" while "the underlying structures are finite."[145] This is particularly true of narrative-parables. The "immediately-given units of the story" are "variable values" and do not determine the meaning.[146] Characters, for example, may proliferate, but their "function"—or their action from the point of view of its significance for the whole plot—is more limited. This is what leads Vladimir Propp to conclude that underlying the variegated "surface structure" of individual narratives there is a "deep structure" or "depth semantics"

[140]   Ricoeur, "Biblical Hermeneutics," 105. Ricoeur says that such a continually pared down text "would tend to become meaningless as it becomes 'pure.'"

[141]   Ricoeur, *Figuring the Sacred*, 158. On the problem of isolating the *ipsissima verba* of Jesus, see Wright, *Jesus and the Victory of God*, 141.

[142]   Ricoeur, *Figuring the Sacred*, 100.

[143]   Working with the canonical text is not a denial that "segments of 'prose commentaries'" are later "inserted in 'poetic declaration'" or that they add "didactic, apologetic, and dogmatic components" that could alter meaning. But against the conclusion that these early developments should be discarded as instances of "allegorizing," Ricoeur points out that "they are not quite exterior to the text"—not only because they are given with the last text but also because they "prolong" the text's "productivity," adding "conceptual elaboration" to the original metaphor or symbol (Ricoeur, "Biblical Hermeneutics," 35).

[144]   Ricoeur, *Figuring the Sacred*, 158; "Biblical Hermeneutics," 105.

[145]   Ricoeur, "Biblical Hermeneutics," 40.

[146]   Ricoeur, "Biblical Hermeneutics," 39, 52. In classifying stories according to "constant values" instead of subject, motif, or meaning, Propp attempts to do for Russian folktales what Saussure does for language itself (in dividing *la langue* and *la parole* and privileging the former). He simply extends a linguistic model to long units of discourse.

reducible to a single meta-folktale defined by a certain succession of func-tions, namely: mischief–intermediate functions–dénouement/reintegration.[147] The prodigal son's action, departure–far journey–homecoming, is emblematic of this pattern. The form, rather than surface elements such as characters or themes, indicates the parable's viable trajectories of meaning. That is what it means to say its metaphorical force derives from "*a structural trait of the nar-rated action.*"[148] Without a clear sense of this, it is difficult to grasp the coher-ence of identifying the storyteller, Jesus Christ, with the prodigal son.

One pressing concern about structuralism, and what becomes poststructur-alism, is that the reduction of surface features to deep functions that are ach-ronical can create a gap between inner structure and any existential or outer reference.[149] The final text is a closed text. We cannot get outside the system, to concrete referents, to meaning, to temporality, to life.[150] In what might be called an "ultra-structuralist approach," the narrative becomes a mere "quotation" of its underlying codes such that, in Barthes' words, "what happens in narratives is from the referential standpoint actually NOTHING. What happens is language alone, the adventure of language."[151] (The similarities with an emotive concep-tion of metaphor and aniconic or paradoxical accounts of parable are notable.)

---

[147]   Ricoeur, "Biblical Hermeneutics," 43. In other words, Propp thinks the "mor-phological" thesis (about what underlies the various forms) leads to a "genetic" thesis, but this is not an inevitable conclusion—even when a basic pattern is acknowledged. Ricoeur denies that any proto-parable is discernible in the case of the parables of Jesus taken as a whole.

[148]   Ricoeur, "Biblical Hermeneutics," 125 (emphasis added).

[149]   Some of Propp's successors, such as Greimas, retain his "logic of narration." However, because "the system of relations between 'functions' is 'achronical,'" certain French structuralists, such as Claude Lévi-Strauss, "reduce even the narration to an underlying combination" or "deep-structure," which undercuts the story's "'chrono-logical' appearance." Ricoeur, "Biblical Hermeneutics," 41, 45, 49. The "syntagmatic sequence" of the narrative is supplanted by "paradigmatic order."

[150]   In short, a structuralist understanding of the narrative form is only "a dead end" when it is used to subordinate the message (individual discourse) to its achron-ical "underlying 'code,'" when it blocks the "return from the deep-structures to the surface-structures." But that would have to be a "dogmatic decision" (Ricoeur, "Bib-lical Hermeneutics," 65, 51). The structuralist *method* is to be distinguished from structuralist *ideology*—or what Ricoeur calls the "for-the-sake-of-the-code-fallacy" (69). Ideology perverts method when, for example, we become enamored of "the message *for its own sake*" (Roman Jakobson), or resolve that "the meaning of a nar-rative is nothing other than the integration of its elements within the closure of its form" (Roland Barthes), or perform a "radical dechronologization of the narrative" with no return to its surface narration (Claude Lévi-Strauss) (51–52).

[151]   Ricoeur, "Biblical Hermeneutics," 51. Ricoeur is translating directly from Barthes. See Roland Barthes, "An Introduction to the Structural Analysis of Narra-tive," *New Literary History* 6, no. 2 (1975): 237–72.

What is forgotten here is the origin of text as discourse, as *communication*. Narrative is "a means of *production*," not simply "a means of classification."[152] As Ricoeur says of narrativity, it is "a rule-governed form of imagination, encoded, yes, but authentically productive of meaning."[153] The strictures of the rules of competence governing narration are precisely the conditions for individual instances of creative performance and interpretation.[154] The way out of the enclosure of the final text, the way beyond reduction to the achronical code, is an appropriate understanding of text as text, of parable as parable—that is, as an encounter between people, an act of communication. Discourse makes use of a code or system precisely in order to convey a message.[155] (This presupposes that the unit of meaning is a sentence; semantics takes precedence over semiotics.) The "triple event character" of discourse is constituted through "a speaker, a world, and a vis-à-vis."[156] Against a certain hackneyed rendition of the Derridian axiom *il n'ya pas de hors texte*, the extralinguistic referentiality of narrative fiction such as parable is inscribed in its definition as communication.[157] In loosening "the first-order reference of ordinary language," poetic language functions to bring forward "the second-order reference."[158] And this is what takes place, paradigmatically, in the metaphorical process of parabolic discourse. Its bracketing and deferral of direct reference does not result in *no* reference but in *indirect* reference or referential excess. Hence Ricoeur's methodological rule of thumb:

---

[152] Ricoeur, "Biblical Hermeneutics," 69 (emphasis added).

[153] Ricoeur, *Rule of Metaphor*, 151.

[154] Ricoeur, "Biblical Hermeneutics," 70; Ricoeur, *Figuring the Sacred*, 151.

[155] Breaking with structuralism at this point, Ricoeur (following Humboldt and Cassirer) reminds us that "the function of language is to articulate our experience of the world, to give form to this experience." His "major argument against the structuralist ideology" is that "a mode of discourse, a literary genre, is nothing more than a means to produce a singular message, to give a *style* to individual discourses" ("Biblical Hermeneutics," 69). "The surface-structure of the 'plot' is not an epiphenomenon, but the message itself" (72).

[156] Ricoeur, "Biblical Hermeneutics," 66. In interpreting a text, we must recall all three dimensions: (1) its backward reference to "a speaker," (2) its forward reference to "an extra-linguistic reality," and (3) the text as "*communication* with an audience."

[157] The claim *il n'ya pas de hors texte* ("there is no outside the text" or "there is nothing outside the text") was first articulated by Jacques Derrida in *Of Grammatology*, trans. Gayatri Chakravorty Spivak (Baltimore: Johns Hopkins University Press, 1976), 158. Unlike some of his successors, Derrida's point is not to deny but to destabilize referentiality.

[158] Ricoeur clarifies here: "The suspension of the referential function of ordinary language does not mean the abolition of all reference" but rather serves as "the negative condition for the liberation of another referential dimension of language and another dimension of reality itself" ("Biblical Hermeneutics," 83–84).

"Structural analysis is complete only when it gives *more* meaning to the 'plot' than does the first naïve reading."[159]

Parable tells us its meaning exceeds its own confines and garners more meaning to the plot through specific narrative features, namely, signs of metaphoricity internal to the story and intertextual resonances within Gospel. Much is made of the "realism" or ordinariness of the parables. This is evident in Dodd's inclusion of the clause "drawn from nature or common life." But a defining feature of parable is a tension between ordinariness and "extravagance."[160] This is perhaps what Dodd is intimating in adding that "the metaphor arrests the hearer by its vividness or strangeness." A common sign of a parable's metaphorical import is the presence of "the *extraordinary in the ordinary*," for example, in "the eccentricity of the modes of behavior to which the Kingdom of heaven is compared" and in "the dénouement of the parables." The quality of oddness or peculiarity is sometimes lost on contemporary readers as we miss certain cultural cues. Consider, for instance,

> the extravagance of the landlord in "The Parable of the Wicked Husbandmen," who after having sent his servants, sends his son. What Palestinian property owner living abroad would be foolish enough to act like this landlord? Or what can we say about the host in the "Parable of the Great Feast" who looks for substitute guests in the streets? . . . And in the "Parable of the Prodigal Son," does not the father overstep all bounds in greeting his son?[161]

Like other modes of "intensification" in biblical discourses (e.g., paradox and hyperbole in proverbs and teachings), parabolic "extravagance" outstrips the realistic confines of a story, "pointing beyond" to "the Wholly Other."[162] It makes "us see a modality which logic"—as well as familiarity, everydayness, literalism, and every form of expectation—"tends to pass over in silence, the logical *scandal*."[163] They safeguard "the *openness* of the metaphorical process from the *closure* of the narrative form."[164] In illuminating the fault line between what is expected from and what is executed in a particular form of

[159]   Ricoeur, "Biblical Hermeneutics," 72.
[160]   Ricoeur, "Biblical Hermeneutics," 115. On the realism of the parables, see Dodd (*Parables of the Kingdom*, 21f.), Jeremias (*Parables of Jesus*, 12), and Amos Wilder (*The Language of the Gospel: Early Christian Rhetoric* [New York: Harper & Row, 1964], 81).
[161]   Ricoeur, "Biblical Hermeneutics," 115. See 116f. for more examples.
[162]   Ricoeur, "Biblical Hermeneutics," 108, 110f.
[163]   Ricoeur, "Biblical Hermeneutics," 121.
[164]   Ricoeur, "Biblical Hermeneutics," 99.

discourse, a literary analysis gives us space to register contraventions and grasp their symbolic import.[165]

Other signs of metaphoricity internal to a pericope include quotations, structural and thematic parallels, postscripts, comparatives, questions, intertextual allusions, and so on. These loosen and complicate roles and identities, stimulating a transfer of significance on a number of levels: from element to element inside the text, from characters to the audience outside the text, from elements within the parable to the speaker of the parable, and finally from the parable to literary context. This is especially evident when the story begins with the introductory phrase "the Kingdom of God *is like.*"[166] But even in cases where signs of metaphoricity stand outside the original speech of Jesus, these clues are not exactly external insofar as they trace a "direction of thought opened up by the text."[167] In the Parable of the Sower (Matt 13:1–23), for example, the inclusion of a prophetic quotation from Isaiah 6:9–10 (LXX) in verses 14–15 opens the boundaries of an otherwise discrete pericope "in the direction of other texts." This *"foyer du foyer"* ("text within the text"), it is like *"l'écoute d'une autre voix"* ("listening to another voice"). From the mouth of Jesus, Isaiah "governs the text from the place of another text" and "indirectly" points to his prophetic presence.[168] This makes us ask about the identity of the speaker, about the relationship between what is said and the one who says it.

Likewise, when a narrator intrudes through allusive postscripts, or "'segment[s] outside the narrative' (*un hors-récit*) where the listener is questioned," this serves to recast identities and roles by muddling the fixed borders between them. In the Parable of the Tenants (or "Wicked Husbandmen"), the identity of the characters inside and outside the parable are suddenly challenged and expanded when the narrator interjects, "What will the owner of the vineyard do?" (Mark 12:9) and quotes Psalm 118:22–23: "The stone the builders rejected has become the cornerstone; the Lord has done this, and it is marvelous in our eyes."[169] In implicating figures and events outside the story itself, the specific configuration of the whole text endows characters (e.g., master/servant, father/son) and actions (e.g., far journey and homecoming) with polyvalence and indeterminacy. The text begins to assimilate, indict, and measure its hearers. It tells us "everyone is *more than* they seem to be."[170] It asks us to keep looking.

[165] Ricoeur, "Biblical Hermeneutics," 115. Literary analysis is thus an important intermediary step between historical criticism and theological interpretation.
[166] Ricoeur, *Figuring the Sacred*, 149.
[167] Ricoeur, *Interpretation Theory*, 88, 92.
[168] Ricoeur, "Biblical Hermeneutics," 60–61.
[169] Ricoeur, *Figuring the Sacred*, 155.
[170] Soskice, *Metaphor and Religious Language*, 114.

It is these internal dynamics that open up the Parable of the Prodigal Son as well. At the end of the parable, the father says, first to the servants (v. 24) and then to the older son (v. 32), "This son of mine [brother of yours] *was dead and is alive again; he was lost and is found.*" This prompts Barth's remark, "If there is any point where we can ask whether there is not finally a direct as well as an indirect christological reference . . . it is in face of these two verses."[171] Aligning Jesus Christ with the "main character" in the story is an interpretive possibility that does not emerge for centuries. In the tradition of *allegoresis*, his presence was readily located in other elements, such as the fatted calf, the father's embrace or right arm, and his kiss—though not in the arc of the wayward son.[172] An interanimating reference to the storyteller himself is signaled here in a number of ways. The repetition of the words "lost and found" ensures that the parables of Luke 15 are taken as a set. Jesus offers the three stories of the lost sheep, coins, and son in response to being questioned about his identification with sinners: "Now all the tax collectors and sinners were coming near to listen to him. And the Pharisees and the scribes were grumbling and saying, 'This fellow *welcomes sinners and eats with them*'" (Luke 15:1–2).[173] In light of this preface, the parable narrates the rabbi's table fellowship with sinners, which runs counter to teachings against this (e.g., Ps 1:1; 119:63; Prov 13:20; 14:7; 28:7). Solidarity is renarrated as a recovery. The sequence "lost and found" is crowned with "rejoicing" (a key term in all three parables), and in the third parable a banquet ensues—"let us eat and celebrate" (15:23). This verse points back to the preface

---

[171]   Barth, *CD* IV/2, 24.

[172]   For example, Ambrose sees Jesus as the calf prepared for the feast (*Expositionis Lucam VII* [PL 15, 1699]). Bonaventure, likely following Jerome, interprets the kiss of the father as the exchange of God and humanity in the incarnation. See *Commentarius in evangelium Lucae*, in *Opera omnia*, vol. 7 (Florence: Ad Claras Aquas, 1895), 395; ET: *St. Bonaventure's Commentary on the Gospel of Luke*, ed. Robert Karris, 3 vols. (St. Bonaventure, N.Y.: Franciscan Institute Publications, 2001–2004).

[173]   In the context of the claim "Jesus is God," this set of parables in Luke 15 forms a metaparable about the character of God that completely upsets human/religious assumptions. Contrary to the teaching against fellowship with sinners (e.g., Ps 1:1; 119:63; Prov 13:20; 14:7; 28:7), the message of Luke 15 is something like: "God is the one who associates with sinners" or "God's righteousness includes solidarity with the unrighteous and lost." To "stand," "sit," and "eat" with the wicked meant to "receive counsel" from them, to be contaminated by them. But eating with outcasts is emblematic of Jesus' prophetic mission to "bring good news to the poor . . . proclaim release to the captives and recovery of sight to the blind," to which we are introduced in Luke 4:18, where, as a boy in the synagogue, Jesus was given the scroll to read from Isa 61:1–2 (LXX)—another telling *"foyer du foyer."* On the symbolic significance of ritual impurity, see Mary Douglas, *Purity and Danger: An Analysis of Concepts of Pollution and Taboo* (New York: Routledge, 2002).

in verses 1–2 and alludes to a major Lukan motif: the celebration of the King-dom of God through feasting with outcasts.[174]

The conclusion of Luke 15 foreshadows 19:10, where Jesus says to Zacchaeus, "The Son of Man came to seek out and to save the lost." This saying has been called "an aphoristic commentary on these [three] parables [Luke 15] as well as the entire Gospel."[175] It resounds in the mouth of the father, as "another voice." It begs the question Barth poses: "To whom does this all refer?"[176] Finally, the words "dead" and "alive again" bring to mind the passion sequence—Jesus' own death and resurrection as well as the promise of life-out-of-death that it represents and effects. Jesus' reference to himself as the one who seeks and saves "the lost" aligns him with the work of God, for salvation is only "the Lord's doing." That designates the "metaphorical" or "indirect" *who*. But *how*? It is not simply by the story, but through Jesus' own lived fellowship and solidarity with "sinners" defended by the story. The coupling of lost/found and dead/alive thus presents a veritable "Gospel within the Gospel."[177] The evocative parallelism of verses 24 and 32 exemplifies the way internal signs of metaphoricity are often instances of narratological metalepsis that directly and indirectly summon meaning through the parable's positioning within a larger context.[178] They illuminate and initiate the broader play of literary context and intertextuality.

This points us to the fact that the critical procedure impelling us to inter-pret a narrative *as a parable* is *narrative embedding*. A parable is simply a "nar-rative within a narrative" or "a narrative recounted by a personage of another narrative that encompasses it."[179] Intertextuality is defined variously, but here

---

[174] See Donahue, *Gospel in Narrative*, 143–44. Luke, even more than the other Gospels, highlights Jesus' table fellowship with the marginalized (e.g., 5:29; 7:33–34, 36–50; 15:1). We often find meals as the context of Jesus' teaching (e.g., 5:31–39; 7:36–50; 10:38–42; 11:37–52; 14:1–24; 22:14–38; 24:20–49). Meals are also an import-ant theme in the parables, e.g., the Parable of the Great Supper (Luke 14:16–24) that precedes the three parables in ch. 15. Compare to Matt 9:13, where Jesus says, "I have come to call not the righteous but sinners."

[175] Donahue, *Gospel in Narrative*, 150.

[176] Barth, *CD* IV/2, 24.

[177] Donahue, *Gospel in Narrative*, 146.

[178] Distinguished from the trope in ancient rhetoric, "*narratological* metalepsis" refers to the porosity between narrative levels and voices, for example between the story proper or *the told* (diegetic level) and the narration or *the telling* (extradiegetic level). Metalepsis is important to storytelling in general but is especially significant in embedded narratives such as the parables. See Gérard Genette, *Narrative Discourse: An Essay in Method* (Ithaca, N.Y.: Cornell University Press, 1983).

[179] Ricoeur, "Biblical Hermeneutics," 60. Ivan Almeida, *L'Opérativité sémantique des récits paraboles: Sémiotique narrative et textuelle; Herméneutique du discours reli-gieux* (Louvain: Peeters, 1978), 117.

it chiefly concerns "the work of meaning through which one text in referring to another text both displaces this other text and receives from it an extension of meaning."[180] The narrative embedding of parables generates "networks of intersignifications" not only (1) within a parable taken in its final form but also (2) among two or more parables, (3) between the parables and Jesus' other sayings, (4) between the parables and the deeds of Jesus, and, most importantly, (5) between a parable and the Gospel narrative, namely the passion sequence.[181] These intertextual relationships are vital to the work of "parabolization"—that is, the metaphorization of the story. They "make meaning move."[182]

The "mediation of the Gospel form" integrally connects the parables of Jesus "with the main topic of the Gospel, the *narrative of the Passion*."[183] This relationship is not simply one of contiguity. Rather, it suggests "a *specific possibility* of interpretation," the possibility of reading "the proclamation of Jesus as 'the parable of God' *into* the proclamation by Jesus of God 'in parables.'"[184] On a textual basis, Jesus becomes the indirect or metaphorical referent of the

---

[180]   Ricoeur, *Figuring the Sacred*, 148. "Intertextuality" is a term borrowed from semiotics and has a range of meanings. According to Daniel Boyarin, intertextuality has three "accepted senses." First, it refers to the fact that "the text is always made up of a mosaic of conscious and unconscious citation of earlier discourse." Second, it means that texts are "dialogical in nature—contesting their own assertions as an essential part of the structure of their discourse." Boyarin says that "the Bible is a preeminent example of such a text." Third, "there are cultural codes . . . which both constrain and allow the production . . . of new texts within the culture." Boyarin's first sense is closest to Ricoeur's use here. The second insight, drawn from Mikhail Bakhtin's work, makes for an excellent point of entry in analyzing the parables but is outside the scope of this study. His third sense is very much in keeping with what has been said about structuralism and narrative above. See Boyarin, *Intertextuality*, 12.

[181]   I am combining and revising two different lists from Ricoeur's "Biblical Hermeneutics" (102) and *Figuring the Sacred* (159–60). Even if the last text results from a redactional process, "the question remains whether the *insertion* of the parable within the larger framework of the Gospel contributes to its *meaning* as a parable" (Ricoeur, "Biblical Hermeneutics," 103). Treatment of the parables as a corpus in connection with the sayings and deeds of Jesus cannot be central to this analysis. I will be focusing instead on the nexus: Parable of the Prodigal Son–Gospel–Salvation History (a now freighted term, I employ it in its most basic sense of the historical shape of the creation–fall–redemption sequence). However, at points I will draw on other parables, sayings, and deeds of Jesus to interpret the Parable of the Prodigal Son, so it is still important to note that together they "constitute a universe of meaning in which the symbolic potentialities of one contribute by means of their common context, to making the potentialities of another explicit" (Ricoeur, *Figuring the Sacred*, 157).

[182]   Ricoeur, "Biblical Hermeneutics," 148.

[183]   Ricoeur, "Biblical Hermeneutics," 104.

[184]   Ricoeur, "Biblical Hermeneutics," 104–5.

parables, including the Parable of the Prodigal Son.[185] Through embedding, the "of" transforms into an "about." Interpreting "a text *through* another text *within* another larger text," the life, death, and resurrection of Jesus resound within the parables and vice versa, such that "from now on, the parables are not only the 'parables of Jesus,' but of the 'Crucified.'"[186] Acknowledging the narratological interplay between parable and Gospel is thus a hermeneutical, not an "artificial" or "allegorizing," decision. It is initiated within the bounds of the narrative form. "The narrative metaphorizes itself."[187]

To summarize, parable is defined as a narrative form that undergoes a metaphorical process, which is initiated textually—contextually, intertextually, literarily. While a parable is not technically "a metaphor," metaphor is indeed essential to understanding the form, function, and meaning of parable. Further, understanding metaphor properly engenders interpretative possibilities of the sort that might otherwise get shut down as tangential impositions.

Figuration, Spiritual Meaning, and the Narrative Outside

Standing back from the problem of definition, a few formal anxieties interlace various attempts to define parable in terms of metaphor in sharp distinction from allegory. They center on parable's supposed (1) opaqueness, (2) (ir)reducibility, and (3) referentiality.

The worry about opaqueness is that if the parables are written or read allegorically, they require a thick interpretive context in order to grasp the meaning. It could seem as if Jesus does not really want to be understood, or at least not by everyone, and that is uncomfortably exclusionary. We must reckon with the hard teaching: "To you has been given the secret of the kingdom of God, but for those outside, everything comes in parables; so that seeing they may indeed see but not perceive, and they may indeed hear but not understand; lest they should turn again, and be forgiven" (Mark 4:11–12; cf. Matt 13:13–18).[188] This passage has led some to view the parables as strategies of exclusion, veiled revelations, riddles intelligible only

---

[185] Ironically, then, taking Christ as the *metaphorical* referent is mistaken for an "allegorical" claim precisely on allegorical grounds—that is, based on the expectation of a one-to-one correlation between figures. But, as I will show, Julian and Barth both resist a simple one-to-one identity between the son and the Son.

[186] Ricoeur, "Biblical Hermeneutics," 102, 105; *Figuring the Sacred*, 150.

[187] Ricoeur, *Figuring the Sacred*, 165.

[188] Dodd says Mark 4:11–20 is not part of the primitive/Jesus tradition but derives from later apostolic teaching. That is how he explains what he calls the "confused" interpretation of the Parable of the Sower that follows it (*Parables of the Kingdom*, 4). Cf. Jülicher and others who take an illustrative view of parable.

to the initiate. Eugene Peterson, among other theologians, compares Jesus' parables to Emily Dickinson's "Tell all the truth but tell it slant."[189] But literary critic Helen Vendler contrasts the two, claiming, "Jesus' motive is esoteric, while Dickinson's is charitable. . . . Her purpose is not to hide it from those preferring untruth, but rather to mediate it, out of kindness, to those as yet too weak to bear its glare."[190] Is Jesus' storytelling deliberately arcane? The idea that only those inducted into a certain symbolic world can access his teaching leads some scholars to reject biblical context and imagery as requisite for meaning. Funk, for example, even denies that "Jesus drew upon Old Testament imagery in the construction of his parables."[191] The appeal of the literary-existential trend is that it does not stumble over the question of how parable continues to communicate so powerfully from age to age and culture to culture, to the learned as well as the unlearned, the religious and the unreligious. Ricoeur's "post-critical naïveté" is widely embraced, along with an appreciation of the text's "*natural* force." It allows "the parable to speak of itself."[192] Hence so many claims about the "realism," "ordinariness," "naturalness," and even the "secularity" of the parables—they are accessible to all.[193] But these assertions can be anachronistic and counterproductive, deemphasizing the Hebrew Bible

---

[189] Eugene Peterson, *Tell It Slant: A Conversation on the Language of Jesus in His Stories and Prayers* (Grand Rapids: Eerdmans, 2008).

[190] In Emily Dickinson's words, "As Lightening to the Children eased / With explanation kind" (Poem 1263). Quite astoundingly, Helen Vendler suggests Jesus' intention is to keep "sinners" on the outside—a claim that runs counter to Jesus' whole life and ministry. See Vendler, *Dickinson: Selected Poems and Commentaries* (Cambridge, Mass.: Harvard University Press, 2008), 431.

[191] Funk specifically disagrees with the view of scholars like Harald Riesenfeld and Birger Gerhardsson that "a common reservoir of images, of references to a system of interlocking images and figures" drawn from the Hebrew Bible is foundational for understanding the parables of Jesus because "the parable would then depend for its significance on the ability of the hearer to catch the overtones, to supply, as it were, out of his own heritage the body of the image, which alone has the power to let the parable speak" ("Old Testament in Parable," 253). While it would be extreme to conclude that the parable is made completely mute without a certain degree of education, how could it not be the case that a religious and literary background informs interpretive competence? See Harald Riesenfeld, "The Parables in the Synoptic and the Johannine Traditions," *Svensk Exegetisck Årsbok* 25 (1960): 37–61.

[192] Perrin, *Jesus and the Language of the Kingdom*, 181.

[193] See, among others, Jeremias, *Parables of Jesus*, 11–12, 19; Dodd, *Parables of the Kingdom*, 10; Wilder, *Language of the Gospel*, 73, 83; Funk sites Lucetta Mowry, "Parable," in *The Interpreter's Dictionary of the Bible*, vol. 3 (Nashville, Tenn.: Abingdon, 1962), 650.

and the Gospel narrative as the dual context of Jesus' storytelling in an effort to sidestep the problem of mediated meaning.[194]

We might see the mediation, opacity, or resistance of parabolic language and its narrative embeddedness not as a genuine obstruction or a method for fencing meaning but as a paradoxical aid—like friction for wheels, gravity for structures, exercise for health. The help is in the hindrance. We could receive Jesus' saying in Mark 4 in light of Ricoeur's observation about the kinship between Jesus' parables and proclamations. As in "woe to those . . ." prophecies, the negative indictment is not absolute but rather serves as a goad for stubborn hearts—much like Ezekiel's outrageous behavior or the grotesque in Flannery O'Connor's short stories. O'Connor captures the essence of the "intensification" or proverbial hyperbole to which Ricoeur refers when she says, "To the hard of hearing you shout, and for the almost-blind, you draw large and startling figures."[195] Parable as "veiled revelation" is neither an exclusionary tactic nor an oxymoron. It is an invitation to pay attention, tarry, enter, uncover.

A second recurrent concern is over the purported reducibility of figurative modes to propositional speech. How do we ensure that narratives and images are not regarded as dispensable? Why do these stories and sayings continue to have meaning for us even after they have been explicated and reduced countless times? Why do they need to be told and retold? Why can we not just toss them aside and extrapolate the pure propositions embedded in them? How do certain images, such as an overjoyed parent embracing a lost child, conjure so much more than a teaching point? Like returning to sit before a familiar work of art, we expect to see anew again and again. As O'Connor says, even when we "find" meaning, it "cannot be drained off and used as a substitute."[196] In the same way that "you can't say Cezanne painted apples and a tablecloth and have said what Cezanne painted," it is insufficient to summarize the Parable of the Prodigal Son with the assertion "God forgives lost children." As Eduard Schweizer puts it, "A musical performance cannot be transmitted didactically without becoming an audible event; neither can the content of this parable [Luke 15:11–32] be captured in a summary statement."[197] Parable, like other arts, must be *performed*. Ricoeur's understanding of parable as an

---

[194] This is evident in Jeremias, *Parables of Jesus*, who downplays Jesus' use of Scripture. For another example of this trend, see Wilder, *Language of the Gospel*, 73f.

[195] Flannery O'Connor, "The Fiction Writer and His Country," in *Mystery and Manners: Occasional Prose* (New York: Farrar, Strauss, and Giroux), 34.

[196] O'Connor, "Fiction Writer," 75. O'Connor is citing John Peale Bishop's observation.

[197] Eduard Schweizer, *The Good News according to Luke*, trans. David E. Green (Atlanta: John Knox, 1984), 252.

ongoing process of metaphorization through retelling holds open the irreducibility and multidimensionality of the form.

The third issue, of referentiality, is closely related. On the one hand, the destabilization of reference is merely of a piece with the claim about irreducibility. Parable is polyvalent, with multiple layers and conflicting senses. Its textually faithful yet diverse interpretations stand side by side and pile up over time. On the other hand, in literary-existential interpretations informed by the New Hermeneutic and poststructuralism or deconstructionism, very often the eventfulness of language becomes the thing itself. In that case, claiming any extradiegetic point of reference is cast off as a form of allegorizing.[198] Here the purpose of Jesus' parables is not so much to teach a lesson but to bring the hearer to a point of crisis. The problem with the "shock and awe" explanation of this phenomenon is that it can suppress the assertorial and reality-depicting potential of metaphorical speech, when the storyteller (and his redactors) very clearly intended to communicate something. However, there is an important insight here, one that loosens referentiality without obliterating it. Resisting or querying the immediate reference of parable is not necessarily about denying meaning beyond the text but about channeling that meaning into a transformational existential encounter. Reference happens *in front of* the text.

The way the opaqueness, irreducibility, and referentiality of the parables can be addressed without flattening them into preknown theological or moral claims alleviates the need to distinguish them sharply from allegories. It becomes clear that much of what is today dismissed as "allegorizing" is more accurately accounted for in terms of figure, type, or even simply allusion, parallel, or metaphor.[199] It is also clear that the telos of figuration is praxis, lived application, which is why structuralism can take Ricoeur only so far.

The word "allegory" is first employed in a Christian context by Paul (Gal 4:22–30).[200] It is used to express a "symbolic transposition" from one history or

[198] *Extradiagetic* means "outside the story" and refers to elements beyond the main narrative that are referenced or implied within it.

[199] De Lubac says traditional exegesis is concerned with types and figures. "Typical meaning" is sometimes exchangeable with "mystical or allegorical meaning, or even with figurative meaning, as in Pascal" (*Scripture in the Tradition*, 15–16). However, for him, "typology" is too narrow and too easily confused with "historical." Following Louis Boyer, de Lubac wants to distinguish Christian spiritual interpretation, based on *correlations*, from "organic allegory" based purely on "imaginary symbolism" (44–45).

[200] Paul says ἅτινα ἐστιν ἀλληγορούμενα—"these things are allegorized" (v. 24)—when he takes Hagar and Sarah as symbols for the two covenants, the first from "Mount Sinai," bringing forth children for slavery (v. 24), the second, "our free mother" from "the Jerusalem above" (v. 26).

story to another.[201] The narrative link unsettles the typical modern distinction between allegories as artificial or esoteric extrapolations and parables as simple "stories *drawn from life*."[202] De Lubac speaks of the transposition of meaning as a "prolongation" of earlier realities, "fulfilling while transfiguring."[203] At points, his description of "spiritual" interpretation is almost synonymous with Auerbach's "figural" interpretation, despite the fact that Auerbach contrasts "the basic historical reality of figures" with "all attempts at spiritually allegorical interpretation."[204] Figural interpretation, for Auerbach, refers to "a meaning first concealed, then revealed" or to the "temporal relation of promise to fulfillment."[205] For example, Paul's assertion that "the law is spiritual" or his construal of Jesus as "the new Moses" are instances in which a figure or type (law, Moses) is redeployed in such a way that it appeals to and enhances "the immediate" (literal, historical, conventional) meaning.[206] In the relation of figure to fulfillment, the one "heralds" the other; the elder serves the younger (Rom 9:12).[207]

Within such language looms the specter of supersessionism.[208] However, de Lubac challenges the view that the symbolic transposition of allegorical or spiritual understanding is something Christians do capriciously in order to commandeer Hebrew Scripture.[209] Rather, it is a textual phenomenon they are

---

[201] De Lubac, *Scripture in the Tradition*, 11–12. De Lubac argues on the basis of Tertullian and Origen that the Christian allegorical interpretation originates with Paul. He points to Tertullian on "*allegorica dipositio*" (*Val.*, ch. 1, 177) and its precedence in "the apostle" (*Marc.*, bk. V, ch. vii, 595), as well as Origen on "*allegorica intelligentia*" (*Comm. Gen.*, h. 5, n. 5, 64), "*allegoriae ordo*" (h. 6, n. 3, 69), and "*allegorias nostras, quas Paulus docuit*" (h. 3, n. 5, 45), etc. Cf. *Medieval Exegesis*, 2:1f.

[202] Dodd, Jeremias, et al.

[203] De Lubac, *Scripture in the Tradition*, 6, 40.

[204] Erich Auerbach, *Mimesis: The Representation of Reality in Western Literature*, trans. William R. Trask (Princeton: Princeton University Press, 1953), 196; and "Figura," trans. Ralph Mannheim, in *Scenes from the Drama of European Literature* (Minneapolis: University of Minnesota Press, 1984), 34.

[205] Robbins, *Prodigal Son / Elder Brother*, 2.

[206] De Lubac, *Scripture in the Tradition*, 43.

[207] Augustine, *City of God* XX.4.

[208] See, for example, Robbins, *Prodigal Son / Elder Brother*, 38. Cf. John David Dawson, *Christian Figural Reading and the Fashioning of Identity* (Berkeley: University of California Press, 2002), 14.

[209] Due to the resonances between them, de Lubac's spiritual interpretation and Auerbach's figural interpretation have both been critiqued for bearing within them a supersessionist bias. See, for example, Jill Robbins on "Figurations of the Judaic," in *Prodigal Son / Elder Brother*. Cf. Kathleen Biddick, *The Typological Imaginary: Circumcision, Technology, History* (Philadelphia: University of Pennsylvania Press, 2003), 5–6. Against "the fantasy of supersessionism," Biddick speaks of the "threat of typological

simply extending, for there is already "an almost constant process of spiritualization at work in biblical history." The Hebrew Bible

> never stops reflecting on the events of Exodus; the departure from Egypt, the so-
> journ and march in the desert, the conquest of the Promised Land. . . . The Proph-
> ets see in them a perfect type of the great exodus which is to come, of the final
> liberation, and of the glory of the chosen people. The psalmists discover in them
> the drama of the interior life, which is every day renewed in every Israelite.[210]

Figuration proceeds through detecting and juxtaposing resonant intertexts, a
movement already present in the texts prior to Christian reflection on them.

This account stands in contrast to that of many modern scholars. Dodd,
for example, does not make the connection between New Testament allegorizing or typologizing and Old Testament allusion, but associates allegory
with Greek mythology and esoterica, which he considers alien to the Jewish
imagination.[211] De Lubac certainly acknowledges the influence of allegory in
Greek rhetoric and myth on Christian reading practices.[212] He admits that
ancient allegory "evokes the idea of an analogy which is artificial, elaborately
detailed . . . an exploitation of image to develop an idea which is already
formed," and he bemoans the fact that "such an evocation corresponds only
too well to what has in fact become the usage of scriptural 'allegory'"—cloying,

---

reversibility." But the fluidity of figuration is already accounted for and welcomed in
the tradition of spiritual interpretation.

[210] De Lubac, *Scripture in the Tradition*, 33. If this is true, it calls into question
the popular view in redaction criticism that in framing Christ's speech as they did,
the New Testament writers were corrupting the original text with alien allegorical
elements, as if symbolism and figuration were not already part of the religious discourse of the day, including Jesus'. Allegorizing or typologizing does not begin with
Philo and the Hellenistic influence on early Christian writing.

[211] Consequently, he is forced to contradict his emphasis on metaphor by reducing parables, in at least one instance, to illustrations. Dodd claims, "The probability
is that the parables could have been taken for allegorical mystifications only in a
non-Jewish environment. Among Jewish teachers the parable was a common and
well-understood method of illustration, and the parables of Jesus are similar in form
to Rabbinic parables. . . . In the Hellenistic world, on the other hand, the use of
myths, allegorically interpreted, as vehicles of esoteric doctrine, was widespread"
(*Parables of the Kingdom*, 4). The association between allegory, myth, and Greek
philosophy is one of the primary reasons so many New Testament scholars wish to
eschew allegory.

[212] However, de Lubac does offer an alternate genealogy. For a brief comparison of
the history of the use of "allegory" in ancient Greek poetry and philosophy vs. in early
Christian thought, see de Lubac, *Medieval Exegesis*, 1–9.

arbitrary, reducible.[213] While wary of the limits of "scientific methods" and "pernicious literalism," de Lubac also integrates the gains of historical criticism and denounces a "hasty flight" to "spiritual significance."[214] Although in ancient and early medieval interpretation, "the so-called mystical or allegorical meaning was always considered as the doctrinal meaning par excellence," from the twelfth century on it is increasingly interiorized and associated with "spiritual fruit" (or piety and morality) such that "mystical" readings become more private, personal, and therefore also subjective or idiosyncratic.[215] By the thirteenth century, Aquinas has to assert, "From the literal [intended] sense alone can arguments be drawn," and, after the Renaissance and Reformation, there is an increasing bias against "spiritual" reading, a kind of "outdoing the Cartesian spirit" that finally devolves into "the prosaic pragmatism of the eighteenth century."[216] But this history of reading includes the observation that, in early Christian interpretation, beginning with Jesus' own reading of Scripture, there is a distinct prolongation of the figuralism of Hebrew narrative.[217] Problems arise when the practice of spiritual interpretation is unmoored from biblical history and scriptural reference.[218]

A literary analysis, such as that of Robert Alter, helps clarify the point. Alter argues that Hebrew sacred history is the beginning of "prose fiction" or "fictionalized history," which, he says, "is the best general rubric for describing biblical narrative."[219] Calling it "fiction" indicates that the biblical writers employ "conscious artistry" and a "particularizing imagination" in the retelling of history, seeking "through the process of narrative realization to reveal the enactment of God's purposes in historical events."[220] The development of Hebrew storytelling, then, is bound up with a certain view of God (as "the God of history") and humanity (as free and fallen agents). In contrast to the "polytheistic genre" of paganism defined by "ritual rehearsal" and "the stable closure of the mythological world," Hebrew literature marks a move toward linear, indeterminate,

---

[213]   De Lubac, *Scripture in the Tradition*, 12.

[214]   De Lubac, *Scripture in the Tradition*, 3.

[215]   De Lubac, *Scripture in the Tradition*, 49, 57.

[216]   E.g., Aquinas, *ST* I, q. 1, a. 10. De Lubac, *Medieval Exegesis*, 60.

[217]   In Luke 24:27, it says that "having begun from Moses and from all the prophets," the resurrected Christ "explained" or "interpreted" (διερμήνευσεν) "to them in all the scriptures the things concerning himself." Similarly, it says, "he opened to us the scriptures" (v. 32) and "he opened their minds to understand the scriptures" (v. 45) (literal translation from the Greek).

[218]   De Lubac, *Scripture in the Tradition*, 12.

[219]   Robert Alter, *The Art of Biblical Narrative* (New York: Basic Books, 1981), 24–25.

[220]   Alter, *Art of Biblical Narrative*, 32.

and liberative accounts of history and human freedom that resemble "life in history" more than the fixed cycles and hierarchies of myth.[221] In tracing this development, Alter notes key conventions of Hebrew narrative, for example, the use of "type-scenes" or "recurrent narrative episodes" involving a certain set of characters, situations, locations, dialogue patterns, and so forth.[222] In much the same way as parable, the storyteller plays with a fixed repertoire familiar to its hearers, concisely conveying a message more through structural omission and novelty than through roles and characters.[223] Alter says, "Much of art lies in the shifting aperture between the shadowy foreimage in the antic- ipating mind of the observer and the realized revelatory image in the work itself."[224] As with parable, the meaning of the story lies in between expectation and realization—*as* a fulfillment, it is also always a transformation.

While Alter does not refer to this leap as "spiritualization" (de Lubac) or "figuration" (Auerbach), his description of the repurposing of inherited forms to generate new insights is akin to them. Soskice draws our attention to the same literary dynamic. Lamenting the loss of the vitality of biblical imagery in the legacies of literalism and historical-criticism, she observes that metaphors in Scripture are "more than simple metaphor—they are almost *emblematic*." While acknowledging that the "repetition of metaphor has often gone hand in hand with typological interpretation and the conviction that certain events in the Old Testament prefigure those in the New," she says:

> We need not commit ourselves to this tenet of faith to make *the essentially liter-ary point* that, in ways similar to the allusive techniques of any literary tradition, certain metaphors and models of God's presence and gracious acts . . . have been used and re-used in the central texts of Christianity and in subsequent expositions of those texts. So, to explain what it means to Christians to say that God is a foun-tain of living water, or a vine-keeper, or a rock, or a fortress, or king requires an account not merely of fountains, rocks, vines, and kinds but of a whole tradition of experiences and of the literary tradition which records and interprets them.

Inquiry into the meaning of recurring metaphors in the tradition, then, would require a "study of gloss upon gloss, use and re-use of the figures that comprise an interweaving of meanings so complex that the possible readings are never exhausted."[225]

---

[221]   Alter, *Art of Biblical Narrative*, 26–27.
[222]   Alter, *Art of Biblical Narrative*, 47, 54.
[223]   Alter, *Art of Biblical Narrative*, 51.
[224]   Alter, *Art of Biblical Narrative*, 62.
[225]   Soskice, *Metaphor and Religious Language*, 158–60 (emphasis added). In the search for the historical Jesus, "Christians both liberal and conservative" have

A better understanding of biblical prose fiction (Alter) and metaphor (Soskice) leads away from the conclusion that theologizing, typologizing, or alluding to and refiguring supposedly flat histories is a later "allegorizing" practice. The story or history is already multi-referential or multi-intentional, recalling past iterations and inviting new inferences. The scriptural reservoir of metaphors and models are already refracted for us, not only through subsequent applications, paraphrases, commentaries, sermons, and retellings, but first of all within the text itself. Storytelling, in practice, undercuts simple theoretical divisions between allegorical and historical, figural and literal, and so on.

In some cases, however, the aversion to so-called allegorizing is not merely a matter of misunderstanding the literary point but appears to be an aversion to the notion that the inner or "spiritual" life of the individual is implicated in the biblical narrative in the present. Like "allegory," "spiritual" is a term that is easily misconstrued. Spiritual means *interior*; spiritualization is interiorization, appropriation. The text makes its claim on the reader's life. Thus the figural or spiritual interpretation of Scripture always marks a "dual passage."[226] While it has been criticized for belying a totalizing impulse (and, concomitantly, supersessionism), it is meant to involve a double transposition from figure (OT/Law) to fulfillment (in NT/Christ) in which the fulfillment itself becomes a figure to be fulfilled again and again (in the interior/soul or community). The "doubleness" is in fact open-ended; it does not stall out at one point in history. A fulfilled figure asks to be refigured, in another way, inside and outside the text. It is endlessly generative. (This is a different sort of indeterminacy.)

Undercutting the stark dualities Christian/Jewish, Spirit/Law, spiritual/corporeal, the "spiritual" understanding of Scripture lies, above all, in its "incarnate" meaning—that is, in seeing Scripture "transfigured by Christ" in his bodily life.[227] In Jesus' person, as in his storytelling, the history of Israel is represented and refigured. As de Lubac says, "The reality of which the Old and even the New Testament contain 'types' is not only spiritual, but is also incarnate. It is not only eternal, but is historical as well. . . . *The spiritual meaning*, then, is everywhere . . . *first and foremost in reality itself.*"[228] The spiritual is embodied in reality; that is why Scripture requires "a global interpretation."[229] As Barth says, "The shadow

---

attempted "to salvage his exact words and acts from the dross of allusion and interpretation with which the gospel writers surrounded them." What they share in common is a literalism that ultimately "equates religious truth with historical facts."

[226] Soskice, *Metaphor and Religious Language*, 17, 19.
[227] De Lubac, *Scripture in the Tradition*, 22.
[228] De Lubac, *Scripture in the Tradition*, xix.
[229] De Lubac, *Scripture in the Tradition*, 22.

of Christ . . . is everywhere at play in the history of the (chosen) people."[230] Inasmuch as "the categories used by Jesus to tell us about himself are ancient biblical categories," de Lubac says, he "causes them to burst forth, or, if you prefer, sublimates them and unifies them by making them converge upon himself."[231] The referent of the parables may be the Kingdom of God, but Jesus is, to use Origen's phrase, *autobasileia*, the kingdom-in-person.[232]

One might see Jesus as a walking nexus of allusions, a convergence of types and type-scenes, himself an intertextual event.[233] He offers himself to be read—in light of a particular history, a particular collection of stories, a particular set of identities.[234] He illuminates them, yes, but they also illuminate him. This is particularly true of the parables of Jesus. The interplay of embedded narratives creates a "symbolic interference" that goes both ways and requires the "mutual interpretation" of both.[235] The vis-à-vis of storytelling as an act of communication produces a "reverberation of the narrative-parable on the person who tells it" and yields figural interpretive trajectories that move in multiple directions.[236] Spiritual meaning is lived meaning; figuration is incarnate and exemplary.

Parable and Reduction

The participatory refiguration of parable in life is assumed in the final clause of Dodd's definition of parable: "The application is left imprecise in order to tease

---

[230]   This phrasing is taken from de Lubac's citation of Barth's sixth Gifford Lecture, "The Revelation of God in Christ" (*Scripture in the Tradition*, 83). The published translation in English reads, "It is His shadow that can be traced clearly or faintly in things great and small, everywhere in Israel's history" (6.2). See Barth, *The Knowledge of God and the Service of God according to the Teaching of the Reformation: Recalling the Scottish Confession of 1560*, trans. J. L. M. Haire and Ian Henderson, The Gifford Lectures (London: Hodder and Stoughton, 1938), 65. De Lubac describes Barth's exegesis as "reminiscent in many ways of the exegesis of the early Fathers" (*Scripture in the Tradition*, 77).

[231]   De Lubac, *Scripture in the Tradition*, 7.

[232]   Origen, *Commentarium in evangelium Matthaei* 14.7.10, in *Origenes. Origenes Werke*, vol. 10.1–2, ed. Erich Klostermann (Leipzig: Hinrichs, 1935–1937).

[233]   For an Old Testament type-scene retold in Jesus himself, consider his interactions with the "woman at the well" in John 4. It bears many of the traits of the familiar betrothal scene that structures, for example, Jacob's encounter with Rachel at the well (see Alter, *Art of Biblical Narrative*, 54f.). The fact that Jesus reenacts this scene in his *life* rather than speech should not prevent us from seeing it as a narrative retelling. If we have trouble making this leap, it is only a testimony to the distanciation of text and life today. Scriptural allusions are no less prevalent in Jesus' actions than in his words.

[234]   This is consonant with what Wright says of Jesus' parables being rooted in Israel's prophetic-apocalyptic tradition of storytelling. See *Jesus and the Victory of God*, 177.

[235]   Ricoeur, "Biblical Hermeneutics," 105.

[236]   Ricoeur, "Biblical Hermeneutics," 164.

the hearer into their own application." Modern and contemporary New Testament parable scholarship is peppered with comments like this, about the way the parables of Jesus interrupt, suspend, expand, revise, and renew the field of human perception. Parable is said to "arrest" its audience through "vividness" or "strangeness," serving as a kind of reproving "shock" tactic that facilitates "a new apprehension of reality," making visible a "kinship" where "ordinary vision" would not otherwise perceive it and "revealing" things irreducible to "a clear language."[237] Jesus' parables interrupt and dismantle the "commonsight" that otherwise "tyrannizes" perception.[238] They have a "revelatory character," a "capacity of imparting to their hearers something of Jesus' vision of the power of God" by producing "an image with a certain shock to the imagination which directly conveys vision of what is signified."[239] Jesus is a "poet-parabler," whose words have

> the power to *provoke new sight*, freed from the weight of habituated usage. The term poet is of course used here in a root sense: not just as creator of verse, but as the creator of threshold language opening onto vistas forgotten or world aborning.... In this sense, Moses was a poet, Socrates was a poet, Jesus was a poet.[240]

The poetic function of parable is a "juxtaposition" that "produces an impact upon the imagination and induces a vision of that which cannot be conveyed by prosaic or discursive speech."[241] Parable "does not 'teach,' in the sense of teaching abstract or timeless truth; it *acts*. It creates a new world."[242]

These comments draw attention to the agency of parabolic language, specifically to the way it inverts the reading relationship. Jesus' sayings "do not invite contemplation of themselves as objects of value but require us to contemplate our lives."[243] According to Rudolf Bultmann's principle, "not only does the interpreter interpret the text, but also *the text interprets the interpreter*."[244] In

---

[237] Dodd, *Parables of the Kingdom*, 5; Jeremias, *Parables of Jesus*, 21; Perrin, *Jesus and the Language of the Kingdom*, 89; Wilder, *Language of the Gospel*, 129; Ricoeur, "Biblical Hermeneutics," 79.

[238] Funk, *Parables and Presence*, 13, 117.

[239] Kissinger (commenting on Wilder), *Parables of Jesus*, 168; Wilder, *Language of the Gospel*, 72.

[240] Crossan, *In Parables*, 17 (emphasis added). Funk, *Parables and Presence*, 17.

[241] Funk, *Language*, 136.

[242] Wright, *Jesus and the Victory of God*, 130.

[243] Robert Tannehill, *Sword of His Mouth* (Philadelphia: Fortress, 1975), 17.

[244] This is Perrin's paraphrase of Bultmann (*Jesus and the Language of the Kingdom*, 10; see 11, n. 17). Similarly, Funk glosses Fuchs in claiming that "the parable is not meant to *be* interpreted, but to interpret" (*Language*, 152).

parable, "the hearer's judgment is precipitated"; the reader is read.[245] The parables function like different kinds of glass: some are "mirrors" that "consistently resist our attempts to turn them into windows" and, through their "reflective opacity," reflect "instead the faces of those who look upon them."[246] The hearer is invited to "unfold with the story" and to "be illumined" by it.[247] Inasmuch as parable bears the reality to which it refers, "the hearer not only learns about that reality" but actually "participates in it" or—better—is "invaded by it."[248]

Perduring within so many statements about parable's capacity to implicate its hearers and transform vision are traces of a technical language originating with phenomenology and, specifically, the philosophy of Edmund Husserl. These make their way into recent parable scholarship, following, among other routes, the path from Martin Heidegger to Bultmann, Fuchs, and Ebeling to later Anglo-American biblical scholars influenced by existentialism and the New Hermeneutic, or, alternately, from Heidegger to Derrida and Ricoeur through deconstructionism and poststructuralism. In contemporary New Testament scholarship, parable is often, and sometimes unwittingly, conceived in Heideggerian terms, as "a privileged instrument for suspending reality by means of the displacement of the ordinary meaning of words."[249] What is latent here are the philosophical techniques of "bracketing" (or *epochē*) and "reduction." "Bracketing" refers to the suspension of "the natural attitude," or our habitual, everyday, theoretical, naïve ways of facing things.[250] "Reduction," in its phenomenological sense, means "to lead back" (*reducere*) rather than its more ordinary use as

[245]   Rudolf Bultmann, *History of the Synoptic Tradition*, trans. John Marsh (Peabody, Mass.: Hendrickson, 1963), 191f. Quoted by Funk, *Language*, 144.

[246]   Crossan, *Cliffs of Fall*, 26.

[247]   Funk, *Language*, 162; Kissinger, *Parables of Jesus*, 169.

[248]   Wilder, *Language of the Gospel*, 92.

[249]   Ricoeur, "Biblical Hermeneutics," 83. Funk, like Crossan, approaches the parables of Jesus as "double paradigms or declensions of reality." While "the first paradigm brings the logic of everydayness to the surface and confirms that logic as self-evident or self-validating," it "is shattered on the second, which disrupts the order of everydayness by reversing certainties or turning things upside down" (*Parables and Presence*, 52).

[250]   Edmund Husserl, "Phenomenology as Transcendental Philosophy," in *The Essential Husserl: Basic Writings*, ed. Donn Welton (Bloomington: Indiana University Press, 1999), 66. According to Husserl, *epochē* is a "method of parenthesizing" and "judgment-excluding" in which the relationship I have to an object is phenomenalized; it becomes something I can look at, contemplate—and even suspend. As Robert Sokolowski explains it, "From the philosophically reflective stance, we make the appearances thematic. We look *at* what we normally look *through*." See Sokolowski, *Introduction to Phenomenology* (Cambridge: Cambridge University Press, 2000), 49–50.

"distill" or "condense." The work of "reduction" is twofold: it involves (1) a whittling down of the subject to "transcendental consciousness" (or what we might think of as a purged, receptive gaze) and (2) a following back of the object to its essence (*eidos*), which is able to more fully appear once the plank in our eye, as it were, has been removed.[251] In short, bracketing and reduction is a process of identifying and setting aside the accidental biases that blind and practicing radical openness to reality in its otherness.

Husserl was primarily concerned with the epistemological subject-object relationship, with the way we view things, the way they appear to us. But a common theme of more recent phenomenology is the inversion of the dynamics of perception, such that the object, for example a text, is said to "constitute" the subject rather than vice versa. This gives rise to phrases such as "counter-intentionality" and "counter-gaze," philosophical correlates of claims in New Testament scholarship related to the experience of being viewed or queried by the parable. As Paul Claudel says, "It would be more exact to acknowledge that it is Scripture which is questioning us."[252] It is noteworthy that devoted readers have long understood their textual relationships in precisely this way. This is because "talk of *epochē* and reduction—is abstraction from literary practice."[253] The philosophical vocabulary merely helps name and clarify the phenomenon. What those who praise the poetic function of metaphor in parable intuit is the way parable as a genre "brackets everyday life and its worldly logic" and "leads back" to the "divine logic" of what we call "the kingdom."[254] Through a dual strategy of defamiliarization and

[251] Transcendental consciousness is that which remains when "the whole world, including ourselves with all our cogitare, is excluded" (Husserl, "Phenomenology," 66). This "phenomenological residuum" can be understood in the broadest sense of the Cartesian cogito: it includes not only "I think" but comprises "every 'I perceive, I remember, I phantasy, I judge, I feel, I desire, I will,' and thus all egoical mental processes which are at all similar to them" (67–68). It is that *something* that remains after bracketing the world—the "I" that experiences, that exists purely as a "dative of disclosure." But something else remains as well. In assuming the phenomenological attitude, "the thing itself" is not discarded but uncovered by way of an "eidetic reduction," or an "intuition" of the *eidos* (essential form) of a thing that endures after all "phenomenological judgment-exclusions" (66).

[252] De Lubac, *Scripture in the Tradition*, 73. See Paul Claudel, "L'Ecriture sainte," *La Vie intellectuelle*, May 1948, 8.

[253] Kevin Hart, "The Christian Reduction," response paper presented at "The Promise of Phenomenology and Scripture" panel at the American Academy of Religion annual meeting, Montreal, November 2009. Hart draws this point out specifically in connection to the parables, which he says are not only "open to a phenomenological reading" but are themselves "an example of phenomenology." See Kevin Hart, *Kingdoms of God* (Bloomington: Indiana University Press, 2014), 19.

[254] Hart, *Kingdoms of God*, 20.

indictment, the parables of Jesus challenge ordinary perception and foster a kind of "counter-experience" in which the hearer or reader is incorporated into another's perspective, God's perspective.

Imaging this experience, we might think of parable as a narrative icon. The visual field of a painted icon inverts ordinary pictorial perspective. In linear perspective, our sight converges on a vanishing point within the frame (/\). By contrast, the icon reverses perspective, placing the vanishing point outside the frame (\/). The viewer becomes viewed. Parable likewise implicates its hearers in a participatory encounter. Where in the Husserlian *epochē* our prejudgments are only temporarily bracketed, in what we might call the "parabolic reduction," our narrative expectation is not merely suspended for a time but finally transformed within lived experience.

There is no reason, then, for a distinctly literary approach to deny that "poetic language aims at reality" or to conclude that the parables impart only paradox and crisis.[255] What parable theory inherits from phenomenology, and would do well to clarify, is a language for the way parable—and, indeed, much good fiction—works on its readers, challenging first order referentiality *in order to* expose other levels of meaning inside, outside, and in front of the text. It not only requires but generates ears that hear and eyes that see. This brings us back to the dynamics at work in scriptural figuration and spiritual interpretation. Allowing oneself to be interpreted, precipitated, invaded, unfolded by the text entails a kind of crisis followed by conversion. Commonly attending the language of conversion is the image of transition from blindness to sight. Consider, among countless examples, Paul's paradigmatic ordeal on the way to Damascus, Augustine's rhetoric throughout *Confessions*, and the famous hymn "Amazing Grace" by slave trader turned abolitionist John Newton—"I once was lost, but now I'm found, was blind but now I see." This is because, in de Lubac's words, "the entire process of spiritual understanding is . . . identical to the process of conversion. It is its luminous aspect."[256]

Children Afield: Two Views from the Parable

If the Parable of the Lost or Prodigal Son functions as a double declension of reality, if it is a narrative icon inverting ordinary perspective, then into what new world are its hearers incorporated? In Luke 15:11–32, the motif of inverted or contested vision is most pronounced in the prodigal's return (v. 20), but it implicitly structures the whole story. As the few key instances of direct speech and dialogue reveal (vv. 12, 17–19, 21–22, 29–32), the younger

---

[255]   Consider Roman Jakobson. Ricoeur, "Biblical Hermeneutics," 83.
[256]   De Lubac, *Scripture in the Tradition*, 21.

son's drama begins with and depends upon a certain perception he has of himself, his father, and the nature of their relationship, which prompts him to set his sights elsewhere and escape his father's oversight.

The action begins with his demand: "Father, give me the share of the property that will belong to me" (v. 12). He relates to his father from within a legal economy of belonging, property, or right. In asking for what is his portion of the οὐσία/βίος (property, livelihood, wealth), the son disobeys the command to honor one's father and mother (Exod 20:12; Deut 5:16). He symbolically expresses his wish that his father were dead, as customarily inheritance was bestowed only at that point. It also reveals something about how the son sees the father, as well as himself. His self-assertion actually bespeaks a sense of subjection. In an effort to be free *from*, the boy denigrates himself, impulsively taking less than his full inheritance and setting off for a "distant" (i.e., gentile) land where he will not be seen squandering his existence, becoming unclean.[257] Yet, from beginning to end, the father's regard for his son serves as a counterpoint to the son's sense of himself and his father. Rather than holding his son or his property hostage, in granting his request, the father treats him as a free individual and—quite unnecessarily—as his legal equal.

After the son depletes his funds, famine overtakes the country, echoing the descent of the Hebrew people into slavery in Genesis 47.[258] He begins "to go without" (v. 14) and is forced to become another man's "indentured servant" tending a heard of pigs (v. 15).[259] This situation is emblematic not merely of poverty but of captivity and ritual impurity. The association with swine is a profound degradation.[260] The story's nadir and turning point consists in the boy "coming to his senses" (v. 17), a flash of recognition after a period of anaesthetization and blindness. He sees his condition and, in a moment of intense hunger, he says to himself,

---

[257] Hultgren, *Parables of Jesus*, 74. "Far country" means "outside of Palestine," where it is impossible to keep kosher (cf. Luke 19:10), ensuring not only spatial but also ritual alienation from family.

[258] In the third year of famine, after losing their money and their cattle, the Hebrew people sold their bodies and their land for sustenance, saying to Joseph, "We cannot hide from my lord that our money is all spent, and the herds of cattle are my lord's. There is nothing left in the sight of my lord but our bodies and our lands. Shall we die before your eyes, both we and our land? Buy us and our land in exchange for food. We with our land will become slaves to Pharaoh; just give us seed, so that we may live and not die and that the land may not become desolate" (Gen 47:18–19).

[259] Hultgren, *Parables of Jesus*, 75.

[260] In the Mishnah, raising pigs is prohibited, and, in the Babylonian Talmud, those who do are called "accursed" (Hultgren, *Parables of Jesus*, 75).

How many of my father's hired hands have bread enough and to spare, but here I am dying of hunger! I will get up and go to my father, and I will say to him, "Father I have sinned against heaven and before you; I am no longer worthy to be called your son; treat me like one of your hired hands." (vv. 17–19)[261]

Envisioning the abundance of the home he abandoned, he resolves to acknowledge his sin and openly endure its expected consequences, being disinherited as "son" and demoted to "servant." The younger son evaluates himself from within an economy of worth or merit and, indeed, survival. If he ever saw himself as a "worthy" child, he certainly does not now. Presenting himself as, at best, "one of your hired hands" (ἕνα τῶν μισθίων σου), he situates himself among the day laborers, even lower in the hierarchy than the household servants (παῖδες) and slaves (δοῦλοι).[262] He conceives of his father's good favor as something earned or, in his case—*spent*. His speech, then, is not a request for forgiveness, much less restoration. While he professes himself a sinner, a degenerate, it is the sudden awareness of the pointlessness of his destitution that drives him home rather than the hope of relational reconciliation.

The father, however, is ready for his son's return—expectant, vigilant, resolute. "While he was still a long way off, his father saw him and had compassion for him" (ἔτι δὲ αὐτοῦ μακρὰν ἀπέχοντος εἶδεν αὐτὸν ὁ πατὴρ αὐτοῦ καὶ ἐσπλαγχνίσθη) (v. 20). There is much commentary on this word ἐσπλαγχνίσθη from σπλαγχνίζομαι.[263] It means: to have compassion or pity, to feel love, or,

---

[261]   In Bernard's allegorization of the parable, it is the figure of Fear (rather than hunger) that awakens the lost heir and Hope that inspires the notion that he return to his father as a *mercenarius* (Luke 15:17), which (corresponding to the second step in the ascent to God in *On Loving God*) is inferior to the filial love with which he began and which his father wishes to restore.

[262]   The latter had stable employment and were considered part of the household. Day laborers had the least reliable income and most tenuous connection to the family and land. For us today, this is somewhat counterintuitive, since day laborers would have had the "choice" to travel from region to region—a fact that we are accustomed to perceiving as "freedom." But, within this cultural framework, it is not mobility or transience but familial security that is desirable.

[263]   The term occurs twelve times in the gospels (Matt 9:36; 14:14; 15:32; 18:27; 20:34; Mark 1:41; 6:34; 8:2; 9:22; and Luke 7:13; 10:33; 15:20). See Helmut Koester, "σπλάγχνον," in *Theological Dictionary of the New Testament*, vol. 7 (Grand Rapids: Eerdmans, 1995), 553–55. Except in the parables of the Good Samaritan, Unforgiving Servant, and the Prodigal Son, it is always applied to Jesus or God (namely in the context of healing) rather than other human characters. But in these parables, it is still "used in reference to persons who reflect divine compassion" (Hultgren, *Parables of Jesus*, 24).

more viscerally, to be moved in one's intestines or womb.[264] As the central verb and "dramatic center" of the whole parable, it focuses us on "the father's compassionate nature."[265] It is worth highlighting the way ἐσπλαγχνίσθη is used in conjunction with εἶδεν: the father *saw* his son and had compassion.[266] It is sometimes speculated that he must have spent his days squinting down the road, patiently waiting for his child's return. How else would he happen to have seen him on this particular day and at such a distance? But this is a pronounced moment in which the extravagance of the story transcends its "realism." Parataxis gathers the action of the father into a single stream, "and while he was still at a distance his father saw him and was filled with compassion and having run he fell upon his neck and kissed him" (καὶ ἀναστὰς ἦλθεν πρὸς τὸν πατέρα αὐτοῦ. ἔτι δὲ αὐτοῦ μακρὰν ἀπέχοντος εἶδεν αὐτὸν ὁ πατὴρ αὐτοῦ καὶ ἐσπλαγχνίσθη, καὶ δραμὼν ἐπέπεσεν ἐπὶ τὸν τράχηλον αὐτοῦ καὶ κατεφίλησεν αὐτόν) (v. 20).[267] The father sees and pities and runs and embraces and kisses—all at once. This sequence of verbs evokes Esau running to meet Jacob (Gen 33:3): "It reveals strong emotion," the visceral pang of love.[268] The father's running would have been surprising to the initial audience.[269] Yet all

[264] This word specifically implies the love of a parent, especially of a mother. "Pity" (mentioned so often in Julian's text) and "compassion" (a pivotal term in the biblical parable) have Latin roots that are virtually synonymous and have a strong connection with motherhood in Hebrew: *raham*/"compassion" is comprised of the same set of consonants as *rahem*/"womb."

[265] See Holgate, *Prodigality, Liberality, and Meanness*, 53. Holgate refers to Menken's word study, which shows that σπλαγχνίζομαι is the central aorist indicative verb of the twenty-three indicatives in the parable. See Maarten J. J. Menken, "The Position of σπλαγχνίζεσθαι and σπλάγχνα in the Gospel of Luke," *Novum Testamentum* 30, no. 2 (1988): 107–14.

[266] We also find "saw and had compassion" linked in Matt 9:36 ("When he saw the crowds, he had compassion for them, because they were harassed and helpless, like sheep without a shepherd"); Matt 14:14 ("When he went ashore, he saw a great crowd; and he had compassion for them and cured their sick"); Mark 6:34 ("As he went ashore, he saw a great crowd; and he had compassion for them, because they were like sheep without a shepherd; and he began to teach them many things"); and Luke 7:13 ("When the Lord saw her, he had compassion for her and said to her, 'Do not weep'"). In the other passages, seeing is implied through proximity. Jesus recognizes those around him and registers their needs, and something is viscerally evoked in him.

[267] This is a literal translation from the Greek. Regarding the phrase "fell upon his neck," compare with Gen 33:4; 45:14; 46:29; 3 Macc 5:49; Acts 20:37.

[268] Schweizer, *Good News*, 249.

[269] They would have seen this as undignified, for "fathers in a first-century Near Eastern environment do not run" (Donahue, *Gospel in Narrative*, 15). In the language of Sirach, "the 'way' a man walks 'shows what he is'" (Sir 19:30).

of this should not necessarily be interpreted, as it so often is, as an act of forgiveness.[270] The father does not follow any conciliatory procedure. His radical openhandedness is, in every regard, "atypical" of his context and defies expectations of even the most favorable welcome a son might have received under the circumstances.[271] The father's watchfulness, the readiness of his welcome, exceeds the ordinary, and this disjuncture opens up the narrative in the direction of "something else, something more" (Ricoeur). This preemptive welcome embodies God's promise to Israel, in the language of Isaiah 65:24: "Before they call, I will answer, / while they are yet speaking I will hear."

In the midst of their embrace, the son speaks directly for the third time. He recites the first part of the speech he prepared, but his father interrupts him at "I am no longer worthy to be called your son," before he can complete his plea, "treat me like one of your hired hands" (v. 21). The son's presentation of himself is immediately contradicted in the following verse, first through the father's ordering the "slaves" (δοῦλοι), with whom the son is thereby contrasted, and then again by the father's inexplicably extravagant hospitality: "The father said to his slaves, 'Quickly, bring out a robe—the best one—and put it on him; put a ring on his finger and sandals on his feet. And get the fatted calf and kill it, and let us eat and celebrate'" (vv. 22–23). Together these symbols convey the son's "full restoration" as heir.[272] They designate his status not simply as a free person but as *master*.[273] This is so in the strongest sense. The younger son's reinstatement as heir implies that he is bound to inherit a "double portion,"

---

[270]   For "in the best circumstances," the father would offer words of forgiveness and "a review of expectations" for the son's "probation" (Hultgren, *Parables of Jesus*, 78).

[271]   Holgate's central thesis is that the "primary frame of reference" for the parable is "neither Jewish midrash nor the practices of the patristic church, but Greco-Roman culture" (*Prodigality, Liberality, and Meanness*, 22). He compares the parable to other Greco-Roman narratives that explore the theme of "liberality" by contrasting prodigal and miser characters (26–38). Jesus' parable differs from these tales, however, in that "the father . . . acts quite differently from the way fathers with covetous sons were conventionally portrayed" (55). In very few cases does Greco-Roman literature include such an indulgent paternal response to sons.

[272]   Hultgren, *Parables of Jesus*, 79.

[273]   Bestowing of a robe is evocative of several biblical scenes: for example, when Rebecca gives Esau's garments to Jacob (Gen 27:15), when Pharaoh enrobes Joseph (Gen 41:42), and Antiochus clothing Philip (1 Macc 6:15). The ring is a sign of authority, usually given to an elder son, which obviously alludes to the many stories of older and younger brothers and the reversal of inheritance or priority. The placing of shoes on someone's feet symbolizes a bestowal of freedom—for a slave lacks shoes—and when the slave places shoes on the son's feet, he acknowledges him as master. See Hultgren, *Parables of Jesus*, 79, n. 43. Jeremias, Marshall, Bailey, Donahue, etc., all highlight this as well.

as was customarily the birthright of the firstborn (Deut 21:17). This becomes a symbol of salvation throughout the Hebrew Bible. In the language of Isaiah 61:7, "Because their shame was double / and dishonor was proclaimed as their lot, / therefore in their land they shall possess a double portion; / everlasting joy shall be theirs."

His lavish gestures (vv. 20–23) are what prompts talk of the prodigality of the *father*. His response is immoderate, heedless, even wasteful—with respect to custom (cf. Deut 21:18–21 on the treatment of a "rebellious son") as well as the remaining estate, which he has been given to steward. A point rarely made, the restoration of such a son is a risk to his own wellbeing and that of the household for which he is responsible. We are made to ask, is the father a bad steward? In this, he parallels the shepherd who leaves a whole fold to retrieve one stray (Luke 15:3–7).

While most interpretations of the parable contrast the two sons, we should not pass over certain rhetorical similarities.[274] First, just as we find the younger son "in the fields" (εἰς τοὺς ἀγροὺς) (v. 15), so too we find the elder son "in the field" (ἐν ἀγρῷ) (v. 25). While the younger son has become the servant of a gentile pig farmer, the older son has worked his father's land alongside the family servants and hired hands. It is frequently noted that the elder son is a figure of loyalty and righteousness. He dutifully remains at home, serving his father's interests, fulfilling the commandments his brother breaks.[275] But the text suggests that both sons are in fact lost, afield. They are *peregrine—per* (through), *ager* (field)—wayward and alien.

Second, mirroring the close succession of and contrast between son (v. 21) and slave (v. 22) in the first part of the parable, in the second part, the elder son comes out of the fields (v. 25) and summons one of the servants (τῶν παίδων) (v. 26). Yet, despite this apparent authority to give orders, the older son sees himself in much the same ways as his younger brother, as another subordinate in his father's household. While the son-servant role is culturally ambiguous and appears continuous in both sons' self-perceptions, the rhetoric and structure of the text strongly distinguishes them.[276]

---

[274] As Donahue says, "Just as the younger son felt that the way to restore the severed relationship was to become a servant, the older brother maintained it by acting as a servant. Between the dutiful son and the prodigal is a bond much deeper than is visible on the surface" (*Gospel in Narrative*, 157).

[275] The older son's words "I have never disobeyed your command" (Luke 15:29) evoke Deut 26:13 (LXX) and refer back to the Pharisees in the parable's audience (v. 1).

[276] The son-servant pairing works on different levels in Scripture. In certain rabbinical and New Testament parables, as well as in parallel Greco-Roman stories, the two are analogous in terms of the *roles* they play—that is, as subordinates to a father-

Third, this is made explicit in the fourth instance of direct speech in the parable when, confounded and angered by his brother's extravagant reception, the older son says to his father, "Look! For so many years I have been *slaving away* for you and I have never neglected a command of yours" (v. 29).[277] He complains to his father that he has never been recognized, saying, "You have never given me even a young goat so that I might celebrate with my friends" (v. 29). In exclaiming, "Look!" and adding "for you," the boy suggests his father has not beheld and approved of his service—even though he chose to live before him, unlike the younger one who fled the father's sight. It is as if the elder brother is asking, "Do you not see me?" Perhaps he bemoans that he has not been rewarded for his many years of service, less because he originally expected as much, and more because he can interpret the banquet for his younger brother only in those terms. He is measuring the time; he is keeping count. It seems he cannot make sense of the brother's welcome apart from that framework, an economy of merit, of reward and punishment. In the brother's complaint, this dichotomy exerts itself; it is present as an unfulfilled expectation (v. 30).

The father's treatment of both sons emphasizes their kinship. While the younger son addresses the father as "Father" (v. 21), the older son refuses to. Yet, in response, the father calls him "child" (τέκνον), an affectionate term of address.[278] Similarly, while the older son distances himself from his brother, referring to him as "this son of yours" (ὁ υἱός σου οὗτος) (v. 30), the father reminds him of their relation, calling the younger son "your brother" (ὁ ἀδελφός σου) (v. 32). In the face of the older son's anger at the injustice of celebrating his profligate brother's return, his father explains, "Child, you are always with me and all that is mine is yours" (πάντα τὰ ἐμὰ σά ἐστιν) (v. 31). With these words the father affirms not only the sonship and heirship of his older child but also his full and present ownership of the estate. The father's use of the word "all" (πάντα) contrasts the younger son's earlier request for

---

master figure (the paterfamilias of the Greco-Roman household codes). Throughout the Hebrew Bible, Israel is referred to as a "servant" as well as a "child" or "spouse." The language of "servant" and "savior" often go hand in hand, where a servant or steward is a viceroy, one who represents, who enacts the will of another. At the same time, throughout the Old and New Testaments, servility is contrasted with right relationship with God. There is a clear soteriological transition from servitude to inheritance (Gal 4:7). A distinction between family bonds and servanthood is also indicated by the Hebrew prophets—for example, in the words of Hosea 2:16: "On that day, says the Lord, you will call me, 'My husband,' and no longer will you call me, 'My Baal' [master]."

[277] The NRSV translates δουλεύω σοι as "I serve you," but it is better rendered "I slave for you."

[278] Hultgren, *Parables of Jesus*, 81.

"part" (μέρος) of the property (v. 12) and the fact that he takes less than the full amount because he departs so hastily (v. 13).[279] This suggests that the younger son in fact asks not for too much but for too little. His request is less *prodigal* than *meager*.[280] This is likewise true of the elder son, whose accusation of the father, "you never *gave me*" (ἐμοὶ οὐδέποτε ἔδωκας) (v. 29), echoes the younger son's demand at the beginning of the story, "Father, *give me*" (πάτερ, δός μοι) (v. 12). The father might have replied, "you never asked," but instead he insists that everything already belongs to him (v. 31), which is to say, "you do not need to ask me." This is yet another sign that the father's view of the son, as "companion" and "co-owner," is incommensurable with the son's view of himself, as a "faithful slave."[281] In his actions and attitude, "the father shatters the self-identity of both sons" defined "in terms of servile obligations."[282]

Stopping short, for now, of the most christologically evocative verses— "dead and alive," "lost and found" (vv. 24, 32)—Luke's parable, in much the same way as Pauline theology (Gal 4:4–7), opposes the condition of servility to that of being a child of God. While the prodigal's story does indeed evoke other chosen younger sons in Scripture—Jacob (Gen 27:1–45), Joseph (Gen 37–48), Gideon (Judg 6:1–23), David (1 Sam 16:6–13)—it would be a strain to claim from the text that the welcome of the younger son implies the rejection of the elder son or that there is somehow a "polar reversal" of their destinies.[283]

---

[279] He took only what was quickly convertible to cash (v. 13)—an early step in the direction of self-ruin.

[280] In this sense, we might play with the Greco-Roman motif of "covetousness" and its attendant prodigal/miser pairing, which Holgate analyzes. Instead of simply aligning the sons younger/prodigal and elder/miser, we have reason to reinterpret the younger son's liberality-gone-awry as a form of meagerness.

[281] Bernard B. Scott says, "Where the son saw himself as a faithful slave, the father views him as a *companion* ('always with me') and *co-owner* of the farm ('all that is mine is yours')." See Scott, *Hear Then the Parable: A Commentary on the Parables of Jesus* (Minneapolis: Fortress, 1989), 21.

[282] Donahue, *Gospel in Narrative*, 157.

[283] If we were to map Jesus' life onto the parable's characters based purely on the parable's literary context (as a defense of his table fellowship with undesirables), it would look like this: younger son = the sinners with whom Jesus consorts; elder son = the righteous religious leaders who criticize Jesus' association with sinners; the father = Jesus, who welcomes sinners of all kinds, including the self-righteous. It is an unfortunate extrapolation to read the father's embrace of the younger son (i.e., Jesus' embrace of sinners, the stray) as a rejection of the elder son (i.e., Jews, law-abiders, the faithful fold). Although, just "as the elder brother is unable to rejoice in the restoration of one who is lost, so, too, the Pharisees and scribes grumble over the reception of 'sinners' by Jesus" (Hultgren, *Parables of Jesus*, 82); the larger point of

Instead a different polarity has emerged. Tracing these heavily freighted terms, "son" and "slave," through the narrative prompts us to draw the distinction elsewhere—not between the two sons, but between the way they both see themselves and the way their father sees them. We might regard the ordinary relation of children to parents—more specifically, in this case, sons to fathers in first-century Palestine—as the "natural attitude" that is meant to be bracketed and excluded in Jesus' storytelling. A certain prejudgment about how sons and fathers or children and parents would ordinarily behave under such circumstances is, to refer back to Alter's description of Hebrew story, the narrative "expectation" that is left in the lurch by the narrative "fulfillment" of *this* father behaving like *this*.

Seizing upon this very specific focal actuality draws attention to the way the story narrates two kinds of perception based on two economies and their attendant values: on the one hand, an economy of "just deserts" (*deservir*: to serve well, to deserve) and, on the other hand, an economy of uncalculating love. Interrupting the first and recruiting its readers in the other, it seems the storyteller is interested in a different conversion moment—not so much that of the wayward boy inside the story, but that of the audience outside the story, whose self-righteousness and shame alike constitute a myopia obscuring vision of self and others. The way the father sees his sons leads back to the compassionate gaze of God. John of Damascus' description of God (θεός) as the one who sees (θεασθαι) and runs (θεειν) is suited to the image of providential love personified in the parabolic father.[284] In his humanly impossible vigilance, he figures the divine "omniseer" or, to use Hagar's formulation—*El Roi* ("the God who sees").[285] His searching gaze and preemptive embrace give us the counter-experience of being beheld and welcomed by God with a visceral affection in light of which deservedness is an unthinkable category.

---

the parable is that those who reject the love of God/the father/Jesus do not therefore seal their own rejection. Even the younger son's rejection of the father himself has no (negative) bearing on the father's reception of him.

[284] John of Damascus, "Concerning What Is Affirmed about God," in *The Orthodox Faith IX*, vol. 9 of *Nicene and Post-Nicene Fathers*, 2nd series, trans. Philip Schaff (Edinburgh: T&T Clark, 2004). He follows a certain etymology of "the second name" of God (θεός), suggesting—as Gregory of Nyssa, Gregory the Great, and many other patristic and medieval theologians do—that θεός comes from θεασθαι, "to see," but also θεειν, "to run." (Plato similarly draws this association between "God" and "running" in *Cratylus*.)

[285] Hagar calls God "*El Roi*" in Gen 16:13 when God reveals to her a well in the desert to save her and her son, Ishmael (which means "God hears"). She says in response, "You are the God who sees me . . . I have now seen the One who sees me" (NIV). Ishmael, the elder son, is not abandoned by God.

In retelling the Parable of the Prodigal Son, the servile self-perception of both sons is meant to be not momentarily parenthesized but thoroughly purged. It does not merely illustrate; it *performs* the perspective of God.[286] There is a redemptive reduction then, one that leads back to reveal but also to remake. This is, paradigmatically, the work of parable.

---

[286] As Wright says, "The parables are not merely *theme*, they are also *performance*. They do not merely talk about the divine offer of mercy; they both make the offer, and defend Jesus' right to make it" (*Jesus and the Victory of God*, 176).

2

Prodigal Christ

"Jesus does not appear in the parable, but only because it is he who tells it and lives it to the point of death does the joy of restoration it recounts become a reality . . . without his ministry the parable would not be true."[1]

—Eduard Schweizer

The Gospels are comprised of stories that "represent little Gospels" within "the larger one," such that we can regard "a single farthing of the Gospel (i.e., the widow's mite) as the key to salvation," a "microcosm" of the whole.[2] Of all the parables of Jesus, the Parable of the Prodigal Son is preeminently "the gospel within the gospel."[3] Embedded in the encompassing narrative of Luke, there is reverberation between story and storyteller, content and context. The symbolic gain of parables from the life in which they are situated is reciprocal. The story of the lost son's far journey does not simply point away from itself toward Christ and the larger creation–fall–redemption story. Rather, the "relation of intersignification" instituted between the smaller and larger narrative produces "a new signification."[4] It comes to "signify something *else*, something *more*."[5] That is why Barth cannot help but ask about what the father's words

1   Eduard Schweizer, *The Good News according to Luke*, trans. David E. Green (Atlanta: John Knox, 1984), 252.
2   Amos Wilder, *The Language of the Gospel: Early Christian Rhetoric* (New York: Harper & Row, 1964), 58–59.
3   Jill Robbins, *Prodigal Son / Elder Brother: Interpretation and Alterity in Augustine, Petrarch, Kafka, Levinas* (Chicago: University of Chicago Press, 1991), 10.
4   Paul Ricoeur, *Figuring the Sacred: Religion, Narrative and Imagination* (Philadelphia: Fortress, 1995), 163.
5   Ricoeur, *Figuring the Sacred*, 161. Ricoeur warns of two interpretive errors: (1) reading the primary narrative without reference to its embedded context and

"this my son was dead and is alive" mean within and for the Gospel as a whole. The strength and coherence of his distinctive christological interpretation of the parable is more evident when laid out alongside its sole precedent, found in Julian's example. Among the deep parallels that emerge between them, we find that (1) each ascends interpretive levels from the plain or literal to the typological or christological in a way that is (2) only intelligible in light of a shared set of intertexts through which they each filter the parable.

Barth's Exegesis of the Parable

Barth's exegesis of Luke 15:11–32 is located in the small text of IV/2, "The Homecoming of the Son of Man," within the larger paragraph "The Exaltation of the Son of Man" (§64). It is noteworthy that Barth refers to this section of *Church Dogmatics* as "the decisive center" of his Christology (IV/2, 105). It is here that he turns to what he calls the "second problem of the doctrine of reconciliation" (sanctification). The first problem of the doctrine of reconciliation (justification) is addressed in IV/1, where the allusive caption "The Way of the Son of God into the Far Country" (§59.1) has already been employed. As these section titles indicate, Barth's application of this story far exceeds his discrete excursus on the parable in §64.2 (21–24). We will return to the contextual significance of the passage, but, for now, the focus will be restricted to his explicit exegetical engagement with the parable.

Although he situates his treatment of the parable at the turning point of *The Doctrine of Reconciliation*, Barth begins by offering a reading that is non-christological. His initial approach to the parable gives express attention to its rendering in the tradition and echoes a fairly common interpretation of its meaning. Barth says that, in a "direct" (*direkt*) sense, the parable "speaks of the sin of man and the mortal threat which comes to him in consequence, of his repentance and return to God, and of the overwhelming grace with which this one who turned away and then turned back to God is received by Him" (IV/2, 21). In other words, at the beginning of his excursus, Barth acknowledges that the most immediate reading of the parable can yield no more than a generic claim about divine grace. He concedes, here, that "a direct christological interpretation" would produce only a "strained interpretation" ("over-interpretation," *Überinterpretation*) (21). In what follows, I trace Barth's

---

(2) failing to consider how the parable might inform the larger story. In their engagement with the Parable of the Prodigal Son, Julian and Barth bypass both pitfalls, perhaps more thoroughly than anyone before them. Their interpretations are not merely original and creative. Rather, we must learn from them about how to not leave the story underinterpreted.

account of the biblical passage, distinguishing and relating the two interpretive layers he discerns, before going on to consider the arc of the christological interpretation of the story he ultimately embraces.

Barth's "Direct" Interpretation of the Parable

Barth's preliminary reading locates the parable in its literary context, from which he derives the "parabolic reference" to sinful humanity. He exegetes the Parable of the Lost Son "in concretion of the parables of the Lost Sheep and the Lost Coin" (21). Consequently, Barth takes for granted that Luke 15:1–2 provides a referential backdrop for the whole narrative picture: "Now all the tax collectors and sinners were coming near to listen to him. And the Pharisees and the scribes were grumbling and saying, 'This fellow welcomes sinners and eats with them.'" On this first level, the father figures God, the younger son the "publicans and sinners" with whom Jesus socialized, and the older son "the scribes and Pharisees" who judge Jesus for the company he keeps. Even on a direct reading, Barth has no trouble expanding these identities so that the son who goes into the far country represents the lost that Jesus came to seek and save (Luke 19:10) while the elder son portrays the righteous who are in need of repentance (Luke 15:7).[6]

Barth acknowledges that the scriptural passage contains within it two parables—the story of the younger son's relationship with the father (vv. 12–24) and the story of the elder son's attitude toward the father and the younger son (vv. 25–32). This fact has led some to speak of "The Prodigal Sons" or to call it "The Parable of the Father's Love." Barth insists instead that the "real message" is located in the first of the two parables, with the story of the elder brother who will not rejoice in his lost brother's homecoming having "only the significance of a contrast in relation to the main statement of the passage." In contrast to many commentators and in keeping with later structuralist readings, Barth sees the younger son, not the father, as the "main character."[7]

---

[6]   Throughout *The Doctrine of Reconciliation*, Barth uses "lost" to stand in for flesh and fallenness. The word gathers together the whole history of humankind, wayward, alienated, distressed. This is evident, for example, in §59, as at many other points. Barth says "lost" sums up "the situation of Old Testament man," of exile, wilderness, the desert-land, and desertedness (Deut 32). In other words, it describes "a history of suffering" (IV/1, 173–74). All of this is evoked in the image of the younger son in an alien (gentile) land.

[7]   Cf. Joachim Jeremias and Luke T. Johnson. Robert Funk's structuralist reading (discussed in my first chapter) provides illuminating support for Barth's claim. The younger son is the "determiner" of the narrative, while the father and the elder son are two "respondents." In an unusual inversion or conflation of roles, we have in the younger son not only the "determiner" (who is usually the authority figure in NT parables, e.g., a father/lord) but also the "recipient of grace" (who is usually one of the respondents). This

According to Barth, the "main statement" of the story is twofold. It concerns, first of all, the "turning away and turning back" of humanity "in relationship to God." Barth is particularly attuned to the outward-homeward movement of the younger son's narrative. In leaving home, he "takes his inheritance," "wastes his substance in riotous living," exiles himself from his father, and makes himself an alien and a slave. In his homecoming, he is welcomed, celebrated, and restored again as child and heir. Second, the quality of the son's reception upon his return tells us "there is not only no diminution but a supreme heightening and deepening of the fatherly mind and attitude of God towards him." Barth's attention to these two elements—(1) the doubleness of the son's journey, and (2) the extraordinary elevation of the son in his homecoming—leads him to an indirect plane of interpretation.

In, With, and Under the Text

For Barth, as for Julian, there is an excess in the parable that cannot be explained or contained by a first-blush reading yet is necessary to its full meaning. Barth infers that this is what many of his predecessors were after in their flawed attempts to connect this story about grace with the actuality of grace in Jesus Christ. Tracing the cracks as paths emerging from his "direct" exegetical groundwork, Barth suggests that even "if there is the danger of a strained interpretation, it is also possible not to do full justice to the passage" and "to miss what is not expressly stated but implied in what is stated, and therefore necessary to what is stated" if we do not attend to "that which is said indirectly" (IV/2, 21–22).[8] Between the overeager and the meager interpretation, Barth commends an interpretation that neither forces nor denies the indirect identity the text itself initiates.

---

analysis of the parable's literary structure is particularly interesting in light of Barth's doctrine of election, where the prodigal Christ is both Judge (in the authoritative position) and Judged (in the dependent position). See Robert Funk, *Parables and Presence: Forms of the New Testament Tradition* (Philadelphia: Fortress, 1982), 50. For different reasons, Eduard Schweizer agrees that "the father is not simply an allegorical equivalent of God." This is textually grounded in the observation that the son distinguishes the father from God ("heaven") in his speech. See Schweizer, *Good News*, 248.

[8]   The translators render Barth's "*Unterinterpretation*" (*Kirchliche Dogmatik* [KD], 22, 23) in terms of not "doing justice" to the text. "*Überinterpretation*" is similarly translated as "strained interpretation." What Barth means by this pairing is clarified by another: to "not say more" but also to "not say less" (24). In other words, Barth does not want to overstate his christological reading to start, but he also does not want to understate what the text itself is suggesting on the basis of its context and "signs of metaphoricity" (Ricoeur).

That Barth has taken us as far as he has in this first "direct" reading is a significant achievement for his subsequent interpretation. While he reiterates that we cannot say "more than this . . . directly," perhaps more importantly, he says, we cannot say less.[9] In addition to claiming that the parable narrates divine grace, Barth maintains its integrity with the preceding parables. This fact alone opens the text up in a number of directions—namely, toward the world in front of the text (Ricoeur). Barth takes for granted that the three parables of Luke 15 cohere as a whole and are therefore inter-referential, that these are the parables *of Jesus*, that the parabolic referents stand outside the text (sinners and righteous), and that the life of Jesus "reverberates" (Ricoeur) upon the text. In other words, it is Jesus' life, action, and character that prompt the whole storytelling episode. This moves us in the direction of the intertextual expansion of the parable that follows.

Before venturing his own indirect reading, Barth surveys precedents for identifying the "presence" that is "not expressly stated in the parable." Among those who try to attend to "that which is said indirectly," Barth highlights Augustine, Christoph Starke (eighteenth century), and Ferdinand Christian Baur (nineteenth century). Their readings are "indirect" because they draw a connection between three figures or groups: (1) "the lost and re-found younger son," (2) "the sinful but penitent *'am ha'aretz* ['people of the land'] of publicans and sinners,"[10] and (3) "the election, calling and redemption of the Gentile world" ("in contrast to Israel as revealed in the elder brother") (IV/2, 22). In the text, "there is no explicit mention of this relationship" among the three groups. But what warrants it is the way *'am ha'aretz* functions elsewhere in the New Testament, particularly in Luke where there is a "very pronounced universalistic" drive. Jesus' inclusion of outcast Jews moves concentrically to encompass gentiles and the rest of the world. In view of this, Barth asks

---

[9]   The "literal" (or direct) reading for Barth, then, is not a matter of "letter" but of intention or intended reference. As for Aquinas, the "literal" sense of a metaphorical story is figurative. Janet Martin Soskice, *Metaphor and Religious Language* (Oxford: Oxford University Press, 2002), 86.

[10]   The ambiguity of the phrase *'am ha'aretz* is significant to the rest of Barth's exposition. It means "people of the land" and has a variety of applications. It can simply stand for the land of Israel, but more often it is used to refer to ignorant or uneducated (rural) Jews, Jews who fail to observe Torah (e.g., John 7:49), as well as (and particularly in the plural, "peoples of the land or lands") Samaritans, non-Jews, or gentiles. In this instance, Barth seems to have in mind the social caste of uneducated and unobservant Jews as well as gentiles. As an undesirable fringe identity, the former points to the latter.

whether a mapping of the salvation of gentiles onto the identity of the younger son is in fact really a "reading into" the text.

With this question, Barth begins to erode his own working distinction between direct and indirect interpretation. He still maintains that certain theological content "is not there" in "direct exegesis." Yet he also suggests that "we cannot really expound the text" without considering what is given "in, with and under what is said directly." This sacramental "in, with and under" appears to be Barth's way of speaking about the fact that the story is animated by another story, that the embedded narrative is not self-contained and therefore not self-explanatory. Through it, within it, "another voice" (Ricoeur) surfaces, directing the story outward, transgressing its structural parameters. The text initiates this—*directly*. The strictly exegetical reading is precisely what opens up the contextual and intertextual reading. The latter, therefore, cannot be brushed off as an "allegorical" imposition. Because of this, "the question also arises whether we have not to take from the text, in the same indirect way, a christological content."

Here again, Barth complicates the distinction between direct (or literal) and indirect (or typological) reading, saying, "It does actually contain this [christological content]—although not explicitly."[11] He denounces the sort of non-christological treatment of the parable one finds, for example, in Adolf von Harnack's *The Essence of Christianity*. On the basis that Jesus is not mentioned in Luke 15, "it is hastily concluded . . . that not the Son and the atonement accomplished in Him but only the Father and His goodness belong to the Gospel preached by Jesus Himself." As a counterpoint, Barth commends Helmut Gollwitzer's christological interpretation of the parable in *Die Freude Gottes* (*The Joy of God*), claiming it is not merely legitimate but actually unavoidable.

Summarizing Gollwitzer, Barth writes, "In the parable, then, Jesus is 'the running out of the father to meet his son.' Jesus is 'hidden in the kiss which the father gives his son.' Jesus is the power of the son's recollection of his father and home, and his father's fatherliness and readiness to forgive." Gollwitzer can render Jesus present in the story in this way because he interprets the passage in light of its setting-in-life described in Luke 15:1–2. The parable renarrates and defends Jesus' practice of "eating with the publicans and sinners." Further,

---

[11]   Again, Barth denies that this is a kind of eisegesis. He claims the text itself suggests the meaning that so many modern historical-critical readers wrongly consider "allegorical."

it presents that action as "a fulfillment" of "the blessing of sinful Israel" rather than "the coronation of righteous Israel." Barth explains:

> Not the theory of a Father-God who self-evidently and consistently pardons, but the miraculous actuality of this act of God, is the non-explicit but indispensable presupposition of the happening between God and man which is envisaged in the relations between father and son described in the parable.

In other words, only abstraction, only generalization, could yield a non-christological reading of the parable. Given "the non-explicit but indispensable" history presupposed by the speech (the history of the parabler and his audience), it is impossible for this little narrative to close itself off to the details and actuality of grace as it is achieved in the life of the one who tells it. Barth insists such a conclusion is in no way "allegorical." Rather, it is simply the result of expositing the text in the context of the rest of Luke and with a view to the larger New Testament message. Barth's claim that christological exposition "does justice to what is there in light of" the text's "background," or "expounds it from its context," correlates with Ricoeur's description of "narrative embedding." The text does this to itself by itself.

While Barth embraces Gollwitzer's "method," he is not entirely happy with the content, primarily because he thinks it still overemphasizes "the action of the father" by deriving "reference to Jesus Christ" only from him. Barth says this "destroys the essential balance of the parable," for "the main figure in the story is the younger son who leaves his father and is lost, but returns and is found again." Overaccentuating the father is an "error" Barth laments as common to "more recent Protestant exegesis." Pressing further than Gollwitzer, he refocuses our attention on the action of the son.

Barth's "Indirect" Interpretation

Partway through his treatment of the parable, Barth commences a new exposition, hoping it can display "the presence and action of the Son of God, and therefore of the atonement accomplished in Him, in what takes place between God and [humankind] as indicated in the parable" (IV/2, 23). He acknowledges, once again, that this cannot be "demonstrated" immediately from the text. On this point, Barth is critical of patristic *allegoresis*, such as Ambrose of Milan's, which he thinks too closely identifies Jesus with minor figures and details in the parable, such as the fatted calf that is slaughtered.[12] At the same

---

[12]   Presumably he has in mind Ambrose's *Expositionis Lucam VII* (PL 15, 1699).

time, Barth freely draws an "analogy" between Jesus Christ and the lost son of the parable. He says that while this cannot be a "simple equation," nonetheless, we cannot "do justice" to the parable

> if we do not see and say that in the going out and coming in of the lost son in his relationship with the father we have a most illuminating parallel to the way trodden by Jesus Christ in the work of atonement, to His *humiliation* and *exaltation*. Or better, the *going out* and *coming in* of the lost son, and therefore the *fall* and *blessing* of [the human], takes place on the horizon of the humiliation and exaltation of Jesus Christ and therefore of the atonement made in Him. It has this as its higher law. It is illuminated by it. (IV/2, 23)[13]

These lines provide at least two signposts for Barth's second approach to the parable. First, in shifting between the language of "parallel" and "horizon," he signals the enclosure of one trajectory, that of the lost Son, within another, that of the eternal Son. In other words, we should not look primarily for similarities between the lost son and Jesus Christ but for the ways in which the latter overtakes and encompasses the former. Second, the precise points of analogy are delimited to the "going out and coming in" (form) of the son and his "humiliation and exaltation" (content).

Barth's renarration of the parable falls into three paragraphs corresponding to the chronology of the story (IV/2, 23–25). He first addresses the going out of the lost son/eternal Son (vv. 11–16). Then he turns to the homecoming of the son/Son (vv. 17–24). Finally, as a kind of epilogue, he considers the story of the elder son (vv. 25–32).

As Barth recounts the parable a second time, he interweaves his initial conclusions with a new christological reference. Starting with the going out of the son, he paraphrases the parable:

> The son comes with his greedy and arbitrary demand, takes his inheritance from the hands of his father, makes his way into a far country and wastes his substance in riotous living . . . and then suffers want in the famine which comes on that land, being glad at last to feed on the husks which do not belong to him, but to the swine which he is charged to keep. (23)

Barth calls this portion of the narrative "the way of [humankind] in its breaking of the covenant with God." This is the "going out" that belongs to sinful humans. The breaking of the relationship with God is seen in concentric circles: "lost Israel," the "publicans and sinners" of the Third Gospel,

---

[13]   Emphasis added.

and gentiles. All of these groups are in some sense "the lost son"—rebellious, disobedient, self-destructive. As such, they cannot be easily mapped onto "the way of Jesus Christ," the obedient Son of God who keeps and does not break the covenant with God.

How can these figures function as a "parallel" for Jesus Christ then? Barth says, "The way of the latter [Christ] *is* in fact the way into the far country of a lost human existence."[14] His journey into the far country is

> the way in which He *accepts identity and solidarity* with this lost son, unreservedly *taking his place, taking to Himself* his sin and shame, his transgression, as though He Himself had committed it, *making* his misery *his own* as though He Himself had deserved it, and all this in such a way that the frightfulness of this far country, the evil of the human situation, is revealed in its full depths only as it *becomes His* situation, that of the holy and righteous Son of God. (23)[15]

In other words, the wandering of the lost son and the Son of God are "parallel" only in a structural sense (fall and incarnation). For Barth, as for Julian, it is more accurate to say that the story of Jesus Christ intersects or crosses the story of wayward humanity. In fact, it not only intersects but intercepts and redirects it. The way of Jesus Christ is "like" that of the lost son only in the sense that it *is* the way of the lost son. It becomes it; it takes over that other history, rewriting it from within. The prodigal son's story occurs within the "horizon" of the history of Jesus Christ. As Augustine says, "*Per ipsum pergimus ad ipsum* [through him we travel to Him]."[16]

[14]   Emphasis added.

[15]   Emphasis added. These lines are highly evocative of Martin Luther's commentary on Gal 3:13, a verse Barth frequently references. Speaking of Christ "being made a curse for us," Luther says: he "hath and beareth all the sins of all men in His body. . . . He received them . . . and laid them upon His own body. . . . He was found and reckoned among sinners and transgressors . . . a companion of sinners, taking upon Him the flesh and blood of those who were sinners. . . . We must wrap Christ, and know Him to be wrapped in our sins, in our malediction, in our death, and in all our evils, as He is wrapped in our flesh and blood. . . . He beareth the sins of the world, His innocency is burdened . . . a suffering Christ, who took upon Him to bear the person of all sinners . . . to overcome . . . the wrath of God in himself . . . to take away the curse in Himself." Luther repeatedly stresses the burdening of Jesus Christ, in his very person and body, that results in the "happy change" by which "we being now clothed are freed from the curse." In his exegesis of this verse, Luther, like Julian and Barth, appeals to the Suffering Servant of Isaiah, upon whom the Lord has "laid the iniquities of us all" (Isa 53:6) as well as 2 Cor 5:21 and Phil 2:7. See Martin Luther, *Commentary on Galatians*, trans. Erasmus Middleton (Grand Rapids: Kregel Classics, 1979), 164–72.

[16]   Augustine, *De Trinitate* XIII.xix, 24.

In highlighting that Christ "accepts identity and solidarity" with the lost son, takes his "place," assumes his "sin," "shame," "transgression," and "misery," and fully indwells the "human situation," Barth alludes, as Julian does, to 2 Corinthians 5:21, which proves to be a defining intertext in Barth's christological interpretation of the parable. It clarifies what Barth has already said about what it means for the Word to take on human "flesh"—not just the human form, but fallen humanity: sinful, dead, perishing, *lost*.[17] He goes on to explain:

> The Word became flesh—not just [human], but the bearer of our human essence, which is marked not only by its created and *unlost* goodness but (in self-contradiction) by sin, so that it is a perverted essence *and lost* as such. If His human essence were sinless as such, how could it be our essence? How could He really be our Brother at this decisive point? How could there be any solidarity with us in our lostness? Would it not mean that the Son of God had become the Son of Man but had not as such taken to Himself our sin and guilt? But if He had not done that, how could He have taken them away, as He has done? He did in fact *bear* them. (IV/2, 92)[18]

The "fatal journey of the lost son," the "pit" into which the Son readily enters, is not merely human embodiment but, necessarily, the embodiment "stamped by human sin." Christ's humanity always has "this twofold sense" (IV/2, 25).

---

[17]   Again, the connection between flesh and lostness is prevalent in Barth's thinking. He says, "'Flesh' in the language of the New (and earlier the Old) Testament means man standing under the divine verdict and judgment, man who is a sinner and whose existence therefore must perish before God, whose existence has already become nothing, and hastens to nothingness and is a victim to death. 'Flesh' is the concrete form of human nature and the being of man in his world under the sign of the fall of Adam—the being of man as corrupted and therefore destroyed, as unreconciled with God and therefore lost" (IV/1, 165).

[18]   Emphasis added. Barth continues the thought: "But He bore them without sin. 'Without sin' means that in our human and sinful existence as a man He did not sin. He did not become guilty of the transgression which we in our human essence commit. He bore an alien guilt, our guilt, the guilt of all men, without any guilt of His own. He made our human essence His own even in its corruption, but He did not repeat or affirm its inward contradiction. He opposed to it a superior contradiction. He overcame it in His own person when He became man. And we can and must say that He overcame it at the deepest level by not refusing to accomplish the humiliation of the Son of God to be not only a creature but a sinful creature, to become and be the bearer of human essence in its inward contradiction, to repent as such, to become the friend of publicans and sinners, to suffer and die as a malefactor with others" (IV/2, 92).

In view of the comprehensiveness of Christ's assumption of the lost son's identity, Barth thinks it is fitting to invert the order of reference. For him, it is not quite accurate to say the prodigal son points to Jesus Christ. Rather, he reflects him, and only faintly so. Barth says the way of the lost son in the parable

> is only a sorry caricature of the going out of the one Son of God into the world as it took place in Jesus Christ, of the humiliation in which, without ceasing to be who He is, but in the supreme exercise and expression of His Sonship and deity, He became poor for our sakes (2 Cor. 8:9).

Before continuing with Barth's retelling of the parable, it is worth clarifying a few points about what has been said thus far.

First, Barth is sometimes criticized for sidelining the reality of other human beings in his relentlessly all-encompassing account of the humanity of Christ.[19] Calling the lost son a "sorry caricature" of Jesus Christ is one of many moments in *Church Dogmatics* that might corroborate such a criticism. However, as the succeeding points indicate—even if Barth's rhetoric sometimes suggests otherwise—the objective is decidedly not to diminish the human; it is to communicate the extremity and conclusiveness of Christ's rooting out of the unnatural, the evil, the sinful from human reality. Second, phrases like "taking his place" and "poor for our sakes" give away that the outward/downward movement of the eternal Son teleologically signals and includes the restoration of the lost son in the parable (who, again, stands for Israel, outcasts, gentiles, and all of humankind). They foreshadow the homecoming of the lost son that always already glimmers on the horizon of the going out of the eternal Son. Third, Barth echoes his treatment of John 1:14 (§64.2) and his description of the "Lord as Servant" (§59) in linking humiliation specifically to the *divinity* of Jesus Christ. Where, historically, *exinanitio* and *exaltatio* are both related to Christ's humanity, Barth assigns the former to Christ's divinity and the latter to his humanity and, by extension, all humanity in him.[20]

[19]   It can particularly appear to be the case in Barth's earlier writings that he suggests "a view of divine heteronomy in which there is no place for free human agency." Daniel L. Migliore, "Commanding Grace: Karl Barth's Theological Ethics," in *Commanding Grace: Studies in Barth's Theological Ethics*, ed. Daniel L. Migliore (Grand Rapids: Eerdmans, 2010), 3.

[20]   This will be addressed at length in ch. 4. See Paul Dafydd Jones, *The Humanity of Christ: Christology in Karl Barth's "Church Dogmatics"* (London: T&T Clark, 2008), 125. This revised set of references corresponds to the language of "Electing God" and "Elected Human" used in §33.

Right after reiterating that the lost son merely caricatures the Son of God, Barth slips in the rather astounding claim: "As away from the heights to the depths, from home to a far country, it is analogous to it. It is similar for all its dissimilarity, like the being of Adam in relation to that of Jesus Christ: τύπος τοῦ μέλλοντος ['the pattern of the one to come'] (Rom. 5:14)." The precise structural points of the analogy are again specified as "going out and coming in" and "humiliation and exaltation." What is remarkable about this statement is the addition of the word "being." The analogy is not simply formal or narratival—it is *ontological*. Between the *being* of Jesus Christ and the *being* of Adam, there is similarity in the midst of dissimilarity.[21] Both preveniently determining the narrative arc of humankind (as the pattern) and retroactively overriding it (through the cross), the humanity of Christ forms and re-forms the story—and, with it, the identity and "essence"—of humanity as such.[22]

Having already signaled that the first movement, the far journey, contains the second in nuce, a homecoming, Barth resumes his retelling of the parable, closely paraphrasing the biblical passage. The son's homecoming consists of two distinct moments. It pivots on his awakening in the far country. As Barth glosses the passage,

[21]   Barth's relationship to the *analogia entis* is a much-debated topic. See the more recent reprisal of the old dispute between Barth and Erich Przywara: John R. Betz, "Beyond the Sublime: The Aesthetics of the *Analogy of Being*," 2 parts, *Modern Theology* 21, no. 3 (2005): 367–411; and 22, no. 1 (2006): 1–50; Kenneth Oakes, "The Question of Nature and Grace in Karl Barth: Humanity as Creature and as Covenant Partner," *Modern Theology* 23, no. 4 (2007): 598–616; and Keith L. Johnson, "Reconsidering Barth's Rejection of Przywara's *Analogia Entis*," *Modern Theology* 26, no. 4 (2010): 632–50. What is clear in this passage, and throughout *Church Dogmatics*, is that inasmuch as Barth "comes around to" an analogy of *being* (and not simply an *analogia relationis* and an *analogia fidei*), it is, in Oakes' words, "ruthlessly Christological" ("Question of Nature," 605). It therefore fundamentally differs from Przywara's account (in which the *analogia entis* is creational). This is because, as Adam Neder explains, "there exists no independent relationship between God and creation apart from Jesus Christ." Neder, *Participation in Christ: An Entry into Karl Barth's "Church Dogmatics"* (Louisville, Ky.: Westminster John Knox, 2009), 30.

[22]   The atonement in Jesus Christ is a "history in which our own history takes place" (IV/3.1, 183). Barth addresses the nature and extent of Jesus' embodiment of the history of Israel and the world in multiple places—e.g., see his description of Christ's *munus propheticum* (IV/3.1, §69.2). As Hans Frei explains, in Jesus' story "we get a cross section of the whole history of events that together make up the people of Israel. He is, in effect, a climactic summing-up of that whole story. The crucial events that happened to Israel at large and constituted Israel as a people happen on a small scale to Jesus, but in such a way that there is now a completion or fulfillment of what is left incomplete in Israel's life." Frei, *The Identity of Jesus Christ: The Hermeneutical Bases of Dogmatic Theology* (Eugene, Ore.: Wipf & Stock, 2013), 131.

The lost son comes to himself among the unclean beasts with whom he associates, remembering the well-being in his father's house which he has exchanged for this imminent death by hunger. He resolves, therefore, to return to his father with a confession of his fault and a request to be received at least as a hired servant (*Tagelöhner*). In execution of this resolve, he sets off on his way.

This is the first moment. It has a certain tone—shame, resignation, resolve, a modest hope for nothing more than survival. But when it comes to the point of executing his plan, the boy's intention is interrupted. "But" (δὲ)—this is the hinge of the younger son's return in verse 20, as well as in Barth's paraphrase of it:

> But [*aber*] the father sees him afar off, and has pity on him, and runs to meet him, and falls on his neck and kisses him—and all this before he has even uttered his confession and request, let alone proved them by corresponding actions of amendment. And beyond all this the father gives the order to clothe the one who has returned with the best robe and a ring and shoes, to bring and slay the fatted calf, and there is a great feast with music (lit. "symphonies," v. 25) and dancing, which annoys the elder son so terribly as he comes home from his conscientious labours. (IV/2, 23)

Reiterating his initial direct reading, Barth calls this the "way back" of lost humanity, as it (1) "turns again to God in repentance and sorrow, sincerely and therefore without claim, eagerly and therefore resolutely," and (2) is "received and accepted again by [God] without hesitation or reservation" because it "belongs" to God (23). Here Barth, like Julian, highlights that all the double movement of going out and coming in, of being lost and found, actually generates "an even greater joy." The rejoicing and celebrating in the parable (vv. 23, 24, 32) reinforces the reality that the return the father spontaneously bestows upon his son is of an utterly different kind than the return the son sets out to "execute" for himself. The son's homecoming is marked by an asymmetry that is precisely the opposite of what is expected.

As he turns to his indirect or deeper reading of this portion of the text, Barth repeats that, just as there is no direct identity between the going out of the lost son and the going out of the eternal Son, "there can be no simple equation of this way with that of the exaltation of Jesus Christ" (24). However, he goes on to say,

> The way of Jesus Christ is primarily and properly the way to [humankind's] home which is not lost but remains, not closed but open: the way to fellowship with God; the way on which Jesus Christ precedes all others as a King who draws them after him to share his destiny; the way to the end of which Jesus

Christ Himself has already come, so that this home of theirs is already visible and palpable to those who still tread it.

This passage forms a complement to Barth's earlier allusion to 2 Corinthians 5. Just as Christ assumes in himself and even becomes the way of lost humanity, he is also in and of himself the way of found humanity. Because he is the former, he is the latter.

The roles of priest and king meet in this passage, at the vertex of the parabola formed by the Son's "going out" and "coming in." Becoming sin, as the priest who makes self-sacrifice, Jesus constitutes the path home, as the king who redistributes his portion to all. That home is "fellowship with God"—which, despite everything, despite exile, waywardness, and every other kind of lostness, is not itself lost but always "open." This home is Christ's destiny and, therefore, humankind's destiny. It is his rightful inheritance and, therefore, the inheritance of all in him. Moreover, Christ himself *is* that home, that fellowship, that reconciliation, that double portion, not merely the path to it.

Rather than clarifying why he makes the leap from parable to speaker, from the way of the lost son to the way of the eternal Son, Barth moves in the other direction, from speaker to parable, asking, "What is the redemptive return of the lost son as seen from this standpoint?"—that is, from the standpoint of Jesus Christ as the way home, the king who shares his destiny. Barth once again downplays the strength of the parallel he draws when he says "the redemptive return of the lost son" is "only a feeble reflection of the entry of the one Son of Man into fellowship with God as it took place in Jesus Christ." Again he claims it is no "more than a copy, an analogy, a type" (IV/2, 24).

At this point, it is worth inquiring as to why Barth is so redundantly circumspect in drawing the association that occupies him in this excursus. Several related considerations could be flagged here. First, Barth is careful to distance himself from "allegorical" readings (by which he means readings that artificially separate form and content), and he is evidently concerned that his christological interpretation could place him in that camp (IV/2, 22).[23] In assiduously avoiding the assertion that the parabolic figure "stands for" the Son, Barth may be trying to protect himself from such an accusation. Second, the language of "echo" and "shadow" is bound up with his account of reconciliation, in which the humanity of Jesus Christ is utterly determinative of human reality, such that the latter can be regarded as derivative of or included in the former. For Christ is the "firstborn of all creation" (Col 1:15).

---

[23]   By "allegorical" Barth seems to mean idealized, ahistorical, abstract, or merely symbolic. His primary concern is that it might be a kind of dehistoricizing or demythologizing of the Christ event (see IV/1, 337).

A third point is closely related. As Barth goes on to say, while the figure in the parable cannot be more than a copy, echo, or type, nor can it be less. It garners all of its meaning from the pattern of the one who has come. Barth says,

> It cannot be more because what he himself is and does and experiences on this way back can only be a very little thing in relation to that of the one Son of Man, and even this very little does not lie within the range of his own possibilities, as though even temporarily he could set himself even in the most perfect fellowship with God.

At the same time, we must remember,

> It is also not less because the little that he is and does and experiences is *carried* and therefore *capacitated* by the great and original and proper being and action and experience of the one Son of Man, being *empowered* by the fact that in Him it is a wonderfully complete reality.[24]

Taking these two sentences together, a few insights are worth emphasizing: (1) While, grammatically, the antecedent to this "no more" and "no less" is the lost son of the parable, Barth clearly has in mind fallen humankind as well. Recall, the indirect identity between the parabolic figure and various people groups was already established in his "direct" reading. Humanity's identity with the lost son does not require the qualifications he makes concerning Jesus Christ's identity with the lost son. What Barth communicates about the relationship between the lost son and the eternal Son can also be applied to the relationship between lost humanity and the humanity of Jesus Christ. (2) "No more" and "no less" are two sides of the same coin—hence Barth's oscillation between, on the one hand, disclaimers that seem to undercut the parallel he is making and, on the other hand, more forceful assertions than a direct reading of the text would otherwise allow. This is actually a way of gaining ground for a larger claim: the narrative-parable is derivative of another story—and so much so that we are forced to regard the Parable of the Prodigal Son as a Parable of Reconciliation. This is perhaps the chief reason why earlier christological readings of the parable do not suit Barth: they cannot be seen as versions of the original template; they simply import discrete christological references in connection with minor details in the story. (3) In the context of the encompassing narrative, there is no viable explanation for the homecoming of lost humanity apart from the "being and action and experience of the one Son of Man." On Barth's

---

[24] Emphasis added.

telling, this story is not, first of all, a story of repentance.[25] Like the parables of the Lost Sheep and the Lost Coin that precede it, it is a story of being lost and found. Of itself, lost humanity cannot repent; it cannot restore fellowship. Its homecoming, its reconciliation, is wholly "capacitated" by another. For Barth, the fact of Jesus Christ is the sine qua non of every human return to God. That is why the "parallel" between the lost son and the eternal Son eventually breaks down. The latter must cross the former.

Finally, inculcating in his readers the view that the lost son is "only" a copy, Barth opens up a new perspective on the parable, one that ensures we locate it within the whole history of God and humankind that culminates in Jesus Christ. In other words, in apparently minimizing the being of the lost son in relationship to the being of Jesus Christ, Barth shores up his soteriological reading. In light of this, his reading is not only not allegorical (whether in the traditional or pejorative sense); it is not straightforwardly typological either (even though that is a term Barth uses), for the chronology runs the other way (not as scriptural figure to christological fulfillment). Yet, methodologically speaking, it is not the case that Barth arrives at this conclusion because he comes to the passage with a rigid christological premise that simply will not allow the text to set its own bounds. Instead, and more fundamentally, it is because he reads intertextually. His reading practice verifies his stated concern about how to "do justice" to or not "under-interpret" the passage. To avoid gleaning too little from the Parable of the Prodigal Son, Barth insists, we must register the presence of Christ given "in, with and under" the story he tells. With this, Barth has placed the onus on non-christological readings to defend what he considers a hermeneutically unjust reticence and irresponsible oversight. In the end, Barth has no wish to attenuate the relationship between the lost son and the eternal Son, as the surface of his rhetoric sometimes suggests.

Having initially set aside the "second parable," the story of the older brother, as merely a foil, when Barth revisits this portion of the narrative, it becomes clear that it is in fact crucial to the whole for at least two reasons: (1) it clarifies the character of the father's love, and (2) the concluding verse in the second parable forms an illuminating parallelism with verse 24 at the end of the first parable.[26]

---

[25]   When addressing the human response to grace, Barth does appeal to the parable in a more conventional fashion as a story of conversion or repentance (§74, passim). But since the material content of reconciliation is objective, the subjective possibilities of the story are not evoked in this context.

[26]   Barth's exegesis puts this saying in v. 28 and v. 32, but in the NRSV, as well as other English translations, the saying to which Barth refers is found in v. 24 and v. 32.

Barth equates the elder brother with the scribes and Pharisees, taking it for granted, based on literary context, that Jesus originally intended for the former to fictionally narrate the character of the latter. According to Barth, the elder brother, and by extension the scribes and Pharisees, form two points of contrast with the younger son, and by extension the publicans and sinners. First, the older son does not share the younger's trajectory (going out and coming in). Second, his reaction to his brother's homecoming reveals that he does not understand the love of the father, namely that it is only increased by the "twofold movement" of being lost and found. Barth says, "He failed to understand, therefore, the fact that in His grace God is the God precisely and exclusively of the man who makes this twofold movement" (IV/2, 24). On Barth's interpretation, this picture of the older son's character is meant to shed light on the scribes and Pharisees in front of the text who do "not reject merely a distasteful doctrine of sin and forgiveness" but also the revelation of God Godself as well as the essence of humanity. For God elects to be the God of *lost* humanity. In this same decision, humanity is determined from eternity as humanity elected and preserved for fellowship with God. In other words, the problem is not just that the elder brother, like Jesus' dissenters, is averse to the gratuitousness, and even injustice, of the father's gracious reception of the son. The greater issue is that refusing the actuality of grace means rejecting (1) the concrete love of God in Christ and (2) the reality of humankind as beloved in Christ. To deny this story about a son who was lost and found is to deny Christ's own loving action and, concomitantly, the good news that, by grace, God and humanity are united in an eternal fellowship that is ultimately deepened and strengthened by the historical process of covenantal rupture and reconciliation.

So, the elder son is by no means a dispensable foil for his younger brother. Instead, Barth maintains, "this elder brother will finally bring Jesus to the cross, not merely because Jesus said about God and the sinner what is said in this parable, but because [Jesus] is the man in whom what is said in this parable . . . is actuality" (24). The problem, then, is *not* that the story tells of a distant "Father-God who self-evidently and consistently pardons," which is offensive to the righteous (22). What gives the whole parable its force is that, embedded in the ministry of Jesus, it identifies *this* individual (the storyteller) as the one in whom God's grace is revealed. According to Barth, "What puts this figure [the elder son] so terrifyingly into the shadows is that it is a personification of the conflict against the actuality of the God-man." What the elder son opposes is none other than Jesus Christ. This story decisively insinuates itself into the world in front of it—and in such a way that it helps effect what it describes: the going out and coming in of the Son of God.

This is the second reason the inclusion of the elder son's story is in fact integral. In light of Barth's recognition of the embeddedness of the parable within Luke 15 and within the whole of the Gospel, the life of Jesus cannot help but "reverberate" on the parable, and vice versa. Barth is attuning his readers to this when he turns to verse 32, "the final saying of the father to his elder son which forms the conclusion of the parable." As the King James Version, the English translation used for Barth's quotation of the verse, reads: "Son, thou art ever with me, and all that I have is thine. It was meet that we should make merry, and be glad: for this thy brother was dead, and is alive again; and was lost, and is found" (vv. 31–32). This concluding statement parallels the words of the father to his servants when he orders them to prepare a feast upon his younger son's return, "Let us eat, and be merry: For this my son was dead, and is alive again; he was lost (had gone off, disappeared), and is found" (vv. 23–24). Barth comments:

> If there is any point where we can ask whether there is not finally a direct as well as an indirect christological reference, and therefore need of a christological exposition, it is in face of these two verses, of this "my son" and "thy brother," of this dead man who was alive again, of this lost man who was found, of the rejoicing which rings out in these words.

We must ask, "To whom does this all refer?" It is precisely at this point that "another voice" breaks into the text, transgressing its narrative enclosure, yielding meaning in excess of its own elements. Dead and alive again—is this not "almost too strong to be applied . . . to the lost son of the parable"? (24–25). Barth does not "press the point." Nor does he have to. For an "*in concreto* christological exposition" is "invited by the text itself" (25). So much so that "even the most cautious exegesis of the parable" must be able to account for the meaning of these startlingly evocative parallel verses.

Ultimately claiming much more than a structural-narratival similarity between the far journeys and homecomings of the lost son and the eternal Son, Barth concludes with a strong a posteriori justification for venturing his christological interpretation. Having initially proposed only an "indirect" reference to Christ, he finally suggests it must be "direct" as well. So much for his disclaimers about not being able to "demonstrate" as much. Barth quips between his quotations of verses 24 and 32, "Yes, this is also *in the text*."[27]

As Eduard Schweizer later puts it,

> Jesus does not appear in the parable, but only because it is he who tells it and lives it to the point of death does the joy of restoration it recounts become a

---

[27]   Emphasis added.

reality. In the parable "there is no room left for any mediator between God and the sinner" (Jülicher); it is all the more incomprehensible, however, without a mediator. It was not simply Jesus the teacher who discovered God to be the father of [humankind]; without his ministry the parable would not be true.[28]

Jesus lives the grace narrated in the parable. Without the storyteller, apart from the mediating analogue of his existence, the story is not true. This is precisely the spirit of Barth's christological interpretation of Luke 15:11–32. It is also Julian's intuition as she makes sense of her dramatic biblical vision. The presence of Jesus is localized in the structure of the younger son's action. The one who "came to seek and to save the lost" (Luke 19:10) does so by becoming the lost.

Julian's Example of the Lord and Servant

Julian receives her Example of the Lord and Servant as the answer to a doubt she expresses earlier about how all could "be well" in light of sin and suffering. It becomes the theological key to her Long Text, "a microcosm for the entire visionary sequence," which leads into an expansive Trinitarian account of the motherhood of God.[29] But, initially, it is introduced as a reply to Julian's question about how God sees humankind. In chapter 50, prefacing the example, Julian restates a theological conundrum that occupies her discussion of the judgment of God (in ch. 45):

> Goode lorde, I see the that thou arte very truth, and I know sothly [truly] that we sin grevously all day and be mekille [very much] blamewurthy. And I may neither leve the knowing of this sooth, nor I se not the shewing to us no manner of blame. How may this be? (50.6–9)

Julian is attempting to reconcile her own experience of the blameworthiness of sin, which coincides with "the comen teching of holy church," with her vision in which God assigns no blame to humankind. These "two contraries" fill her with dread because she is "lefte in unknowing how he beholde us in our sinne" (50.16–17). To be more precise, she sees *that* God beholds sinful humans with no manner of blame; the problem is that she cannot account for *why*, in the face of what she has been taught about divine judgment. She longs "to see in God how he seeth" sinners (line 18). Through her lengthy periphrastic meditation, Julian slowly uncovers the quality of God's judgment revealed in a multilayered gloss of the Parable of the Prodigal Son (chs. 51–52).

---

[28]   Schweizer, *Good News*, 252.
[29]   Kevin McGill, *Julian of Norwich: Mystic or Visionary?* (New York: Routledge, 2006), 81.

The Example and the Properties of Understanding

Chapter 51 begins, "And then oure curteyse lorde answered in shewing, full mistely, by a wonderful example of a lorde that hath a servant." In the showing itself, which spans lines 6–51, Julian beholds "in bodely liknesse" two figures: a lord and a servant. She sees the servant standing before his seated master. He is sent out to do his master's will, but he departs so eagerly and hastily that he immediately falls into a hollow and is injured in such a way that he is unable to get up. As Julian narrates the sequence,

> The lorde sitthe solempnely in rest and in pees. The servant stondeth before his lorde reverently, redy to do his lordes wille. The lorde loketh upon his servant full lovely and sweetly, and meekly he sendeth him into a certaine place to do his will. The servant not onely he goeth, but sodenly he sterteth and runneth in gret hast for love to do his lordes wille. And anon [immediately] he falleth in a slade, and taketh ful gret sore. And that he groneth and moneth and walloweth and writheth. But he may not rise nor helpe himselfe by no manner of weye. (lines 6–14)

But the real crisis for the wounded servant is that, from the pit, he is unable to see the nearness of his lord and be comforted by him. She says,

> And of all this, the most mischefe that I saw him in was failing of comfort. For he culde not turne his face to loke uppe on his loving lorde, which was to him full nere, in whom is full comfort. But as a man that was full febil and unwise [weak and foolish] for the time, he entended to [focused on] his feling and enduring in wo [suffering]. In which wo he suffered sevene gret paines. (lines 15–19)

The pains the servant suffers because of his fall are enumerated here but left uninterpreted. Julian says he suffers: (1) soreness and bruising, (2) the full weight of his body, (3) weakness from the first two, (4) blindness and a feeling of being so stunned that he hardly recalls his love for the lord, (5) the possibility that he may never be able to get up, (6) the experience of being alone, and (7) the difficulty and terribleness of the place where he now lies (lines 20–27).[30]

---

[30]   The seven pains the servant suffers have no connection with the "seven deadly sins," which Walter Hilton, for example, uses in *The Scale of Perfection*, trans. John P. H. Clark and Rosemary Dorward (New York: Paulist, 1988) to describe the fall's impact on the soul. See Nicholas Watson and Jacqueline Jenkins, eds., *The Writings of Julian of Norwich: "A Vision Showed to a Devout Woman" and "A Revelation of Love"* (University Park: Pennsylvania State University Press, 2006), 274. Rather, according to Colledge and Walsh, the pains allude to the description of the Suffering Servant in Isaiah. Edmund Colledge and James Walsh, S.J., eds., *A Book of Showings*

Of these pains, Julian calls the sixth—feeling alone—the most "mervelous," which is to say, the most painful. This corresponds to her seeing "the most mischefe" in the servant's lack of comfort. The worst aspect of the situation is the apparent separation between servant and lord.

Julian begins to examine this picture for (1) any fault in the servant and (2) whether the lord "shuld assigne in him ony maner of blame" (lines 29–30), but discovers neither. First, there is no fault in the servant because "only his good will and his gret desyer was cause of his falling. And he was as unlothful [innocent] and as good inwardly as he was when he stode before his lorde, redy to do his wille" (lines 31–33).[31] Second, she sees no blame, for "his loveing lorde full tenderly beholdeth him." The loving look of the lord has a "doubil chere [expression]." On the one hand, the "outwarde" expression is one of "gret rewth and pitte [sorrow and compassion]." On the other hand, in his "inwarde" and "more gostly" expression, Julian says, "I saw him hyely enjoy [rejoice]" that he will restore his servant "by his plentuous grace" (lines 34–38).[32]

This second aspect of the lord's gaze is clarified for Julian when "saide this curtyse lorde in his mening [intent]":

> Lo, my beloved servant, what harme and disses [trouble] he hath had and taken in my servis for my love—yea, and for his good will! Is it not skille [reasonable] that I reward him his frey [fright] and his drede, his hurt and his maime, and all his wo? And not only this, but falleth it not to me to geve him a gifte that be better to him and more wurshipful [honorable] than his owne hele [well-being] shuld have bene? And els me thinketh I did him no grace [would not be doing right by him]. (lines 40–45)[33]

Julian reiterates that it "behoveth nedes to be" (i.e., is good and necessary that) the "deerworthy [much-loved] servant . . . shulde be hyely and blissefully rewarded withoute end, above all that he shulde have be if he had not fallen" (lines 46–49). The servant will be elevated above his initial condition, and his suffering itself will be transformed into blessing (line 50).

---

to the Anchoress Julian of Norwich, 2 vols. (Toronto: Pontifical Institute of Medieval Studies, 1978), 133.

[31] "Unlothful" is translated variously as "innocent" and "unhateful" by Watson and Jenkins, and, at times, "ready" by Elizabeth Spearing.

[32] Julian repeatedly describes the double "chere" of the lord/father toward the servant/son as "compassionate" and "rejoicing." These are both central terms in the prodigal son's homecoming in Luke.

[33] This is one of the many passages in which it is clear that the identity of the figure in the example is overlain with that of the Suffering Servant of Isaiah.

The vision leaves off here, yet Julian's rumination on it continues for many years. She understands that it is the answer to the desire she expressed (ch. 45 and 50) concerning how God sees humanity in its sin (line 55). But for a long time "full understanding" eludes her because, "in the servant that was shewed for Adam," she "sawe many diverse properteys that might by no manner be derecte [attributed] to single Adam" (lines 56–58). The confusing overflow of Adam's "properties and conditions" is part of the reason why Julian could not comment on the example earlier, when she recounts her other "showings" in the Short Text. She had not yet worked out the meaning of the doubleness of the servant. Sensing that the "misty example" contains further "privities [secrets]" (line 60), Julian grasps one level of the example, which she calls "gostly in bodely liknesse," long before she grasps the other, "more gostly withoute bodely liknes" (lines 3–4).[34] The polyvalence of the story forces Julian to reflect on her hermeneutical process before offering a twofold interpretation that bears resemblance to Barth's.

Julian speaks here of three "properties" or modes of learning that overlay the double interpretation Julian is about to offer (lines 63f.).[35] Using Trinitarian language to describe her progressive insight as "thre . . . so oned" and "thre as one" (lines 67–68, 69), she obliquely evokes the Augustinian "psychological" trinity of "memory, reason, and will."[36] The first property, she says, is "the beginning of teching that I have understonde therein in the same time" (line 64). By this Julian means the lesson itself and whatever she is able to grasp directly, plainly, or at first blush. Typically, this first mode of learning is associated with the phrase "I saw" and involves straightforward recollection.[37] This includes the way Julian initially recounts the Example of the Lord and Servant and brings it to life visually. The second property is "the inwarde lerning that I have under-

---

[34]   Interestingly, while the form of the *exemplum* is meant to clarify or illustrate, Julian receives this example more as a riddle. It is her retelling that clarifies it. See Watson and Jenkins, *Writings of Julian of Norwich*, 276.

[35]   The relationship between the three properties and two levels is not crystal clear. Watson and Jenkins delineate the first (lines 73–102), second (lines 103–227), and third (lines 228f.). However, Julian freely slides between them, particularly the first two. This makes sense, since she has already indicated that "theyse thre [ortals] be so oned . . . that I can not nor may departe them" (lines 67–68). For our purposes, I am treating the narration of the showing as recollection (the first property), the first interpretation of it as the inward learning (the second property), and the second interpretation as "ghostly without bodily likeness," or her constructive conceptualization of the whole (the third property).

[36]   Watson and Jenkins, *Writings of Julian of Norwich*, 276; see notes on lines 68–69.

[37]   Watson and Jenkins, *Writings of Julian of Norwich*, 276; see note on line 64.

stode therin sithen" (line 65). This concerns Julian's prolonged meditation on and reasoning through the details of the example, especially those that were earlier "indefferent [meaningless]" to her "sight" (line 76). This second "inward" or "ghostly" teaching is usually attended by the verb "understand."[38] Going over the givens again, meditation yields a layer of reflection that includes Julian's own thoughts and questions. It corresponds to the first interpretive level, much like Barth's "direct" reading. The third property or type of insight has to do with "alle the hole revelation, fro the beginning to the ende" (lines 65–66). It seeks coherence with other scriptural and theological knowledge and involves synthesizing either an individual showing or *A Revelation* as a whole. This covers what Julian is doing in her second interpretation of the example.

In making explicit the interpretive modes and layers at work in her retelling of the example, Julian prepares her readers to not take what she has recounted simply on the surface, as having to do with a fictional lord and a servant.[39] It is presented as a metaphorized narrative with theological import, as expected of any homiletic *exemplum*. Some commentators and translators simply refer to it as a parable or "story-revelation." Its meaning is "shewed double" (line 3), according to the distich of spiritual interpretation, indicating that Julian regards the teaching itself as having the status of Scripture. Like the parables of Jesus, it must be beheld again and again, "gostly" and "*more* gostly*," deeper and deeper still (Ps 42:7). Although Julian offers hints of the full insight she had achieved by the time she retells it, she slowly and circuitously leads the reader along the same path she pursued for many years as she pieced together clues to the "how much more" of the story's meaning.

The Example Shown Double

In her first interpretation of the example ("gostly in bodely liknesse"), Julian recognizes it as a fall narrative.[40] She tells us that the lord who sits in rest and peace is God and the servant standing before him is "shewed for" Adam (lines

[38] Watson and Jenkins, *Writings of Julian of Norwich*, 276; see note on line 65.

[39] A strictly literal reading of the story is of course possible and might have been misleading for Julian's contemporary audience since, as Watson and Jenkins point out, there are many similarities between Julian's example and contemporary Romances (*Writings of Julian of Norwich*, 282). Julian may be borrowing from this genre to tell a different kind of story.

[40] I am focusing on Julian's analysis as spiritual interpretation, but she also examines the story according to a list of topics that are commonly found in rhetorical manuals (e.g., Cicero's *De ortals rhetorica* 1.24). She follows the sequence "Who, Where, What" or, under the topic "Who," "Name, Nature, Manner of Life"

85–86). She grasps the purpose of the example on this level as clarifying "how God beholdeth alle manne and his falling. For in the sighte of God alle man is one man, and one man is alle man" (lines 87–88). This is an obvious allusion to 2 Corinthians 15:22 and Romans 5:12. So although she says in the servant "one man was shewed at that time" (line 87), the language "one man is alle" is an early signal that the identity of the Adamic figure exceeds what can be said of fallen humanity per se. Because she only fully understands the initial sense when she understands the whole, there are such signs of her second reading within the first throughout.

Julian again observes that the main problem with the servant's fallenness is that he is "turned fro the beholding of his lorde" so that he cannot see that "our lorde commende and aprove . . . nor he seeth truly what himselfe is in the sight of his loving lord" (lines 91–95). She concludes that "only paine blameth and ponisheth" while "oure curteyse lorde comforteth and socurreth [helps]" (lines 99–100). This distinction maps onto the contrast between human and divine judgment Julian describes as competing "domes" in chapter 45.[41] Her detailed descriptions of individual elements of the story—the lord's location and manner of sitting, the servant's location and manner of standing, their clothing, the colors, eyes, and so on (see lines 103–10)—reinforce her perception of the lord's "lovely [loving] loking" as pure grace, generous, merciful, and full of compassion (line 109). Insofar as the gaze of the lord is mixed, it is a "semely medelur [fitting mixture]" of (1) "rewth and pitte," which is "erthly," and (2) "joy and blisse," which is "hevenly" (lines 112–14).

At this juncture, Julian switches without notice from "lord/e" to "fader," saying the father has compassion ("rewth and pitte") inasmuch as Adam falls, but rejoices (has "joy and blisse") in "the falling of his deerwurthy son, which is even with the fader" (lines 114–16). This implicitly signals her shift toward a second interpretation plane. Julian is beginning to speak of more than the general relationship between God and humanity through the lord and servant. In referring to the "deerwurthy son . . . even with [equal to] the fader," she identifies the servant as the Son and makes an unmistakably Chalcedonian affirmation of his divinity and coequality with the Father.

In her second approach to the example ("more gostly withoute bodely liknes"), the lord/father is identified with the first person of the Trinity and the servant/son with Jesus Christ, the second person of the Trinity. While, to this point, Julian has been reading the servant's misstep as a fall into sin

---

and "Expression, Clothing, Gesture, Action." See Watson and Jenkins, *Writings of Julian of Norwich*, 276; notes on lines 79–84.

   [41]   This will be explored at length in ch. 3.

and suffering (Gen 3), now the "falling" of the eternal Son is connected with salvation (Phil 2). The "merciful beholding" of God (the Father) is manifest in the Son, who "descended downe with Adam into helle, with which continuant pitte Adam was kepte fro endlesse deth" (lines 117–18), as well as the Spirit, in whom "this mercy and pitte dwelleth with mankinde into the time that we come uppe into heven" (118–19). Julian discerns a threefold in the loving gaze of God, assigning the sending of the servant (creating and begetting) to the Father, the falling of the servant into the slade (redeeming) to the Son, and the comforting presence (sustaining) to the Spirit (not yet explicitly mentioned).

As the example illustrates, this salvific and sustaining look is precisely what the fallen servant cannot see. Like Athanasius, Anselm, and others before her, Julian speaks of fallenness as "blindness" to "oure fader, God, as he is." Wondering why God became human, she reasons that, because of human blindness, God must appear "homely [familiar]" (line 122).[42] At the same time, Julian clarifies "we ought to know and beleve that the fader is not man," as if to explain that the incarnation is appropriated to the Son alone. She says the lord's appearance as a man sitting on the barren earth indicates that the fallen servant (Adam) is now "not alle semely [not entirely fitting] to serve of that noble office" (line 124). Yet God's "owne citte" and "dwelling place" is meant to be the human soul (line 125). So the "kinde fader wolde adight him non other place [would not prepare for himself another place] but to sit upon the erth, abiding mankinde . . . till what time by his grace his deerwurthy sonne had brought againe his citte into the nobil fairhede [state of noble beauty] with his harde traveyle."[43] In other words, the lord/father is shown in a barren place because he is waiting patiently for his dwelling among humans to be restored by his servant/son. By the physical details of the lord/father—his billowing blue clothing and darkness of his eyes and face—Julian understands him to be generous and steadfast in the effort to restore the fallen servant/son "by his plentuous grace" (line 136).

Julian proceeds to note other signs that the identity of the servant is Jesus Christ, a possibility that only comes into view gradually. In particular, she explores the doubleness of the servant's appearance, outer and inner (lines

---

[42]   Elizabeth Spearing translates "homelyhed" as "familiarity." As A. C. Spearing notes, in Julian's emphasis on the "homeliness" of God, the word retains "the full emotional resonance of *home* itself, including friendliness, familiarity, intimacy, without the pejorative associations it has in American English" (introduction to *Revelations of Divine Love*, trans. Elizabeth Spearing [New York: Penguin, 1998], xix).

[43]   According to Watson and Jenkins, this language alludes to medieval romance narratives of "lost kingdoms." As they point out, the irony in Julian employing this familiar framework is that she is arguing *the* kingdom has never actually been lost (*Writings of Julian of Norwich*, 280; note to lines 128–29).

139f.). Outwardly, she sees he is simply clothed, "as a laborer which was dis-
posed to traveyle" (line 140). What is curious to Julian is that although he is
just being sent out for the first time, he already looks like he has been traveling
or travailing (the play on this word is suggestive throughout *A Revelation*).[44]
She later recalls this image of Christ on earth as if he "were on pilgrimage"
(81.5). He is clad in

> a whit kirtel [white shift], singel [thin], olde, and alle defauted [deficient], dyed
> with swete [stained with sweat] of his body, straite fitting [close-fitting] to him
> and shorte [i.e., a peasant's garment] . . . seeming as it shuld sone be worne uppe
> [worn out], redy to be ragged and rent [torn up for rags]. (51.142–44)

In other words, he is poor, dirty, weary, and unfit for service. The unseemliness
of the servant's appearance renews her inquiry about how the lord looks on
him with such affection and compassion.

By way of explanation, Julian turns to the inward meaning of the servant,
saying, "In him was shewed a ground of love," and this love between lord and
the servant is "even [equal]" (lines 147–48), language that implies divinity.[45]
Her reference immediately following this to "the *wisdom* of the servant" (line
149) points to the incarnate Wisdom of God and the figure of the "Suffering
Servant" of God (Isa 40–55).[46] But rather than clarify these claims here, Julian
simply retells the basic trajectory of the example again in a different way (lines
149–56). She says the servant's wisdom is that he perceives what he could do
that would bring worship to the lord, which is what sets him out on his journey. Julian says, "For love, having no regarde to himselfe nor to nothing that
might fall of him, hastely deed sterte and runne at the sending of his lorde to
do that thing" (lines 150–52). A clear gloss on Philippians 2:7, this explains
the second aspect of the father's mixed gaze (line 116)—not pity for the fall of
Adam but rejoicing over the descent of his beloved Son.[47]

---

[44]   According to Soskice, "In Julian's Middle English, 'travails' carries three
meanings: Christ labours with us (gives birth), sorrows with us (shares our travails),
and, in doing both, 'travels' with us on our way" (*Kindness of God*, 151).

[45]   The resonance with Augustine's account of the Trinity is pronounced here.
The Spirit is the love that obtains between the Father and the Son.

[46]   In Colledge and Walsh's analysis, this is Julian's most important scriptural
allusion (*Book of Showings*, 133). The example narrates the identity of the "Suffering
Servant" in Isaiah. Cf. James Walsh, S.J., *The Revelations of Divine Love of Julian of
Norwich* (London: Burns & Oakes, 1961), 31–32.

[47]   Paul says Jesus Christ, "though he was in the form of God, / did not regard
equality with God / as something to be exploited, / but emptied himself, / taking the
form of a slave, / being born in human likeness. / And being found in human form,

In his wisdom, the servant sees that "ther was a tresoure in the erth which the lorde loved" (line 157).[48] Julian describes the treasure as "a mete [food] which is lovesom [appetizing] and plesing to the lorde" (lines 158–59). Perplexing details and mixed metaphors abound: there is no food or drink to serve the lord, the lord has only one servant (when a real lord would have had many), and the servant is being sent out "that he shuld do the grettest labour and the hardest traveyle that is: he shuld be a gardener" (lines 159–65). So the servant is sent out to toil, till, plant, water, harvest, prepare, and present the lord with his treasure (lines 164–69). A bizarre amalgam of imagery, the allusions included shed some light on its meaning. First, the reference to treasure is connected with the Kingdom of God (Matt 13:44). Second, the careful preparation of abundant food and drink indicates feasting—a prevalent theme in the parables of Jesus, especially Luke (e.g., 15:11–32 and its context, 15:1–2), as well as throughout Scripture—symbolic of the eschatological union of God and humankind. Third, the specification of the laborer as a gardener reminds us of John 20:15, where Mary Magdalene meets the resurrected Christ but mistakes him for the gardener. Julian's description of the gardener and his "travail" evokes many scriptural passages concerning the life-giving and sustaining work of God.[49] These charged details begin to coalesce as Julian wonders "fro whens the servant came." The lord has everything within him, wanting nothing; there is nothing without or outside him. Who is this servant, then, who can give something so important to such a lord—and where did he come from?

Finally, Julian unambiguously puts it together that the fallen servant represents not only Adam but also the second person of the Trinity, who is Jesus Christ. She says,

> In the servant is comprehended the seconde person of the trinite, and in the servant is comprehended Adam: that is to sey, all men. And therfore whan I sey "the

---

/ he humbled himself / and became obedient to the point of death—/ even death on a cross" (Phil 2:6–8).

[48] This must have been a particularly confusing detail in the example that Julian held back because it did not make sense on the surface apart from her secondary (christological) interpretation.

[49] For example: "For I will pour water on the thirsty land, / and streams on the dry ground" (Isa 44:3); "you shall be like a watered garden, like a spring of water, whose waters never fail" (Isa 58:11); "those who drink of the water that I will give them will never be thirsty. The water that I will give will become in them a spring of water gushing up to eternal life" (John 4:14); "neither the one who plants nor the one who waters is anything, but only God who gives the growth" (1 Cor 3:7); etc. See also Gen 2:5, which suggests that tilling the land is part of humanity's vocation.

sonne," it meneth the godhed, which is even with the fader; and whan I sey "the servant," it meneth Cristes manhode, which is rightful Adam. (lines 179–82)

Julian is careful to distinguish Christ's humanity (outward/servant) from his divinity (inward/son), specifying that his "manhode" includes Adam or "alle man" (lines 182, 187) while he is equal to the father in his "godhed." She begins to indicate the difference by using "servant" for his union with Adamic humanity and "son" for his equality with God. These distinctions are signaled in the details of the story. For example, Julian says the "nerehed [nearness]" of the servant to the Lord signifies that he is the son (divine) while the son's standing on "the left side" signifies that he is Adam (human) (lines 182–84). Similarly, "by the wisdom and the goodnesse that was in the servant is understond Goddes son" (line 192), but "by the pore clothing as a laborer . . . is understonde the manhode and Adam, with alle the mischefe and febilnesse that foloweth" (lines 193–94). His white tunic is human flesh; its narrowness is poverty; its shortness is servitude and work; its worn appearance is because of Adam; its flaws and sweatiness show human travail (lines 207–10). But for all these subtleties, Julian claims that, in the servant, "oure good lorde shewed his owne son and Adam but one man" (line 195).

Julian's story is clearly a soteriological example then; it is not merely about the fall of Adam. It depends upon the Pauline identity of Adam and Christ as corresponding representatives of humanity (Rom 5) as well as the logic of Hebrews 2:9–17, in which the "pioneer" of salvation is made perfect through suffering (lines 179f.).[50] Reflecting on Christ's incarnation and passion, Julian goes on to clarify:

---

[50]   Heb 2:9–17 reads,

But we do see Jesus, who for a little while was made lower than the angels, now crowned with glory and honor because of the suffering of death, so that by the grace of God he might taste death for everyone. It was fitting that God, for whom and through whom all things exist, in bringing many children to glory, should make the pioneer of their salvation perfect through sufferings. For the one who sanctifies and those who are sanctified all have one Father. For this reason Jesus is not ashamed to call them brothers and sisters, saying, "I will proclaim your name to my brothers and sisters, / in the midst of the congregation I will praise you." And again, "I will put my trust in him." And again, "Here am I and the children whom God has given me." Since, therefore, the children share flesh and blood, he himself likewise shared the same things, so that through death he might destroy the one who has the power of death, that is, the devil, and free those who all their lives were held in slavery by the fear of death. For it is clear that he did not come to help angels, but the descendants of Abraham. Therefore he had to become like his brothers and sisters in every respect, so that he might be a merciful and faithful high priest in the service of God, to make a sacrifice of atonement for the sins of the people. Because he himself was tested by what he suffered, he is able to help those who are being tested.

By Adam I understond alle man. Adam fell fro life to deth: into the slade of this wreched worlde, and after that into hell. Goddes son fell with Adam into the slade of the maidens wombe, which was the fairest doughter of Adam—and that for to excuse Adam from blame in heven and in erth—and mightily he feched him out of hell. (lines 186–91)

For Adam, the "slade" or pit is sin and death, but, for the Son, it is a double descent to earth, Mary's womb, and hell. Translating the christological hymn of Philippians 2 again, she continues:

Notwithstonding that he is God, even with the fader as anenst [with respect to] the godhead, but in his forseeing purpos—that he woulde be man to save man in fulfilling the will of his fader—so he stode before his fader as a servant, wilfully taking upon him alle oure charge [burden]. And than he sterte full redely at the faders will, and anon he fell full lowe in the maidens wombe, having no regarde to himselfe ne to his harde paines. (lines 202–7)

On this level, the "readiness" of the servant belongs to Christ, not Adam, and his hard pains are salvific, not merely the consequence of sin. His desire, his "ghostly thirst," is to recover the lost treasure on earth. Julian now sees in the example that in the servant the Son stands before the Father saying, "Lo, my dere fader, I stonde before the in Adams kirtel, alle redy to starte and to runne. I wolde be in erth to don thy worshippe, whan it is thy will to send me. How long shall I desyer it?" (lines 211–13).[51] The picture is evocative of Hebrews 2, where, having been "made lower than the angels" (i.e., human) (v. 9), Jesus says, "Here am I and the children whom God has given me" (v. 13)—which is to say: here I am holding the children of God within my own flesh. Julian reiterates this oneness: "All is the manhode of Crist. . . . Jhesu is all that shall be saved, and all that shall be saved is Jhesu" (lines 218, 225–26). She alludes to such passages as 1 Corinthians 12:12 and Colossians 1:18 when she explains, "For he is the heed, and we be his membris" (lines 218–19). It is apparent, then, that the example illustrates not only the fall but also salvation, incarnation, and the hypostatic union.

The predominant biblical image of salvation to which Julian appeals is of mutual inclusion or enclosure: all humanity re-membered in Christ's body as he "puts on" the flesh. After years of reflecting on and reasoning

---

[51]   Julian alludes to Mark 13:32: "But about that day or hour no one knows, neither the angels in heaven, nor the Son, but only the Father." Although she is referring to the incarnation at first, by the end of the passage she has shifted her attention to the judgment for which the righteous wait.

through the example, Julian finds her answer to the question concerning how to reconcile God's gracious judgment with the blameworthiness of fallen humanity. For "oure good lorde Jhesu [hath] taken upon him all oure blame, and therfore oure fader may nor will no more blame assigne to us than to his owne derwurthy son" (lines 197–99). In becoming incarnate, the second person of the Trinity absorbs the blame of fallenness and eagerly assumes "alle our charge," the burden that properly belongs to Adam, in order to restore humankind in the eyes of God. In his going out, the servant expresses God's pity for human suffering, and, in his return of God's treasure, there is great rejoicing. The narrative shape of the biblical parable and its key themes are recognizable here.

"Oning" in the Trinity

Julian comes to understand that the servant's descent into the slade stands for both fall and restoration. In one sense, then, the "doubleness" of the servant simply involves a plurality of reference (Adam, humankind, the individual "soul," Christ). The whole story can be narrated differently with respect to each referent. It can retell the fall as well as kenosis and incarnation. This is a doubleness of *interpretive* layers. But in another sense, the doubleness of the servant depends upon an interweaving of the referents such that the various interpretive strata of the example produce quite another story. In fact, it is only as Julian sees them entwined that the different aspects of the servant reveal the meaning of the example. The two trajectories do not simply parallel one another; they are integrally related. Christ's fall intercepts and redirects Adam's fall. It is not so much that the one narrative tells two stories of descent—one concerning the fall and another the incarnation. The manner in which Julian's interpretation unfolds suggests that these two events must be understood, on another level, as one event, concerning one person (Jesus Christ), taking place at once—*in the Trinity*.

After identifying the servant/son with the second person of the Trinity, in her second interpretation of the example, Julian says, in good Augustinian fashion, "The lorde is God the father; the servant is the sonne Jesu Crist; the holy gost is the even love which is in them both" (lines 184–85). She asked to see how God sees humankind. But when she sees Adam and Christ as one, and all in Adam, she also sees Christ situated within the Trinity, clad in weary human flesh, standing ready before God the Father, prior to his incarnation in time. She writes:

Thus was he the servant, before his coming into erth, stonding redy before the father in purpos, till what time he wolde sende him to do the wurshipful deede by which mankinde was brought again into heven. (lines 200–202)

In other words, Julian beholds in the example an intratrinitarian event, a "rightful oning" (line 186) that precedes and governs Christ's temporal atonement.

This passage mirrors her shocking claim: "When Adam felle, Goddes sonne fell. For the rightful oning which was made in heven, Goddes sonne might not be seperath from Adam" (lines 185–86). That Christ falls into Mary's womb *because* Adam falls into sin is one thing; that God's Son falls *when* Adam falls, quite another. What could this mean? Here she speaks rather modestly of this heavenly atonement being a reality "in purpose." Elsewhere she uses the language of "intent" and "foresight." But it is bound up with her claim that "ther was right noght [nothing at all] betwen the godhede and the manhede" (line 208). The "rightful oning which was made in heven" (line 186) takes on eternal dimensions as Julian turns to the third "property" in the method of spiritual interpretation she lays out earlier (lines 63f.) in order to venture an interpretation of the whole.

Julian revisits, for the third time, the many "previties" (line 231) of the narrative-image she was shown, excavating additional meaning as she goes. The passion narrative emerges more clearly. She now circles back to some of the details in light of the pattern of the Gospel story, drawing out a threefold decent. Julian reinterprets the meaning of the servant's attire in light of her other visions of Christ's crowning, scourging, and crucifixion (lines 246–53). She speaks of the fall into Mary's womb succeeded by a further fall into death and finally a going down into hell. Beginning with Christ's conception and incarnation, Julian says the sitting of the father or lord "betokeneth the godhede," God dwelling in rest and peace. The standing of the servant to the left indicates the servant's travail and his unworthiness as fallen. The start or origin belongs to his divinity, while the running or labor belongs to his humanity. The beginning, or leaping up, is from the father, "into the maidens wombe," and the falling is "into the taking of oure kinde." The "grete sore" born in this fall "was oure flesh" (lines 232–39).

At the nadir of his descent, Julian speaks of Christ "yelding the soule into the faders hand, with alle mankinde for whome he was sent" (lines 252–53). His "body ley in the grave till Easter morrow" yet "fro that time he ley never more" (lines 256–57). In both cases Christ's "yelding" is a twofold play on the word: loss and gain, surrender and victory. At this point we encounter one of several mentions of the harrowing of hell in Julian's text. She says the servant "beganne furst to show his might" and "raised uppe the gret root oute of the depe depnesse, which rightfully was knit to him in hey heven" (lines 254–56). "Great root" may be a play on words that means "mighty company," and it could also allude to "the root of Jesse," associated with the redeemer throughout the Bible.[52] The latter sense can, of course, encompass the former—and this seems to be the case in the following lines, where Julian speaks of the "foule dedely flesh, that Goddes son toke upone him" (in Adam's "kirtle"), being cleansed, restored, and made "fair and richer than was the clothing which I saw on the fader" (lines 259–62).[53] Christ is the root of that renewed humanity. In him is included a great multitude, symbolized by the "largenesse" of the "garments of salvation" (Isa 61:10) (line 296).

Having discerned in the imagery of her example Christ's multitiered descent (incarnation, suffering, death, hell), Julian sees—as if without interval—the servant again before the lord, but now richly adorned and clothed. No longer standing to the left, he sits on the right hand of the father—an unmistakable allusion to, perhaps even a translation of, the Apostles' Creed, as well as Hebrews 8:1.[54] Julian sees the servant standing with "a crowne upon his hed of precious richenes" (line 269), and this image evokes her initial vision of Christ, crowned with thorns (in Revelation 1). She continues, "It was shewede that 'we be his crowne,'" referring back to Revelation 9 (ch. 21–23), which "was shewed for the joy and the blisse of the passion" (23.10–11).[55] There Julian speaks of "alle the trinite wrought [works or at work] in the passion of Crist" (23.24) and mentions the Trinitarian rejoicing over the treasure "wonne . . . with his hard traveyle" (51.243–44). "Which

[52]   Watson and Jenkins think "root" is a variant of "rout," which refers to a crowd, here those who were kept in hell until Christ's harrowing (*Writings of Julian of Norwich*, 286).

[53]   Aelred of Rievaulx has a similar vision of Christ in Adam's tunic (Colledge and Walsh, *Book of Showings*, 16).

[54]   In *The Lay Folks Mass Book*, this part of the creed is translated, "Now syttus he on his fadur righte honed in maieste." Heb 8:1 similarly speaks of a high priest set on the right hand of the majestic throne in heaven. See Colledge and Walsh, *Book of Showings*, 544; and T. F. Simmons, ed., *The Lay Folks Mass Book: The Manner of Hearing Mass, with Rubrics and Devotions for the People, in Four Texts, and Offices in English according to the Use of York, from Manuscripts of the Xth to the XVth Century* (London: N. Trubner, 1879).

[55]   In ch. 23, Julian speaks of the various ways the passion is shown to her. Four of those modes concern Christ's suffering on earth (and can be identified with the first gaze of the lord, which is marked by pity or compassion and is directed toward fallen humanity). The fifth mode concerns the joy and bliss of the passion, which is invisible on earth but experienced in heaven (this can be identified with the second divine gaze, which is marked by enjoyment and constitutes an insight into intratrinitarian relations).

crowne"—humanity restored—"is the faders joy, the sonnes wurshippe, the holy gostes liking, and endlesse, mervelous blisse to alle that be in heven" (lines 270–71). Humankind is the crown that on earth is seen in thorns and, *at the same time*, seen in heaven as precious jewels (the great treasure for which the gardener in the example labors).[56] The descent of the servant effects the raising up of humankind. The standing to the right (exaltation) includes and depends upon the standing to the left (humiliation). They are two sides of the same event.

In a rare application of nuptial imagery, Julian writes, "Now is the spouse, Goddes son, in pees with his loved wife, which is the fair maiden of endlesse joy" (lines 276–78). But, characteristically, she quickly shifts and blends her metaphors, saying, "Now sitteth the son, very God and very man, in his citte in rest and in pees"—and, concluding on a Trinitarian note—"which his fader dighte to him of endlesse purpose, and the fader in the son, and the holy gost in the fader and in the son" (lines 279–80). Both images, of bride and city, capture the motif of "wonning" or being-at-home-with that pervades Julian's Christology.[57] Here, as throughout her theology, the Trinity is seen to include humanity, and, in some sense, for Julian, this is eternally so.

Prodigality and Intertextuality

What is apparent from attentive encounters with these retellings is that they are richly intertextual. In both Julian's example and Barth's exegesis, the Parable of the Prodigal Son is overlain with (1) the Genesis 2–3 account of creation and fall, (2) the narratives of Israel's captivity, exodus, and exile, and especially the "Suffering Servant" imagery of Isaiah 40–55, (3) the Gospel story in which "the Word became flesh" (John 1:14), an "offering for sin" (Isa 53:10), even sin itself (2 Cor 5:21), (4) the event of divine condescension (Phil 2:6f.), and (5) the Pauline Adam-Christ identity (Rom 5:14f.; 1 Cor 15:22).[58] Recourse to this broader biblical framework, we will see in subsequent chapters, is not

---

56   The mixture of metaphors is logically unsustainable but suits the highly textured and many-layered nature of the reality Julian is attempting to narrate in this one example. Humankind is Christ, his garments, his crown (of thorns and jewels), as well as the treasure on earth or the "mete" (food) for which the lord longs and for which he toils.

57   "Wonning" can mean "dwelling," and some manuscripts render it that way, but, according to Watson and Jenkins, its more specific sense is "being at home" (*Writings of Julian of Norwich*, 40).

58   This selection is not meant to exclude the other biblical allusions and evocations present in their retellings. But we find the biblical elements I have identified are mapped onto one another more explicitly.

an instance of capricious "allegorization" or an imposition of an "ecclesial" template, as might be argued from a strictly historical-critical perspective.[59] Rather, as Barth maintains, to "do full justice to the passage" itself, to not leave it "under-interpreted," we must also attend to the relationship between the parable and the rest of the story (IV/2, 22).

Mirroring Christ's incarnation (birth–death–ascension) and passion (crucifixion–burial–resurrection), the prominent structural feature of the Parable of the Prodigal Son is the double movement of separation and reunion: descent and ascent, fall and restoration, going-out and homecoming, *exitus* and *reditus*, humiliation and exaltation, desolation and consolation, sacrifice and reward. It is not primarily the conventional stock characters (father/son, master/servant) that give the story its force and significance. Rather, it is this double movement, activated within a scripturally freighted setting. If we can say, "Jesus Christ *is* the prodigal son," it because Christ's character is manifested and determined by his traversing the same circuit—lost and found, dead and alive. His self-identity and his identity with the younger son are indicated (differently) by the same narrative arc.[60] The fallen son/servant "is" Adamic humanity "is" Christ by virtue of the downward/upward and outward/homeward sequence that is transferred and redoubled.[61]

---

[59]   Insofar as it attempts to dissociate the "original" speech from its interpretation. Ricoeur, *Figuring the Sacred*, 158.

[60]   Rather than an equation between the fictional figure and a real person (i.e., the prodigal son = the eternal Son), what we have here is more topologically associative: the direction and destiny of the prodigal son mirrors that of the eternal Son (and vice versa). It is the *course* of the younger son (rather than, say, his motives or his character) that tells us something about the second person of the Trinity. The referent of the narrative outside of the narrative shares the same structure/movement only in a certain way. Hans Frei's understanding of narrative identity is of some help here. However, at issue in parabolic identity is not how Jesus is identified *as himself* (i.e., in Frei's words, "is what he *does* uniquely, the way no one else does it") but how he is identified *as another* (in traversing the identical course, differently) (*Theology and Narrative*, 12). Narrating this identity-with-another is not simply a matter of the intention-action of the subject. In Julian's and Barth's retellings, we know *who* because we know *where*.

[61]   Throughout biblical, rabbinic, and medieval homiletic parables, there is an ambiguous correspondence between the figures of the "son" and the "servant." On the one hand, they are sometimes interchangeable, or at least fluid—sometimes the servant is like a son to the master, or the son works for the father like a beloved servant. On the other hand, some parables highlight the polarity of the roles of son (heir/free and wealthy) and servant (slave/dispossessed) (e.g., Luke 15). In the Synoptic Gospels, this tension is complicated by the intentional portrayal of Christ, Son of God, as the Suffering Servant of Israel.

At the center of the lost son's trajectory lies a certain topography—the pit or pigsty, Sheol, the grave—which is definitive of the geographical and figurative place: the far country (*regio longinque*)—the region of unlikeness (*regio dissimilitudinis*), the land of wandering, the wilderness.[62] This distant land at the heart of the parable stands over against the lost paradisiacal home, origin and telos of the narrative circle. Conjuring the psalmist's words, "my soul hath been long a sojourner" (Ps 119:5–6), "the place of my pilgrimage" (Ps 118:54) is counterposed with "all my ways are in thy sight" (v. 168) (DRA). In the same way, the thematic counterpoint to the younger son's peregrination—to his lack of citizenship, connection, and place—exceeds the polar earthly topos of his abandoned family home and evokes the horizonless scope of God's sight.[63]

Rereading the parable alongside Julian's and Barth's structurally resonant retellings, a few things come into view: (1) the parable works on multiple theological levels, (2) this is largely a function of its intertextual interpretation, and (3) it narrates the work of atonement by virtue of its narrative structure or plot. But something more is beginning to emerge as well: (4) the content of the parable presses back into the Trinity. The doctrinal implications of elevating the parable to a third plane of theological signification are fleshed out in what follows.

---

[62] The multivalence of the topos of "the pit" is evident in the language of Ps 139:8, "If I go up to heaven, you are there . . ."—the second half of which is translated variously: "If I make my bed in the *depths*, you are there" (NIV), ". . . go down to the *grave* . . ." (NLT), ". . . make my bed in *sheol* . . ." (NASB, ESV), ". . . lay down with the *dead* . . ." (ISV), ". . . make my bed in *hell* . . ." (KJV). *Regio dissimilitudinis* is Augustine's term, borrowed from Plotinus, found in *Confessions* I.18.28 and VII.10.16. It indicates the post-lapsarian condition of having become "unlike" God. It is closely associated, especially in the later tradition (e.g., Bernard and William of Saint-Thierry), with the *regio longinqua* of Luke 15. See Mette B. Bruun, *Parables: Bernard of Clairvaux's Mapping of Spiritual Topography*, Brill's Studies in Intellectual History 148 (Leiden: Brill, 2007), 188. This locus is both literal (in Genesis: outside of the garden; in the parable: the foreign land) and metaphorical (in both cases: the condition of sin, of having lost/diminished the image of God). Distance means dissimilitude. By contrast, the nearness of Christ (in his going out) is initiated by and is effective because of his likeness to God as God.

[63] I think of William Thompson's insight here that "the New Testament is to be read in a psalmodic manner" and that Christology is in some sense "Psalmody." Thompson, *The Struggle for Theology's Soul: Contesting Scripture in Christology* (New York: Crossroad Herder, 1996), 44. It is likewise difficult to return to the Psalms without hearing deep resonances with the narrative of the prodigal son and its mixture of theological themes superscribed in the life and identity of Jesus Christ.

3

Prodigal Mother

"Our savioure is oure very moder,
in whome we be endlessly borne
and never shall come out of him."

—Julian of Norwich (57.40–43)

"Grace is God."

—Julian of Norwich (63.8)

The Example of the Lord and Servant is the center of Julian's Long Text, narrative condensation of her whole theology, and hinge for her Trinitarian turn. Because she presents it as a response to her inquiry about the meaning of sin and suffering, this has led some readers to locate its interpretive key in the prior revelation and elevate "teleological theodicy" as the primary theme of her work.[1] The tension between the human condition and divine love is certainly a, if not the, keynote in Julian's thought.[2] However, the significance of the example, as a deliberate counterexample to prevailing images of divine judgment, only fully unfolds in the succeeding chapters where she expounds the motherhood of God on the basis of the loving look of the lord (chs. 52–63). Glossing the Parable of the Prodigal Son as she does (ch. 51) enables Julian to renarrate divine judgment as pure grace (ch. 45) and lay the groundwork for

---

[1]   Denise Baker, *Julian of Norwich's Showings: From Vision to Book* (Princeton: Princeton University Press, 1994), 85, 89. The example is found in Revelation 14, and Baker's analysis is rooted in Revelation 13. She reads the example as a revision of the prevailing Augustinian interpretation of Gen 3 and Rom 5. As opposed to Augustine's "etiological" theodicy, which is concerned with the origin of human sin, Julian focuses on the end, restoration.

[2]   Though I think her struggle with the tension is best seen as an expression of Julian's love for God. It is this desire to love God well that leads her to see God's love properly.

her subsequent reflection on divine motherhood (chs. 53–63). While, on the face of it, these adjacent portions of her text move in different directions, their thematic continuity is rooted in a fairly diffuse but systematic account of the atonement that is, in turn, coordinated with a Trinitarian vision of predestination. Tuning her reader's perception to the way God regards humankind in its fallen condition in and through Christ, Julian moves through a set of relational analogies that are not disconnected. She progressively specifies the "tender beholding" of God, first as a judge, then as a lord and father, finally landing on the title "mother."

Two Domes

The Example of the Lord and Servant is offered as Julian's solution to a set of contradictions that preoccupy her. Most basically, her showings portray God as "unblaming" despite the patent blameworthiness of sin, which means they do not line up with the church's teaching on divine wrath and damnation. These and related tensions are foregrounded at the beginning of the showing in which the example is embedded (Revelation 14). There she introduces a distinction between "two domes" or ways of beholding (ch. 45), a concept that becomes "fundamental to the argument of chapters 45–63."[3] Julian's lengthy commentary on the "two domes" and attendant "contraries" is integral to understanding not only the example but also the theology of God's motherhood that follows.

The "Fair Dome" of God and the "Medeled" Deeming of Humanity

Julian commences the showing in which the example is embedded by saying, "God demeth [assesses or judges] us upon oure kindely [created] substance . . . and this dome is of his rightfulhede [justice]." But "man demeth upon oure changeable sensualite, which semeth now one and now another" and is "medeled [mixed]" (45.1–4). She is alluding, as she often does, to the logic of Isaiah 55:8, "For my thoughts are not your thoughts, / nor are your ways my ways, says the Lord," and 1 Samuel 16:7, "The LORD does not see as mortals see; they look on the outward appearance, but the LORD looks on the heart." In Julian's words, "For otherwise is the beholding of God, and otherwise is the beholding of man" (52.58).

"Deme" (v.) is a legal term that Julian uses to describe God's judgment of the soul after death (ch. 8). "Dome" (n.) bears related connotations. In this passage (45.1–4), it is explicitly connected to God's justice or righteousness. The mod-

---

[3]   Baker, *From Vision to Book*, 258.

ern English "doom" comes from "dome," and "doomsday" from "domesday," or Judgment Day. Similarly, "deming" is related to "daming," which can mean "condemning" or simply "judging" (v.) as well as "judgment" or "perception" (n.).[4] Julian's idiosyncratic use of these terms stands out against the backdrop of the doomsday preaching and final judgment imagery of her contemporaries.[5] Consider, for example, the extremely popular mid-fourteenth-century English poem *The Pricke of Conscience*, which reads:

> Alle sal haf [shall have] gret drede that day,
> bath gude and ille [both the good and the evil], als we here clerks
>   [clerics] say.
> Thar sal be nouther aungel na man [neither angel nor man]
> That they ne sal [shall not] tremble for dred than [then].[6]

The tone of these lines, prevalent in Julian's day, is antithetical to her own writing on the "dome" or judgment of God. While still thematically bound up with the question of salvation and damnation, her use of "dome" is suggestive of the active or constructive role judgment plays in perception. It implies the interrelatedness of seeing and assessing without reducing God's judgment to its negative or condemnatory function.

The first of the two "domes" Julian discusses in chapter 45 of *A Revelation* is said to proceed from God's "own high endlesse love" (lines 11–12). She describes it as "fair," "swete," and "delectable" (lines 12, 14). In "alle the fair revelation," by which she appears to mean not only this showing (Revelation 14) but the whole "revelation of love," Julian claims, "I saw him assigne to us no maner of blame" (line 13). In the preceding showing (Revelation 13), she similarly asserts, "As we be ponished here with sorow and with penance, we shall be rewarded in heven by the curtesse love of oure lord God almighty. . . . For he beholdeth sinne as sorow and paines to his lovers, in whom he assigneth no blame for love" (39.29–30). Forming an almost constant refrain, interweaving her texts are descriptions of God's kind "chere [expression]" as glad, thankful, loving, piteous, compassionate, and joyous. In other words, it seems

---

[4]   Baker, *From Vision to Book*, 164, 396.
[5]   Such discourses reflect a certain kind of reaction to outbreaks of the plague, which struck England five times between 1347 and 1406. Julian's text implicitly counters the common message of clerics and monks that the plague is divine punishment. Anne Hunt, *The Trinity: Insights from the Mystics* (Collegeville, Minn.: Liturgical, 2010), 99.
[6]   Quoted by Nicholas Watson and Jacqueline Jenkins, eds., *The Writings of Julian of Norwich: "A Vision Showed to a Devout Woman" and "A Revelation of Love"* (University Park: Pennsylvania State University Press, 2006), 224.

Julian already has the answer to the question she is asking; the answer itself has generated the question. Julian's concern is not so much how God sees fallen humanity but how it is possible that God sees humans in this way, in the way revealed to her.

The root of Julian's uncertainty about God's "fair dome" appears to be two-fold: (1) she experiences herself (and humankind) as unworthy, and (2) her experience is consonant with the teaching she has received from the church. These sources constitute the second "dome" Julian describes in chapter 45. The definitive feature of this other judgment is that it is of mixed quality, namely, that it includes wrath. Julian says of human self-judgment, "somtime it is good and esy, and somtime it is hard and grevous" (45.4–5). Referring to the church's authority, Julian says "by this dome, methought that me behoveth nedes to know myselfe a sinner" and that "sinners be sometime worthy [deserve] blame and wrath" (45.16–18). However, she says, "And theyse two"—that is, blame and wrath—"culde I not see in God" (lines 18–19). She goes on to order the two "domes," calling the judgment of God the "higher dome" and the teaching of the church the "lower dome" (lines 20–21). Inasmuch as human judgment is "good and esy," it participates in the higher dome and "longeth to the rightful-hede [righteousness, justice]" (line 6).[7] But inasmuch as it is mixed or "hard and grevous," Julian says, "oure good lorde Jhesu reformeth it by mercy and grace thorow [through or by] vertu of his blessed passion" (lines 7–8).

The easy/hard contrast hearkens back to the lines, "For [the workes of our lord] be fulle good, and *alle* his domes [judgments] be esy and swete [easy and sweet], and to gret ees [comfort] bring the soule that is turned fro the behold-ing of the *blind deming of man* into the fair, swete deming of our lorde God" (11.27–29).[8] Here Julian reckons the lower human dome unseeing—which is to say, sinful—whereas God sees truly and thus looks kindly upon the soul.[9] Throughout *A Revelation*, "mercy" and "grace" consistently define God's dealings with sin. They reform and repair the harsh deeming of fallen humans—hence Julian's later claim, "I saw no wrath but on mannes perty [part, side]," but even this "forgeveth he in us," as attested by "his lovely chere of ruth [mercy] an pitte [compassion]" (48.5–10). Wrath is thus construed as a kind of rebelliousness and opposition to God's love and forgiveness.

---

[7]   Julian's claim runs directly counter to the dominant view. As Baker explains, "The fear of such a wrathful judge pervades the medieval preoccupation with penance. . . . The themes of guilt and punishment came to dominate verbal and visual pastoral instruction" (*From Vision to Book*, 83).

[8]   Emphasis added.

[9]   Blindness is Julian's foremost image for sin.

While Julian sets up a strong opposition and ordering between the two modes of "deeming," she claims they are "accorded [harmonized] and oned [united]" and that both "shall be knowen . . . in heven without ende" (45.9–10). This seems to be because she specifies the sinful human form of judgment as "the dome of holy church" (line 15). She feels she "might by no weye leve the lower dome" and wonders "in what manner . . . the dome of holy church herein techeth is tru in [God's] sight" (line 23). Throughout her writing, Julian carefully situates her showings and their interpretation within the church's teaching and, on the face of it, denies any contradiction between them. As she writes in chapter 9,

> In all thing I believe as holy church precheth and techeth. For the faith of holy church, which I had beforehand understonde—and, as I hope, by the grace of God willefully kept [consciously observed] in use and in custome [according to practice and tradition]—stode continually in my sighte, willing and meaning never to receive onything that might be contrary therto. (9.18–23)

In particular, Julian is concerned about the teaching she has received that some will be damned (Revelation 13), when she herself sees no one among the "reproved." She writes:

> And one point of oure faith is that many creatures shall be dampned: as angelis that felle out of heven for pride, which be now fendes [see Isa 14:12–15], and man in erth that dyeth out of the faith of holy church [those who die outside the faith]—that is to sey, tho that be hethen—and also man that hath received cristondom and liveth uncristen life, and so dyeth oute of cherite [outside a state of charity]. All theyse shalle be dampned to helle withoute ende, as holy church techeth me to beleve. And stonding alle this, methought it was unpossible that alle maner of thing shulde be well, as oure lorde shewde in this time. (32.33–40)[10]

In other words, Julian does not understand how she can hope for all things to be well if what she has been taught about hell and damnation is true. This puts her in a bind, which is reflected in the way her rhetoric vacillates.

That the precise relationship Julian sets up between divine and human or ecclesial judgment on this point remains ambiguous is reflected in the wide

---

[10] Watson and Jenkins point out that these are the "traditional categories into which the damned are divided: fallen angels, anyone not a Christian, and wicked Christians" (*Writings of Julian of Norwich*, 222). A parallel statement can be found in Walter Hilton's *The Scale of Perfection*, trans. John P. H. Clark and Rosemary Dorward (New York: Paulist, 1988), book 2.3.

range of perspectives among Julian's commentators. Some believe she finds a way to resolve the two, while others maintain it is a mysterious paradox that she finally embraces, and still others see an insoluble disjunction or deliberate contradiction.[11] It is difficult to dispute that Julian never fully reconciles divine and human judgment in her writings.[12] The instances in which she appears

[11]   For Colledge and Walsh, the *exemplum* enables Julian to "reconcile" the two "domes" through a kind of double vision. Edmund Colledge and James Walsh, S.J., eds., *A Book of Showings to the Anchoress Julian of Norwich*, 2 vols. (Toronto: Pontifical Institute of Medieval Studies, 1978), 141. It is a matter of coordinating the inward (blameless substance) and outward (blameworthy sensuality) dimensions of the human. As her position develops, they argue, Julian begins to see the matter from both sides and learns to accept "what the church teaches . . . that we should accuse ourselves . . . to a Lord who is loving and merciful." Baker similarly maintains that Julian deals with "the apparent contradiction between her showings and the church's teaching about God's wrath" by drawing a distinction between the "inner" and "outer" aspects of human existence. But, in her view, it is "because humans can see only the outward manifestation of the lower part, or sensuality," that it is said to be "appropriate for them to blame themselves for sin" (*From Vision to Book*, 104). By contrast, Turner sees the "domes" in "harmony," as two "sources" that make up "a single, complex, indivisible whole." Denys Turner, *Julian of Norwich, Theologian* (New Haven: Yale University Press, 2011), 82. Turner admits that Julian "does not see in her shewings what the Church teaches about the damnation of sinners, and the Church does not teach what she sees in her shewings about the Lord's not condemning them" (69). Yet he contends there can be no disjunction between Julian's showings and the Church because "Christ *is* the Church" (72). This "resolution" bears the quality of "paradox," a notion that pervades Turner's reflection on Julian as well as his thought in general. He interprets Julian's questions about salvation and damnation through the lens of her paraphrase of Luke 18:27—"that is unpossible to the[e] is not unpossible to me" (32.42)—saying, "It does not seem right to conclude that, contrary to the teaching of the Church, God will pull off the 'impossibility' of saving everyone. It seems a more natural reading of what Julian says that the impossibility of which the Lord speaks refers to her problem of *seeing* how the damnation of many can be made consistent with God's making 'althing wele'" (107). Turner concludes, "Julian is certain that many are damned" (72). However, this is precisely what she says she doubts. Colledge and Walsh resolve the conundrum differently, recalling that "in all of her visions of Christ's Passion she saw none of the reproved, except only the devil himself" (*Book of Showings*, 106). They claim that "this accords exactly with the Church's teaching, which, in affirming eternal damnation, has never defined that anyone is in hell, except only the devil." This is certainly compatible with Catholic dogma, as de Lubac and Balthasar see it. However, Julian does not seem to be aware of such a solution; rather, she is convinced the official teaching is that some creatures are damned (40.33).

[12]   Watson and Jenkins do not detect any resolution between the "contraries." Instead, they maintain that "*A Revelation* here [in ch. 32] makes quite explicit the tension between what 'holy church techeth' and what Julian interprets her vision to imply" (*Writings of Julian of Norwich*, 222). They point to a parallel passage in *Piers*

to endorse the human "dome" or the teaching of the church typically take the form of a question—"How could it be that . . . ?"—or are posed conditionally as "Methought . . ."—a qualification implying uncertainty or a change of mind. This rhetorical move permits Julian an "exploratory" approach while enabling her to nuance scriptural and theological evidence from the tradition and avoid contradicting the church explicitly.[13] Without ruling out the possibility, she defers hope of their integration to the end of time (32.46f., 85.9–10). In the interim, she turns her attention to subtly reforming the story her readers tell themselves by pointing to the higher dome of God (45.7).

Julian directly challenges "sin's story about itself," insinuating that sometimes theology reinforces a sinful narrative.[14] As a corrective, she recounts the gracious judgment of God, implicitly through her retelling of the Parable of the Prodigal Son (ch. 51) and more overtly in her devotional instruction concerning self-knowledge and divine wrath (ch. 46). Here Julian attempts to practice the instruction of "holy church" to "know thyself," which she connects with the awareness of one's own sinfulness (45.16–17). She traces the ecclesial position not simply to cast doubt on it but to reframe and rewrite it pastorally, slowly infusing it with her own perspective and setting up her readers to receive her example as an authoritative counterexample to leading accounts of salvation and atonement.[15] A few passages shed light on her revisionary approach.

Highlighting the tension between the "two manner of beholdings"—God's gracious manner and "the comen teching of holy church" (46.13–16)—Julian says, "Methought it behoved nedes [it seemed necessary to me] to se and to

---

Plowman that exhibits "a similar resistance to orthodox salvation theology." Interestingly, William Langland, like Julian, alludes to Luke 18:26–27: "Those who heard it [Jesus' words to the Rich Young Ruler] said, 'Then who can be saved?' He replied, 'What is impossible for mortals is possible for God.'" Focusing on v. 26 shifts the problem away from the damnation of some to the salvation of any. The impossible possibility here is a matter of how anyone can be saved, a question Julian implicitly poses throughout. Watson and Jenkins highlight the ongoing tension between the two domes in ch. 45 and following. As they see it, "the church's teaching on sin is clearly subordinated to that of the revelation" (see 45.20–21). In Julian's restatement of the prevailing teaching on damnation (32.33–40), she is "following this argument only to cast doubt on it."

13   Turner, *Julian of Norwich*, 14.

14   Turner, *Julian of Norwich*, 99. This is a marvelous turn of phrase, although Turner never seems to acknowledge that Julian aligns "sin's story" with the "church's story," contrasting both with "God's story."

15   As discussed in the preface, the narrative form of medieval *exempla* is inherently linked to the production of cultural and ecclesial authority. See Larry Scanlon, *Narrative, Authority, and Power: The Medieval Exemplum and the Chaucerian Tradition* (Cambridge: Cambridge University Press, 2007).

know that we be sinners and do many evilles . . . wherfore we deserve pain, blame, and wrath" (46.21–23).[16] But then she says, "Notwithstanding alle this, I saw sothfastly [truly] that oure lorde was never wroth [angry] nor never shall. For he is God, he is good, he is truth, he is love, he is pees" (lines 24–25). In a certain sense, Julian's inability to see wrath in God is not out of the ordinary, given the dogma of divine impassibility with which she would have been familiar. This denial could merely be a logical extension of the classical view that God does not suffer the "passions."[17] However, throughout her Long Text, Julian also decenters a prominent account of atonement in which the satisfaction of divine anger plays a key role.[18] Throughout her writing, God is good and *therefore* not wrathful. She says, "For I saw truly that it is against the properte of his might to be wroth [angry], and against the properte of his wisdom, and against the properte of his goodness" (lines 26–28). It is as if Julian is viewing the situation from God's side and trying to recruit her readers into that perspective. She says, "Betwen God and oure soule is neither wrath nor forgevenesse in his sight" (lines 30–31). Julian thus implicitly aligns her perspective with God's.

It seems disjointed that having disputed ecclesial teaching on sin and claiming divine insight, Julian could conclude, "Now I yelde me to my moder holy church, as a simpil childe oweth [ought to]" (line 41). But this is a common pattern in her thought: it proceeds by looping back on itself—questioning, repeating, repairing, assenting. Given the "spiral" shape of her thought, it can be difficult to make out whether it comes to rest, and where.[19] In a similar passage, Julian teaches, "It longeth us [is proper for us] to have thre manner of knowing":

> The furst is that we know oure lorde God. The seconde is that we know ourselfe, what we ar by him in kinde [as created] and in grace [as redeemed]. The thirde is that we know mekely what ourselfe is, anemptes [as regards] our sinne and anemptes our febilnes. (72.43–45)

---

[16]   The word "methought," here and elsewhere in Julian's writing, has the effect of undermining what she is about to say. It does not constitute an assertion so much as a stage on the way to understanding.

[17]   Watson and Jenkins interpret ch. 31 of *Revelations* along these lines.

[18]   For example, Anselm's assertion in *Cur Deus Homo*, in the mouth of Boso, that "the wrath of God is nothing but his desire to punish" (ch. VI). Anselm of Canterbury, *Opera omnia*, 6 vols., ed. Franciscus Salesius Schmitt, O.S.B. (Edinburgh: Thomas Nelson and Sons, 1936-1961), 2:54. See Baker, *From Vision to Book*, 101.

[19]   Turner, *Julian of Norwich*, 4.

While the awareness of sin is integral to self-knowledge, there are a number of important nuances in Julian's teaching that distinguish it from the view of divine wrath and punishment that she is attempting to reshape. She strongly differentiates human nature (kind) from sin. She recommends to her "even-cristen" that they look at themselves not only or primarily as sinners but, first, as loved by God; second, as they were meant to be and truly are in Christ; and lastly, as they are in their fallen state. Even in this "third manner of knowing," the self is not simply equated with its sinfulness (cf. 52.59; cf. 52.60). The lesson corresponds closely to Julian's prior teaching that, although "unnethes the creature semeth ought to the selfe [the creature scarcely seems of any value to itself]," it should "beknowen [recognize] that [it] is made for love" (44.15–16). What Julian demonstrates for her readers is how the usual disciplines of self-examination and confession can lead back not merely to shame but to the experience of "God in fulhed of joye" (46.4).

When Julian revisits this theme later on, it sounds as if she retracts her prior assertions and concedes that the "lower dome" may be right about condemnation and punishment (ch. 77). She closely follows the content of other instructional manuals on the matter of self-accusation and ascesis (77.11–39):

> Than is this the remedy: that we be aknowen of oure wrechednes and fle to oure lorde. . . . And se we thus . . . "I knowe wele I have deservede paine, but oure lorde is almight, and may ponish me mightly; and he is all wisdom and can ponish me skillefully; and he is alle goodnesse, and loveth me tenderly."[20]

Here the stress falls on words like wretchedness, punishment, and pain. The confession that this is "deserved" seems to be justified in the subsequent paragraph on "penance." But, again, Julian persistently points back to God's perspective, reminding her readers that while God "can" and "may" treat humans otherwise, God is in fact good and therefore loves tenderly (lines 14–15). While, at the beginning of the passage, Julian refers to the knowledge of one's own "wretchedness" as the "remedy" (line 11), by the end she has revised the claim to "the remedy is that oure lorde is with us" (line 34). And not only that—the remedy is seeing the triune rejoicing of God in the passion and knowing that Jesus is "keping us and leding into fulhed of joy" (i.e., into the life of God) (lines 34, 38). So she softens the ascesis of hard "penance" to "meek [humble] accusing," insisting that "he [God] seyeth: Accuse not thyselfe

---

[20] Cf. *Ancrene Wisse*, part 5, on the practice of self-accusation. Anne Savage and Nicholas Watson, *Anchoritic Spirituality: "Ancrene Wisse" and Associated Works* (New York: Paulist, 1991).

overdon mekille [much too much]" (77.27–28).[21] In God's view, the "wo" of life is already enough suffering and should not be compounded by "the sin of self-accusation" (line 30).[22] This is not to suggest Julian downplays the reality of sin. The point is she gets "humility" right as the mean between self-denigration and pride. Proper humility is not self-excoriating; it trusts the judgment of God as that of a compassionate parent.

Reading the preceding passages in light of the Parable of the Prodigal Son and Julian's retelling of it, the presiding message seems to be that while the prodigal son's confession—"I am no longer worthy to be called your son"—is indeed "deserved," his father's economy is patently not one of "just deserts" but of grace and "glad giving." As such, his "rejoicing" and hospitable welcome forms the true and ultimate word, the word by which the son's self-presentation must be measured.[23] In short, self-blame is only "appropriate" in an ambiguous way. The picture Julian paints is one in which (1) humans are indeed sinful and it behooves them to recognize that they are in need of God's grace, but (2) because of their sin, they accuse themselves too harshly and focus inordinately on their own littleness and fallenness.[24] Thus to say it "longeth" or belongs to *fallen* humankind to judge itself in this way is not necessarily to condone it. It is genuinely fitting if it leads back to grace. But as a form of self-accusation, it is a symptom of sin, contradicted by grace and destined to be forgiven.

Julian thus disconnects the practice of self-knowledge from characterizations of God as punishing and angry and consigns such a view of God to the sinful lower dome. This is an artfully pastoral way of calling into question the whole theology of atonement that typically undergirds much devotional instruction. In her view, the greater spiritual obstacle is not sin but "a sinful

---

[21]   This is said in the context of "false dread."

[22]   Watson and Jenkins, *Writings of Julian of Norwich*, 364.

[23]   As will be addressed in ch. 4, this differs markedly from Barth's use of the younger son's confession throughout §74. Despite the fact that election and reconciliation override sinful humanity's self-assessment, Barth considers the son's view of himself an "obedient" one. Julian, in stark contrast, is suggesting that conformity to God means accepting God's gracious view of the human situation and abandoning humanity's own economy of merit.

[24]   In no way do I mean to associate "littleness" and sin—on the contrary, such an association arises from the judgment of the sinful "dome." "Little" is a key term in Julian's example of a hazelnut (ch. 5), and it appears throughout her writing as an expression of the contrast between human beings and God. But for her, human littleness or lowliness never translates into insignificance. It is used not to put humans in their place but to highlight the amazing attentiveness of God, even toward what is so small.

theology of sin."[25] Julian claims, "Either it [wrath] cometh of failing of might, or of failing of wisdom or of failing of goodnesse, which failing is not in God, but is in oure party [is on our side]. . . . For we by sin and wretchedness have in us wrath" (48.7–9). "Wallowing" is "idolatrous," then, because it is predicated upon a false image of God.[26]

Substance, Sensuality, and the "Godly Will"

As she brings her initial reflection on divine and human judgment to a close, Julian seems to change subjects, saying, "Oure kindely [created or natural] substance is now blisseful in God" (lines 34–35). The mention of "substance" at this juncture brings us back to the opening lines of the chapter where she says God judges according to "oure kindely substance" while humans and "mother church" judge according to "oure changeable sensualite" (lines 1–4). The types of judgment are linked to two aspects of the human. The issue is not simply two ways of seeing the same thing, then, but two things seen. This is an important part of the solution to the problem of how God regards sinful humanity. It corresponds in complicated ways with the Adam-Christ identity of the fallen servant in her example or the lost son in the biblical parable.

Julian does not unpack the distinction between "substance" and "sensualite" made in chapter 45 until after the example, which is what renders it intelligible to her. The doubleness of the servant revealed in chapter 51 continues to preoccupy her in chapter 52, where she moves into divine motherhood, and it forms a preface to the content that follows in chapter 53, concerning the "godly will," up through chapter 57, where she loops back to human substance and sensuality. Moreover, all that Julian says about substance, sensuality, and the will is located in the context of her devotional instruction about self-knowledge, which interweaves the whole of Revelations 13 and 14. For Julian, as for Augustine and Calvin, there is no knowledge of the self that is not bound up with knowledge of God.[27] Further, there is no knowledge of God that is not mediated by Christ's humanity—hence setting a sustained reflection on human nature inside her inquiry into the dynamics of salvation. While Julian is simultaneously interpreting her example, addressing common spiritual practices, quibbling with church

---

[25] Turner, *Julian of Norwich*, 103.
[26] Turner, *Julian of Norwich*, 105.
[27] For Julian, as for Calvin and Augustine, "all knowledge is mediated by self-knowledge and . . . self-knowledge is itself mediated by the knowledge of God." See Charles T. Mathewes, "Augustinian Anthropology: *Interior intimo meo*," *Journal of Religious Ethics* 27, no. 2 (1999): 195.

teaching, and offering pastoral support, the surface content is interlaced with deep systematic claims about the meaning of the atonement.

Distinguishing substance and sensuality is not unique to Julian, nor is her mention of a divided will.[28] This demonstrates Julian's familiarity with Latin theology and medieval anthropology.[29] She draws upon Augustine's psychological *vestigia trinitatis*—"oure soule is a made trinite like to the unmade blessed trinite" (55.33–34). Likewise underlying her terms is Augustine's interpretation of Genesis 1:27 in book 12 of *De Trinitate*, where he locates the image of God in the mind (*mens*), which he divides into two parts, associating higher reason or *sapientia* with men and lower reason or *scientia* with women.[30] Julian uses the words "substance" and "sensuality" in their Middle English senses as loose translations for Augustine's "higher" and "lower reason," in much the same way as Richard Rolle and Geoffrey Chaucer did.[31] Substance is "a synonym for existence" and simply refers to the fact that humans are created *ex nihilo* and therefore have their being in a participatory sense in and from God.[32] Sensuality refers to the "natural capacity for receiving physical sensation understood as an inferior power of the soul concerned with the body."[33]

---

[28]   See, for example, Hilton, *Scale of Perfection*. Echoing Augustine, Hilton writes, "The higher part is compared to a man, for it should be master and sovereign, and that is properly in the image of God, for by that alone the soul knows God and loves him. The lower part is compared to a woman, for it should be obedient to the higher part of reason as woman is obedient to man, and that lies in the knowledge and rule of earthly things [and] . . . at the same time always to have an eye raised to the higher part of reason, with reverence and fear, in order to follow it" (book 2.13, pp. 213–14).

[29]   Julian may have been exposed to it through William of Saint-Thierry's *The Golden Epistle*, which Colledge and Walsh believe to have influenced her (*Book of Showings*, 45).

[30]   Baker, *From Vision to Book*, 108–9, 125. For a detailed analysis of this technical vocabulary, see ch. 5, "Reconceiving the *Imago Dei*: The Motherhood of Jesus and the Ideology of Self."

[31]   Baker maintains that Julian uses "sensualite" as "the Middle English equivalent for the Augustinian lower reason" (*From Vision to Book*, 128–29). Denys Turner's more existential paraphrase can be seen to reflect the same basic distinction between "substance"/*ortals* and "sensuality"/*scientia*. He says "sensuality" refers to "our being in time and history," "our selfhood insofar as it is inserted into history and time and worldly experience." "Substance," on the other hand, refers to "our being as created and eternally held in the knowledge and love of God" or "our selfhood insofar as it is in God" (*Julian of Norwich*, 187).

[32]   Baker, *From Vision to Book*, 119.

[33]   Baker, *From Vision to Book*, 193. Quoting from Hans Kurath, Sherman McAllister Kuhn, and Robert E. Lewis, eds., *The Middle English Dictionary* (Ann Arbor: University of Michigan Press, 1954), 436.

What is marked about Julian's application of this technical language is the way she borrows accepted distinctions but manages to disrupt their usual dualistic and androcentric interpretations.[34] In the literature with which Julian would have been familiar, substance and sensuality respectively map onto the pairs good and evil, divine and human, spirit and body, and masculine and feminine.[35] William of Saint-Thierry, for example, renders higher and lower reason in terms of *anima* (soul) and *animus* (spirit):

> The soul [*anima*] is something incorporeal, capable of reason, destined to impart life to the body. It is this which makes men animal, acquainted with the things of the flesh, cleaving to bodily sensation. But when it begins to be not only capable but also in possession of perfect reason, it immediately renounces the mark of the feminine and becomes spirit [*animus*] endowed with reason, fitted to rule the body, spirit in possession of itself. For as long as it is soul it is quick to slip effeminately into what is of the flesh; but the spirit thinks only of what is virile and spiritual.[36]

Sensuality, *anima*, or lower reason is that part of the soul that has dealings with what is corporeal. Substance, *animus*, or higher reason, on the other hand, has a purely spiritual—even divine—quality about it. William's teaching recapitulates the common ancient and medieval association between women and the body (matter–*mater*–mother), addressed by Caroline Bynum among others.[37] It also partakes of the Neoplatonic or dualistic bias against the body. Where Augustine attempted to maintain the full spiritual equality of male and female,

[34]   On Julian's reworking of the traditional sexist exegesis of Gen 1–3 that undergirds these concepts, see Sandra J. McEntire, "The Likeness of God and the Restoration of Humanity in Julian of Norwich's *Showings*," in *Julian of Norwich: A Book of Essays*, ed. Sandra J. McEntire (New York: Garland, 1998), 3–33. Drawing on Mikhail Bahktin's account of dialogical language, McEntire details "the inner dialogue that Julian undertakes with the dominant discourse," which demonstrates "the structure of resistance and revision" (12). This is evident, for example, in the way "Julian appropriates the inferior female body for an image of humanity and its salvation and hereby reverses Augustine's anthropology" (17).

[35]   This is but one of many examples of Julian's creative and sometimes idiosyncratic use of phrases, distinctions, and concepts that she would have come across in devotional manuals, in preaching and teaching in the church, and in whatever theological treatises were available to her.

[36]   William of St. Thierry, *The Golden Epistle: A Letter to the Brethren at Mon Dieu*, trans. Theodore Berkeley, O.C.S.O., vol. 4 of *The Words of William of St. Thierry* (Spencer, Mass.: Cistercian, 1971), 79.

[37]   Caroline Walker Bynum, *Jesus as Mother* (Berkeley: University of California Press, 1982); and idem, *Fragmentation and Redemption: Essays on Gender and the Human Body in Medieval Religion* (New York: Zone Books, 1991).

the connection between women and materiality invariably belies this, in his own writing and more so in that of his successors, as the body becomes associated with the "flesh" or sinful nature.

Human sensuality is implicitly suspect in Julian's theological climate, to say the least. Perhaps because of the usual dualisms and the ambiguity of her terms, some of Julian's commentators align substance with what Julian calls the "godly" will and sensuality with the "bestely" or sinful will.[38] However, their relationship is not so straightforward. Julian mentions the two wills in chapter 37, where she is attempting to explain how it can be true both that "I shuld sinne" (line 1) and that "we be that [God] loveth, and endlesly we do that he liketh" (lines 17–18). Her conviction is unwavering that "he loveth us now as welle while that we be here as he shalle do when we be there before his blessed face" (lines 18–20). But how can God rejoice in sinners, now and already? She seems to be suggesting that the presence of good will is requisite for divine favor. The problem of the divided will is, for her, the problem of intimacy with God. Julian writes,

> For in every soule that shalle be saved is a godly [good] wille that never assented to sinne, nor never shalle. Right as there is a bestely [base] wille in the lower party that may wille no good, right so there is a godly will in the higher party, which wille is so good that it may never wille eville, but ever good. (37.14–17)

These lines resonate with William of Saint-Thierry's *Golden Epistle* as well as a number of other writers with whom Julian would have been familiar.[39] They also echo Paul's words in Romans 7:15–20:

> I do not do what I want, but I do the very thing I hate. . . . For I know that nothing good dwells within me, that is, in my flesh. I can will what is right, but I cannot do it. For I do not do the good I want, but the evil I do not want is what I do. Now if I do what I do not want, it is no longer I that do it, but sin that dwells within me.

In light of this, Julian's occasional confession "I do nought but sin" (see 36.4 and 82.13) makes more sense alongside her insistence on the presence

---

[38]   The relationship between the "godly" will and substance is complicated and ambiguous. There is scholarly disagreement over whether they are synonymous. For example, compare Watson and Jenkins' (*Writings of Julian of Norwich*) notes on chs. 37, 53, and 57 to ch. 6 in Turner's *Julian of Norwich*. Turner rightly cautions that we not draw a precise identity between them. Yet, Julian herself connects them, and they function in parallel ways as she reasons through the double reality of human fallenness (in Adam) and exaltedness (in Christ).

[39]   Colledge and Walsh, *Book of Showings*, 109.

of a good will. There is a commonly recognized gap between desire and ability. This is caused not by "me" (my humanity as such) but by "my flesh" (σάρξ) or sinful nature (Gal 5:17). Paul, like Julian, is affirming the enduring presence of good will in fallen humanity when he speaks of *the good I want* over against *the evil I do not want—but do*. Similarly, there is a sense in which, for him, the true "I" is distanced from the *sin* that *does what I do not want*. On its own, the self is a divided self—and its true identity (good will) is corroded by evil actions in the world.[40] The division between will and deed is related to another: substance and sensuality are bifurcated in the fall. However, the two do not map onto one another in a simplistic way. It is not so much that the sensuality *is* the beastly will, but, rather, the beastly will results from the division in that which was meant to be one. This is an important nuance.

Julian does coordinate the experience of the two "contraries" with the Pauline language of "inner" and "outer" realities in 2 Corinthians 4:16 (see 19.21–27). She says we are "full" in our substance and "fail" in our sensuality. Because of this, it would be easy to identify the higher with the spirit (perfect) and the lower with the body (imperfect). However, Julian's text withstands such an interpretation. In chapter 53, she says the "lovely, gracious, shewing" (the example) revealed to her that "in ech a soule that shall be safe is a godly wille that never assented to sinne, ne never shall" but "continually it willeth good and werketh good in the sight of God" (53.7–11). In the following lines, the "godly" or "goodly" will gets linked up with "substance." However, a comparable relationship is never directly established between sensuality and the "bestely" will.[41] In this way, Julian eschews the sort of identification William Flete makes, in *Remedies against Temptations* (fourteenth century), between the "bestely" part of the soul and the "sensulalite," which he says "is ever incligninge downwarde to sin."[42]

---

[40]   Cf. ch. 63. According to Baker, Julian's "conception of the *imago Dei* may be influenced, either directly or indirectly, by that of Bernard of Clairvaux," who "moves the *imago Dei* from the mind . . . to the will" (*From Vision to Book*, 116). This means that, if the real image is located in the will (manifest as a desire for the good) and that is not eviscerated by the fall (as Paul's comments imply), then, in "substance," the human is still "godly"—i.e., in God's likeness.

[41]   On the "beastly" will, see Watson and Jenkins (*Writings of Julian of Norwich*, 98, 260); Baker (*From Vision to Book*, 117); and Turner (*Julian of Norwich*, 196). After retelling the Example of the Lord and Servant, mention of the lower or "bestely" will drops off.

[42]   See Watson and Jenkins, *A Vision*, in *Writings of Julian of Norwich*, 98, nn. 8–11.

Instead, Julian mixes her terms, speaking of "oure kinde [natural] sub-stance." This evokes created nature, "oure fair kinde," that Christ assumes in the incarnation. Similarly, she uses the phrase "oure sensual soule," a pair-ing that resists the identification of sensuality with the body per se. More-over, the entire contrast between substance and sensuality takes place within a discussion of the soul, not the relation between body and soul (56.2f.).[43] Julian states that "theyse two perties . . . the heyer and the lower . . . is but one soule" (55.40–41). Thus, Turner, among others, rightly argues against a dual-istic reading of Julian's anthropology.[44] In Julian's treatment of it, sensuality is not regarded as the source of sin. In fact, sometimes her use of substance and sensuality parallels "created nature" and "fallen nature," implying a vital distinction between the "natural"—whether pre- or postlapsarian—and the "unnatural," which vies against the creaturely nature that God creates, loves, and sustains. For example, she writes, "So sothly [truly] as sinne is uncleane, so sothly sinne is unkinde [unnatural]" (63.12–13). In this manner, Julian con-sistently distinguishes fallen creation from sin and evil per se—as so many theologians and religious teachers, then and now, fail to do, with dreadful con-sequences for theological anthropology. The third term is crucial.

For Julian, "the 'sensualite' is a more ambiguous, and more positive, aspect of the soul" than it was for Flete and many of her other contemporaries.[45] In fact, "Julian's respect for the sensuality" may be her "most important contri-bution to the theology of the *imago Dei*"—one we would do well to integrate

[43]   Substance and sensuality are polyvalent terms deployed variously in different contexts. Julian herself makes a number of amorphous shifts in predication, not all of which have I examined. Despite my claim that substance and sensuality typically refer to dimensions of the human soul or of the humanity of Christ, they do some-times get aligned with divinity and humanity, respectively, or with the figures in the *exemplum*, the lord and servant. For example, Julian says that "oure sensualite [humanity], by the vertu of Cristes passion, be brought up into the substance [God/ origin]" (56.30–31). But this alignment is not an equivalence. Nor are the pairings divinity/humanity and lord/servant made to correspond to a soul/body polarity. To further muddle any such identification, the lord and the servant get recast as dimen-sions of the soul rather than the relation between God and humanity (see 52.70f.).

[44]   Turner, *Julian of Norwich*, 187, 189. The overlap of substance and sensuality is actual and, on occasion, experienceable (for example, in prayer or in love). As Turner says, "What we most truly are in our historical created existence is what we are in our origin in God," and "what we most truly are is what we most truly desire" (our substance in God) (173–74).

[45]   Watson and Jenkins, *Writings of Julian of Norwich*, 260. Kerri Hide similarly notes that Julian's concept of "sensuality" includes but also exceeds the physical body. Hide, *Gifted Origins to Grace Fulfillment: The Soteriology of Julian of Norwich* (Col-legeville, Minn.: Liturgical, 2001), 84.

today.[46] The non-opposition of substance and sensuality is ensured first, on account of creation and, second, on account of incarnation. Julian says, "Oure kinde, which is the hyer party, is knitte to God in the making [creation]; and God is knit to oure kind, which is the lower party, in our flesh taking. And thus in Crist oure two kindes be oned" (57.14–16). Similarly, she says of the godly will, linked with substance, "We have all this blessed will hole and safe in oure lorde Jhesu Crist" (53.13). When Julian claims of human substance or essence that "oure kinde [nature] is in god hole," she is referring to the union of the "lower" and the "higher" "kindes" in Christ (line 12). As she goes on to explain it, "our substance is in God," kept secure in each person of the Trinity (57.50; 58.50–53), and the "sensualite" is that which "the secund person hath taken," drawing both parts of humanity into God (57.16, 18). So both the substance and the sensuality "knit" humankind into God. Neither poses an obstacle to union and reconciliation. Rather, the problem is that fallenness divides sensuality and substance, which are originally one in the prototype of humankind and true image of God, Jesus Christ.[47]

The complex anthropological implications of such passages have been thoroughly examined by Julian's commentators.[48] While her technical vocabulary remains opaque in ways, stepping back and situating these enigmatic reflections about substance and sensuality in the context of her larger point, it is clear that they are intended to reinforce her theory of the atonement. Through a rather elliptical discussion of the will and the soul, what Julian is trying to show is that the truth of humankind exists only in and through Jesus Christ.[49] She puts it unequivocally: "But no man ne woman take this singularly to himselfe, for it is not so: it is general. For it is [true in] oure precious moder Crist, and to him was this faire kinde dight [assigned]" (62.23–24). Given the rest of her thought, it would of course be incongruous for Julian to claim humankind is or has something in and of itself, independently of the grace of God mediated by Christ. The language of gift and giving interweaves her discussions of creation and salvation. She often reminds her audience that all that is good is from God and that all human goodness—wherever it emerges in the creation–fall–redemption sequence—is essentially participatory. But, more specifically, Julian is asserting

[46]   Baker, *From Vision to Book*, 129.
[47]   Turner, *Julian of Norwich*, 194.
[48]   See, for example, Baker's *From Vision to Book* and Turner's *Julian of Norwich* as well as Hide's *Gifted Origins*.
[49]   As Watson and Jenkins comment, "The redemption of humankind is understood as the uniting of the sensuality and the substance in Christ as perfect and collective human being. *Human selfhood thus emerges as incoherent except in Christ*" (*Writings of Julian of Norwich*, 304 [emphasis added]).

that what belongs to Christ belongs to humanity by virtue of their shared "kind." This is the meaning of the identity of Adam and Christ:

> God knit him to oure body in the maidens wombe, he toke oure sensual soule. In which taking—he us all having beclosed in him—he oned it to oure substance, in which oning he was perfit man. For Crist, having knit in him all man that shall be saved, is perfete [complete] man. (57.35–38)

This "beclosure" or mutual enclosure of "kindness" becomes one of Julian's leading images for the atonement, alongside closely related terms such as "knitting" and "oning." She particularly uses "beclosure" to describe the integral Adam-Christ identity, but it is also applied to the divine-human relationship more broadly. With clear maternal evocations, it appears throughout Julian's account of divine judgment and atonement and prepares the way for her more explicit description of God as Mother.

Atonement as Beclosure

The "dome" of the Lord is finally unblaming because of the divine-human union in Christ. All that Julian says about judgment is grounded in her systematic understanding of the atonement. Her story functions as a sophisticated christological and soteriological counterexample. While Julian is keenly attuned to the parameters of Chalcedonian Christology here, the vividness of her depiction of the reconciliation accomplished in the passion of Christ can submerge its incisive theological claims. But this is itself of theological import. Such visually animated description may be owing to Julian's contemplative practice, among other factors, but the effect is that it focuses her hearers on a face, a sequence of actions, a relationship, a history. It enacts her point—grace is not abstract. It is a name, a person, a relationship. "Grace is God," Julian says—not an idea (63.8).

Several related clarifications help bring into focus the highly relational and imagistic presentation of the atonement that undergirds Julian's example as well as her account of the "two domes" that precedes it and her reflection on the Motherhood of the Trinity that follows. According to Julian, (1) the at-one-ment of God and humanity in Christ is best imaged as a kind of mutual enclosure where (2) Christ becomes a portal into the intratrinitarian life and we see (3) God's meaning in predestination is unalloyed love, so radically and primordially that (4) we must speak of an eternal atonement in God, which is (5) the end-in-the-beginning ensuring that all things must be well.

Beclosure

A series of interlocking images form a special point of access to Julian's account of atonement as a kind of mutual "beclosure" or enclosure of humanity-in-Christ and God-in-Christ. Julian repeatedly refers to God as the one in whom "all" are "enclosed" or "beclosed." Augustine's *interior intimo meo* similarly resonates throughout her writings. She paraphrases him: "God is more nerer to us than oure owne soule" (56.9). While this mutual being-in becomes the explicit theme of the last showing, it already permeates Revelation 14. Julian says, "Our soule wonneth [dwells] in God. Our soule is made to be Goddes wonning [dwelling place]; and the wonning of our soule is God" (54.7–8). Evoking 1 John 3–4, John 1:14, and John 17, Julian plays on the words "oning" (uniting) and "wonning" (dwelling), indicating that union takes place through the dwelling-in-and-with God and the human in Christ. God is humankind's home, and vice versa. "'We be all in him beclosed.' And he is beclosed in us" (57.44–45).[50] This relation, established "in the beginning" and manifest in creation, is recapitulated and deepened through the incarnation.

Reflecting on her initial vision of the bleeding head of Christ, which shows the "homely loving [intimate love]" of "our good lord," Julian says,

> I saw that he is to us all thing that is good and comfortable to oure helpe. He is oure clothing, that for love wrappeth us and windeth us, halseth [embraces] us and all becloseth [wholly encloses] us, hangeth about us for tender love, that he may never leeve us. And so in this sight I saw that he is all thing that is good. (5.1–5)

The whole meaning of the ensuing passion sequence is connected to Julian's experience of Jesus as the clothing that completely surrounds her—wrapping, winding, embracing, enclosing. This language of being clothed in Christ derives from an important set of scriptural metaphors for the reality of atonement, salvation, and reconciliation. (See, for example, 1 Cor 15:22; 2 Cor 2:17; Col 1:27; 2:7; 2:10; Gal 3:27; and Eph 2:10; among many other passages.) The

---

[50]   This being-at-home-with-and-in one another is probably the most accurate sense in which there is nothing "between" human substance and divine substance. In a rather controversial passage, Julian writes, "Thus is the kinde made rightefully oned to the maker, which is substantial kinde unmade, that is God. And ortals it is that ther may ne shall be right ortals between God and mannis soule" (53.38–40). Turner has argued against the suggestion that Julian is an autotheist based on the claim that she cannot see a difference between human and divine substance (*Julian of Norwich*, 175f.). Similarly, I think her comments are ultimately indicative not of a divine-human union of substance but of wills.

image of salvation and forgiveness as a garment, signaling personal and social identity, or shelter, evoking home and protection, is common throughout the Hebrew Bible as well (e.g., Isa 61:10). Related metaphors portray God dwelling in God's "city," another form of enclosure.

This web of imagery is pronounced in Julian's example and comprises a primary figure for atonement throughout her work. The "answer" to Julian's stated conundrum—"some are damned . . . all shall be well"—is a narratival reframing of the problem that renders Adam "alle man" in Jesus Christ, as seen in the example. In other words, her solution is to point to an identity, an identity within an identity. It is not a proposition but a relationship, not an equation but a complex character. It is given as a picture, a montage of events and features juxtaposed and woven together. In her example, she describes the Son of God "afore the fader in Adam kirtle [garment]" (i.e., Adam's flesh), saying he "stode before his fader as a servant [Phil 2:7]" and, "wilfully taking upon him alle our charge [burden]," he "fell full lowe in the maidens wombe" (51.206–7). Julian notes the doubleness of the servant before God: "In the servant is comprehended the seconde person of the trinite, and in the servant is comprehended Adam: that is to sey, all men" (lines 179–80). "Comprehended" means "grasped" or "known"—and, in this sense, Julian simply communicates that she recognizes both the Son of God and all humanity signified in the figure of the servant. Yet it also means "encompassed" or "circumscribed"— the servant (Jesus Christ) contains humanity along with the second person of the Trinity. Christ and humankind are seen in the same figure because they are ontologically in-and-with one another. Julian explains: Christ "falls into" a "taking of our kinde," "for love," and, in so doing, confirms that he "made mannes soule to be his owne cite [city] and his dwelling place" (lines 124–25).

Julian's use of "oning" (uniting) and "wonning" (dwelling) is bound up with her depiction of Christ as the representative or head of humanity. She says, "He is the heed, and we be his membris" (lines 218–19) (1 Cor 12:12). In him humankind is incorporated—embodied, gathered together, and taken up into the Trinity in Christ, set "before [the lord] in himselfe present [into his own presence]" (line 176). Julian thus claims, "Alle is the manhode of Crist [all people are (in) Christ's humanity]" (line 218). For, paraphrasing Paul, "in the sighte of God alle man is one man, and one man is alle man" (lines 88–89). This "one man" is Jesus Christ, the second person of the Trinity, "in whom we be alle enclosed" (53.27). Just as Christ assumes, and indeed becomes, human flesh (John 1:14), humanity in turn "puts on" Christ (Rom 13:14). He clothes himself in humanity and humanity in himself.

Placing the emphasis on being-in—borne-in, seen-in, sheltered-in— enables Julian to describe the atonement in a way that is less mechanistic and more organic or relational than many juridical or substitutionary construals. If atonement as "beclosure" is a kind of "exchange" or "substitution," then it must be of a distinctly perichoretic sort. While it sometimes goes hand in hand with legal and economic language in Julian's text (e.g., "deem," "rightfulhede," "again-buying"), evoking clothing and enclosure plays up the narrativity or drama of juridical metaphors and pushes the issue of identity and character to the fore. Particularly when addressing the question of blame, Julian relies on the language of "assignation"—which is functionally synonymous with "imputation" but also connotes a more personal sense of character ascription. In stressing the way clothing and shelter designate, ensure, and construct identity and relationship, the concept of substitution is not simply supplanted but expanded. Substitution becomes more than a simple this-*for*-that, a strict exchange of discrete subjects or statuses. For Julian, it involves a complication or incorporation, of identities, histories, and attributes: this-*in*-that and vice versa. The atoning incorporation-into and being-enveloped-by-Christ is inherently transformative. We see this in that the overtones of Julian's account of the atonement are "medicinal" rather than "forensic."[51] The reidentification of humanity in Christ is healing, from the inside out (indwelling) and also from the outside in (putting-on).

In other words, the way Julian talks about God seeing humanity *in* Christ is distinct from any account in which God sees Christ *instead of* the human. The overall effect of her depiction of the atonement as being-seen-in does not present Christ as a shield, veil, or lens—something that blocks, overlays, or merely filters. Instead, her use of the language of being-in-Christ implies an inextricability of the sort we find in Adam's first words in Genesis, "This at last is bone of my bones and flesh of my flesh," or, to use the maternal analogy Julian prefers: "Our savioure is oure very moder, in whome we be endlessly borne and *never shall come out of* him" (57.40–43).[52] This exceptional image warrants further unpacking, but for now the point is that God's judgment meets Christ and humanity at once and as one, like a woman with child.

This casts light back on Julian's description of the "dome" of the Lord. The pairs sensual/substantial, inner/outer, and goodly/sinful are indeed reflected

---

[51]   Baker points out that, in contrast to Bernard's litany of pains from sin, in her example, "Julian articulates the servant's suffering in medical and psychological rather than forensic terms" (*From Vision to Book*, 98). The same can be said of the servant's redemption, particularly inasmuch as his stumbling doubles as the "fall" or condescension of Christ. Baker goes onto claim that "in Julian's parable the lord regards the servant as a compassionate healer rather than a just judge" (185).

[52]   Emphasis added. Julian has a sort of nesting-doll image here: humanity inside mother Jesus inside mother Mary.

in the divine gaze. But the higher way of seeing is not double in the same way human judgment is. While the latter is alternately permissive and accusing (and perhaps each at the wrong time), divine judgment expresses *one thing*—love—in *two modes*—compassion and rejoicing. The divine bifocality that corresponds to the "beclosure" of the atonement is not to be mistaken, then, for a polarity of grace and damnation, love and hate, election and reprobation. It is not a medley of pity and blame, as in Augustine, Anselm, Calvin, and so on.[53] As Julian recounts it, the two sides of God's "tender" look are *pity* toward human suffering and *bliss* over the restoration of humanity in Christ—and this is because of the mutual enclosure of Christ and humankind.

A Trinitarian Portal

Bound up with the image of being-(seen-)in-Christ is a claim about the revelation of God in Christ. Just as true humanity is constituted in him, for Julian, true divinity is revealed in him. But what Julian is saying exceeds an assertion about the historical atonement per se. She is also asserting that the suffering love of Christ is a portal into the intratrinitarian love that is the divine life. When Jesus shows his wounded side (Revelation 10), it is "as if he had saide: 'My darling, behold and see thy lorde, thy God, that is thy maker and thy endlesse joy. See thin owne brother, thy savioure. My childe, behold and see what liking and blisse I have in thy salvation, and for my love enjoye with me'" (24.11–14). Jesus' body is as an opening into the Trinity, where what is beheld is God's love for humankind and rejoicing over salvation. It is in this same sense that, when she witnesses "the servant fall," Julian says her "understanding" is "led into God" (52.40–41), and she sees that "the trinite is comprehended in Crist" (57.16–17).

Julian prefaces her very first vision, of the suffering of Christ crowned with thorns, by stating that this sight comprehends and specifies the Trinity. She says it encapsulates much of what is to follow in subsequent showings concerning the incarnation and the "oning" between God and humankind (1.3–7). Beholding "the garland of thornes . . . pressed on [Jesus'] blessed head" and "the red bloud trekile downe . . . hote and freshely, plentuously and lively," Julian remarks, "Right so, both God and man, the same that sufferd for me," and claims, "it was himselfe that shewed it to me, without any meane [intermediary]" (4.1–5). She continues

---

[53]   For a detailed reading of how Julian's soteriology differs from the prevailing Anselmian position, see Baker, *From Vision to Book*, 92, 100–106. See also Turner, *Julian of Norwich*, 126; and Edmund Colledge, *The Medieval Mystics of England* (New York: Charles Scribner's Sons, 1961), 21, 87; and Joan Nuth, "Two Medieval Soteriologies: Anselm of Canterbury and Julian of Norwich," *Theological Studies* 53 (1992): 611–45.

by affirming that "the trinity is God, God is the trinity," and alerting her readers that "this [the Trinity] was shewed in the first sight and in all" (4.7–11). In other words, Julian wants us to know from the outset that her graphic showings of the visceral suffering of Christ are intrinsically triune. Hence the hermeneutical principle that follows, "For wher Jhesu appireth the blessed trinity is understand, as to my sight"—the Trinity is understood wherever Jesus appears (4.11).

Julian is careful to maintain that all three persons of the Trinity are involved in the suffering love of Christ and active in the work of salvation. Although she appropriates the suffering of the passion to "the maidens sonne," she sees "alle the trinite wrought in the passion of Crist" (23.23–24) and says, "I saw in Crist that the father is" (22.11). "Crist shewed" her the "werking of the father," namely "that he geveth mede [reward] to his sonne Jhesu Crist" (lines 9–12). Where she addresses the same showing in the Short Text, Julian refers to God as the "blissedfulle trinite of oure salvation" in which "the fadere is plesed, the sone is worshipped [glorified], the haly gaste likes" (ST, sec. 12).[54] A strong sense of the perichoretic unity of the persons of the Trinity appears through-out her writing, and she constantly alternates her stress on appropriation and unity. When Julian writes that in the incarnation, "God is knit to oure kind," she adds, "The trinite is comprehended in Crist," before assigning the incar-nation specifically to "the secund parson" or "mid person" of the Trinity. In short, while she upholds the orthodox view that only the Son is incarnate, she also emphasizes that all three persons are implicated in "oure flesh taking" (57.15–18). In fact, Julian later extends the triad most commonly applied to the persons of the Trinity directly to "moder Jhesu," saying, "He is almighty, all wisdom, and all love" (61.33).

An important assertion throughout these passages is that the Trinity is accessed through the economy of salvation and not otherwise. Julian's vision of the Trinity depends upon the Gospel love of Jesus reanimated in her visions. Though her mind is finally taken up into the triune motherhood of God, she does not abstract from the concrete manifestation of divine love in Christ's suffering that yields her intratrinitarian insight.

The Meaning Is Love

Julian's phrase "love is oure lordes mening" becomes a hermeneutical prin-ciple akin to Augustine's *regula caritatis* found in *De doctrina christiana*.[55]

---

[54]   Watson and Jenkins, *Writings of Julian of Norwich*, 89.
[55]   Augustine writes, "Whoever thinks he understands divine scripture or any part of it, but whose interpretation does not build up the twofold love of God and neighbor, has not really understood it. Whoever has drawn from scripture an

She wants her readers to know that, whatever she has written, its truth is hemmed in at every point by God's unalloyed love.[56] While the text clearly commences, "This is a revelation of love . . . ," Julian perhaps feels the need to reiterate this throughout, and especially in conclusion, in order to set up guardrails for her readers who are accustomed to quite a different account of divine judgment. As intricate, strange, dense, and apocalyptic as Julian's prose can be at times, there is nothing willfully codified about the message. That is not to say her showings do not require diligent interpretation, on her part and ours, but Julian regards the purpose as unambiguous. She explains in her beautiful concluding passage:

> And fro the time that it [the revelation] was shewde, I desyerde oftentimes to witte [know] that [what] was our lords mening [intention]. And fifteen yere after or mor, I was answered in gostly [spiritual or intellectual] understond-ing, seyeng thus: "What, woldest thou wit thy lordes mening in this thing? Wit [know] it wele, love was his mening. Who shewed it the? Love. What shewid he the? Love. Wherfore shewed he it the? For love. Holde the therin, thou shalt wit more in the same [Hold yourself in this, and you shall know more of the same]. But thou shalt never wit therin other withouten ende [you will never perceive anything else in it for all eternity]." (86.13–16)

Julian is telling us this is God's own authorial intent through her showings and the Gospel narrative, which they recount. What is given to her, what she gives to her readers, is a *self*-revelation of God. As she has emphasized throughout her showings, God's intention is pure goodwill for the beloved, not a mixed bag of love and wrath, and this is guaranteed because of who God is.

"Love" is the Lord's meaning, but, as happens with the repetitive use of a single word, its sense begins to erode. What exactly does Julian want us to understand by "love"? She consistently sets up a special relationship between love and goodness. Goodness is cast primarily in terms of caregiving and near-ness. We see this, for example, in Julian's initial description of Christ clothing humanity with himself (5.1–5). The passage begins and ends with the attribu-tion of the word "good" to Christ. Its meaning is concretely filled out in the

---

interpretation that does fortify this love, but who is later proven not to have found the meaning intended by the author of the passage, is deceived to be sure, but not in a harmful way, and he is guilty of no untruth at all" (1.36.40). See *On Christian Doctrine*, trans. D. W. Robertson Jr. (Upper Saddle River, N.J.: Prentice Hall, 1997).

[56]   Where Augustine emphasizes the "double" love of God and neighbor, saying humans do not need instruction to love themselves, Julian maintains a triple love throughout. She thinks humans need to hear that they are loved, and much of her teaching is oriented toward getting people to see themselves as such.

middle by his comforting and caring action—he "wrappeth . . . windeth . . . halseth . . . all becloseth" and "hangeth about us." This purpose of this action is twice affirmed as "for love" and "for tender love." The bond is such that "he may never leeve us." At the end of her revelation, she tells us,

> And I sawe fulle sekerly [very surely] in this and in alle, that or [before] God made us he loved us, which love was never sleked [quenched], ne never shalle. And in this love he hath done alle his werkes, and in this love he hath made alle thinges profitable to us. And in this love oure life is everlasting. (86.17–20)

Love is defined in terms of what it *does*. Love desires the good of the beloved, and is never slaked. Love lends life. It comforts and restores. It is ever present. Love is constant and reliable. It binds and does not detach. It is reparative, transforming everything to the benefit others (Rom 8:28).

Julian's use of "love" is plainly linked to the character of God manifested in the history of creation and redemption. Her chief triad for the persons of the Trinity, "Maker, Keeper, Lover," is illustrated particularly vividly in her example of the hazelnut, a metaphor for creation (5.7–13). The conclusion of Julian's final chapter simply recapitulates this earlier example, where she says,

> [God] shewed a little thing the quantity of a haselnot [hazelnut], lying in the palme of my hand as me semide [it seemed to me], and it as a rounde as any balle. I looked theran with the eye of my understanding, and thought: "What may this be?" And it was answered generally thus: "It is all that is made." I marvayled how it might laste, for methought it might sodenly have fallen to nought [perished] for littlenes. And I was answered in my understanding: "It lasteth and ever shall, for God loveth it. And so hath all thing being by the love of God."
>
> In this little thing I saw three properties: the first is that God made it, the secund is that God loveth it, the thirde is that God kepeth it. But what is that to me? Sothly [truly], the maker, the keper, the lover.

Julian describes creaturely being as contingent, borrowed; it has life only by God's grace. To a certain extent, she is merely endorsing the common teaching of Scripture and the church that creation is actively sustained by God at every point. But in her reflection on the hazelnut, she specifies that this action is the foremost expression of God's love. God grants life—that is love; God watches over, preserves, and restores—that is love. The gift of existence is defined as an act of love. All that is made is sustained not by sheer "being" but by a being specified at every point as Love. In other words, God the creator is not at all construed as a disinterested or distant life-source. Thirst or longing is one of

Julian's primary features of both human and divine love. Creation expresses God's visceral desire for the beloved. It is not theologically insignificant that Julian locates this longing in eternity.

Eternal Atonement

Speaking of Christ's passion, Julian says this "love was without beginning, is, and shall be without ende" (22.40). Her *Revelation* is peppered with similar assertions, particularly in Revelation 14, adjacent the example. In the final lines of her Long Text, she elaborates the same point, claiming, "In oure making we had beginning, but *the love wherin he made us was in him fro without beginning*, in which love we have oure beginning" (86.20–22).[57] In one sense, there is nothing particularly novel about Julian's view of God's love for the world as eternal. If it were otherwise, in Thomas Aquinas' words, "it would follow that something would come anew into the Divine Mind," which cannot be the case given the simplicity and eternity of God.[58] However, that she goes further than her predecessors is seen, first, through her oblique narration of predestination through the retelling of the parable and, second, in her inclusion of humanity in the Trinity throughout the Long Text.

Immediately following the Example of the Lord and Servant, Julian offers an account of election, a doctrine she refers to in terms of "rightful knitting and endlesse oning" (53.17). Julian comments, "God began never to love mankinde . . . righte so the same mankind hath be [been], in the forsighte of God, knowen and loved fro without beginning in his rightful entent [providence]" (53.17–18, 21–24). As in the language of Psalm 139:13, "For it was you who formed my inward parts; / you knit me together in my mother's womb," Julian associates "knitting" with human procreation, one of her primary images for creation, redemption, and union with God. But "rightful knitting and endlesse oning" is, more specifically, Julian's language for "predestination."[59] She describes an "eternal atonement" in God that implies divine self-election. The predestination of the Son is construed as an intratrinitarian decision in which the second person of the Trinity is "oned" with "alle" humankind. As Julian puts it:

> God, the blisseful trinite, which is everlasting being, right as he is endless fro without beginning, righte so it was in his purpose endlesse to make mankind; which fair kind [human nature] furst was dight [assigned to] the second person. And when he [Christ] woulde [desired it], by full accorde of alle the trinite,

---

[57]   Emphasis added.
[58]   Aquinas, *ST* IIIa, q. 24, a. 1.
[59]   Baker, *From Vision to Book*, 111f.

he made us alle at ones [all in an instant, or all in one]. And in our making he
knit us and oned us to himselfe, by which oning we be kept as clene and as noble
as we were made. (58.1–6)[60]

"Or God made us he loved us" echoes Ephesians 1:4, "He chose us in Christ
before the foundation of the world."[61] She also seems to be glossing Colossians
1:15–17, "He is the image of the invisible God, the firstborn of all creation; for
in him all things in heaven and on earth were created. . . . He himself is before
all things, and in him all things hold together." Human election is election
through Christ.[62] Again, this is in line with "the teaching of mother church."
Aquinas writes, "By one and the same act God predestinated both Christ and
us."[63] However, while Aquinas carefully restricts the predestination of the Son
to his humanity, Julian's comments produce an image of "endlesse oning"
between God and humanity in the second person of the Trinity.[64]

---

[60]   I am following Watson and Jenkins' interpretation in putting "Christ" in
brackets following "he" (*Writings of Julian of Norwich*, 306). Although one might
expect "God" to be the subject here, they argue that the context suggests otherwise
(see the following sentence). This reading suits Julian's Christology more generally
as well. She highlights the role of Christ as creator throughout her writing.

[61]   Aquinas quotes this passage in *ST* Ia, q. 23, a. 4. He points out that chosenness
presupposes love in the order of reason. Julian may also have in mind a passage like 1 Pet
1:20, "He [the lamb of God] was destined [chosen, known] before the foundation of the
world, but was revealed at the end of the ages for your sake."

[62]   Baker thinks Julian understands the order of election and predestination after
Peter Lombard's summary of Rom 8:30: "*preadestinando non existentes, vocando
aversos, justificando peccatores, glorificando mortals* [by appointing beforehand the
nonexistent, by calling those who turned away, by justifying sinners, and by glorify-
ing mortals]" (*From Vision to Book*, 114). See Lombard, *In Epistolam ad Romanos 8*
(PL 191, 1451). Aquinas too clearly distinguishes election and predestination, but
reverses the order (for him election precedes predestination, and both depend upon
love). Aquinas says, "The reason of this is that predestination, as stated above (a.1),
is a part of providence. Now providence, as also prudence, is the plan existing in the
intellect directing the ordering of some things towards an end; as was proved above
(q.22, a.2). But nothing is directed towards an end unless the will for that end already
exists" (see *ST* Ia, q. 23, a. 4). However, I will use the terms without drawing a sharp
distinction between them, because (1) Julian uses neither word and the words she
does use correspond only loosely to either, (2) where they appear in the Greek NT
the meanings are usually similar if not interchangeable, and (3) Barth uses them
interchangeably.

[63]   Aquinas, *ST* IIIa, q. 24, a. 4.

[64]   Aquinas writes, "We must attribute predestination to the Person of Christ:
not, indeed, in Himself or as subsisting in the Divine Nature, but as subsisting in the
human nature" (*ST* IIIa, q. 24, a. 1).

Referring to the incarnation of the Son, Julian describes the "flesh" that "the secund person hath taken" as already belonging to him. She says that "which kind furst to him was adight," in other words, human nature was first given to him (57.16, 18). Julian suggests that the second person of the Trinity is predestined eternally not only to become incarnate but also to bear humanity in himself within the triune life before the creation of the world. So it would be out of keeping with Julian's reflection on predestination to speculate, as Aquinas does, "If Christ were not to have been incarnate, God would have decreed men's salvation by other means."[65] Instead, we find her reasoning that God's Son fell when Adam fell because of this prior "oning . . . made in heven," by which "Goddes sonne might not be seperath from Adam" (51.185–86). Julian does not speak of the predestination of humanity in Christ as an idea, a prior "plan of salvation" that could have been worked out differently. Rather, predestination is an ontological bond between Adamic humanity and Jesus Christ that consists in God's assignment of humanity to Godself in the second person of the Trinity. Christ, for Julian, is predestined not to fulfill a task that could be performed otherwise but to be "all in all," not merely to do but to be the reconciliation of God and the world in himself (2 Cor 5:19). Julian writes, "And by the endlesse entent and assent and the full acorde of al the trinite, the mid person wolde be grounde and hed of this fair kinde [human nature] out of whom we be all come, in whom we be alle enclosed, into whom we shall all wenden [go]" (53.25–28). The second person, or mid person, is ground and head of humanity, origin and culmination, bearer and lord. The temporal atonement enacted in the incarnation derives from and reinforces the eternal atonement or "beclosure" of humanity in God.[66] The divine-human union in time has the quality of a repetition.[67] It echoes an occurrence that has already taken place in the eternal Son vis-à-vis Father and Spirit.

---

[65]   Aquinas, *ST* IIIa, q. 24, a. 4.

[66]   This calls into question Turner's claim that Julian is "unable to make any sense of the Incarnation . . . except as a response of the divine love and compassion for the predicament of fallen humanity" (*Julian of Norwich*, 209). "Response" is contingent. For Julian this "oning" is preordained. She does not describe the incarnation primarily as a solution to a problem. Nor does her language suggest that election, fall, and atonement are simply willed all at once. She goes further than this. The atonement in time arises from and is always already included in the eternal atonement—and not as an idea but as an ontological bond. The incarnation is not preordained as one of any number of possible solutions to sin (Aquinas); it is inscribed in the eternal love of God, in God's eternal will to dwell with and in humankind.

[67]   We have a modern Catholic precedent for this sort of reasoning in the Trinitarian theology of Hans Urs von Balthasar: see *Mysterium Paschale*, trans. Aidan Nichols, O.P. (San Francisco: Ignatius, 1990); and *Theo-Drama: Theological Dramatic Theory*, vol. 5, *The Last Act*, trans. Graham Harrison (San Francisco: Ignatius, 1998). His notion

Julian's conception of predestination as a kind of atonement is paramount to her argument that God is without blame or anger (ch. 45f.). As an "answer" to her question about how God regards fallen humanity, the example narrates not simply grace or salvation but also election. Julian attends to the second half of Ephesians 1:4: it is in order "to be *holy and blameless* before him in love" that "he chose us in Christ before the foundation of the world." Election goes hand in hand with blamelessness. It is "an ontological relation between the elect and the Trinity for all eternity that precludes their damnation."[68] In the words of Romans 8:29, "For those he foreknew he also predestined to be conformed to the image of his Son, so that he might be the firstborn among many brothers."[69] This is why all is said to be well, despite the reality of sin and suffering, despite the teachings of the church on damnation. "Grace is God," not a reaction or solution, but an eternally secure knitting of humankind into the Trinity through the being of the Son.

All Shall Be Well

In her final comment on the contrary "domes" at the end of the Long Text, Julian says, "For in the beholding of God we falle not, and in the beholding of oureselfe we stonde not . . . but the beholding of oure lord God is the higher sothnes [truth]" (82.24–26).[70] Reiterating what she has already said about the two "domes," these lines evoke the difference in the Parable of the Prodigal Son between the way the father sees his sons and the way they see themselves. Sin or blindness does not perceive the higher truth of God's "loving look" (85.1). But "whan the dome is geven"—that is, on the day of

---

of Ur-events in God that are recapitulated in time is influenced by Hegel and Barth. It seems like Julian is saying something similar in speaking about the atonement as an eternal and inward happening in God that "wants" to be achieved outwardly—e.g., her claim that grace and mercy (i.e., world/time) are better than unrealized love is interesting in this connection.

68   Baker, *From Vision to Book*, 111.

69   According to Baker, this is the scriptural warrant for Julian "integrating the doctrines of predestination and the *imago Dei*" (*From Vision to Book*, 111). Rom 8:1, 31–35 also undergirds Julian's teaching on predestination in ch. 53f.: "There is therefore now no condemnation for those who are in Christ Jesus. . . . If God is for us, who is against us? He who did not withhold his own Son, but gave him up for all of us, will he not with him also give us everything else? Who will bring any charge against God's elect? It is God who justifies. Who is to condemn? It is Christ Jesus, who died, yes, who was raised, who is at the right hand of God, who indeed intercedes for us. Who will separate us from the love of Christ?"

70   As Kevin McGill paraphrases, "We cannot . . . stand in our own sight. In the sight of God however we do not and cannot fall but are safe and secure." *Julian of Norwich: Mystic or Visionary?* (New York: Routledge, 2006), 113–14.

judgment—then, Julian says, we will see what has been true all along: "We have been in the foresight of God loved and knowen in his endles purpose fro without beginning, in which unbegonne love he made us." So, the judgment of God is something to look forward to; it will reveal a love without beginning or end. And we will not ask why or if it could have been otherwise but will see that "it is wele" as is (85.9–12).

This most famous of Julian's sayings resounds throughout Revelations 13 and 14 (27.10–11; cf. 31.2–4; 34.20–21)—"Alle shalle be wele, and alle shalle be wele, and alle maner of thinge shalle be wel." The immediate context of this permutation of the phrase is a discussion of the "behoveliness" (fittingness or necessity) of sin. When Julian ventures the hypothesis that all would have been well had humanity not sinned, she is answered by the Lord, "Sin is behovely [fitting], but alle shalle be wele" (27.9–10). The claim is closely connected with Julian's enigmatic vision of the momentous eschatological deed God performs in the future (32.19f.; 36.1f.). But the reassurance that "all shall be well" is rooted in what has already happened, not only in the historical atonement but in the eternal "oning" of election. The end must be well because of this beginning.[71]

This maxim is Julian's translation of the Hebrew *shalom*.[72] It is frequently found situated within her discussions of salvation and, more specifically, "the glorious asseeth [atonement, reparation]" (29.9f.) Julian calls the atonement, or the "asseeth-making" of Christ, "more wurshipfulle for mannes salvation withoute comparison than ever was the sinne of Adam harmfulle" (lines 10–13). Julian is alluding here to the "how much more" of grace (Rom 5:20), a passage she elsewhere translates, "So much oure mede [reward] is the more for we geve him occasion by oure falling" (39.38–39). Falling is a felix culpa for Julian, then.[73] As horrific as she understands human sin and suffering to be, she believes the

---

[71]   This is an implication of Kerri Hide's reading of Julian's account of the atonement (*Gifted Origins*, 110).

[72]   In Julian's writing, the maxim lacks the triumphalistic ring it might take on when removed from its context. "Shalle" should not simply be translated into the future tense, "will." It is more like "must," which has the force of an imperative (carrying a sense of necessity) while also expressing the quality of hope, which is always defined by uncertainty (or at least awaits fulfillment). According to Hunt, this saying "effectively translates the Hebrew *shalom*" (*Trinity*, 103).

[73]   Julian sees in the lord's "chere," or expression, that "mightely he enjoyeth in his falling, for the hye [high] raising and fulhed of blisse that mankinde is to come to, overpassing that we shuld have had if he not had fallen" (52.38–40). God delights in the "falling" of the Son because it results in the homecoming and exaltation of humankind.

fall is a necessary and even gainful part of the divine-human union.[74] This is so, in Julian's reasoning, because (1) it provides the conditions for the appearance and recognition of God's love and (2) grace and mercy constitute a deepened intimacy between God and the world and an increase in God's good pleasure in creaturely reality. In the same sense, her Example of the Lord and Servant retells the heightening of the father's love and elevation of the son embodied in the parable (Luke 15:22–24). How better to model the great reward occasioned "by oure falling" (39.38–39) than in a mother's compassionate embrace of her injured child? All is well because of her presence and consolation.

The Motherhood of God

Julian's exposition of the example in chapter 51 presses into chapter 52, which begins:

> And thus I saw that God enjoyeth [rejoices] that he is our fader, and God en-
> joyeth that he is our moder, and God enjoyeth that he is our very spouse, and
> our soule his loved wife. And Crist enjoyeth that he is our broder, and Jhesu
> enjoyeth that he is our saviour. (52.1–4)

It is here that Julian broaches the motherhood of God for the first time. Missing from the Short Text, the concept is essentially tied to her later revisions, particularly the Example of the Lord and Servant that prompts them. While it seems to signal a change in subject matter, Julian's Trinitarian excursus on the motherhood of God is in no way disconnected from the narrative that precedes it. Rather, beginning "and thus," it is clear that "the opening paragraph of chapter 52" is "the *culmen contemplationis* of the parable."[75] The example as well as the atonement images of beclosure, wonning, and containment culminate in Julian's perception that "as verely as God is oure fader, as verely is God oure moder" (59.10). The chapters that follow should be read as an extended meditation on the homecoming of the lost son, where home is figured in maternal terms as the womb and bosom of God.

The Meaning of Motherhood

Through her theological retelling of the parable, Julian shifts from imaging the divine-human relationship in terms of a lord and servant to a father and son and finally to a mother and child. To grasp the significance of this development

---

[74]   While little is known about Julian's life, many commentators speculate from her writings, context, and late entry into religious life that she had been a mother who lost her family to the plague. Her sense of human suffering is deep and personal. She does not offer this comfort naively or from a place of security.

[75]   Colledge and Walsh, *Book of Showings*, 139.

in metaphors, it will be helpful to address Julian's application of relational and gendered language. Julian's creative interaction with the traditional gendering of God has been the subject of much scholarly interest, and rightly so. The priority she, a medieval English laywoman, so freely grants divine motherhood in her final chapters indeed warrants amazement as well as analysis. Although it may sound radical to post-Reformation, post-Enlightenment Christian ears, the application of the title "mother" to God and, especially, to Christ would not have been unfamiliar to Julian or contrary to the tradition she inherits. At the same time, she would have been aware that God is primarily figured in masculine terms and her divergence from this pattern is undoubtedly meaningful. To make sense of her use of maternal language, there are a number of qualifications to keep in mind.

First, the cultural significance of Julian's feminine naming of God is not immediately self-evident to modern readers. The terms "mother" and "father," like "woman" and "man," are fluid and do not bear exactly the same meaning at all times in all places. Gendered images take on personal connotations as well, in connection with the experience of the writer. It is important to be cautious when drawing conclusions based on present-day assumptions about what a fourteenth-century anchorite means by "mother."[76] The precise theological and cultural import of her language will be examined in what follows.

At the same time, second, in view of certain physiological givens of sex, there are some common associations that are intelligible to most readers based on the experience of ordinary life—for instance, the bodily demands of pregnancy, childbirth, and caregiving. In this sense, the function of "mother" is analogous to other religious metaphors based in nature, for example, the warmth and light of the sun, a physical phenomenon with which nearly all humans are familiar. Although it can be an emotionally evocative image, strictly speaking the "nursing mother" is more of a biological fact than a psychological insight, hence its universal evocativeness apart from the culturally specific and personal gender markers attending it. (Implied here, of course, is the critical distinction between "gender," as socially constructed, and "sex," as biologically given, as well as an awareness of their practical overlap and reciprocal influence on one another.)[77]

Third, gendered language is rarely, if ever, morally neutral. It bears the impress of a patriarchal "social imaginary" that is inherently androcentric and

[76]   See Bynum, *Jesus as Mother*, 7.
[77]   On this distinction and its theological relevance, see, for example, Serene Jones, *Feminist Theory and Christian Theology: Cartographies of Grace* (Minneapolis: Fortress, 2000), 8 and 24–48.

sometimes misogynistic as well.[78] The dynamics of sex and gender are caught in a system of hierarchical dualism that is difficult to efface from thought and language, even for those who wish to subvert it. Thus the mere addition of feminine titles for God does not by itself dismantle dominant biases and may even reinforce them.[79] This is certainly true of Julian's writing. For example, in feminizing the caregiving of God, she at once elevates women and reinscribes a social pattern in which women are subordinated in certain roles and spheres of influence.

Fourth, gendered language for God, whether masculine or feminine, is fundamentally anthropomorphic and metaphorical. That is to say, when we call God "father" or "mother," we are drawing on certain dimensions of the realities of women and men as human models for imagining and speaking about the divine, who is radically Other.[80] Julian understands both that God transcends sex and gender and that these created traits may be reflective of and applicable to the creator by virtue of the *imago Dei*.

Fifth, because, in Ricoeur's words, "the symbol gives rise to thought," there are at least a couple of intrinsic benefits to breaching the hegemony of masculine imagery by drawing upon women's bodily experience the way Julian does. It subverts the idolatrous tendencies of an over-literalizing imagination, reminding us that, in Julian's words, "the fader is not [a] man" (51.23). Tempering of the temptation to reify metaphors is thus a theological good. There is an ethical gain as well: it dignifies the reality that women are also *imago Dei* and *capax Dei*, that "men" in general are not closer to God, more suitable for

---

[78]   The studies on this connection are manifold. Caroline Walker Bynum's comment on the comprehensiveness of the problem in the religious milieu in which Julian found herself is emblematic: "The misogyny of the later Middle Ages is well known. Not merely a defensive reaction on the part of men who were in fact socially, economically and politically dominant, it was fully articulated in theological, philosophical and scientific theory that was centuries old. *Male* and *female* were contrasted and asymmetrically valued as intellect/body, active/passive, rational/irrational, reason/emotion, self-control/lust, judgment/mercy and order/disorder. In the devotional writing of the later Middle Ages, they were even contrasted in the image of God—father or Bridegroom—and soul (*anima*)—child or bride" (*Fragmentation and Redemption*, 151).

[79]   See Rosemary Radford Ruether, "The Female Nature of God: A Problem in Contemporary Religious Life," in *God as Father?* ed. Johannes-Baptist Metz and Schillebeeckx, Concilium 143 (Edinburgh: T&T Clark, 1981), 66.

[80]   As discussed in the first chapter, in metaphor "we *speak* of one thing or state of affairs in language suggestive of another." Metaphors are based on models, in which "we *regard* one thing or state of affairs in terms of another." See Janet Martin Soskice, *Metaphor and Religious Language* (Oxford: Oxford University Press, 2002), 50–51 (emphasis added).

representing God, or in any sense more similar to God than "women" in general. This is a truth exclusively masculine naming invariably conceals.[81]

Finally, we should avoid falling into the sort of easy gender binarism in which one might regard Julian's turn to the motherhood of God after renarrating the Parable of the Prodigal Son, with its all-masculine cast, as a conceptual or thematic rupture. Such an assumption would be antithetical to the integrity of Julian's text as well as broader trends in medieval women's writing. Julian's teaching on the motherhood of God both consolidates and expands the theological contents of the example. This coordinates with Caroline Walker Bynum's finding that female writers in the high and late Middle Ages were significantly less likely than male writers to use feminine and masculine imagery in dichotomous ways.[82] In shifting from the pairings lord/servant or father/son to mother/child, Julian is elucidating, nuancing, and intensifying rather than overturning the description of the divine-human relationship captured in her retelling of the parable. In other words, we should not be so preoccupied with the *gender* evocations that we miss the gender *evocations*. The same should be said of paternal language for God in Scripture and theology.

The Kindness of Mother

This last point is crucial for understanding Julian's specific sense of motherhood. Her application of relational titles to God depends upon a basic non-opposition of gendered terms such as father and mother, brother and sister, or spouse and child. This is seen in a variety of interrelated ways, for example, in (1) her focus on kinship titles, (2) her free multiplication and mixing of names and triads, (3) the prominence of the word "kind" in her thought, and (4) her nongendered translation of the Tetragrammaton. Such patterns of naming

---

[81]   See Paul Ricoeur, "Conclusion: The Symbol Gives Rise to Thought," in *The Symbolism of Evil* (New York: Harper & Row, 1969); and "Fatherhood: From Phantasm to Symbol," in *The Conflict of Interpretations: Essays in Hermeneutics*, trans. Don Ihde (Evanston, Ill.: Northwestern University Press, 1974). Cf. Janet Martin Soskice's chapter "Calling God 'Father,'" in *The Kindness of God: Metaphor, Gender, and Religious Language* (Oxford: Oxford University Press, 2007). Taking the "Song of Moses" (Deut 32) as paradigmatic, Soskice writes, "Both paternal and maternal imagery are given in quick succession, effectively ruling out literalism, as does the equally astonishing image of God as a rock giving birth" (79).

[82]   Bynum, *Fragmentation and Redemption*, 165. For a number of reasons, when referring to God or the self, women writers are more inclined "to fuse male and female images" and are less averse to "role reversal" than their male counterparts (186, 170). In other words, even if female writers tacitly accept a hierarchical dualism of male and female, there is a gender fluidity found in their texts that contrasts the dominant (masculine) theological tradition in which difference is stressed.

help bring into focus the theological function of Julian's maternal language in affirming God's "kindness."

To understand the full weight of Julian's invocation of God as "mother," it must be grasped as "the centre-piece of a theology configured by *kinship*."[83] As Soskice argues, what Julian achieves through "mother" is what "father" is meant to accomplish in Scripture. There are "three registers" in such "biblical anthropomorphic titles": (1) "those appropriate to offices of *governance*, for instance, where God is Lord, King, and Judge," (2) "those related to offices of *service*, in which God is Shepherd, Watchman . . . Servant" or "Teacher" (which fits into either of the first two categories), and (3) "those representing the offices of *love*—Father, Brother, Son, Spouse, Lover."[84] The "offices of love" are "the most intimate, because they are all . . . kinship titles." They are mutually implicating—"if I am your kin, then you are mine." Thus to say that "God is our Father, or Christ our brother, is . . . to make a strong claim not only about God but about us."[85] Soskice concludes, then, that "the principal reason why the biblical writings are so dependent on gendered imagery . . . is not because its writers were so very interested in sex, or even hierarchy as subordination, but because they were interested in kinship."[86] This is true of Julian's writing as well; it is for the same reason that she emphasizes what she calls the "kind" and "condition" of motherhood.

Julian avails herself of the rich array of names, figures, and metaphors for God in the theological tradition she inherits: friend, lover, spouse, lord, trinity, father, mother, brother, son, servant, nurse, grace, wisdom, love, and so on. She draws on classical triads for Father, Son, and Spirit such as might (power), wisdom, and goodness (54.21) or kind (nature), mercy, and grace (59.29), while sometimes reordering or reassigning some of the terms, as in the triad goodness, kindness, and grace (59.11–12). She also generates her own formulations, such as life, love, and light or "mervelous homelyhed," "gentille curtesse," and "endlesse kindhede" (83.4–5).[87]

---

[83]   Soskice, *Kindness of God*, 126 (emphasis added).

[84]   Soskice, *Kindness of God*, 1 (emphasis added).

[85]   Soskice, *Kindness of God*, 2. Soskice writes, "Once one has a brother or a sister, one *is* a brother or a sister."

[86]   Soskice, *Kindness of God*, 4.

[87]   It is difficult to translate this triad in a few modern English words. They are all tensive images and historically contextual phrases. "Mervelous homelyhed" means something like "high nearness" or "great hominess"; it stresses the proximity and accessibility of God the Father. "Gentille" and "curtesse" are both courtly terms. Julian's use of "gentle" is something more like "genteel" or what is meant by "gentle" in the older sense of "gentleman." "Courtesy" refers to lordly condescension. She is

"Kind" is perhaps the most conspicuously recurrent word in Julian's theological vocabulary. She often refers to the "kindnes of moderhode" or the eternal "kindhede" of God. The ordinary Middle English senses of the word include "natural" or "essential" (adj.) and "nature" or "kin" (n.).[88] When Julian refers to God as "kinde unmade," she means that God's nature is uncreated and eternal. In the phrase "kinde goodnes of God," "kind" means "natural"; God is good by nature. Julian also uses the word adjectivally in phrases like "kind love" (60.4) or "my kind mother" (61.40). The meaning here differs from contemporary connotations of "kindness" as "niceness," "friendliness," "considerateness," and so on. It is sometimes ambiguous whether Julian means "natural" or "good" or both. This is because "kindness" becomes almost "synonymous" with "goodness" in her thought.[89] Playing on this, Julian says:

> God is kind [good] in his being: that is to sey, that goodnesse that is kind [essential], it is God. He is the grounde, he is the substance, he is the same thing that is kindhede [being], and he is very fader and moder of kindes [created natures]. (62.9–12)

Julian, as so many theologians before her, is asserting that God is being, origin, and substance. But, in these lines, she is simultaneously filling in the content of God's being: God is loving-kindness. Elizabeth Spearing thus translates "kind" (n.) not simply "nature" but "kindly nature."[90] In the language of Titus 3:4–5, "When the goodness and loving-kindness of God our Savior appeared, he saved us . . . according to his mercy, through the water of rebirth and renewal by the Holy Spirit" (Gk. χρηστότης and φιλανθρωπία, lit. "kindness" and "love of humankind"). The identity between good and God is so complete that Julian can invert the order of predication: what is essentially good—"it is God" (line 10). This point is made in the first sentence of the passage, with an *inclusio*

---

referring here to the Son's royalty and humility. "Endlesse kindhede" means something like "eternally kind nature." The Spirit, the nature of God, is kindness. The complexity of Julian's use of "kind" will be explained below.

[88]   Soskice, *Kindness of God*, 5.

[89]   Watson and Jenkins, *Writings of Julian of Norwich*, 318.

[90]   Cf. Colledge and Walsh, *Book of Showings*, 611, n. 13. Interestingly, the Wycliffe Bible translates this passage as "when the benignity and humanity of our Saviour God appeared." *Philanthropia*, love of humankind, is simply translated "humanity." Not too differently, Julian uses "fair kind," i.e., humankind, to designate the goodness of human nature in a number of places. That is to say, "kind"—whether divine or human—seems to have positive connotations even without the qualifiers "good," "fair," and "loving." Reference to "the humanity of God," then, fundamentally implies the *goodness* of God.

(God . . . god) structured as a *chiasmus* (God . . . being . . . goodness . . . god). As Julian goes on to assert more straightforwardly, "Thus is kind [nature] and grace of one accorde: for *grace is God*, as unmade kinde is God" (63.7–8).[91] God is not sheer, undefined divine essence. God is who God is in relationship with humankind. God's kind is kind.

This claim is integral to Julian's creative translation of the Tetragrammaton (Exod 3:14) as "I it am." Julian tells us in Revelation 12, "Often times oure lorde Jhesu saide":

> I it am, I it am. I it am that is highest. I it am that thou lovest. I it am that thou likest. I it am that thou servest. I it am that thou longest. I it am that thou de-sirest. I it am that thou meneste [intend]. I it am that is alle. I it am that holy church precheth the and techeth thee. I it am that shewde me ere to the [showed myself to you]. (26.4–8)

Rather than treating God's self-naming before Moses as a statement of abso-lute being, "I am that is," Julian retains and intensifies the highly particular relational character of the utterance as it appears in Exodus: "I am the God of your father, the God of Abraham, the God of Isaac, and the God of Jacob. . . . I have observed the misery of my people who are in Egypt; I have heard their cry on account of their taskmasters. Indeed, I know their sufferings, and I have come down to deliver them from the Egyptians, and to bring them up out of that land to a good and broad land, a land flowing with milk and honey" (3:6–8). She personalizes it to her own devotional situation—"I it am that *thou* . . ."[92]

In view of her hermeneutic *wherever Christ appears the Trinity is under-stood*, it is unsurprising that putting these words from Exodus in Jesus' mouth transforms them into a Trinitarian epithet. This is more readily apparent in the "I it am" statements that follow in chapter 59:

> I it am, the might and the goodnes of faderhode. I it am, the wisdom and the kindnes of moderhode. It I am, the light and the grace that is all blessed love. I it am, the trinite. I it am, the unite. I it am, the hye sovereyn goodnesse of al

---

91   Emphasis added.

92   Three times, God uses some variation of the following while addressing Moses: "The LORD, the God of your ancestors, the God of Abraham, of Isaac, and of Jacob, has appeared to me, saying: I have given heed to you and to what has been done to you in Egypt. I declare that I will bring you up out of the misery of Egypt, to the land of the Canaanites, the Hittites, the Amorites, the Perizzites, the Hivites, and the Jebusites, a land flowing with milk and honey" (Exod 3:16–17). God's reference to Godself is a relational history, not merely a statement of transcendent being and power.

manner [of] thing. I it am that maketh the to love. I it am that makith the to
long. I it am, the endlesse fulfilling of all true desyers. (59.11–16)

It is remarkable how, in both passages, Julian carefully avoids gendering her
translation of the divine name, even when it is applied to Jesus. In conjunction with her assertion "as verely as God is oure fader, as verely is God oure
moder" (line 10), using "it" rather than "he" asserts a basic orthodox tenet:
while different sexes are included in the image of God (Gen 1:27), God transcends creaturely being.

Both sets of "It I am" statements also reinforce a central assertion of Julian's
kindness language: God is as deeply within the soul as comprehensively surrounding it. While maintaining the otherness of God's being, she sees no gulf
between creator and creature on account of this difference. Conjuring Augustine's phrase "more inward to me than my most inward part" and prefigur-
ing Eberhard Jüngel's inversion of Aquinas' analogical configuration—"a still
greater similarity . . . in the midst of a great dissimilarity"—Julian portrays God
who is most high as her nearest kin.[93] Her triadic and maternal naming nearly
always contains this tension between high/low or other/near or above/within
and produces the assertion that God's power is in proximity. If Julian adopts
motherhood as the crowning metaphor for the divine-human relationship, it
is because it is seen to best embody the naturalness of divine-human kinship
that is the focal point of her theological imagination and message. Nearness is
definitional for love, and, in her experience, the "kindness of motherhood" is
the closest, surest, safest, and dearest bond and relation (60.12).

Maternal Naming in Medieval Spirituality

While the creativity and distinctiveness of Julian's theological vocabulary is
unmistakable in these passages, what she means when she calls God "mother"
is also informed by her medieval religious context in a variety of ways. Her
sentiment is clearly situated within the longstanding "Anselmic tradition of
devotion to the motherhood of God in Christ," which draws particular cultural and biological associations between human mothers and the salvific
work of Christ.[94]

---

[93]   See Augustine, *Confessions* 3.6.11; Eberhard Jüngel, *God as the Mystery of the
World: On the Foundation of the Theology of the Crucified One in the Dispute between
Theism and Atheism*, trans. Darrell Guder (Edinburgh: T&T Clark, 1983), 288.
[94]   Gordon S. Wakefield, "Anglican Spirituality," in *Post-Reformation and Modern*, vol. 3 of *Christian Spirituality*, ed. Louis Dupre and Don E. Saliers (New York:
Crossroads, 1996), 282. See Anselm's prayer 10 to St. Paul: *Opera omnia* 3:33 and
39–41, 168.

Recent scholarly interest in feminine and especially maternal theological language tends to focus on its use in women's writing in the thirteenth and fourteenth centuries. But, after the patristic period, it first reappears in twelfth-century works by men and is especially popular among Cistercian monks.[95] There is no reason to regard the motherhood of God as a specifically "feminine insight."[96] Instances of feminine language for God in the Middle Ages are found in the works not only of Anselm of Canterbury but of Peter Lombard, Stephen of Muret, Bernard of Clairvaux, Aelred of Rievaulx, Guerric of Igny, Isaac of Stella, Albert the Great, Bonaventure, Gertrude the Great, Adam of Perseigne, Helinand of Froidmont, William of Saint-Thierry, Mechtild of Magdeburg, Marguerite d'Oingt, Richard Rolle, William Flete, Catherine of Siena, Bridget of Sweden, Dante Alighieri, Thomas Aquinas, and Margery Kempe, among others.[97] These writers draw from scriptural precedents such as Deuteronomy 32:11, 32; Isaiah 49:15; 66:13; Matthew 23:37; and John 16:12; as well as the personification of Wisdom as a woman in the Hebrew Bible (e.g., Prov 8). Although feminine imagery is handled differently by individual authors, there are a number of generalizations that can be made about its broad significance within the context of medieval spirituality.[98]

An increasing emphasis in the high Middle Ages on the approachability of God is reflected in an affinity for earthy and relational imagery, for example, God nursing, caring for children, gently chiding, and giving birth.[99] Such language is especially linked to the humanity of Christ but is also driven by affirmations of the creation of humankind in the image of God and connected to union with God in the Eucharist. As Bynum points out in her study *Jesus as Mother*, a few basic "stereotypes" concerning women, namely mothers, are at work "in spiritual writers from Anselm to Julian."[100] The first has to do with

[95] Bynum, *Jesus as Mother*, 111–12. Bynum undercuts the assumption that "such a devotional tradition is particularly congenial to women and therefore must have been developed by or for or about them."

[96] Bynum, *Jesus as Mother*, 140.

[97] This is a partial selection of medieval writers from a list compiled by Bynum. There are, of course, patristic examples as well, including Gregory of Nyssa and Augustine.

[98] Bynum provides an analysis of the associative nuances in writers of different sexes and from different periods (*Jesus as Mother*, 162, 173).

[99] Bynum, *Jesus as Mother*, 129. Bynum explains that such language reflects an "increasing preference for analogies taken from human relationships, a growing sense of God as loving and accessible, a general tendency toward fulsome language, and a more accepting reaction to all natural things, including the physical human body."

[100] Bynum, *Jesus as Mother*, 131.

women's generativity and bodily sacrifice in procreation. According to medieval medical theories, "the female in some sense provides the matter of the
foetus, the male the life or spirit."[101] The physical suffering of women in labor
is embraced as a fitting symbol for Christ's material sacrifice on the cross.

Motherhood is, second, specially connected with love, tenderness, and,
most of all, empathy or compassion. "Mother-love" is construed as "instinc-
tive and fundamental." This is why Bernard uses *mater*, in contrast to *magister/
dominus*, to redefine the authority of abbots in terms of care. He frequently
describes the mother as "one who cannot fail to love her child."[102] The assumption here is that a father or lord may or may not express such love while a
mother does so almost automatically, by virtue of the physical and emotional
bonds of childbirth and caregiving. Closely related, third, there is a strong link
between mothering and feeding or nursing. Given the connection in medieval
physiology between breastmilk and blood, the breasts and wound of Christ
are often "interchangeable" symbols of his life-giving sacrifice.[103] Similarly,
Christ figures maternally in the Eucharist, as the one who nourishes his children with his own body and blood. Because of this, Bynum says, "the female
parent seems to have been particularly appropriate to convey the new theological concerns, more appropriate in fact than the image of the male parent if we
understand certain details of medieval theories of physiology."[104]

These associations surface in Julian's writing as well. For example, in her
teaching on substance and sensuality, Christ figures as mother in a double
sense—in creation (nature, birth) and incarnation (grace, rebirth) (59.32–33).
She makes an explicit connection between Christ's passion and women's labor,
saying that "in the taking of oure kind [nature] he quickened [conceived] us,
and in his blessed dying upon the crosse he bare [bore] us to endlesse life"
(63.25–26). Similarly, she speaks of "oure very moder Jhesu" who "bereth
[bears] us to joye," "sustaineth us within him," "traveyled [labored] into the full
time," to "suffer the sharpest throwes [birth pangs] and grevousest paines that

[101] Bynum, *Jesus as Mother*, 133, n. 80.
[102] Bynum, *Jesus as Mother*, 116. Cf. Bernard's commentary on the canticle.
[103] On the "wound" in medieval writing, see Caroline Walker Bynum, "The
Female Body and Religious Practice in the Later Middle Ages," in *Fragmentation
and Redemption*, 181–238.
[104] Bynum, *Jesus as Mother*, 132–33. Significantly, milk was thought to be repro-
cessed blood. Throughout late medieval spiritual writings, we find an intuitive
connection between the pierced side of Christ, milk, blood, water, "honeycomb" (Ps
19:10), and hiding in "the clefts of the rock" (Song 2:14). For a similar reason, the
pelican becomes a symbol for Christ's sacrifice, as a mother pelican was believed to
pierce her own side to feed her babies if food was unavailable.

ever were or ever shalle be" (60.16–19). In such passages, Julian echoes the gendering of Christ's humanity as feminine in her religious milieu (see 58.32–36). Like other writers, she selects the term "mother" because she thinks, of all the models of human relationship available, "the moders service is nerest, reediest, and sekerest [surest]" (60.12). Speaking of Christ's "moderhed of kind [natural] love, which kinde love never leeveth us" (lines 1–4), she maintains that God never fails to have compassion because of who God is. Mother God attends her "deerwurthy children" and oversees them "full tenderly" for this is "the kinde and condition of moderhed" (lines 44–45). In other words, Julian, like Bernard, imagines the mother as one who cannot help but remember and care for her children; it is her very "nature."

In keeping with her devotional tradition, Julian associates the breast of the nursing mother with the wounded side of Christ on the cross. She writes, "Jhesu, he may homely lede us into his blessed brest by his swet, open side, and shewe us therein perty of the godhed and the joyes of heven" (lines 34–35). Christ's bosom or side reveal God's rejoicing over lost humanity. Julian likewise compares the mother who "may geve her childe sucke her milke" with the Eucharist, saying that "oure precious moder Jhesu" who "may fede us with himselfe" through "the blessed sacrament that is precious fode [food] of very life" (lines 25–27). It is evident, then, that Julian relies on many of the same connotations as her predecessors and contemporaries. Her use of maternal imagery is firmly rooted in this broader tradition and would have been familiar to her readers.

Despite clear precedents for maternal naming of God, it remains a fairly minor theme among patristic and medieval theologians until Julian. When motherhood is evoked in the discourses she inherits, it usually pertains to the incarnate Son or, occasionally, God, as one image among many. But Julian's revelation culminates in a focused meditation on the motherhood of the Trinity that recapitulates everything else she has said. Here she makes a striking contribution in extending maternal language to the Son with respect to his divinity and, therefore, broadening its application to the Father and the Spirit.[105] Her ascription of the "office" of motherhood to Christ demonstrates these theological developments.

The Office of Motherhood

It is only after the soteriological example in chapter 51 that motherhood emerges as Julian's central model for conceiving of God and the divine-human relationship.

---

[105] Colledge and Walsh, *Book of Showings*, 154.

The imagery is integrally connected to the atoning work of Christ described there. In her Trinity of father, mother, and lord, "motherhood" is specially "inpropred [appropriated]" to the second person (59.34–36). Julian writes:

> I beheld the werking of alle the blessed trinite, in which beholding I saw and understode these thre propertes: the properte of faderhed, and the properte of motherhed, and the properte of the lordhede in on God. In oure fader almighty we have oure keping and oure blesse, as anemptes oure kindely substance, which is to us by oure making fro without beginning. And in the seconde person, in wit and wisdom, we have our keping, as anemptes oure sensuality, oure restoring, and oure saving. For he is oure moder, broder, and saviour. And in oure good lorde, the holy gost we have oure rewarding and oure yelding [payment] for oure living and oure traveyle, and endlessly over-passing alle that we desyer in his mervelous curtesy of his hye, plentuous grace. (58.15–24)

Julian maps the "properties" of fatherhood, motherhood, and lordship onto familiar triads such as power, wisdom, and goodness/love or creation, redemp-tion, and grace (cf. 58.47–52). She also develops her own assignments, such as substantial keeping and blessing (Father); sensual keeping, restoring, and saving (Son); and rewarding, yielding (giving), and surpassing expectation (Spirit). While fatherhood is typically keyed to creation or being and moth-erhood to mercy and grace (see lines 37–46), Christ is not only "oure moder sensual" but also "oure moder substantially" (lines 31–32).[106] In other words, motherhood is appropriated to the Son on account of not only his humanity but also his divinity.

The quality of motherhood "longeth" to the Son and is assigned to him largely because of the gendered evocations of her theological tradition. But Julian also makes several significant constructive moves here. First, while in patristic and medieval theology, the roles or "offices" of Christ are identified as "king, prophet, and priest" (Aquinas), Julian speaks of "the very office of a kinde nurse" (61.56) and "the service and the office of moderhode" (60.9).[107] Calling Christ "oure

---

[106] The work of the Spirit is absorbed into the property of motherhood at this juncture. Julian seems to be saying the Spirit performs the motherhood of Christ.

[107] The *munus triplex Christi* is an important doctrine in Reformation and Reformed theology, associated with Calvin in particular. The *munus duplex* of priest and king is thought to be more common in medieval theology; see Barth's remarks on the matter (*CD* IV/3.1, 5f.). However, Christ's threefold role of prophet, priest, and king derives from patristic thought (it is used by Justin Martyr, Jerome, and Chrysostom among others) and is found in medieval theology as well. Aquinas, for example, writes, "Christ was to be king, prophet, and priest. Now Abraham was a

moder, broder, and savioure" effectively translates and encapsulates for her what is meant by Jesus' royal, prophetic, and priestly roles (53.21).

Second, Julian combines the images of heirship and rebirth in her soteriology. As Soskice observes, Julian's "originality lies in her alignment of Paul's language of atonement as fraternal kinship (Christ, the firstborn of many brothers), with the second birth imagery of the gospels," which is maternal.[108] Motherhood and brotherhood are often paired in her description of the work of salvation in such a way that they seem to define one another. Evoking scriptural passages such as John 1:10–13 and Ephesians 1:3–6, "Julian's theology of 'at-one-ing' . . . is grounded in the biblical insight that through Christ, believers become the *kin* of Christ, either adoptively or by new birth."[109] Julian stresses Christ's comprehensive recapitulation of Adamic humanity with the recurrent phrase "alle is the manhode of Crist" (51.218). In a conflation of biological relations, it is as the firstborn among many siblings that Christ becomes mother of all.

Julian's composite kinship language reinforces the image of "beclosure" and graphically exemplifies salvation as incorporation into the body of Christ. In one of her most dramatic passages about being-in-Christ, she describes Christ gladly looking into his own pierced side, and "ther he shewed a fair, delectable place, and large inow [enough] for alle mankinde that shalle be saved to rest in pees and in love" (24.3–4). Playing on the association between wound and womb, images like this fuse Christ as firstborn son/brother and Christ as mother. His open side not only creates but reveals his capacity to bear the whole world in himself.

Calling Christ "moder and broder" also goes hand in hand with other intimate illustrations of being-in-and-with. For example, Julian describes what she calls the "updrawing" of humanity into Christ—"in which thurst [desire] he hath drawen his holy soules that be now in blisse. And so getting his lively mebris [living members], ever he draweth and drinketh, and yet him thursteth and longeth" (75.4–6). Registering the double meaning of "draw," she portrays God as bringing "his holy souls" so close that it is as if they are "his living members," "drafted" into God by an insatiable "thirst" for intimacy with them.[110]

Third, the convergence of motherhood and brotherhood in her thought reflects the way Julian tightly interweaves the doctrines of predestination,

---

priest . . . (Gn. 15:9). . . . He was also a prophet, according to Gn. 20:7. . . . Lastly David was both king and prophet" (*ST* IIIa, q. 31, a. 2; cf. q. 22, a. 1).

[108] Soskice, *Kindness of God*, 145.

[109] Soskice, *Kindness of God*, 144–45.

[110] Watson and Jenkins, *Writings of Julian of Norwich*, 358.

creation, and redemption, all of which come under the common designation: atonement. The "office of moderhode" (60.11) is assigned primarily to Christ, then, not because it is strictly temporal and embodied, and therefore inappropriate to the Father and Spirit. Rather, it is because (1) in him there is an intensification of the motherhood of God (he is mother *twice*—in creation and in recreation), (2) he is the one who reveals and provides access to the motherhood of the Trinity, and (3) as the eternal firstborn he is the preeminent instance of the mutual enclosure that, for Julian, constitutes atonement.[111] In short, even in its christological focus, Julian's maternal naming of God varies from the pattern of her tradition. It is of a piece with her assertion that it is the second person who manifests the motherly "kindness" of the Trinity.

Further, Julian extends the property of motherhood to Father and Spirit as well. This insight constitutes a marked theological development over late medieval devotion to "moder Christ."[112] Several passages demonstrate Julian's extraordinary contribution. First, toward the end of Revelation 14, Julian references the motherhood of all three Trinitarian persons quite directly:

> I understood thre manner of beholdings of motherhed in God. The furst is grounde of oure kinde making. The seconde is taking of oure kinde, and ther beginneth the moderhed of grace. The thurde is moderhed in werking, and therin is a forthspreding by the same grace, of length and brede, of high and of depnesse without ende. (59.37–41)

While, in the preceding paragraphs, Julian distinguishes the properties of fatherhood, motherhood, and lordship (ch. 58f.), here she designates motherhood as a quality of Father, Son, and Spirit.[113]

As throughout Julian's writing, "kind" is associated with creation and the work of the Father, incarnation and grace with the Son, and the "spreading

[111] Of course, *as* appropriated, any quality is shared, due to the perichoretic unity and the simplicity of God.

[112] For a more detailed analysis of the motherhood specifically of Christ, see Baker, *From Vision to Book*, 107–34.

[113] Baker, among others, assumes these three manners of beholding all apply to Christ, given the context. But I agree with Colledge and Walsh that Julian is speaking of the motherhood of the Trinity. This is apparent in the way she maps the forms of motherhood onto a triad that she repeatedly uses for the persons of the Trinity in their traditional ordering and numbering, viz. kind, incarnation, and grace, or creation, redemption, and grace. Julian often uses "mercy and grace" or "grace and mercy" without regard for the order when she is speaking of the work of the Son and the Spirit. She makes it clear that it is the same work. But "forthspreading," or the dissemination of grace, is assigned in a more limited way to the Spirit. This makes sense as Julian understands the Spirit as "the Spirit of Christ" (Rom 8:9).

forth" of the grace of Christ with the Spirit. Julian maintains a certain Trinitarian ordering in the mission of salvation: "Oure fader willith, oure mother werketh, oure good lorde the holy gost confirmeth" (lines 24–25). The active triad "willing, working, confirming" affirms the unified counsel of Trinitarian persons in the decision to create and redeem humankind. Although she assigns "will" to the Father here, Julian often singles out the self-reflexive deciding of the Son as well. She says, for example, that "in oure very moder Jhesu oure life is grounded in the forseeing wisdom of himselfe fro without beginning" (63.23–24). The accent of 59.24–25 falls less on the anterior willing of the first person and more on the visibility or palpability of the action of the Son and the Spirit: they phenomenalize the shared divine will and fold humankind into it. It is possible, as Baker notes, that Julian "uses the phrase *forth spredyng* to translate *diffusa* in Rom. 5:5: 'The charity of God is poured forth in our hearts, by the Holy Ghost who is given to us.'"[114] Julian describes the "moder Crist" working integrally with "the thurde person, the holy gost" as "grace werketh with mercy" (58.38, 41–43). The Spirit extends the work of Christ, spreading it forth in the hearts of believers.

In a second direct reference to the motherhood of the Trinity, Julian says, "We be brought againe, by the motherhed of mercy and grace [Son and Spirit], into oure kindly stede where that we ware made by the moderhed of kind love [Father], which kinde love never leeveth us" (60.1–4). The motherhood of mercy and grace (Son and Spirit) leads back to the motherhood of kind love (Father). It is not simply the case that God is father (as the Father) *and* mother (as the Son). Rather, the Spirit enlarges the motherhood of the Son "tille alle his deerwurthy [much-loved] children be borne and brought forth" (63.19–20) and returns those children to the motherhood of God the Father. Julian thus describes God's work in the economy of salvation in the usual sequence Father–Son–Spirit (59.24–25), but the human encounter with God is structured Spirit–Son–Father (61.1–4). The appropriation of salvific activities yields a Trinity of motherhood: Mother–Mother–Mother. And so the prayer Jesus teaches Julian to pray begins, "My kind moder, my gracious moder, my deerworthy moder . . ." (61.40–41).

Third, there is a pronounced moment in which Julian predicates motherhood of God by way of supereminence, indicating that she sees "mother" as more than a metaphor for God in Christ.[115] She writes, "This faire, lovely worde, 'moder,' it is so swete and so kinde in itselfe that it may not verely be saide of none, ne to none, but of him and to him that is very mother of life and of alle" (60.39–41). She continues, "To the properte of moderhede longeth kind love,

---

[114]   Baker, *From Vision to Book*, 194.
[115]   Watson and Jenkins, *Writings of Julian of Norwich*, 312.

wisdom, and knowing; and it is God." Motherhood is God. Julian appears to regard motherhood, in much the same way Aquinas does fatherhood, as a divine perfection rather than merely an image drawn from life.[116] There is none who is truly mother but God; God is this relation itself, love itself, wisdom itself, truth itself, giver of all life.

Motherhood emerges as the most appropriate and comprehensive model for visualizing the mutual enclosure of humanity and divinity in creation, incarnation, and salvation. Such a high view of the divine name "Mother" is the outworking of Julian's claim that humankind is eternally cherished and borne in the second person of the Trinity. But the quality of motherhood would not necessarily be extended to the Father and Spirit as well if it were only applied to the son by virtue of his incarnation and passion, his "sensuality" or humanity. Julian, however, plainly conceives of the Son's motherhood as an attribute of his divinity or substance, and therefore common to all three persons of the Trinity. Motherhood most perfectly displays a condition that always already includes the possibility of another. In that sense, the motherhood of the Trinity is already implied in Julian's earlier teaching on atonement, where her leading motif for reconciliation with God is being-in-and-with—God in the human in God—a condition uniquely exemplified by a pregnant body. Julian tells us that this "beclosure" or mutual "indwelling" is the subject of her final revelation (Revelation 16). The theme forms bookends for her more direct teaching on divine motherhood in chapters 58–63 and is closely related to it.

Example of Mother and Child

Motherhood emerges as the highest and deepest relation of kinship in Julian's theology in large part because of the theological, cultural, and biological associations that accrue to it. Yet there is another salient reason it becomes her predominant model for God's relationship to humankind in Christ: it aptly sums up the depiction of God's compassionate gaze in the Example of the Lord

---

[116] See Aquinas, *ST* Ia, q. 13, a. 6. Julian does not offer a theory of language, so this point could be overstated. Perhaps Julian is only indicating here that motherhood makes for the very *best* creaturely model for God. However, she does state that motherhood should be ascribed to God first and foremost, which constitutes a reversal of the order of predication (moving from God to creature) on par with Aquinas' assertion that fatherhood is predicated of God by way of supereminence. Per Soskice's account of metaphor, both motherhood and fatherhood are models drawn from life that generate good metaphors for conceiving of God, but God is neither father nor mother in an unequivocal sense.

and Servant.[117] The image is produced by the narrative and can be read as a commentary on it.[118] The property of motherhood characterizes the lord/father figure as well as the servant/son figure in Julian's showing. It is readily apparent, in light of what has already been said, how the motherhood of the Son maps onto the servant—his readiness to serve, his self-sacrifice, his bodily "traveyle" and labor (51.129).[119] The fraught relationship between kenosis and femininity is certainly at play here.[120] Yet there are indications in Julian's text that she is simultaneously recasting the lord or father as mother, in a way that undercuts many of the assumptions and polarities she otherwise assumes from her culture and theological tradition. First, glossing Philippians 2:6–8, Julian uses the complementary terms "homeliness" and "courtesy" to describe God's transcendent nearness. Second, she commends to her readers the "property of child" in correspondence to God's "condition of motherhood." With both moves, Julian construes the father in the parable as a motherly father.

The two adjectives Julian favors when referring to God are "homely" and "courteous." They form a prominent pair (4.15; 26.3). "Homely and courteous" becomes a way for Julian to talk about things like the immanent-transcendence of God, the greater similarity between God and the creature in the midst of a great dissimilarity, the union and distinction of divinity and humanity in Christ, the attitude of love and reverence warranted by God's presence, and so on.[121] Taken together, this pair helps her vividly describe a God who is "kind"

---

[117] The addition of the example utterly redefines the Long Text. As Watson and Jenkins' commentary shows throughout, Julian is constantly looking forward and backward to the example when she rewrites her revelations. It becomes her lens for interpreting many other passages in the Long Text. For "motherhood" to sum up the example is for it to sum up the whole *Revelation*.

[118] As Soskice notes, mothering images appear "after and largely by way of what Julian calls the 'wonderful example' of the Lord and his servant" (*Kindness of God*, 143).

[119] One of the primary Middle English senses of "trauayl" (or "traveyle") is "pains of childbirth, labor" (Kurath, Kuhn, and Lewis, *Middle English Dictionary*, 3f.). Julian retains this maternal sense when she speaks of the servant/son being sent to travail, travel, or labor "in the erth" for the lord's treasure (humankind). Cf. A. C. Spearing, "The Subtext of *Patience*: God as Mother and the Whale's Belly," *Journal of Medieval and Early Modern Studies* 29, no. 2 (1999): 310.

[120] On the complexities of this association, see Sarah Coakley's essay "*Kenōsis* and Subversion: On the Repression of 'Vulnerability' in Christian Feminist Writing," in her *Powers and Submissions: Spirituality, Philosophy and Gender* (Malden, Mass.: Blackwell, 2002).

[121] For more on the definitions of and relationship between "homely" and "courtesy," see Joan Nuth, *Wisdom's Daughter: The Theology of Julian of Norwich* (New York: Crossroad, 1991), 74.

or kin, fully at home with and immanent to humankind, but who is also "kind unmade"—"above" and "beyond" creaturely reality: transcendent.

Julian refers to God's "homely loving" (5.2) and frequently speaks of the "homelyhede" or "homeliness" of God (7.35). In her Middle English use, "homely" means "familiar," "intimate," "plain," or "homey."[122] It is connected to the word "comfortable" (i.e., comforting), and both indicate nearness and tender care. "Homely" is especially used to describe God's love, and, like "kindness," it has domestic and familial overtones. According to Watson and Jenkins, "to treat people in a 'homely' way is to treat them as equals."[123] God's desire to be intimate and familiar with humankind is central to Julian's message. Homeliness coordinates with motherhood and service in rather obvious ways.[124]

If "homely" evokes a domestic context and intimacy among equals, "courteous" brings to mind a courtly setting and its attendant social order. "Courteous" goes hand in hand with the term "lord," which Julian uses throughout her writing and which figures particularly prominently in the Example of the Lord and Servant as well as the earlier example of solemn king and poor servant (7.27–35). "Curteyse" (courtesy) connotes courtliness, politeness, and generosity of the sort a good lord would have toward his subordinates. It is the way in which a superior graciously condescends to an inferior without making her feel inferior.

In the same way that the title "Lord" is applied to God and to the Father, but also to the Son and the Spirit, "courtesy" is not strictly appropriated to one person of the Trinity. However, in a number of places, it is specifically connected to the condescension of Christ and his suffering love. This illuminates Julian's meaning. She includes an *exemplum* about a glad or courteous giver in which she alludes to Philippians 2:6f. Describing Christ, Julian says, "The curtesse gever setteth at nought alle his cost and alle his traveyle (labor)" (23.32–33). "Courtesy" becomes a way of referring to the loving condescension or kenosis of God in Christ.[125] Similarly, when Julian refers to "oure curtesse lorde" in chapter 40, she describes him as forgiving, "of fulle glad chere," "with frendfulle

---

[122] These connotations are retained in British English today.

[123] Watson and Jenkins, *Writings of Julian of Norwich*, 136.

[124] In the medieval world, the home was the place of birth, as well as death, and most forms of intimate caregiving, nurturance, and healing in between.

[125] Of course, "condescend" is not used in its popular contemporary sense ("show feelings of superiority; be patronizing"). Precisely the opposite. To condescend is to *be* superior but show no signs of regarding oneself as superior, such as showing disdain for inferiors. I am using "condescension" in its etymological sense as "to descend" (*descendere*) "with" or "together" (*con*); or, more vividly, in the Greek: συναπάγω, to be identified with (συν) and lead away (απάγω) (Rom 12:16).

[friendly] welcoming" (40.9–10). His wish is for his "dere darling" to "see" his "loving" and know his grace and mercy (lines 10–14). Divine courtesy is without blame and compassionately regards all humans as "children" (28.28–30). After the Example of the Lord and Servant, Julian says, "For oure lorde God is so good, so gentil [honorable], so curtesse that he may never assigne defaute [fault] in whome he shall be [to whom he shall] ever blessed and praised" (53.5–6). God's "honor" or lordliness is expressed in raising up the lowly, not in lording it over them, in forgiving, not in finding fault. What her *exempla* figuring a king or lord exemplify is the "grete homelyhede" of God, that God's highness is manifest in a kind of lowliness.

While, in Julian's writing, the language of courtesy is closely linked to lordship and fatherhood, positions of elevated status, it is also extended to motherhood (61.36). In fact, rather than dividing them up, assigning courtly imagery to Father God and homely imagery to Mother God, as one might expect given medieval conventions around gender, "mother" becomes Julian's leading image for the courteousness of God. After her example about the courteous giver, she goes on to describe the gladness of the lord (Christ) as he looks into his wound and sees an ample space for all (24.1f.; see above). This image of Christ making space to bear the world is an early presaging of her later development of the mother/child theme. As in the example in chapter 51, the courteousness of the lord is that he treats his subordinate with a motherly attitude, not like a servant, referring to her as "my darling . . . my childe" (24.12–13).

Julian later offers a less pronounced devotional example of mother and child that clarifies her christological Example of the Lord and Servant. In the same way as God's motherhood epitomizes God's homeliness and courteousness, the gaze of the mother is paradigmatic of all that Julian says about the loving look and unblaming judgment of the Lord (ch. 45 and ch. 51). These themes coalesce in a number of places, particularly in two parallel passages where Julian considers the proper human attitude toward God's graciousness, using parental imagery to explain the relationship between love and fear or reverence. There is an appropriate human courteousness toward God that corresponds to but is qualitatively different from God's courteousness toward humankind. However, it is patently not a kind of servility.[126] Julian maintains that "fear" is appropriate in the face of the properties of God's fatherhood and lordship, while "love" is appropriate to the property of God's good-

---

Theologically, "condescension" specifies the divine posture of downward mobility or ταπεινοφροσύνη (lowliness of mind, humility) (Phil 2:3, 6f.).

[126] Julian describes believers in heaven as "courtiers" (Watson and Jenkins, *Writings of Julian of Norwich*, 358).

ness (74.20–21). Here, as throughout her earlier comments on sin and self-accusation, she avoids describing God as in any way wrathful or "dreadful." In these lines, she offers pastoral guidance for humbly approaching God as sinners. She rules out unholy and excessive apprehension and commends what she calls "reverent drede" (line 27).[127] Julian says, holy fear (i.e., reverence) "maketh us hastely to fle fro alle that is not goode and falle into oure lordes brest, as the childe into the moders barme [bosom]" (lines 29–30). These lines echo an earlier passage in which, recommending contrition in the penitential process, Julian explains that "oure curtesse moder" does not wish "that we flee away, for him were nothing lother [less pleasing]" but "that we use the condition of a childe"—and flee *toward* (61.36–37). The "reverent dread" Julian describes is that of a "meke childe" crying out to its mother for help and pleading for mercy in distress (lines 39–41). In other words, this "fear" is a form of trust. What the child is actually "afraid" of, in our common use of that word, is "all that is not good" (i.e., *not* God), that from which it should flee into the bosom of Mother God (74.29). In the face of human frailty and sin, "be we seker [we are certain]" that God "useth the condition of a wise moder" and "wille [wants] then that we use the properte of a childe, that evermore kindly trusteth to the love of the moder in wele and in wo" (61.43–46).

Julian's example of "a wise mother" thus frames the divine-human relationship in terms of the caregiving role of parenthood. In a surprising reversal of the usual application of soteriological "debt" metaphors, Julian refers to "the kinde and condition of moderhed" as a "debt" that God willingly assumes toward humanity (60.24). This debt is defined by attention and availability. To "use the property of a child" is to make the debt reciprocal, to take on the corresponding attitude of "true loving." She writes, "I sawe that all oure det [debt] that we owe by Gods bidding to faderhod and moderhod is fulfilled in trew loving of God, which blessed love Crist werketh in us" (lines 53–55).[128] In other words, what is "owed" is not the slaving of the elder brother or the prodigal son's servile penance. Both the divine and the human debts are pictured

---

[127] She enumerates four manners of dread in much the same way as other Middle English devotional texts. For examples, see Watson and Jenkins (*Writings of Julian of Norwich*, 354). Holy "dread" is her way of talking about human "courteousness" toward God, which corresponds to God's toward humans. But it does not take on the contemporary connotations of "dread" at all. Explaining the integration of love and fear, Julian says, "And thus we shalle in love be homely and nere to God, and we shalle in drede be gentille and curtesse to God, and both in one manner, like even" (73.39–40). In other words, as Julian clarifies elsewhere, although we shall be close to God, we shall not be disrespectful.

[128] She may be alluding to Exod 20:12 here: "Honor your father and your mother."

in bodily terms, emphasizing physical proximity—the mother offers her very body, and the child takes physical shelter in her arms (60.17, 23, 25, 33, etc.). Julian's vivid language makes the intensity of God's longing, nearness, and care palpable. She says, "He wille have alle oure love *fastened* to him" (60.52).[129] Fastening or binding echoes Julian's earlier claim that Christ "wrappeth," "windeth," "halseth" (embraces), "becloseth," and "hangeth about" his children (5.1–5). It is nuptial and familial, synonymous with cleaving. Perhaps alluding to Augustine's instruction, "*Embrace the love of God, and by love embrace God,*" Julian commends the property of child to cling to the mother's nearness and in this way render what is "owed."[130]

It is precisely "servile dread," the sort of shame that makes one run away and hide, that Julian is attempting to rout out in her pastoral guidance about how to approach God meekly, respectfully, and trustingly in prayer. *Nosce te ipsum*, "know thyself," takes on a variety of meanings in medieval contemplative writing.[131] Often it is used to put the human in her place: know that you are a sinner. This is how Julian presents it in chapter 45 in reference to the "dome" of "holy church." In view of early disputes over the Delphic precept γνῶθι σεαυτόν, it could mean "know that you are not [a] god," as Apollo is said to have intended it, or "know your true, ideal self—the soul," as Plato interprets it.[132] Julian's instruction seems closer to the latter. Self-knowledge is preeminently the knowledge of being regarded by God as a beloved child. Although the self is still in some sense divided, *simul justus et peccator*, the determinative judgment of God remains singular. The two "cheres" or expressions of God show one love in two modes—pity and delight, compassion (Luke 15:20) and rejoicing (vv. 24, 32). If God is not divided in God's "deeming" and God's "dome" defines the reality of humankind, then, despite the fact of sin, humans have no right to see themselves otherwise. The soul is integrated in God's gaze. To know oneself is to see one's "substantial" self, held eternally in the Trinity, mirrored perfectly in Christ's eternal humanity, loved from without beginning. The awareness of one's sin is indeed beneficial or "behovely" (fitting), but only insofar as it reveals one's "blindness and feebleness" and functions redemptively to facilitate the realization, "We be Cristes children" (54.29). Conforming to God's vision of her children is

---

[129] Emphasis added. This echoes the "suttel knot" passage (53.50f.).

[130] Augustine, *De Trinitate* VIII.8.12.

[131] Watson and Jenkins, *Writings of Julian of Norwich*, 262.

[132] The injunction is interpreted in numerous other ways as well. See, for example, Eliza Gregory Wilkins' dissertation, *"Know Thyself" in Greek and Latin Literature* (University of Chicago Libraries, 1917), 60f.

part of paying "the debt of love." To "come to oneself," in the language of the parable, is to remember the "condition of child" and anticipate God's ever-available maternal affection. As in Luke 15, the mother's rejoicing increases when her children "flee" to her for comfort.

We might refer to these chapters as the Example of Mother and Child and see them as an elaboration of the Example of the Lord and Servant in chapter 51. "Homely" and "courteous" are not dichotomous terms for Julian, nor are "fatherhood" and "motherhood." They do not counterbalance one another, as "justice" and "mercy" are sometimes made to do. On the contrary, they are integrally related. Both are used to describe God's undividedly magnanimous attitude. For Julian, the two coincide paradigmatically in a mother's regard for her children, an image that constitutes another answer to Julian's question about how God views fallen humanity (chs. 61, 74). The trajectory of the shift from lord/servant to father/son in chapter 51 is prolonged in Julian's turn to the "office of motherhood" and "the condition of the child." Her maternal description of God defines, rather than dislocates, the paternal and filial focus of the biblical parable as well as the courtly imagery of Julian's example. At once lordly and homely, courteous and lowly, chiding and embracing, she teaches her children to see themselves *as children*, and not slaves. The gracious lord, the loving father, is like a mother. This brings to mind Rembrandt's famous depiction of the prodigal son being embraced upon his return.[133] Rembrandt paints the father's arms in two distinct manners: the left hand appears more conventionally "masculine"—strong, calloused, firm—while the right hand is more conventionally "feminine"—soft, gentle, open.[134] In the same way, Julian's examples of divine love conjure for us a "motherly father."[135]

---

[133] See Rembrandt Harmenszoon van Rijn's oil painting *The Return of the Prodigal Son*, completed ca. 1667–1668, in the Hermitage Musuem collection in St. Petersburg.

[134] See Henri Nouwen's reflection on Rembrandt's painting in light of the parable: *The Return of the Prodigal Son: A Story of Homecoming* (New York: Doubleday, 1992).

[135] Jürgen Moltmann, "The Motherly Father: Is Trinitarian Patripassionism Replacing Theological Patriarchalism?" in *God as Father?* ed. Johannes-Baptist Metz and Edward Schillebeeckx, Concilium 143 (Edinburgh: T&T Clark, 1981), 52–53.

4

Prodigal Son of God

"Grace is the very essence of the being of God. Grace is itself properly and essentially divine. . . . God Himself is it."
—Karl Barth (*CD* II/1, 356)

"In being gracious to man in Jesus Christ, He also goes into the far country. . . . He does not pass him by as did the priest and the Levite the man who had fallen among thieves. He does not leave him to his own devices. He makes his situation His own."
—Karl Barth (*CD* IV/1, 158–59)

Julian's Example of the Lord and Servant illuminates Barth's exegesis of the Parable of the Prodigal Son in surprising ways. It also anticipates important doctrinal ramifications of his identification of the second person of the Trinity with the lost son. For Barth, as for Julian, the parable comes to narrate not only atonement and reconciliation but also election and, finally, the very essence of God. The set of scriptural predicates that yields the association between Jesus Christ and the wayward child has everything to do with the way the story finally presses back into the divine life.

Parable of Retrieval

In his exegesis of Luke 15:11–32, Barth speaks of a "parallel" between the lost son and the Son of God. However, it is clear that the two narrative planes intersect, such that the parable does not tell distinct stories that can be set side by side—one about God and humanity in general and another about Jesus Christ in particular. Nor is it quite a matter of one story with two meanings, one literal or direct and the other metaphorical or indirect. Instead, the interpretive layers interpenetrate one another, become knit together, such that the second level figures as the *how* of the first. In Barth's direct exposition of the parable, fallen humanity is met immediately by God's grace. But, in Adam Neder's words, "Barth's premise is that *grace is not a thing*."[1] It is a name. In its actuality, it is none other than Jesus Christ himself. Humans as such do not return to God, and certainly not on their own. So while, in Barth's interpretation, the parabolic going-out is double—(1) the fall of Adamic humanity, and (2) the condescension of the Son of God—the homecoming is singular: it takes place in Jesus Christ alone. As a figure for humankind lost and perishing, we can only make sense of the son's restoration in light of this second actuality, the atonement. The eternal Son follows the lost son into the far country in order to carry him back to the Father in himself. "No one comes to the Father except through me" (John 14:6).

Within each of the three "lost and found" parables in Luke 15, the larger claim of the Gospel reverberates. Like the parables of the Lost Sheep (Luke 15:3–7) and the Lost Coin (Luke 15:8–10) that precede it, the Parable of the Lost Son is a parable of *retrieval*.[2] While Barth's surface reading of the parable is based on a common pattern of sin and repentance, his deeper engagement emphasizes pursuit and retrieval instead. There seem to be at least two theological reasons for this shift in emphasis. First, like the sheep in the first parable, once lost, humans are incapable of finding their way back on their own.[3] The distance is insurmountable—hence the parallelism of lost/dead, found/alive. Being found and made alive again, one certainly cannot do for oneself. Second, finding one's own way back is simply not a requirement of grace. Something Barth says in his later excursus on miracles (in §64) illuminates this:

> In these stories it does not seem to be of any great account that the men who suffer as creatures are above all sinful men, men who are at fault . . . who are therefore guilty and have betrayed themselves into all kinds of trouble. No, *the important thing about them in these stories is not that they are sinners but that they are sufferers.* Jesus does not first look at their past, and then at their tragic present in the light of it. But *from their present He creates for them a new future. He does not ask, therefore, concerning their sin. He does not hold it against them. . . . The truth is obvious . . . that the evil which afflicts mankind*

---

[1]   Adam Neder, *Participation in Christ: An Entry into Karl Barth's "Church Dogmatics"* (Louisville, Ky.: Westminster John Knox, 2009), 49.

[2]   See Eberhard Jüngel, *God as the Mystery of the World: On the Foundation of the Theology of the Crucified One in the Dispute between Theism and Atheism*, trans. Darrell Guder (Edinburgh: T&T Clark, 1983), 155–57.

[3]   For Barth, it is only derivatively that can we speak of individual or collective recognition and experience of this return. Materially insignificant to reconciliation, it is not part of his interpretation of the parable at this juncture in his thought. But see §74 for Barth's use of the parable in connection with the Christian life.

is in some sense a punishment; that "the wages of sin is death" (Rom. 6:23). But *there is no trace of this consideration* in the miracle stories. (222–23)[4]

Out of humanity's present suffering, God in Christ creates a future, without consideration for the sin that caused it. While the human counterpart of sin is repentance, the divine counterpart is unblaming grace, embodied in the seeking and finding of the triple parables of Luke 15. Barth is critical of what he sees as an overemphasis in Reformed theology on repentance because it overlooks the real "power" of the gospel "as a message of mercifully omnipotent and unconditionally complete liberation from φθορά [destruction], death and wrong." Barth asks, "How could Protestantism as a whole, only too faithful to Augustine . . . orientate itself in a way which was so one-sidedly anthropological (by the problem of repentance instead of by its presupposition—the Kingdom of God)" and miss the issue of "humanity itself" (233), which is precisely God's concern in Christ? What we must learn to recognize in the parable is that "God retrieves us."[5] After all, it is "while he was still far off" that the father sees and has compassion on the son (Luke 15:20).

Parable of Election

The fourth volume of *Church Dogmatics* is strewn with evocative statements identifying this story of a son who was lost and found as the Parable of Reconciliation. Barth explicitly sets his account of atonement and reconciliation within the frame of Luke 15: "The event of atonement and the actuality of [humanity] reconciled with God can be described by those who know it only in the words of Luke 15:2: 'This man receiveth sinners, and eateth with them'" (83). Barth also borrows the narrative structure of the parable, saying, for example, "The reconciliation of sinful and lost [humanity] has, above all, the character of a divine condescension, that it takes place as God goes into the far country" (IV/1, 168). The parable becomes a thumbnail of all the doctrinal elements of incarnation and atonement. It dramatizes what might otherwise be distilled into christological and soteriological categories. In fact, we should regard the whole of *The Doctrine of Reconciliation*, in Alan Lewis' words, as a

---

4   Emphasis added. This shows that Barth, like Julian, combines (1) a Pauline-Augustinian position regarding the nature and consequence of sin with (2) an affirmation that God addresses humans not primarily as guilty sinners but as sufferers oppressed by a mutual enemy. The sentiment underlying Barth's remark about the way Jesus regards humans is remarkably similar to Julian's: "For he beholdeth sinne as sorow and paines to his lovers, in whom he assigneth no blame for love" (39.29–30).

5   Jüngel, *God as the Mystery of the World*, 155–57.

"monumental and imaginative reconstruction of Christology upon the scaffold of the Prodigal Son narrative."[6]

This is clearly indicated in a number of ways, by (1) the parable's pivotal location within *The Doctrine of Reconciliation* (between IV/1–2), (2) being prefaced and coordinated with John 1:14, which, in Barth's view, contains the entirety of reconciliation in nuce, (3) the fact that Barth chooses this particular story to structure and explicate the whole of his Christology, and (4) the network of scriptural references that pervades these portions of *Church Dogmatics*. The first few points are integral to one another, for the immediate context of Barth's exegesis reflects the embeddedness of the parable in the encompassing narrative structure of the Gospel such that the prodigal's story encapsulates the meaning of *vere homo*, *vere Deus* and maps onto a whole set of classical terms related to the person and work of Jesus Christ.

It is on the cusp of his account of the humiliation and self-giving of God (justification) and the exaltation or restoration of the human (sanctification) that Barth turns to the Lukan parable. At the beginning of IV/2, Barth says of what he calls the twofold material content of reconciliation,

> When the whole of this subject is before us, we can hardly fail to think of the New Testament passage which in every age . . . has always been valued by the Church (with all kinds of different interpretations) as central to the whole New Testament and especially the Synoptic tradition. I refer to the so-called Parable of the Prodigal Son, the son who was lost [*verlorenen*] and was found again [*wiedergefundenen*] (Lk. 15:11–32). (IV/2, 21)

While Barth asserts that "we can hardly fail to think of" the lost son at this juncture, the connection is in no way self-evident to most interpreters of the parable. The story on its own, excerpted from its literary and historical context, does not suggest a christological vision of reconciliation at all.[7] But Barth seamlessly interweaves the language of the Parable of the Prodigal Son with that of John 1:14 and of the Gospel story more broadly.[8]

---

[6]   Alan Lewis, *Between Cross and Resurrection: A Theology of Holy Saturday* (Grand Rapids: Eerdmans, 2003), 192.

[7]   In other words, a historical-critical reconstruction of the "original" text, which pries it away from its setting in Luke's proclamation of the good news, cannot yield a genuinely theological interpretation.

[8]   One reason this pairing of John 1:14 with the Lukan parable (read as having a christological reference) is significant is that it enables Barth to hold together the dialectical tension between the Synoptic and Johannine pictures of Jesus Christ. See George Hunsinger, introduction to *Thy Word Is Truth: Barth on Scripture*, ed. George Hunsinger (Grand Rapids: Eerdmans, 2012).

Although not exclusive to this portion of *Church Dogmatics*, it is particularly pronounced in *The Doctrine of Reconciliation*, throughout IV/1–2, and especially in §59 and §64 taken together. In these paragraphs, Barth consistently links the contours of the polyvalent Lukan narrative with classical terms and schemas for Christ's "being and history."[9] In addition to (1) the *unio hypostatica* or *vere homo et vere Deus*, Barth relates elements of the younger son's story to (2) the doctrines of justification and sanctification as well as revised accounts of (3) the *munus triplex Christi* and (4) the *status duplex*.

First, Barth introduces and frames his whole exposition of the parable in terms of John 1:14.[10] The parable is retold as an extended reflection on the more compact account of reconciliation, "the Word became flesh." Barth calls this verse "the center and theme of all theology," "the whole of theology in a nutshell."[11] More specifically, it is the briefest narrative condensation of the hypostatic union or "the two elements in the event of the incarnation" (IV/2, 20). Prefacing the parable, he says of the Johannine verse, "If we put the accent on 'flesh,'" the verse is "a statement about God." We claim that "without ceasing to be true God . . . God went into the far country by becoming human" in God's second "mode of being as the Son—the far country not only of creatureliness but also of corruption and perdition" (IV/2, 20, rev.). On the other hand, "if we put the accent on 'Word,'" John 1:14 becomes a statement about the human. We claim that

> without ceasing to be human, but assumed and accepted in his creatureliness and corruption by the Son of God, the human—this one Son of Man—*returned home* to where He belonged . . . to fellowship with God . . . to the presence and enjoyment of the salvation for which He was destined. (20, rev.)[12]

---

[9] In line with his actualist ontology, Barth refuses to treat person and work separately and prefers the language of "being and history" or "event."

[10] Barth similarly links John 1:14 with Luke 15:11–32 in his *Dogmatics in Outline*, where he paraphrases it: "Into this alien land God has come to us" (trans. G. T. Thompson [New York: Harper & Row, 1959], 109). He also addresses this verse at length in I/2, §15.2. While this portion of IV/2 constitutes a development on his earlier comments (given the ontologically relevant discoveries of II/2), it is clear that in §15 he already sees it as a condensed narration of the hypostatic union. Or, rather, he sees the dogmatic concept "very God and very man" as a mere "description" of what he regards as "the central New Testament statement" found in John 1:14 (I/2, 132).

[11] In a letter to B. Gherardini, May 24, 1955. Eberhard Busch, *Karl Barth: His Life from Letters and Autobiographical Texts*, trans. John Bowden (Philadelphia: Fortress, 1976), 380–81, n. 196.

[12] Emphasis added.

Barth says this "going out" of "the Son of *God*" and this "coming in" of "the Son of *Man*" constitute the "one inclusive event" of the atonement that "took place in Jesus Christ" (21).

Barth concludes the excursus on Luke 15:11–32 by returning to the "main theme" in which it is embedded—that Jesus Christ is as truly human and truly God (25). But he claims, "The doctrine of the two natures cannot try to stand on its own feet or to be true to itself. Its whole secret is the secret of Jn. 1:14—the central saying by which it is described. Whatever we may have to say about the union of the two natures can only be a commentary on this central saying" (IV/2, 66). This makes explicit what is already implicit in the context of Barth's exegesis. Barth believes "the doctrine of the two natures cannot try to stand on its own feet"—that is, without the narrative "the Word became flesh" elaborated in the Lukan parable. He thus sidelines "two natures" language in favor of a more dynamic parabolic thinking of the "two sides or directions or forms of that which took place" in "the common *actualization* (*Gemeinsame Verwirklichung*) of divine and human essence" (IV/1, 133; IV/2, 113, 116).

Second, it is clear from this that the parable embodies the *duplex gratia* of justification and sanctification. The doctrine of justification is retold as the Son's "far journey" (IV/1), and the doctrine of sanctification as the Son's "homecoming" (IV/2). The double movement of the atonement rewrites the whole history of Israel and the world, once and for all, and constitutes the final truth of the human, justified and sanctified before God. Barth appeals to Ephesians 4:9f. and the inextricability of Christ's descent/justification and ascent/sanctification, which he similarly connects with the integral double movement of the parable.[13] Closely related to the double grace of salvation, third, in his treatment of the *munus triplex Christi*, Barth orders Christ's offices priest–king–prophet (respectively corresponding to IV/1, IV/2, and IV/3). He diverges from Calvin's ordering prophet–king–priest, which he says otherwise "comes closest to our own reconstruction" (IV/3.1, 5). But what occupies Barth in IV/1–2 is the *munus duplex* or "union in opposition" of priest and king, the lamb slain and the lion of Judah (Rev 5:5), more commonly evoked in ancient and medieval theology.[14]

---

[13]   Immediately preceding his excursus on the Parable of the Prodigal Son, Barth explains the content of John 1:14 with that of Eph 4:9f.: "Now that he ascended, what is it but that he also descended first into the lower parts of the earth. He that descended is the same also that ascended up far above all heavens that he might fill all things" (21).

[14]   See *CD* IV/3.1 (5f.) for Barth's account of the development of the *munus duplex* into the *munus triplex*. Because Barth's interaction with Luke 15:11–32 primarily concerns the twofold material or "objective" content of the doctrine of reconciliation (IV/1–2) and he does not attend to Christ as prophet or "Mediator"

Fourth, Barth maps the structure of the parable onto what is addressed in Reformed and Lutheran Christology as the *status duplex*, or two states of Christ, while upsetting the pattern of reference in keeping with his exposition of John 1:14 (IV/1, 132). On "the older Lutheran" account, the two states, *exinanitio* (humiliation) and *exaltatio* (exaltation), (1) both belong to Christ's humanity, (2) correspond respectively to his crucifixion and resurrection, and (3) are thus ordered successively.[15] By contrast, for Barth, humiliation and exaltation (1) correspond respectively to the divinity and humanity of Christ, (2) are both rooted in the event of the incarnation, and (3) are thus two sides of the same event (see IV/1, 106; IV/2, 110)[16]—hence the mirror statements: the Lord becomes Servant, and the Servant becomes Lord. Barth's primary "innovation" here is that he interprets the states "strictly together, as two perspectives on a single reality, the doctrines of Christ and the atonement."[17] Equally significant, however, is his "crucial switch of reference," applying the sacerdotal "going out" or abasement of justification to God and the royal "return home" or exaltation of sanctification to the human.[18]

In other words, the two states describe the first two offices taken together: Jesus Christ is a priestly, self-sacrificial king, or, in Barth's language, "the Judge Judged." The offices are, in turn, aligned with the two sides of reconciliation—justification and sanctification. Barth thus returns the doctrines of *duplex gratia*, *munus duplex*, and *status duplex* to their shared narrative root by superimposing them on the Parable of the Lost Son. The simple syntax of John 1:14 indicates the oneness of the reality upon which this set

---

until IV/3—and, concomitantly, the "subjective" realization of reconciliation on the side of humans—I am leaving aside his treatment of the third office for now.

[15]   Barth also notes the Reformed version of the doctrine, which differs in that the object of the two states is the divine Logos rather than the *humanum* of Christ (see IV/1, 133). In both cases, Barth's concern is that they do not capture the cooperation of divine and human action in the unified person of Jesus Christ.

[16]   To offer but one of many examples, Barth says in §58, "We have not spoken of two 'states' (*status*) of Jesus Christ which succeed one another, but of two sides or directions or forms of that which took place in Jesus Christ for the reconciliation of man with God. We used the concepts humiliation and exaltation, and we thought of Jesus Christ as the servant who became Lord and the Lord who became servant. But in so doing we were not describing a being in the particular form of a state, but the twofold action of Jesus Christ, the actuality of His work: His one work, which cannot be divided into different stages or periods of His existence, but which fills out and constitutes His existence in this twofold form" (IV/1, 133).

[17]   Hans Vium Mikkelsen, *Reconciled Humanity: Karl Barth in Dialogue* (Grand Rapids: Eerdmans, 2010), 151; Lewis, *Between Cross and Resurrection*, 192.

[18]   Paul Dafydd Jones, *The Humanity of Christ: Christology in Karl Barth's "Church Dogmatics"* (London: T&T Clark, 2008), 125.

of doctrines "comments"—for "the Word became flesh" does not suggest a going out, on the one hand, and *then* a return, on the other. It is "a single action," not "two different and successive actions." Barth retains the language of "exchange," both in his paragraph on John 1:14 and in connection with the parable, saying "in its literal and original sense the word ἀποκαταλλάσσειν ('to reconcile') means 'to exchange'" (21). But he resists giving the impression that the exchange is a mechanical or symmetrical this-for-that. For it is a matter not simply of the man Jesus in the place of other humans but of the Son of God in the place of humanity. Throughout Barth's account, the cross belongs, first of all, to God (IV/1)—and that means "victory" for humankind (IV/2).[19] That the Lord (God) goes out, becomes Servant (incarnate) (§59), means that the Servant (Christ and humanity in him) comes home, becomes Lord (restored to fellowship with God) (§64). In the *Word* becoming flesh, the creature is brought home, embraced and contained in Christ.

The principal dialectics of reconciliation in IV/1–2 correspond to the narrative structure of parable as follows:[20]

Structural Elements of the Lukan Parable (IV/2.2):	The Going Out of the Prodigal Son	The Homecoming of the Prodigal Son
Johannine Accent:	The Word Became *Flesh*	The *Word* Became Flesh
Standpoint and Direction:	Above to Below	Below to Above
The Twofold Material Content of Reconciliation:	The Lord as *Servant* (IV/1)	The Servant as *Lord* (IV/2)

[19]   This is the principal claim of §59: "Because He is the servant of God, He is the servant of all men, of the whole world . . . He is the man in the parable who when invited to a wedding did not take the chief place but the lower (Lk. 14:10), or even more pointedly (Lk. 22:27) the One who serves His disciples as they sit at meat, or even more pointedly (Jn. 13:1–11) the One who washes their feet before they sit down to meat. . . . *The true God*—if the man Jesus is the true God—*is obedient*" (IV/1, 165; emphasis added).

[20]   My chart leaves out Christ's third office (*munus propheticum*), which Barth treats in IV/3. For a more comprehensive outline of Barth's Christology, see Jones, *Humanity of Christ*, appendix 1, 266. Barth's retelling of the parable could also be mapped onto his reinterpretation of other doctrines I cannot treat here, such as the *communicatio idiomatum, communio naturarum, communicatio gratiarum, communicatio operationinum,* and *participatio Christi.* The *logos asarkos* and Barth's *anhypostatic/enhypostatic* Christology, I will address briefly below.

Ontological Emphasis:	Divinity of Jesus Christ	Humanity of Jesus Christ
Person:	Son of *God*	Son of *Man,* Jesus of Nazareth
Office:	Priest	King
State:	Humiliation (of God)	Exaltation (of the Human)
Soteriological Emphasis:	Justification	Sanctification
Subject/Object:	Electing God (II/2) Reconciling God (IV/1)	Elected Human (II/2) Reconciled Man (IV/1)
Scriptural Image:	Lamb of God	Lion of Judah

These pairs are not component parts or consecutive moments. Shifting from the first to the second problem of reconciliation, Barth says, "In the turn which we have now to execute there can be no question of seeing a new thing, but of seeing the old in a new way. We have not to consider a second thing, but the first one differently" (IV/2, 5). The parabolic form provides a narrative lens that allows us to see these sides at the same time as the same event—not sequentially, but the same differently. Neder notes that "the most conspicuous, innovative, and brilliant feature of Barth's doctrine of reconciliation is his determined attempt to retranslate the whole of it into a history."[21] It is the story of a son who was lost and found that enables Barth to retell the "twofold movement" (*Doppelbewegung*) of this history (IV/2, 7), to look out from both "christologico-soteriological standpoints" at once and as one (IV/3.1, 6).[22]

Intertextual Predication and the Christology of the Parable

While there is considerably more to be said about Barth's Christology on its own terms, of significance here is the way he engages traditional christological categories by integrating them with the language and narrative structure of the Parable of the Lost or Prodigal Son.[23] It is also noteworthy that the precise

[21] Neder, *Participation in Christ,* 39.
[22] For Barth a strong theology of the cross gives rise to a theology of glory. They are two sides of the same.
[23] For treatments of Barth's Christology, see, among others I have mentioned, George Hunsinger, "Karl Barth's Christology: Its Basic Chalcedonian Character," in *The Cambridge Companion to Karl Barth,* ed. John Webster (Cambridge:

content given to both the classical schemas and the meaning of the parable depends upon the intertextuality of his scriptural interpretation.[24] Although he readily employs the technical language of the classical tradition and is keenly attuned to historical-doctrinal developments, Barth also builds up his Christology in another way: by collecting and coordinating scriptural predicates. A particular set of intertexts lend coherence to his alignment of christological and parabolic elements. This brings into focus the identity enacted by Christ and his action narrated in Scripture.[25]

In identifying the Gospel as its encompassing narrative, Barth firmly situates the content of the story within the horizon of Jesus' life, death, and resurrection. This structurally justifiable move opens up an interpretive trajectory for the Lukan passage that very few commentators, if any before Barth besides Julian, have noticed. However, Barth's christological rendering, like Julian's, depends upon other shared intertexts as well. In the first part of his doctrine of reconciliation, especially in §59.1, these include Romans 5:14f., 2 Corinthians 5:21, Isaiah 53:10, and most importantly Philippians 2:5f. Although Barth's

---

Cambridge University Press, 2000), 127–42; Bruce L. McCormack, "Karl Barth's Historicized Christology," in *Orthodox and Modern: Studies in the Theology of Karl Barth* (Grand Rapids: Baker, 2008), 201–34; Neder, *Participation in Christ*; and Jones, *Humanity of Christ*.

[24]   To be clear, my interest in Barth's *inter*textuality is not to be confused with the "*intra*textual" understanding of Barth that Bruce McCormack critiques in his essay "Beyond Nonfoundational and Postmodern Readings of Barth," in *Orthodox and Modern*, 109–65. Based on George Lindbeck's comments in "Barth and Textuality," McCormack defines "intratextual theology" as "without reference to God, the world, history, metaphysics—anything outside or beyond the text" (133). See Lindbeck, "Barth and Textuality," *Theology Today* 43, no. 3 (1986): 362. By contrast, Kathryn Greene-McCreight uses "intratextual" in reference to Barth's *exegesis* to indicate that "it is the text which governs the interpretive process rather than historical-critical reconstruction." Greene-McCreight, *Ad Litteram: How Augustine, Calvin and Barth Read the "Plain Sense" of Genesis 1–3* (New York: Lang, 1999), 202. However, the important point is that an *inter*textual approach (in Ricoeur's sense) emphasizes the coordination or cross-pollination of meanings within texts without ruling out the extratextual reference that brings centripetal force to such meanings. Barth is clearly a "realist" in McCormack's sense, as are the biblical writers. This fact should not call into question "narrative theology" (as it seems to do for McCormack at one point [*Orthodox and Modern*, 113, n. 9]). Rather, that the proper Subject of theology is a Name and a History (not an abstract nature) warrants recourse to narrative logic. By the same token, *name* and *history* signal an extragrammatical reality-reference.

[25]   In Paul Jones' words, Barth "effectively discards the language of 'nature' in his mature Christology" (*Humanity of Christ*, 28). For similar reasons, Barth is wary of the language "the God-man (θεάνθρωπος)," saying it "obliterates the historicity of the subject" and obscures "the event of the co-ordination of the two predicates" (IV/2, 115).

writing is shot through with salient references, this set provides the narrative support his christological interpretation reading of the parable requires.[26]

For Barth, as for Julian, the alignment between Jesus and the younger son in the parable is grounded in the Adam-Christ identity of Romans 5 and 1 Corinthians 15. Inasmuch as the prodigal son represents fallen humanity, we can identify him as Adam. This is something Barth clearly assumes in his "plain" or "direct" reading of the text. However, if we identify the son as Adam, we must also say that all that he is and does has been recapitulated by Jesus Christ. This alone raises the question as to a relationship between the parabolic son and the eternal Son. But, as Hans Frei observes, "In Luke, Jesus' identity is signified in terms of Adam, in whom Israel, humanity, and God are all directly connected. Luke's procedure is reminiscent of Paul's bringing together the first with the second Adam, who is Christ (Rom. 5:14, 1 Cor. 15:21–22)."[27] So Julian and Barth may not be creating a new theological connection through intertextual interpretation so much as registering and amplifying an intertextual dynamic already at work within Luke.

In Christ's solidarity and identity with Adam, there is an asymmetry and a surplus, which Julian and Barth coordinate with the "how much more of grace" they both emphasize in their readings. Justification entails no simple economy of exchange, tit for tat. Jesus does more than mirror and match Adam. "The free gift is not like the trespass" (Rom 5:15). This is one of the reasons that Barth cannot simply "equate" the parabolic son with the Son of God. As in Julian's retelling, the identity of Jesus Christ contains but also exceeds that of prodigal humanity.

Becoming the "second Adam" means assuming *sinful* human flesh, and so exhaustively that we can say Christ becomes "sin itself" (2 Cor 5:21). This is critical for Barth's Christology. He defines "flesh" as "the concrete form of human nature . . . under the sign of the fall of Adam . . . corrupted and therefore destroyed . . . unreconciled with God and therefore *lost*" (IV/1, 165).[28] He says, "In 2 Cor. 5:21 we have it in a way which is almost unbearably severe: 'He (God) hath made him to be sin who knew no sin.' . . . He was made a curse for us, as Paul unhesitatingly concluded from Dt. 21:33 (Gal. 3:13)" (165).

---

[26]   Barth's writing is shot through with wide-ranging scriptural references from both testaments, making it difficult to isolate any one set of passages as primary. Yet certain texts do stand out, either because of the frequency of their occurrence or because their logic determines an overarching theological point.

[27]   Hans Frei, *The Identity of Jesus Christ: The Hermeneutical Bases of Dogmatic Theology* (Eugene, Ore.: Wipf & Stock, 2013), 131.

[28]   Emphasis added.

Assuming flesh, becoming lost, becoming sin is what it means that "in Christ God was reconciling the world to himself" (2 Cor 5:19).

"Becoming sin" is also intimately linked with having "compassion," which is conceptually and rhetorically central to the Parable of the Prodigal Son.[29] This connection is apparent in Barth's excursus on the σπλάγχνα of God and the man Jesus (IV/2, 184f.). Commenting on the verse, "But when [Jesus] saw the multitudes, he was moved with compassion on them, because they fainted, and were scattered abroad, as sheep having no shepherd" (Matt 9:36; cf. Luke 1:78; 15:20), Barth says, of this word ἐσπλαγχνίσθη:

> The expression is a strong one which defies adequate translation. [Jesus] was not only affected to the heart by the misery which surrounded Him—sympathy in our modern sense is far too feeble a word—but *it went right into His heart, into Himself,* so that *it was now His* misery. He took it from them and *laid it on Himself* . . . He Himself *suffered in their place* . . . Jesus had made [their cry] His own. (184)[30]

The compassion of God in Christ is by no means a form of disinterested mercy. It is fundamentally self-implicating. Compassion means: laden with an alien burden, in the place of and for the sake of another. Taking the masses "into his heart" in this way, Jesus embodies the whole history of humankind, miserable and perishing. He refigures in himself the people of God captive and wandering in the desert, Israel in exile, the psalmist descending into the pit, the Jewish boy humiliated in gentile land and wasting away feeding pigs. He stands under their "curse" (Gal 3:13) as its "Bearer" (IV/2, 92). What Barth is saying is that divine compassion is a kind of substitution, but only as an intimate kind of assumption.

---

[29]   Barth makes the connection between compassion, substitution, and the Parable of the Prodigal Son more explicit in *The Humanity of God,* where he says, "In this divinely free volition and election, in this sovereign decision . . . God is *human.* His free affirmation of man, His free concern for him, His free substitution for him—that is God's humanity. . . . Is it not true that in Jesus Christ, as He is attested in the Holy Scripture, genuine deity includes in itself genuine humanity? There is the father who cares for his lost son, the king who does the same for his insolvent debtor, the Samaritan who takes pity on the one who fell among robbers and in his thoroughgoing act of compassion cares for him in a fashion as unexpected as it is liberal. And this is the act of compassion to which all these parables as parables of the Kingdom of heaven refer. The very One who speaks in these parables takes to His heart the weakness and the perversity, the helplessness and the misery, of the human race surrounding him . . . takes them to his heart and sets Himself in their place." Karl Barth, *The Humanity of God,* trans. John Newton Thomas and Thomas Wieser (Richmond, Va.: John Knox, 1960), 51.

[30]   Emphasis added. Compare to the parallel passage in Barth's exegesis of Luke 15:11–32 (IV/2, 23) cited above and the note on Luther's *Commentary on Galatians.*

Jesus bears the weight of human flesh as its "head," the representative and servant of the people. When Barth says, "The New Testament describes the Son of God as the servant, indeed as the Suffering Servant of God," he is alluding to Isaiah 53, which serves as another important hermeneutical intertext throughout his doctrine of reconciliation and specifically in connection with the parable (IV/1, 164). Jesus Christ is preeminently the "servant" who "has borne our infirmities and carried our diseases . . . stricken, struck down by God, and afflicted . . . wounded for our transgressions, crushed for our iniquities . . . oppressed . . . like a lamb that is led to the slaughter . . . like an offering for sin" in order to bear many "offspring" and "make many righteous" (Isa 53:4–7, 10–11). That Barth frequently merges the language of Son and Servant is not without scriptural precedent. Explaining his decision to address the doctrines of justification and sanctification under the headings "The Lord as Servant" and "The Servant as Lord," Barth says:

> There is at least one stratum in the tradition, still maintained in the 2nd century, in which Jesus Christ (Mt. 12:18; Acts. 3:13, 26; 4:27, 30) is not called υἱός [son], or rather this concept is given a particular nuance in reminiscence of David and the Servant of the Lord (Is. 53) and He is called the holy παῖς θεοῦ [child or servant of God]. (IV/1, 194)[31]

The son/servant relationship is ambiguous in Scripture (e.g., Gal 4:1). On the one hand, the meaning of sonship is *heirship*, which is antithetical to the kind of servanthood that involves captivity or abjection (e.g., Exod 20:2; Gal 4:7). On the other hand, inheritance involves assuming responsibility for something or someone and is therefore a kind of service and self-giving.[32] Barth tends to stress the latter.

Although the pairing Judge/Judged is prominent in his discussion of justification, Barth also construes the sonship and servanthood of Christ in vividly

[31]   See Barth's analysis of the christological triad servant–friend–child (IV/1, 94–95, 99).

[32]   This is the emphasis in Barth's later construal of human vocation in terms of obedience and service (§74). Christologically, however, Barth primarily defines the second person's sonship in terms of servanthood defined as subordination. At times, he does acknowledge the first sense of sonship, describing sin by contrast as bondage, slavery, or subservience (IV/2, 93, 384, 405). While there are scriptural passages exhorting us to be servants/slaves of God, a different distinction is usually being made in these cases. See, e.g., Rom 6:15–23. We also encounter a paradoxical mixing of metaphors (free because bound). Even so, I would suggest that, because of the horror of its reality, slavery is not in fact a good metaphor for the divine/human relationship—and certainly not soteriologically speaking. Yet Paul "speaks in human terms," as he says, because of his audience's "natural limitations"—namely, the constriction of their imaginations by slavery to sin (v. 19).

sacerdotal terms, which is particularly true in reference to Isaiah 53. He coordinates it with the picture of reconciliation found in 2 Corinthians 5. The main content of the Son's servanthood is his self-offering. He is the priest who stands in as the sacrificial lamb. As Barth says, earlier servant figures such as Moses, David, Jeremiah, the psalmist, "and, above all, the significant figure of the Servant of the Lord in Isa. 53" are "projected shadows of the one Lamb of God which taketh away the sin of the world" (172).[33] So while it is true that Barth tends to maintain continuity in the meaning of son and servant, the tension between these roles is also indispensable to his Christology. Jesus Christ is not just a servant in the sense that we call monarchs and rulers "servants." He is not just a filial "right-hand man." He becomes "a *slave*" (II/2, 605). He assumes all that is hostile to the glory of his deity as the Son of God and to the dignity of his humanity as a child of God. He is servant both because of and despite his identity as *vere homo et vere Deus*. That is what it means that he takes on "flesh" and becomes "sin." As the Suffering Servant, "He is the Owner and Bearer, the Representative and Lord of [*this*] life"—lost and perishing (IV/2, 375; see IV/1, 29–30). His reign is concealed in the degradation of his servile death.

Undergirding these other intertextual connections, Philippians 2 overlays Barth's reading of the Parable of the Prodigal Son and shapes his account of reconciliation. In fact, much of IV/1 reads as an elaboration of the content of the first part of the christological hymn. As Barth glosses the passage:

> "He emptied (ἐκένωσεν) Himself (that is, of His divine form: He renounced it) and took the form of a servant" (v. 7); and again, "He humbled (ἐταπείνωσεν) Himself, and became obedient unto death, even the death of the cross" (v. 8). In the words of Paul Himself: "He who was rich became poor" (2 Cor. 8:9). In Heb. 5:8, "He who is the Son learned obedience in what He had to suffer." (IV/1, 165)

Barth prefers the language of "condescension," "humiliation," and "obedience" to that of "kenosis." This is due to the various associations that accrued around kenosis as "self-emptying" in a certain vein of kenotic theology.[34] Describing

---

[33]   At many similar moments, Barth appeals to Isa 53, as when he claims Christ "fulfills [God's] judgment by suffering the punishment which we have all brought on ourselves" (IV/1, 252).

[34]   Barth does not restrict the meaning of Phil 2:7–8 to Christ's human nature, as do those who uphold the *extra Calvinisticum* or an absolute *logos asarkos*. However, he also opposes the view of the "modern 'kenotics'" that "self-emptying" involves "a partial or complete abstention not only on the part of the man Jesus as such but on the part of the Son of God, the Logos Himself, from the possession and therefore the power to dispose of His divine glory and majesty, a κένωσις κτήσεως . . . the idea of a self-limitation of God in the incarnation (or, to put it in the categories of the so-called doctrine of the attributes, the possibility of a *genus tapeinoticum*)" (IV/1, 182).

the kenotic work of Christ, Barth opts for terms such as servanthood, humility, obedience, poverty, and suffering. For example, summarizing the condescension of the Son, Barth writes, "God is not proud . . . he is humble" (IV/1, 159). What is most important about this, in connection with his christological interpretation of the parable, is Barth's insistence that the form of the servant does not contradict or constrict the form of God but is precisely a function of it. In this regard, his construal of kenosis departs from seventeenth- to nineteenth-century Neo-Lutheran and Reformed treatments of it.[35] It is worth referencing him at length on this point. Barth says,

---

Calling attention to the seventeenth-century debate between the schools of Giessen and Tübingen, Barth explains that "adopting a statement of Martin Chemnitz the Giessen party taught a genuine κένωσις χρήσεως, an at any rate partial abstention by the man Jesus, in the *exinanitio*, from the use of the majesty imparted to Him. Jesus Christ *regnavit mundum*, but *non mediante carne*, only *qua* Logos, only in the power of His deity. But in Tübingen, following J. Brenz, there was taught a far more subtle κρύψις χρήσεως, an abstention by the man Jesus in the *exinanitio* only from the visible use, a *retractatio* and *occultatio* of the revelation of His power, or positively, a majesty of the Son of God which is, in fact, exercised and operative and actual, but concealed." The problem is heightened in the late nineteenth- to early twentieth-century "alternative" of Gottfried Thomasius and "the more extreme" Wolfgang Gess: "a partial or complete abstention not only on the part of the man Jesus as such but on the part of the Son of God, the Logos Himself, from the possession and therefore the power to dispose of His divine glory and majesty, a κένωσις κτήσεως" (183). Just as Barth is concerned about any construal of the *communicatio idiomatum* in which Christ's humanity is divinized, he is wary of any version in which Christ appears dedivinized.

   [35]   In Sarah Coakley's assessment of kenotic Christologies, we can discern six distinct historical interpretations of what the kenosis means for the relationship between two natures of Christ: (1) a temporary "relinquishing" of "the divine powers that are Christ's by right" (of which Martin Chemnitz' position seem to be a variant) (11); (2) a "pretending" to relinquishing divine power while retaining it (based on Barth's description, John Brentz could be located here); (3) a "choosing *never to have* certain (false and worldly) forms of power" (Coakley considers the Giessen school a variant of this type, although, for them, kenosis is specifically "operative" in the human rather than the divine nature) (11, 17); (4) a "*revealing*" that divine power is inherently "humble"; (5) a "taking on" of human reality "but without loss, impairment, or restriction of divine powers" (Hilary, Cyril, and Alexandrian interpreters of Chalcedon); and (6) "a temporary retracting (or withdrawing into 'potency') of *certain* characteristics of divinity" during Christ's incarnate life (Thomasius and other late nineteenth- to early twentieth-century Lutheran and British kenoticists) (18–19). See "*Kenōsis* and Subversion: On the Repression of 'Vulnerability' in Christian Feminist Writing," in *Powers and Submissions: Spirituality, Philosophy and Gender* (Malden, Mass.: Blackwell, 2002), 3–39. On the basis of the following passage—which is representative of Barth's view—it seems Barth, like Hilary and Cyril, could be situated within Coakley's fifth type since he maintains that kenosis is a *divine* (rather than strictly human) work that involves ontological gain rather than loss.

It was not to [Christ] an inalienable necessity to exist *only* in the form of God, only to be God, and therefore only to be different from the creature . . . He was not committed to any such "only." *In addition* to His form in the likeness of God He could also—and this involves at once a making poor, a humiliation, a condescension, and to that extent a κένωσις—take the form of a servant. He could be like man. . . . He had this other possibility: the possibility of divine self-giving to the being and fate of man. He had the freedom for this condescension, for this concealment of His Godhead. He had it and He made use of it in the power and *not with any loss, not with any diminution or alteration of his Godhead.* That is His self-emptying. It does not consist in ceasing to be Himself as man, but in *taking it upon Himself to be Himself in a way quite other than that which corresponds and belongs to His form as God.* His being equal with God, he can also go into the far country and be there, with all that involves. And so He does go into the far country, and is there. According to Phil. 2 this means His becoming [human], the incarnation. (IV/1, 180)[36]

What often gets translated "self-emptying" or "self-giving" is thus defined rather in terms of an assumption, a "taking it upon Himself to be Himself" in another way. Inasmuch as it is a "renunciation," it is a renunciation not of being God but of *only* being God. It means the freedom to be God and be an-other too, to be "more than" God alone. Taking on another form, the form of the human, is Barth's definition of divine "self-giving." This "humility," this ability, is not "alien" but "proper" to God (193). It belongs to Christ to be equal with the Father (divine) not despite but because of his ability to identify with the lost son (human). Condescension is not foreign to deity; it is not an infringement of but a manifestation of it.

The descent or humility of God expressed in Philippians 2 is consistently narrated in the language of the parable (e.g., 158, 164, 168, 180, 203). The kenosis (Phil 2:7) or "far journey" of the Son (Luke 15) is coordinated with becoming flesh (John 1:14), being the second Adam (Rom 5), becoming sin and a curse (2 Cor 5:21; Gal 3:13), being the Suffering Servant (Isa 53), and so on. These vital intertexts (esp. Rom 5:14f.; 2 Cor 5; Isa 53:10; and Phil 2:5f.) amplify one another, and their content fills out what Barth means by "condescension" and "humiliation" with "the concrete biblical form of these qualities and of God Himself" (II/2, 135). Again, he does not apportion this lot to the humanity of Christ but to his deity: "He is His own master in such a way that He can go into the far country" and genuinely become lost humanity without thereby losing himself (IV/1, 204). Atonement is not a matter of the substitution of the perfect humanity of Jesus for sinful humanity. It is a mat-

---

[36]   Emphasis added.

ter of God Godself in the place of the sinner, the wayward servant, the fallen son. God is revealed as the one who enters into the pit, the pigsty, the grave. Barth concludes, "The *forma Dei* consists in the grace in which God Himself assumes and makes His own the *forma servi*" (187).[37] The divine form, the divine essence, is grace.[38] God is God's grace.

That Barth's intertextual interpretation of the parable exceeds the parameters of a strictly soteriological reading is readily apparent then. To see Jesus Christ following after prodigal humanity, in salvific solidarity with the lost son, is not a strain once we recognize the structural resonances in the scriptural images and narratives with which Julian and Barth overlay the parable. What is startling in his retelling, as in Julian's, is not that the "fall" of Christ succeeds humanity's but that it is said to coincide with, or rather precede, it—an assertion that ultimately pushes atonement back before creation into the doctrine of God proper.

Parable of Election

The most prominent connection between the parable and the atonement is the twofold structural parallel of "going out" and "homecoming." But Christ further relates to the younger son's trajectory as "the way"—the guide and also the path.[39] Barth says he is "primarily and properly *the way* to that home of man . . . the way to . . . fellowship with God," and, on this way, "He *precedes* all men as a King who draws them after Him" (IV/2, 24).[40] He is first on the circuit outward and homeward and constitutes that circuit in himself. It is for this reason that Barth claims we must see the story of the "refound son" as only a

---

[37] Notably the word κένωσις appears only once in the Bible. Therefore, as an exegetical rule, Barth is absolutely right to avoid defining it on its own terms (as "emptying") and to discern its meaning, instead, by reference to other closely related passages.

[38] Barth makes multiple comments to this effect in II/1. For example, "Grace is the very essence of the being of God. Grace is itself properly and essentially divine. . . . God Himself is it" (II/1, 356); and "His whole being . . . is simply grace" (358). The claim about grace as a divine perfection is radicalized in Barth's reworking of election in II/2. As Robert Jenson explains it, for Barth, "God is not a thing but an *event*. And the event which is God is exactly the event of Jesus' self-giving to his fellows." *God after God: The God of the Past and the God of the Future Seen in the Work of Karl Barth* (New York: Bobbs-Merrill, 1969), 72.

[39] Using the plurivalent "way" (*Weg*), Barth reminds us that the peregrination of the younger son is not only a matter of waywardness and alienation. It also evokes, more positively, holy pilgrimage (which Julian mentions), obedience to God, the "royal way" of Num 20–21, the narrow entry of the kingdom, the imitation of Christ, and so on. There are different ways of going-through-the-land (*per-ager*).

[40] Emphasis added.

"reflection," "caricature," or "shadow" of the eternal Son and his journey. Jesus Christ follows, but only inasmuch as he precedes—and not in the fact of his being only, but in this quality of his being: his prodigality. How can he be the original prodigal Son? According to the logic of election.

Barth's christologically grounded account of election (in §32–33) prefigures his later retelling of reconciliation through the Parable of the Prodigal Son. The language of the parable and the trajectory of his interpretation of it are already present in II/2, where becoming the "lost son" is one of the primary images used for the content of the divine decree. Barth asks, "Who is the Elect? He is always the one who 'was dead and is alive again,' who 'was lost and is found' (Lk. 15:24)" (124). He goes on to say:

> As the beginning of all things with God we find the decree that He Himself in person, in the person of His eternal Son, should give Himself to the son of man, the lost son of man, indeed that He Himself in the person of the eternal Son should *be* the lost Son of Man. (157)

God does not become lost and prodigal by a historical accident, as an afterthought or a response to creation gone awry. God wills from before time to be prodigal in love, to be *the* original prodigal in and as the eternal Son, the second person of the Trinity. "It is not accidental. It could not be otherwise" (IV/1, 176). For, in election, God has always already sought out lost humanity, has always already "made the being of this other His own being" (II/2, 121).[41]

The Doctrine of Election

This is an uncommon way of framing the doctrine. It constitutes a "revolutionary refashioning" of election.[42] Without this development, it is difficult

---

[41]   The connection between the Parable of the Prodigal Son and Barth's refashioned doctrine of election is all the more striking in that the dynamic between the prodigal son and his elder brother evokes the story of Jacob stealing Esau's birthright, a story that is commonly cited as evidence for the sort of Calvinist double predestination Barth specifically rejects ("Jacob I loved, but Esau I have hated"; Mal 1:3; Rom 9:13). Instead, for Barth, the younger son represents, on one level, the history of Israel, Israel in exile, disobedient Israel. But, precisely for that reason, the younger son also symbolizes, on another level, outcasts of all kinds, even gentiles. Becoming prodigal, Jesus Christ takes on both identities as the dual facets of human sin ("pride" and "sloth").

[42]   Jones, *Humanity of Christ*, 38. With the doctrine of election, as with the rest of *Church Dogmatics*, we must remember that "Barth has not simply taken over unchanged *any* doctrinal formulation of the ancient or the Reformation churches. He has reconstructed the whole of 'orthodox' teaching from the ground up. It is not the case that he simply tinkered with the machinery" (McCormack, *Orthodox and Modern*, 16).

to grasp the coherence of Barth's identification of the prodigal son with Jesus Christ (in §59 and §64). In fact, according to McCormack, the subsequent interpretive "christocentrism" of *Church Dogmatics* is really "a function of his doctrine of election."[43] The excursus on Luke 15:11–32 in VI/2 is no exception. Because Barth's radical reworking of election undergirds his later interpretation of the parable, it is worth briefly reiterating a number of its distinctive features.

Most fundamentally, Barth comes to believe that election is only intelligible in light of Jesus Christ, who is himself the concrete revelation of the will of God. For this first insight, he is indebted to Pierre Maury's paper on election in 1936, which prompted him to revise his doctrine as it had been laid out in §18 of the *Göttingen Dogmatics*. Barth integrated Maury's central thesis: "Outside of Christ, we know neither of the electing God, nor of His elect, nor of the act of election."[44] This leads him to reject any presentation of the doctrine as an abstract principle or *decretum absolutum* that has priority over or meaning apart from the Gospel. He says it is "a concrete decree," having as its content a "name," a "person." "This decree is Jesus Christ," therefore "it cannot be a *decretum absolutum*" (158).[45] In Barth's view, the christological reference must shape the details of the doctrine at every point. Election is not to be thought of as "secondary" or "supplementary" to the revelation of God in Christ (89–90).

Second, election means "self-election." It is a "decision" (*Entscheidung*) God makes with respect to Godself, and it demonstrates that God is "lord" even of God's own being.[46] In other words, "the primary object of election is not humankind but God."[47] That God is "the One who loves in freedom" is a recurrent claim throughout *Church Dogmatics* (II/1, 257). Based on his exposition of Exodus 3:14, Barth says God is "*free also with regard to His freedom*, free . . . to use it to give Himself to this communion and to practice this

---

[43]   McCormack, *Orthodox and Modern*, 87.

[44]   Pierre Maury, *Erwählung und Glaube*, Theologische Studien 8 (Zurich: EVZ, 1940), 7. Quoted in English by Bruce L. McCormack, *Karl Barth's Critically Realistic Dialectical Theology: Its Genesis and Development 1909–1936* (New York: Oxford University Press, 1995), 457.

[45]   Barth rejects the notion found in Calvinist theology and the Canons of Dordt of predestination as an absolute decree of God that has a "self-sufficient" basis outside of or before Jesus Christ.

[46]   I will continue to use Barth's word "decision" with respect to the divine decree but acknowledge it is heavily freighted with later debates over Barth's voluntarism (which I am setting aside, along with most ontological questions, in order to focus on narrative and character).

[47]   McCormack, "The Sum of the Gospel," in *Orthodox and Modern*, 57.

faithfulness in it, in this way being really free, free in Himself" (303).[48] That is to say, "the concept of being is measured by the concept of God," rather than vice versa.[49] In Jüngel's paraphrase, "God's primal decision to go into the far country is certainly not a decision forced upon [God] from the far country, not something *foreign to* [God], but [a] *free* decision."[50] Against the view that God is absolutely unconditioned, Barth holds up "the picture of the Son of God who is self-conditioned and therefore conditioned in His union with the Son of David" (II/2, 134). Election, then, is God's free self-specification or "self-constitution" as the covenant-partner, Lord, and Shepherd of humankind (54).

Third, Christ is not merely the object or means of executing election, but, as the Son of God, he is also the *subject* of election.[51] It is not enough to consider Christ "the most illustrious *example*" and "the brightest *illustration*" of predestination and grace," as Calvin does, following Augustine.[52] In that case, Christ becomes "only" an "organ which serves the function of the electing will of God, as the means toward the attainment of the end" (65). However, "the electing of the Father and that of the Son are one and the same." The "self-ordination" of God is the self-ordination of the Son (89). Jesus Christ is also the electing God, the active subject of election whose existence is productive rather than merely illustrative of its meaning.

Fourth, election has no meaning other than grace. For Barth, "election" is always short for "the election of divine grace" (from Rom 11:5, ἐκλογὴν

---

[48]   Emphasis added. See II/1, §§28–31 on God's lordship or freedom with respect to God's own being. Jones says of Barth's treatment of Exod 3:14, "Crucial to Barth's presentation is his construal of decision (*Entscheidung*) as an ontological category descriptive of God's capacity for, and enactment of, self-definition. . . . God decides on God's character" (*Humanity of Christ*, 68–69). This ontological claim sets the stage for the highly particular content of the divine self-definition presented in II/2, especially in §§32–33.

[49]   Eberhard Jüngel, *God's Being Is in Becoming: The Trinitarian Being of God in the Theology of Karl Barth; A Paraphrase*, trans. John Webster (London: T&T Clark, 2001), 78. God is not an Unmoved Mover but the Self-Moved Mover. See *CD* II/1, 268.

[50]   Jüngel, *God's Being Is in Becoming*, 15.

[51]   The distinctive trouble with "the older Protestant tradition" is that "we cannot fix our gaze and keep it fixed on Jesus Christ, because the electing God is not identical with Christ but behind and above Him, because in the beginning with God we have to reckon with someone or something other than the οτος of Jn. 1:2 . . . a decision of the divine good-pleasure quite unrelated to and not determined by Him" (II/2, 110). Contrary to the view of election as a "principle which has priority over the person and work of Jesus Christ, so that Jesus Christ is to be understood as the mighty executive organ" of the divine decision, Barth maintains that Jesus Christ is both the subject and the object of election, electing God and elected human (IV/3.1, 175).

[52]   Calvin, *Institutes* II.17.476 (emphasis added).

χάριτος) (9–10). It is, all the way through, an expression of God's basic and unalloyed loving-kindness toward humans.[53] As Barth says, "What takes place in this election is always that God is *for us*" (25, emphasis added). Election is "in favour of this other" (10) and to its "advantage" (121). Its goal is fellowship (*Gemeinschaft*) (121). Election is not "neutral," then, but has the definite character of love, or "good-pleasure" (134, 157). Barth understands "the original ordination of [humankind] to salvation and of salvation for [humankind] as the meaning and basis even of the divine creative will" (IV/1, 19). It "is grace, loving-kindness, favor" (II/2, 28). It has the character of "self-giving" (121). It is thus "the Gospel *in nuce*" (14).

Consequently, fifth, election can be regarded as a "double predestination" only in a very peculiar and limited sense. According to Barth, the root problem with the traditional presentation of predestination is that "the divine election and the divine rejection came to be spoken of as inter-connected divine acts similar in character and determination," as "a double divine decision from all eternity . . . with two parallel sides" (16).[54] At one point Barth says, "The verdict of God to which faith subjects itself is two-sided" (93). It is a verdict that "disowns and renounces" but also "recognizes and accepts" (94). But Barth rejects the kind of "double predestination" in which the elect and the reprobate are conceived as two classes of humanity, the one eternally beloved and the other eternally condemned. Instead, Barth claims that election "is not a mixed message of joy and terror, salvation and damnation. Originally and finally it is not dialectical but non-dialectical" (13). There is no "equilibrium" between God's "Yes" and "No" (134). "It is altogether Yes" (13). This "Yes" is "without any if or but, without any afterthought or reservation, not temporarily but definitively, with a fidelity which is not partial and temporal but total and eternal" (31). This is true for humanity precisely because predestination is indeed "double" in a different sense—that is, with respect to its primary referent: Jesus Christ, who is both the electing God and the elected human (162).[55] It is not

---

[53]   See §30, where Barth addresses the meaning of "grace" at length.

[54]   Barth says, "We cannot be too soon, or too radical, in the opposition which we must offer to the classical tradition" (13). He specifically calls out Augustine and the Reformers because, for them, "predestination means quite unequivocally double predestination" (17). Likewise, Barth rejects what he calls Calvin's "fatal parallelism" of the concepts of election and rejection" (see *Institutes* III.21.5).

[55]   In §32, Barth focuses on undermining the equation of election with the traditional version of "double predestination." He emphasizes the divine "Yes" in this portion of II/2, without much mention of an attendant "No." In §33, however, Barth affirms a "double decree," but only because by this point he has invested it with a new meaning. Under the heading "double decree" and "double predestination," Barth

an either/or for humans; it is a both/and for Jesus Christ. He is himself the "double decree." In him, God elects reprobation, the negative side, for Godself, "refusing to let it be our foreordination in any form" (166, 172). There is no remainder. To the extent that "predestination does contain a No, it is not a No spoken against [humans]" (166). "It is God Himself who is rejected," and for that reason "predestination is the non-rejection of the human" (167, rev.). As McCormack says, reprobation is "a moment on a way which God goes with His people; a way whose goal is election."[56] The end is "implicitly" that it may never be the "portion" allotted to humanity or any segment of it. As Barth glosses Romans 8:1, "There is no condemnation—literally none" (II/2, 167). He is thus able to maintain what Calvin could not, that "there was no divine predisposition towards evil, but only 'a divine predisposition towards salvation (election)' *for all* lost" humans.[57]

That is to say, sixth, there can be no *decretum generale* that is not rooted in the prior election of Jesus Christ (78). Election is only ever election "in him," in the same sense that salvation is salvation "in him." He is the first among the elect—not as the beginning of a series, but as the one who gathers and represents all others in himself. In Barth's succinct definition, "In the beginning with God was this One, Jesus Christ. And that is predestination" (II/2, 145).

In view of this, seventh, it goes without saying that Barth's version of predestination is decidedly *supralapsarian*.[58] This means the election (and reprobation)

---

treats the "passive" and "active" determinations of Jesus Christ. Reprobation receives greater attention here, but it is assigned wholly to Christ rather than a certain segment of humanity.

[56]   McCormack, *Karl Barth's Critically Realistic Dialectical Theology*, 457.

[57]   Busch, *Karl Barth*, 442.

[58]   The central question in seventeenth-century Reformed debates over the object of predestination is this: When we say that God from all eternity elected (or rejected) humans, was God thinking of *homo creabilis et labilis* (humanity yet to be created and to fall) or *homo creatus et lapsus* (humanity already created and fallen)? Supralapsarianism is the position that God forms creatures for salvation or damnation *before* the creation and fall of the world. In this case, God's confrontation with evil and sin is not a "later and additional struggle in which God is dealing with a new and to some extent disruptive feature in His original plan. On the contrary, it must be thought of as an element in that original plan itself" (II/2, 128–29). Barth names certain Calvinist exponents here (e.g., Beza, Bucanus, Comarus, Maccovius, Heidanus, and Burmann) but does not appear to have Calvin himself in mind. He thinks it is unclear whether Calvin really develops a supralapsarian position, although he certainly made statements that move in that direction (127). Over against supralapsarianism, infralapsarians maintain that the object of election is created and fallen humanity. This becomes the dominant view at the Synod of Dort. Barth relies on Turrettini to express the important distinc-

of Jesus Christ precedes creation and fall as God's *"first* thought and decree" with respect to the world. Barth presses this point further than his supralapsarian predecessors by including election in the doctrine of God, not merely as God's first act *ad extra* but, again, as God's own self-electing. In Jones' words, "God elementally intends the incarnation."[59] This is so thoroughly the case for Barth that we can say God's "intention to attain genuine companionship with humankind is basic to God's being."[60]

Finally, this primal "self-ordination" and its manifestation and fulfillment in creation and incarnation do not detract from or contradict God's glory. Rather, bringing it back to Barth's interpretation of Philippians 2, "It is in being gracious . . . that God sets forth His own glory." The election of grace "is how the inner glory of God overflows" (121). Barth thus refrains from opposing God's righteousness and mercy, God's being *in se* and God's activity *ad extra* and *pro nobis*, God's freedom and love, divine glory and human glory.[61] In being faithful to the covenant with Abraham, Israel, and Isaac, God is also being perfectly faithful to Godself.

Eternal Atonement

This construal of election raises what Jüngel calls "the christological question of the significance of the *finite* being of Jesus Christ, and therefore, of the *death* of Jesus Christ for the being of God."[62] Of concern is whether God's self-determination in election and incarnation "constitutes" God's triunity and/or entails a "transformation" of divine being, a question that continues to

---

tion within infralapsarianism, which does not regard reprobation as an original intent in creation. Rather "man is the object of the eternal predestination precisely in the situation in which God knows him as the one whom He will encounter in time" (131). Otherwise, predestination would appear neither just nor merciful. Barth's own position is emphatically supra- rather than infralapsarian. However, its character differs markedly from its seventeenth-century antecedents in that (1) Jesus Christ is the proper object of election and reprobation, and (2) he does not give equal weighting to election and reprobation (140). For a different reading of Barth on this point, see Shao Kai Tseng, *Karl Barth's Infralapsarian Theology: Origins and Development 1920–1953* (Downers Grove, Ill.: IVP Academic, 2016). Tseng argues Barth's doctrine of election retains infralapsarian elements.

[59] Jones, *Humanity of Christ*, 84.

[60] Jones, *Humanity of Christ*, 126.

[61] As Barth says in *Humanity of God*, "How could God's deity exclude His humanity, since it is God's freedom for love and thus His capacity to be not only in the heights but also in the depths, not only great but also small, not only in and for Himself but also with another distinct from Him, and to offer Himself to him?" (49).

[62] Jüngel, *God's Being Is in Becoming*, 3.

be interrogated by a growing number of theologians.[63] While it is difficult to ignore the ontological underpinnings of Barth's christological interpretation of the parable, I have been drawing out another focal point to show how the parable narrates not only reconciliation but also, and therefore, election.[64] Keeping the meaning of his theological retelling as descriptive and textually grounded

[63]   For two positions on one side, see George Hunsinger, "Election and the Trinity: Twenty-Five Theses on the Theology of Karl Barth," *Modern Theology* 24, no. 2 (2008): 179–98; Paul Molnar, *Divine Freedom and the Doctrine of the Immanent Trinity* (London: T&T Clark, 2002); and Molnar, "The Trinity, Election, and God's Ontological Freedom: A Response to Kevin Hector," *International Journal of Systematic Theology* 8, no. 3 (2006): 294–306. For related positions on the other side, see, for example, Bruce L. McCormack, "Grace and Being: The Role of God's Gracious Election in Karl Barth's Theological Ontology," *The Cambridge Companion to Karl Barth*, ed. John Webster (Cambridge: Cambridge University Press, 2000); Kevin Hector, "God's Triunity and Self-Determination: A Conversation with Karl Barth, Bruce McCormack and Paul Molnar," *International Journal of Systematic Theology* 7, no. 3 (2005): 246–61; and Jones, *Humanity of Christ* (esp. ch. 2). As Paul Nimmo concisely articulates the problem, "If the incarnation of Jesus Christ is thus constitutive of the being of God in eternity, then, it must be the case that, for Barth . . . the act of election logically precedes the triunity of God." Nimmo, "Election and Evangelical Thinking," in *New Perspectives in Evangelical Theology: Engaging with God, Scripture, and the World*, ed. Tom Greggs (London: Routledge, 2010), 34. Similarly, in Paul Jones' interpretation, "[Barth] undertakes a thoroughgoing integration of his doctrines of God and Christ, whereby God's sovereign elective act—God's extreme love for humanity, realized by way of the incarnation—*transforms* God's eternal being" (*Humanity of Christ*, 65 [emphasis added]). Significantly, Bruce McCormack revises his earlier position, moving away from the idea that Trinity is a function of election for Barth and instead claiming "election and triunity are equally primordial in God." See McCormack, "The Doctrine of the Trinity after Barth: An Attempt to Reconstruct Barth's Doctrine in Light of His Later Christology," in *Trinitarian Theology after Barth*, ed. Myk Habets and Phillip Tolliday (Cambridge: James Clarke, 2021), 113.

[64]   I am mostly sidestepping the debate over the ontological ramifications of election for several reasons: (1) it is beyond the scope of my topic to treat all the attendant doctrinal and metaphysical issues; (2) others have already done so sufficiently and at length (see note above); (3) by its nature, the matter falls outside the purview of the narrative frame I have assumed because (4) when we limit our attention to *who* God is, rather than *what* God is, the metaphysical questions about self-constitution become secondary. "Who" concerns character, personality, identity—they are narratival. While I believe Barth's exegesis of the parable reinforces his account of the election of grace in II/2 as a "self-determination" of God in God's second way of being, I am not addressing how this works on an ontological level. To enter that discussion would require protracted attention to questions concerning God's aseity, immutability, eternity, and temporality, among other issues. I am likewise setting aside whether or how the Son's assumption of human flesh has a "retroactive" impact on his eternal being and many of the questions about what this would mean for Barth's configuration of the so-called "immanent" and "economic" trinities.

as possible, the attention has been on what Barth is trying to say about divine character, or will, rather than divine being—if that is indeed something else.[65] The "God" of which we speak is not any God, much less an abstract "divine nature," but, Barth is very clear, it is the God of Abraham, Isaac, and Jacob, the God of Israel incarnate in Jesus of Nazareth. This "is" defies any counterfactual or hypothetical description of God's essence apart from God's love for the world revealed in Christ. A narrative approach is a matter of playing up and putting into practice Barth's own assertion that theology must begin and end with the particular name and (hi)story of Jesus Christ (II/2, 4). For his "name is not merely a cipher"—it is the thing itself (IV/1, 21). And a name can only be narrated. The Parable of the Lost Son appears on a third interpretive level to narrate this whole account of election. It is more than a "parable of the kingdom." On Barth's retelling, it is the Parable of God. It recounts the primordial prodigality of God in God's second way of being.

"The doctrine of election is the sum of the Gospel," as Barth concisely summarizes the matter in the précis of §32 (II/2, 3). It is the "best" word because it tells us that "God elects humanity," that "God is for humanity" as "the One who loves in freedom." Election "is grounded in the knowledge of Jesus Christ,"

---

[65]   Admittedly, a narrative or parabolic approach of this sort may pose challenges for theological ontology—something revisited in the conclusion. I am not considering, as is so often the case in classical doctrines of God, what or who God is apart from God's decision in favor of fellowship with the world. To do so would be to depend on, inadvertently I assume, a counterfactual and thus, ironically, still involves construing God's being anthropomorphically—in terms of the past ("was"), a hypothetical ("would have been"), and/or temporality or spatiality ("before"). A major criticism, from the side of "perfect being theology," of the view that the atonement (election and incarnation) has a retroactive "effect" on the being of God is that this implies "change" in God, which is thought to be an anthropomorphic misunderstanding of deity. But Barth's point is precisely that the notion of an abstract "supreme being" who cannot freely self-determine for relationship with the world is an idolatrous constraint imposed on (and by) theology. According to Barth, God has freely elected a real relation with the world in the second person of the Trinity (II/2, 6–7). As Jüngel notes, Barth's choice of accent is action rather than ontology such that God's *will* comes to define God's essence (*God's Being Is in Becoming*, 6). Like Jüngel, Hans Theodor Goebel notes a shift in emphasis from *CD* I, on God's "ability," to *CD* II, on God's "will." Goebel, "Trinitätslehre und Erwählungslehre bei Karl Barth: Eine Problemanzeige," in *Wahrheit und Versöhnung: Theologische und Philosophische Beiträge zur Gotteslehre*, ed. Dietrich Korsch and Harmut Ruddies (Gütersloh: Gütersloher Verlagshaus Gerg Mohn, 1989), 147–66. Cited by Jones, *Humanity of Christ*, 64, n. 15. This is an interesting similarity with Julian, who treats all that God "might" and "can" do as hypothetical. She contrasts the naked "power" of God with what God *has done* in actuality—"loveth tenderly"—which reveals God's "heart." See Julian's Long Text, 77.11–15.

and, by the same token, "it is part of the doctrine of God," for, again, "God's election of humanity is a predestination not merely of humanity but of God Godself." The doctrine has as its "function" that it "bear basic testimony" to the fact that "eternal, free and unchanging grace" is "the beginning of all the ways and works of God." Barth thus rejects the common premise that "election" refers to a two-pronged decision God makes with respect to the salvation and damnation of certain individuals, whether before or after creation and fall. For him, election is fundamentally a matter of the identity and character of the second person of the Trinity. The divine decree is a person, a relationship. It is a matter of God's "basic" decision to be united with humanity in the most intimate and costly way (25). It is a "primal relationship" (52).

The inextricable interpenetration of the doctrines of reconciliation and election is evident throughout II/2 and IV/1–2. Moving seamlessly between the pairings "Reconciling God"/"Reconciled Man" and "Electing God"/"Elected Man," Barth describes election as an "eternal covenant" and regards this covenant as "the presupposition of reconciliation" (III/1, 97). Frequently referring to "the eternal decree" in terms of the Son's "journey into the far country," he speaks of the exaltation of "the Royal Man" as the fulfillment of God's eternal self-determination in election for fellowship with humankind (e.g., IV/1, 22, 158–59, 170, etc.).[66] This doctrinal coinherence is confirmed quite explicitly when Barth makes claims such as: the doctrine of election is the "mystery of the doctrine of reconciliation" (II/2, 89), or: "the grace and work and revelation of God has the particular character of election" (IV/1, 170). Likewise, the point is made when he asserts, "*The doctrine of election is the last or first or central word in the whole doctrine of reconciliation. . . .* But the doctrine of reconciliation is itself the first or last or central word in the whole Christian confession" (II/2, 88).[67] According to Barth, election is oriented toward reconciliation, which is the secret to its truth. The subject matter is always, in his words, "the doctrine of the election *which took place in Jesus Christ*" (II/2, 89, emphasis added). Barth says, "Reconciliation is revelation."[68] Election, too, is revelation.

---

[66]   In fact, according to Busch, Barth considered titling his doctrine of reconciliation "the doctrine of the covenant" (*Karl Barth*, 377).

[67]   Emphasis added.

[68]   "Reconciliation is revelation" is a phrase central to Barth's treatment of Christ's *munus propheticum* (IV/3.1, 8, 38, 182), not treated here, and sums up an important network of claims running through *Church Dogmatics*. Perhaps most significantly, it echoes Barth's pervasive epistemological assertion that the truth of God is genuinely accessible through Jesus Christ (38). As Barth says, Christ "Himself is the 'epistemological principle'" (IV/1, 21). In him, God genuinely becomes

His intertextual application of the parable gives content to what he believes election reveals about God. In particular, the Son's becoming lost, his taking on of the wayward one's burden, is consistently paired with "condescension" and shapes its meaning. Again, Barth himself avoids the word "kenosis" for particular reasons, but in *Church Dogmatics* II/2 the downward/outward and upward/homeward structure of the parable is frequently overlain with the language and logic of Philippians 2, as it is later in IV/1–2. Election is an eternal self-giving in the Trinity, one that contains and grounds the temporal kenosis of incarnation and the cross.[69] Barth speaks of the ἐκλογὴν χάριτος as a "movement" and "primal history," which he calls "the form of the deepest condescension" (9–10). He says, for example, "It is love which is merciful in making this movement, this act of condescension, in such a way that in *taking to itself* this other, it *identifies* itself with its need, and meets its plight by *making it its own concern*" (10).[70] Condescension is a moving-toward and an identifying-with. Barth says, "This self-identification is identical with the decree of His movement toward man" (91–92). As he explains at the beginning of his exposition of election, "Jesus Christ is indeed God in His movement toward [*Zuwendung*] [humanity] . . . Jesus Christ is the decision [*Entscheidung*] of God in favor of this attitude or relation [*Verhalten*]. He is Himself the relation" (II/2, 7).

Christ is God's compassionate condescension in election as in reconciliation; he is the divine decree and self-determination of God for fellowship with humanity; he is God's comportment toward or way of regarding humanity;

---

an "object" (IV/3.1, 217) or a phenomenon for human understanding. This enables Barth to sidestep Kant's relegation of "God" to the category of *noumenal* or unknowable in his *Critique of Pure Reason*. As Jüngel puts it, that "the prophetic office of Jesus Christ discloses his being in his work of reconciliation as a speech-event" is "Barth's staring-point for overcoming the 'subject-object' schema" (*God's Being Is in Becoming*, 14, n. 1). Concomitantly it is an ontological affirmation: the grace of God in Jesus Christ is the essence of God Godself (II/1, 351). Thus it is also a claim about the nature of reconciliation: Jesus announces the twofold material content of justification and sanctification as he enacts and achieves it (and this announcement is none other than the self-announcement of God) (IV/3.1, 8, 38f.). Finally, it is applicable anthropologically in that through reconciliation in Christ we have the true disclosure of humanity—in its creatureliness, sinfulness, and transformation (e.g., IV/2, 384; IV/3.1, 106–7, 182, etc.)—as well as the absurd reality of evil and "nothingness" (*das Nichtige*).

69   See Hans Urs von Balthasar, *Mysterium Paschale*, trans. Aidan Nichols, O.P. (San Francisco: Ignatius, 1990); and *Theo-Drama: Theological Dramatic Theory*, vol. 5, *The Last Act*, trans. Graham Harrison (San Francisco: Ignatius, 1998).

70   Emphasis added.

and he is in himself God's binding relation to humanity. Barth writes in *Dogmatics in Outline*,

> In this one [person] God sees everyone, all of us, as through a glass. Through this medium, through this *Mediator*, we are known and seen by God. . . . Before His eyes from eternity God keeps [us], each [of us] . . . in this One; and not only before His eyes but loved and elect and called and made His possession. In Him He has from eternity bound Himself to each, to all. (91)

Along the same lines as Gollwitzer's interpretation of the parable—where Jesus Christ is the "running out" and the "kissing" of the father—we might say Jesus Christ is the "seeing and having compassion" of the father. He is God's being-toward-and-for the lost son reflected in the father's patient and compassionate gaze. He is that compassion in person, that "desire . . . to *take from* them [the masses] their misery and *take* it *to* Himself" (Matt 9:36) (IV/2, 185).[71] To have compassion is defined here as taking the place of the other, bearing another's suffering. It is only a "taking away" as a "taking to" and "taking up" (219). It consists of an assumption, an "enburdenment" (II/2, 172, 206, etc.).[72] "Taking to Himself the radical neediness of the world" is the same as "reversing its course to the abyss" (IV/1, 213). What Christ takes to himself is not merely the earthly burden of humans but divine reprobation. God "willed to make good" human rebellion "not by avenging" but by "interposing" Godself (IV/2, 227), by "bearing the inevitable wrath and perdition" that otherwise would have "destroyed" God's chosen covenant partner (II/2, 166). Reminiscent of Augustine's description of what happens when desire encounters an obstacle to its fulfillment, Barth speaks of "wrath" as the "consuming fire of God's love," its underside, destined to pass away.[73] In this way, "God makes Himself responsible for the one who became an enemy," assuming all of the "consequences" (124).

---

[71]   Emphasis added.

[72]   Paul Jones uses the words "enburden" and "enburdenment" in reference to Barth's claim that, in Christ, God takes on the burden of human flesh and divine judgment. It is a way of speaking about substitution: Christ's enburdenment "disenburdens" humankind. See *Humanity of Christ* (43, 163, 209, 236). Barth's emphasis on Christ's laying upon himself the burden (or in Julian's language, "charge") of sinful humanity echoes that of Luther, in his commentary on Galatians.

[73]   Barth says, "The divisive No of the wrath of God, which is the consuming fire of His love, lay on the old man, destroying and extinguishing him," but "God Himself" is the "old man"; "God Himself had to come down, to give Himself, to sacrifice Himself" (IV/1, 400–401).

In other words, election is a kind of *eternal atonement*.[74] In Christ the *logos asarkos* is always the *logos incarnandus* (the Word to-be-incarnate).[75] Even though "the human nature (body and soul) of Jesus only came into existence at a particular point in time," for Barth, "God qua Son is never not humanized."[76] In the same way, for Barth, the "atonement" is not primarily a task Jesus performs at the end of his earthly life, like a cog in the machine of salvation.[77] His whole account of predestination combats such an understanding of reconciliation. He says, "*Salvation is* fulfillment . . . of being . . . being which is hidden in God, and in that sense (distinct from God and secondary) *eternal being*" (IV/1, 8).[78] Atonement is Jesus Christ. He is the at-one-ment of God and the world in himself. If Jesus Christ is the "form of it as well as the content," and if the "he" of the atonement is "God in God's second way of being," then the atonement "takes place" *in God* (IV/1, 137).[79] It is there "in the beginning, in His primal decision, in Jesus Christ, at the place where alone He can be known

[74]   Jüngel, following Barth, speaks of this as an "eternal covenant" (*God's Being Is in Becoming*, 89; *CD* III/1, 97), clarifying what Barth means by "primal relationship" (*CD* II/2, 52).

[75]   Concerning the distinction and relationship between the *logos incarnandus* and *logos incarnatus* in Barth's theology, in contrast to that of his seventeenth-century Reformed predecessors, see McCormack, "Grace and Being," 184–87. In short, after II/2 and certainly by IV/1, for Barth, the Son is not "the Logos *simpliciter* (the abstract metaphysical subject)" but the one who has always already designated himself for atonement (229). Cf. IV/1, 181.

[76]   McCormack, "Grace and Being," 187. Jones, *Humanity of Christ*, 148.

[77]   I do not mean to perpetuate a false dichotomy here. In view of Barth's actualist ontology, inasmuch as the atonement is something Jesus Christ does, it is who he is. His actions are not accidental to his essence. That is the point.

[78]   Emphasis added.

[79]   There are two major issues I have glossed over in this sentence. First, Barth prefers the language "mode of being" or "way of being" to "persons" to describe the members of the Trinity. His concern is that we might imagine God in terms of the modern conception of persons. Second, Barth's understanding of the personal union of Jesus Christ is close to Cyril's, rather than Nestorius'. In other words, the proper subject of the hypostatic union is not the human, or the human and God together, but strictly the eternal Son of God. As he explains, "The unity of God and man in Christ is, then, the act of the Logos in assuming human being" (I/2, 162; see also 165). Barth upholds the ancient doctrine that Jesus' humanity is *enhypostatic* and *anhypostatic*. As McCormack explains this, "*Anhypostasis* makes the negative, anti-adoptionistic point that this human 'nature' had no independent existence alongside the Word. *Enhypostasis* is the positive corollary. It says that this human nature acquired its existence in the existence of God, in the mode of being of the eternal son" (McCormack, "Karl Barth's Historicized Christology," in *Orthodox and Modern*, 211). See, for example, I/2, 163f.; and IV/2, 91.

as God" (II/2, 92). This is what "grace" is—that God is Godself and another. As Barth says,

> It is a relation *ad extra*, undoubtedly. . . . It is a relation in which God is self-determined, so that the determination belongs no less to Him than all that He is in and for Himself. Without the Son sitting at the right hand of the Father, God would not be God. But the Son is not only very God. He is also called Jesus of Nazareth. (7)

In grounding election in the actuality of reconciliation, Barth clearly moves away from the classical doctrine of "no real relations" in God (6).[80] The divine relation to the world is mediated in and through Jesus Christ, who "is Himself the relation" (7). In Paul Nimmo's summary of Barth's point, "Jesus Christ is . . . the second member of the trinity, not just in respect of God *ad extra*, but also in respect of God *ad intra*."[81] Put more straightforwardly in *The Humanity of God*: "In Him [Jesus Christ] the fact is once for all established that God does not exist without [humankind]. . . . In this divinely free volition and election, in this sovereign decision . . . God is *human*."[82]

The Son of God is the original prodigal one—the divine decree himself, the "primal relationship" with the world, the eternal atonement. He is this not first of all in the economy of salvation as "the second Adam," but, in election, as the firstborn of all creation (Col 1:15) and, in creation, as the one who "in the beginning" wills fellowship with creatures in himself (vv. 16–19). The prodigal son's trajectory is a shadow of the eternal Son's kenotic self-ordination to establish this relation. It is because that "depth" is already borne in the identity of God in God's second mode of being that Barth maintains that Christ "precedes" lost humanity, that he is the way back and in himself the very embodiment of home (IV/2, 24). He is the appearing, the phenomenalizing, of God's basic *philanthropia*. The parable embedded in the life of Christ points to a divine compassion so deep and visceral that it prompts a pursuit, a substitu-

---

[80]   Barth does this without compromising the freedom and self-sufficiency of the divine life. In fact, rather than jeopardize these traits, Barth's move is to radicalize them: God is so free with respect to God's being that God can establish this relationship to the world *within* Godself. For Barth, God's being does not have rules that can override God's own desire for fellowship with another.

[81]   Nimmo, "Election and Evangelical Thinking," 34.

[82]   Barth, *Humanity of God*, 50–51. This is an important passage that clearly links election, incarnation, divine compassion, substitution, and the Parable of the Prodigal Son (see 51). One can certainly reject the claim, on various metaphysical grounds, that God is eternally human (e.g., see Molnar), but it is difficult to argue this is not what Barth is saying given so much textual evidence.

tion and exchange, wholly benefiting and in favor of the lost. It tells us that God's eternal will is humankind (II/2, 179), that the human condition was taken "right into [God's] heart" (IV/2, 184). Echoing Origen, Barth says, "In this self-giving"—in this far journey, this at-one-ment—"He was the Kingdom of God come on earth" (IV/2, 184).[83] For, "the heavenly Father, His kingdom which has come on earth, and the person of Jesus of Nazareth are not quantities which can be placed side by side, or which cut across each other, or which can be opposed to each other, but they are practically and in effect identical" (IV/1, 161). Grace, the grace that takes place in the parable between the father and son, is God's own "self-attestation" and "self-demonstration" (IV/3.1, 11, 48). It is not just something God does; it reveals who God is.[84]

Barth thus assiduously avoids any "hidden decision," "obscurity," or "twofold mystery" in the divine will (II/2, 156, 147), about which Augustine and Calvin (and, on Barth's reading, even Aquinas) are forced to speculate.[85] The dialectic between the divine "yes" and "no" "is not sealed up as a paradox but broken open teleologically: 'God wills to lose in order that [humans] may gain.'"[86] To put it unambiguously, "the truth of *God* is loving-kindness towards [humans] . . . and nothing else."[87] (This assertion is a gloss on Titus 3:4, ὅτε δὲ ἡ χρηστότης καὶ ἡ φιλανθρωπία ἐπεφάνη τοῦ σωτῆρος ἡμῶν θεοῦ, translated literally, "when the kindness and love-of-humankind of God our savior appeared.") The eternal decision to self-determine as loving-kindness is the basis for what unfolds in the history of salvation. Election reveals that God is never without this human other. But that is not all it reveals about God for Barth.

Prodigal Slave

Barth's application of the language and structure of the parable to the Trinity is less readily apparent than in his treatments of reconciliation and election. The connection is absent from his discussion of revelation and Trinity in the first volume of *Church Dogmatics* and receives little explicit attention in his

---

[83]   See Origen, *Comm. Matt.* 14.7.10.

[84]   Again, this is a point of contention among Barth scholars. But there is consensus among a certain set of interpreters that the self-determination of divine election is in some way ontologically relevant for God (although there are differences in terms of the manner and extent of this self-determination). See especially Jüngel, Balthasar, McCormack, Hector, Jones, et al.

[85]   See II/2, 16–17.

[86]   Jüngel, *God's Being Is in Becoming*, 92. As Jüngel says, "*Praedestinatio gemina* [double predestination] . . . is *praedestinatio dialectica* [dialectical predestination]." Cf. II/2, 162.

[87]   Barth, *Humanity of God*, 52.

doctrine of God.[88] Where it appears most prominently is §59 (IV/1), "The Obedience of the Son of God." This portion of *The Doctrine of Reconciliation* is more than an exposition of the justificatory work of Jesus Christ, the first part of the twofold movement of the incarnate Son. It constitutes a development on the doctrine of the Trinity presented in I/1. Although Barth's stated topic here is the reconciliation of God and the world in Christ, he does not restrict himself to reflection on the economy of salvation. His later description of the Son's relationship with the Father "tenders a Trinitarian amplification of the doctrine of election" and, by extension, of the doctrine of God.[89] At key points Barth broaches reflection on the immanent Trinity, most notably where he proposes the *theologoumenon* of *göttlichen Gehorsam* or "divine obedience" (§59.1, IV/1, 193, 196).

Here he addresses the anterior conditions within God for the Son's actions in the economy. Describing the downward orientation God eternally adopts in God's second mode of being, Barth is also narrating the intratrinitarian relations that enable this movement.[90] In Jüngel's paraphrase of Barth's divine ontology, the "precedence of God in his primal decision shows that God's being not only 'proceeds' on the way into the far country but that God's being is *in movement* from eternity. God's being is moved being . . . moved by *God*."[91] Similarly, Eugene Rogers says of Barth's understanding of the relationship between the Father and the Son, "In the Trinity the Father is eternally sending the Son and receiving him back, the story of the Prodigal collapsed into a single, integral movement."[92] What Jüngel and Rogers detect is the way Barth uses the parable to retell intratrinitarian relations and divine processions. Mapping Philippians 2 onto Luke 15, we are sent back to a divine basis for the

---

[88]   In the first volume of *Church Dogmatics*, there are very few references to the lost or prodigal son, and most of them are applied anthropologically. However, in one interesting passage, Barth intimates the direction of his later exegesis of the parable, where he says, "We hear of a lost son: 'this thy brother was dead and is alive again' (Lk. 15:32). Who can that be?" See §16 of I/2 (216). In the second volume, explicit references to the "lost son" show up about half a dozen times in connection with statements about Christ.

[89]   Jones, *Humanity of Christ*, 9. The doctrines of election and reconciliation are so integral to Barth's concept of God's being that it would be helpful had Barth rewritten his doctrine of God after the discoveries of II/2.

[90]   This is why, when assessing the way Barth configures the immanent Trinity and economic Trinity, commentators must deal with this portion of *CD*.

[91]   Jüngel, *God's Being Is in Becoming*, 14–15.

[92]   Eugene F. Rogers Jr., *Sexuality and the Christian Body: Their Way into the Triune God* (Oxford: Blackwell, 1999), 198.

Son's "journey into the far country" that presses beyond the appearing of God's loving-kindness (Titus 3:4).

Divine Obedience as Kenosis

Throughout his account of election, Barth contrasts the wisdom of God's grace with the limitations of the human imagination (e.g., II/2, 22, 33). God's prodigality is regarded in human terms as a kind of "foolishness." Alluding to the Parable of the Prodigal Son in his comparison of Jesus to the Good Samaritan, Barth describes atonement as "something unnecessary and extravagant, binding and limiting and compromising" (IV/1, 158). He goes so far as to say God is "affected," "disturbed," "harmed," and "assaulted" (IV/2, 401). Barth insists that humans could not "invent" a God like this, who "does not hold aloof," like a human lord, but comes so near as to be implicated in the course of the world (IV/1, 158). In the beginning, the Son of God went into "the far country" and "gave Himself up . . . hazarded Himself" (II/2, 161; cf. IV/2, 401). This is election; this is reconciliation.

Against the human conception of a "lord," "furnished with sovereignty and authority and the plenitude of power, maintaining and executing his own will," Barth points to the humility of Christ in Gethsemane (163–64). Acknowledging what a "scandal" and "offense" it is for human understanding to accept the mystery that "for God it is just as natural to be lowly as it is to be high, to be near as it is to be far, to be little as it is to be great, to be abroad as it is to be at home" (192), Barth exhorts, "We have to hold fast to this without being disturbed or confused by any pictures of false gods" (187). He claims, "There is a humility grounded in the being of God," in the "obedience" of the Son (193), saying,

> The Almighty exists and acts and speaks *here* in the form of One who is weak and impotent, the eternal as One who is temporal and perishing, the Most High in the deepest humility. The Holy One stands in the place and under the accusation of a sinner with other sinners. The glorious One is covered with shame. The One who lives forever has fallen prey to death. The Creator is subjected to and overcome by the onslaught of that which is not. In short, the Lord is a servant [*Knecht*], a slave [*Sklave*]. And it is not accidental. It could not be otherwise. (IV/1, 176)[93]

---

[93]   Where the word *Knecht* could refer to the status of a (paid) household laborer and is used to translate various senses of "servant" in the Bible, *Sklave* is the German word used for the kind of abject chattel slavery we associate with seventeenth- to nineteenth-century colonial slavery and the trans-Atlantic slave trade. See *KD*, IV/2, 192.

When he says, "The way of the Son of God into the far country is the way of obedience," he has in mind not simply the human life of Jesus but an "obedience which takes place in God Himself" (192, 195). The humility, obedience, servanthood, and, indeed, *slavery* of predestination and atonement is appropriated to the Son in a distinctive way. Extrapolating from the identity between the eternal Son and the man Jesus, Barth concludes there must be "an above and a below, a *prius* and a *postorius*, a superior and a junior and subordinate" that "belongs to the inner life of God," that obtains between Father and Son (IV/1, 195, 201). The one is called "origin," the other "consequence" (209). He goes so far as to say God's "divine unity consists in the fact that in Himself He is both One who is obeyed and Another who obeys" (201). This is what the Son elects in his election by the Father.[94] So Barth's explanation of God's "attitude" in election (§§32–33) and justification (§59) gives a very particular picture of the relationship between the first and second persons of the Trinity. A christologically grounded understanding of election leads back not merely to the claim that "God is human," "God is loving-kindness," or "God is grace." Rather, Barth concludes that God's humanity has as its antecedent the intratrinitarian subsequence and subjection of Son to Father.

Barth lands on the radical assertion of eternal obedience for a complex of reasons that may be illuminating for broader conversations about kenosis. Among them we might take special note of a few. First, there is the precedent in the scriptural narrative from which he is attempting not to abstract. Obedience and disobedience are significant concepts in the drama of creation, fall, and salvation. Barth frequently describes sin in terms of disobedience and salvation in terms of obedience.[95] More specifically, Philippians 2:8 ("obedient to death") and Jesus' prayer in Gethsemane that "not my will, but thine be done" (Luke 22:42; cf. Mark 14:36; Matt 26:39, 42) are passages to which Barth consistently appeals.[96] They sum up, for him, the entire network of scriptural pred-

---

[94]   See Jüngel, *God's Being Is in Becoming*, 88.

[95]   This is so from the very start of *Church Dogmatics*. See Barth's description of Christ as the "second Adam" (Rom 5), in which he is already coordinating his salvific "obedience" with his refusal to grasp after the form of God (Phil 2) and those opposing it to Adam's sin in the mode of "pride" (I/2, 157).

[96]   He says, "We remember again the prayer in Gethsemane, and also the fact that in Phil. 2:8 His ταπεινοφροσύνη [lowliness of mind or humility] is explained in terms of a becoming obedient, and in Heb. 5:8 His suffering in terms of a learning of obedience. . . . Rom. 5:19 tells us unmistakably that through the obedience of one many shall be made righteous, and in 2 Cor. 10:5 Paul shows us that it is his aim to bring every thought captive to the ὑπακοὴ τοῦ Χριστοῦ [obedience of Christ], an expression which surely has to be understood as a *Gen. sub.* as well as a *Gen. obj.*" (IV/1, 193–94). Among related passages, Barth also quotes John 10:18, "No man taketh it [my life]

icates and identities that converge in Christ's person and work—especially, the Adam-Christ relationship so central to a Pauline account of reconciliation and his retelling of the parable. In the garden of Gethsemane, we have a poetic mirroring and rewriting of the disobedience of Adam and Eve in the garden of Eden. In Hans Frei's words, "In all four Gospels and in the other writings of the New Testament, it is the motif or quality of obedience that is stressed in regard to the person of Jesus."[97]

Second, this whole history of obedience and disobedience is attributable to the *eternal* Son because, in Barth's view, "the true God" is "identical" (*identisch*) with "the lowly and obedient man Jesus of Nazareth" (199). This is so by virtue of (1) his personal simplicity as the Son and (2) the *communicatio idiomatum* between his divinity and humanity.[98] Barth believes that "divine obedience" is a necessary conclusion if we want to avoid treating reconciliation as "the kind of economy in which [God's] true and proper being remains hidden behind and improper being, a being 'as if'" (198). His aim, Jüngel says, is to rule out "the opposition between a *deus nudus* and a *deus incarnatus*."[99] There is, as Barth puts it, an

> inward divine relationship between the One who rules and commands in majesty and the One who obeys in humility and is identical with the very different relationship between God and one of His creatures, a man. God goes into the far country for this to happen. . . . He takes into unity with His divine being a quite different, a creaturely and indeed sinful being. To do this He empties Himself, He humbles Himself. But . . . He does not do it apart from its basis [*Grund*] in His own being, in His own inner life. He does not do it without any correspondence [*Entsprechung*] to, but as the strangely logical final continuation of, the history in which He is God. (IV/1, 203)

The way of Jesus Christ is reflected in the inner life of God. It corresponds to and is continuous with the eternal relationship between Father and Son. In John Webster's words, "The one whom we encounter in salvation is God as God truly is."[100]

To add to these well-trodden points, there is, third, a textual explanation of Barth's choice. Not only in his excurses on kenosis but also throughout

---

from me, but I lay it down of myself. I have power to lay it down, and I have power to take it again. This commandment have I received of my Father" (166).

[97]   Frei, *Identity of Jesus Christ*, 112. Frei calls "obedience" the "clue to his identity."

[98]   For an explanation of Barth's reworking of the doctrine, and its connection to the *communio naturarum*, see Jones, *Humanity of Christ*, 134–35.

[99]   Jüngel, *God as the Mystery of the World*, 53.

[100]   John Webster, "Translator's Introduction," in Jüngel, *God's Being Is in Becoming*, xii.

The Doctrine of Reconciliation, "obedience" collocates with the phrases "self-emptying" and "self-humbling" (IV/2, 193). It specifies them. It seems *Gehorsam* becomes a kind of shorthand for the content of Philippians 2:7–8, which is so central to Barth's Christology and his intertextual interpretation of the parable. Christ—"who, though he was in the form of God" (v. 6) was "found in human form" (v. 7)—

> v. 7 *emptied* himself (ἑαυτὸν ἐκένωσεν),
>> having *taken the form of a servant* (μορφὴν δούλου),
>>> having been made (or born) in human likeness, and . . .
> v. 8 *humbled* himself (ἐταπείνωσεν ἑαυτὸν)
>> having become *obedient* (ὑπήκοος) to death,
>>> even death on a cross.

"Obedient to death" forms a parallelism with "having taken the form of a servant" and concretely fills out the meaning of the Son's servanthood and incarnation. As a rhetorical climax—and, correspondingly, the nadir, the deepest depth, of Christ's downward narrative—this term does not merely reiterate but crowns and completes the antecedent main verbs and their clauses. It focuses us on the lowest point of Christ's self-abasement—"*even* death on a cross."

Having a textual as well as a theological basis for accentuating the word, Barth lets "obedience" govern what is meant by "kenosis." *Gehorsam* helps him handle a concept that he thinks causes theological confusion, namely by preventing any appearance of ontological diminution.[101] It altogether shifts our attention away from abstract considerations of "being" to concrete descriptions of "act." It more vividly depicts the character of Christ's "far journey" than a word like "condescension," which, taken alone, risks leaving a purely formal impression or inviting scripturally remote speculation about how divine lowliness works. It steers us clear of questions like *"What is emptied in Christ's self-divestment?"* and orients us toward the actuality of his existence as witnessed in the Gospels. The culmination of the parallel verses in "death on a cross" corresponds to the climax of the Gospel narrative. "Obedience unto death" is therefore tied to the course and telos of Jesus' life as well as to the salvific undoing of human fallenness and its consequences (Rom 5:12–19).[102] In short, *Gehorsam* is language that concretizes

---

[101] See the discussion of kenosis on pp. 188–91 and related notes.

[102] The connection with Jesus' prayer in Gethsemane is significant. However, Barth does not leave it at "obedience [submission] to death," but, in view of Jesus' submission ("not my will but yours be done"), it becomes "obedience *to the Father.*" For a detailed treatment of Barth's excursus on Gethsemane, see Paul Jones, *Humanity of*

and historicizes the character of divine self-giving. It both sums up and sets the scriptural boundaries for reflecting on what is meant by the less determinate terms "self-emptying" and "self-humiliation."

The Subjection of Sons

Barth's decision to give priority to "obedience," while intelligible and perhaps methodologically unavoidable for him for these reasons among others, also elicits a number of questions. For example, are there exegetical grounds for elevating "obedience" over the other parallel "kenotic" terms in the christological hymn? What justifies the choice? Does it become a presiding concept that crowds out equally important descriptors of Jesus Christ? Can the word adequately imply the teleological orientation of humiliation toward exaltation Barth otherwise asserts (IV/2)? Should it be extended to the eternal Son with little analogical or metaphorical qualification? Is *divine* obedience a necessary claim in view of Jesus of Nazareth's submission of his will to that of God the Father in the garden of Gethsemane, or is Barth overliteralizing from a human model for God? Why does this action get reified in a "ranking" and "ordering" of persons and relations? Does that undermine the actualism that otherwise prompts the application of "obedience" to God? It seems Barth is using *Gehorsam* to redefine the Son's procession, his "being-posited," but is a formal conception of processions compatible with his later actualist account of the Trinity (IV/1, 209)? Or is this a problematic residuum of the Trinitarian apparatus he leaves behind? Bound up with such questions is a challenging set of concerns that centers on the human models for obedience upon which Barth draws.

His application of "obedience" to the Son's relationship to the Father depends upon a distinct understanding of human sons and fathers.[103] He admits that in employing the title "Son," we are merely drawing an "analogy," which is marked by "similarity in dissimilarity" (III/2, 324; IV/1, 209–10). For example, he says, "What we call 'Son' points in the right direction, but does not reach the fullness of what is here in question," and "the history in which God is living God in Himself can only be indicated and not conceived by our terms son and father and spirit" (209–10).[104] However, Barth thinks "we have no better" language. His pinpointing of the analogical similarity is revealing. He asks,

---

Christ (229f.); and "Karl Barth on Gethsemane," *International Journal of Systematic Theology* 9, no. 2 (2007): 148–71.

[103] In §41 and §45, Barth addresses the parent/child relationship in a way that accounts for maturation and eventually equality (e.g., see III/1, 185; III/2, 218–19). But in §59, he construes fatherhood in a more permanently hierarchical way.

[104] Because there are dimensions "the term cannot bring out," it is "true but inadequate" (IV/1, 209–10).

"What does it mean: Son of God?" and concludes that we use this term for the second person of the Trinity on the basis that

> it can convey the natural determination [*die natürliche Bestimmung*] of a son to subjection [*Unterordnung*] to a father, the self-evident presupposition that a son owes obedience [*Gehorsam*] to a father, the mutual relationship revealed in what a father can expect and demand of a son and also in the way in which a son has to respect the will of his father [*ein Sohn den Willen seines Vaters zu respektieren hat*]. (209)

"Son" is shorthand for being under, owing compliance, and deferring to the will of another.

Barth defines "obedience" (*Gehorsam*) in terms of "subjection" (*Unterordnung* or *Abhängigkeit*) in other places as well (e.g., IV/1, 96, 98). In his discussion of election, he says, "In what Jesus does everything is genuine obedience, real subordination, even subjection [*Unterwerfung*]—not at all the self-exaltation of man to the throne of God, but very definitely the work of a servant, indeed a slave [*Sklave*] of God" (II/2, 605). The Father is "the One who disposes," and the Son is "the One who complies" (IV/1, 209). This is "a position" that cannot be "reversed." That the irreversible ordering of one over the other is the definitive point of similarity between human fathers/sons and the divine Father/Son is reinforced in Barth's discussion of the "*quasi* fatherly character" of other forces (e.g., kingdom, unbelief, the devil, etc.) (210).

"Subjection to the will of another" is a telling feature to foreground in the filial analogy and raises an array of concerns. Why reduce the relation to power or order rather than to "loving-kindness," which is otherwise the keynote of Barth's late theology? On what basis should we accept *Unterordnung* as the most accurate point of similarity in the dissimilarity between Trinitarian persons and human families? Is "subjection" a "natural" and "self-evident" relationship between sons and fathers? Perhaps if Barth has in mind small children and their caregivers. However, in that case, "subjection" and "compliance" (*Fügsamkeit*) could only figure as a means to a more fundamental end: the protection and nurturance of those presently incapable of caring for themselves. In most cases, even this sort of dependence would not be a definitive or enduring "determination" in the relationship.[105] Further, in a human model, the burden of "self-giving" should fall to the parent rather than the child. So

---

[105] Healthy children typically grow to become peers of their parents, as Barth acknowledges throughout III/1–2. But in those instances where disability means dependency is not a developmental stage, we would still not define the person's need for care in terms of subordinance or subjection. "Service" would fall to the adult, the so-called "superior," not the dependent.

"obedience" as "subjection" could no longer comprehensively translate divine "self-giving," otherwise so central to the movement of Luke 15 filtered through Philippians 2. At most, it would be an instance or mode, and not necessarily the most conspicuous one. However, it seems Barth does not have in mind parents and children in general, and certainly not mothers and daughters, but specifically fathers and adult sons.[106] These familial terms are invested with cultural and personal import for Barth, as the mother/child dyad is for Julian. It is surely meaningful that, in drawing from this model, Barth accentuates the subjection or subordination of the son rather than, say, the dependence of the child on the parent and care of the parent for the child, as Julian does.

Barth explicitly coordinates the superordination of the Father and subordination of the Son with other roles or identities as well—namely, men and women, especially husbands and wives. As Faye Bodley-Dangelo explains, Barth "transmutes a paternal relation to a marital relation and renders fatherhood-sonship analogous to sexual difference hierarchically construed."[107] This has led some critics to conclude there is a "dimension" to Barth's "presentation of the Son's obedience" that involves a "crude hierarchicalism" that "must be adjudged ethically and doctrinally injurious." As Jones suggests, Barth's relational analogies "expose" his "incorrigible sexism" and have a "corruptive influence" on his theology.[108] There are a number of illuminating critiques and correctives to Barth on this point.[109] In short, the concern is that Barth draws an *analogia relationis* in which superordination, precedence, willing, and initiative are assigned to the

[106] Where in *CD* III, subordination is temporary for the child (and only permanent for the woman), in Barth's later use of these analogies, "son" indicates ongoing subordination.

[107] Faye Bodley-Dangelo, *Sexual Difference, Gender, and Agency in Karl Barth's "Church Dogmatics"* (London: T&T Clark, 2020), 126.

[108] Jones, *Humanity of Christ*, 212–13.

[109] See especially Bodley-Dangelo, *Sexual Difference*; Jason Springs, "Following at a Distance (Again): Gender, Equality, and Freedom in Karl Barth's Theological Anthropology," *Modern Theology* 28, no. 3 (2012): 446–77; Lisa P. Stephenson, "Directed, Ordered, and Related: The Male and Female Interpersonal Relation in Karl Barth's *Church Dogmatics*," *Scottish Journal of Theology* 61, no. 4 (2008): 435–49; and Katherine Sonderegger, "Barth and Feminism," in *The Cambridge Companion to Karl Barth*, ed. John Webster (Cambridge: Cambridge University Press, 2000), 258–72. See also Jacquelyn Grant, *White Women's Christ and Black Women's Jesus: Feminist Christology and Womanist Response* (Atlanta: Scholars Press, 1989), 70–75; Clifford Green, "Liberation Theology? Karl Barth on Women and Men," *Union Theological Seminary Quarterly* 29 (1974): 228–29; Green, "Karl Barth's Treatment of the Man-Woman Relationship: Issues for Theological Method," in *Reflections on Bonhoeffer*, ed. Geoffrey B. Kelly and C. John Weborg (Chicago: Covenant, 1999), 228–37; and Cynthia Campbell, "Imago Dei Reconsidered: Male and Female Together," *Journal for Preachers* 4, no. 2 (1981): 9–14.

man, and subordination, subsequence, compliance, and receptivity to the woman.[110] While he wants to foreground human agency and action, Barth's choice of analogies betrays a theological imagination bound by a certain conception of order.[111] This is decisive for the comparison he elevates here.

According to Barth, the sexes "stand in a sequence . . . Man has his allotted place and woman hers" (*CD* III/4, 168). He goes on:

> Man and woman are not an A and a second A whose being and relationship can be described like the two halves of an hour glass, which are obviously two, but absolutely equal and therefore interchangeable. Man and woman are an A and a B, and cannot, therefore, be equated. . . . A precedes B, and B follows A. Order means succession. It means preceding and following. It means super- and subordination. (168–69)

Man and woman are not equal; they do not have interchangeable positions. Man is himself in his precedence and woman is herself in her subsequence. The hourglass cannot be flipped so the woman is on top. Why? Because "a certain strength and corresponding precedence are a very general characteristic of man, and a weakness and corresponding subsequence of woman" (III/2, 287). Aligning man with God/Jesus and woman with Israel/church, Barth calls

---

[110] While he tries to rule out domination and abuse as disordered forms of male headship, Barth categorically opposes equality as a path to that end (*CD* III/4, 168–69). On this point, see Bodley-Dangelo, *Sexual Difference*, 170–72. Barth says, "Man speaks against himself if he assesses and treats woman as an inferior being, for without *her weakness and subsequence* he could not be man. And woman speaks against herself if she envies that which is proper to man, for *his strength and precedence are the reality without which she could not be woman*" (III/2, 287, emphasis added).

[111] Barth is fond of saying things like, "The supremacy of man is not a question of value, dignity, or honour, but of order" (III/1, 301). Notably, Bodley-Dangelo challenges the view of most critics that the difficulty with Barth is the way he maps ordered binaries onto one another. She argues that the real issue is his account of human agency, namely that he offers one christological pattern but restricts it to men whenever he broaches the question of sexual difference. "The problem," she says, "is not that the 'I' in §45.2 occupies a privileged place over the 'Thou,' but rather that the agency exhibited in §45.2 and patterned after the movement of the divine agent comes to be fully appropriated only by the male in §45.3" (*Sexual Difference*, 131–32, n. 13). The emphasis of Barth's I/Thou anthropology is that the individual "resists the reduction or dissolution of individual identity and agency into social relations" (133). At the same time, Bodley-Dangelo acknowledges that, in IV/1, Barth does in fact draw a static analogy of relations for Father/Son, which is what I am interrogating here (126, n. 10). Her focus is on Barth's ethics in III/1–4.

this pattern "the rule which is valid both in and outside love and marriage" and claims that "the only alternative is disorder" (III/2, 310–11).[112]

Such a "problematic ordering of the sexes" can be traced back to "the privileged place the male occupies in imitating Christ" throughout Barth's thought.[113] This is evident, for example, in his reading of the Genesis creation narratives (III/1, §41.3), where Adam is "carefully patterned after Christ's agency" while Eve figures the church "in its absolute subordination to Christ" (III/2, 316). She is "the paradigmatic female model of agency specifically in her silent decision to refrain from decision and to consent to be the object of Adam's election."[114] As Barth says of Eve, "She does not choose; she is chosen. . . . She thus chooses herself by refraining from choice . . . as [man's] elect" (III/1, 303). In other words, the problem is not simply a matter of order, that one is categorically above and the other categorically below. More fundamentally, this arrangement is predicated upon the woman prescinding from exercising free agency in deference to the will of her "Lord" (306). While Barth claims to have christological grounding here, as Jason Springs has shown, "freedom" is the "root and crown" of Barth's own christologically inflected I/Thou anthropology (CD III/2, §45.2), and this undermines the sort of unidirectional dynamic between the sexes that supports his later presentation of the Son's obedience.[115]

Barth's description of man and woman as A:B sheds light on Barth's father/son analogy. These are dual instances in which the model of the immediate family bears great weight for his conception of God.[116] He attempts to distance the "binary of sexual difference from its instantiation," in particular "conventions and mores" or biological and psychological explanations. However, as his population of the concept "son" demonstrates, he works with "unexamined" stereotypes that are "deeply embedded in social conventions" and thus "unwittingly makes resource to a natural theology by transforming cultural

---

[112] Barth discusses sexual difference throughout his ethics (CD III), particularly in §41, §45.3, and §54. For some characteristic comments, see III/1, 199, 301–12; III/2, 287; and III/4, 118, 150–73. For other places where Barth appeals to an analogy of relations, see esp. III/1, 185; III/2, 218–19.

[113] Bodley-Dangelo, Sexual Difference, 141.

[114] Bodley-Dangelo, Sexual Difference, 83. Bodley-Dangelo points out that "for Barth sequential order does not inevitably subordinate the second term," but "it does so relentlessly when the second term is woman" (128).

[115] Springs, "Following at a Distance," 469. Reading Barth against Barth, Springs considers what "a Christocentric account of gender equality" would look like (467).

[116] Barth keeps Paul's Christianization of the Greco-Roman household codes intact. Following passages like Eph 5:20f., he aligns subordinates—children, women, and slaves (see esp. IV/1, 189).

assumptions into a divinely imposed ought."[117] As pernicious as the social and ethical implications of these analogical associations may be, the point here is that they disclose Barth's vision of God, in which the Son is a subordinate subject, servant, or slave. The problem is not merely the oppressiveness of the models themselves but that Barth resorts to them because he conceives of the subjection of the Son as eternal and unilateral. To be clear, at issue is not whether it is fitting for there to be something like "kenosis," submission, or vulnerability in God or, for that matter, between humans.[118] Nor is it a question of whether obedience is an authentic dimension of the existence of Jesus Christ.[119] Rather, what requires interrogation is the precise content, basis, and priority Barth gives the term.

Toward Enburdenment

Various charges have been leveled against Barth's later presentation of the Trinity, in *CD* IV/1–2, from the standpoint of classical Trinitarianism.[120] A number of scholars have offered correctives to his hierarchical social ordering by appealing to the equality and perichoresis of intratrinitarian persons.[121] However, difficulties arise when attempting to apply the more ancient and conventional aspects of the Trinitarian apparatus with which Barth works in I/1 to his description of the Trinity in §59 and following. After reformulating

[117]   Bodley-Dangelo, *Sexual Difference*, 160.

[118]   Again, see Coakley's essay "*Kenōsis* and Subversion," in *Powers and Submissions*, 3–39.

[119]   T. F. Torrance, among others, maintains as much without converting this incarnational fulfillment into an intratrinitarian basis.

[120]   We see this in Paul Molnar's concerns in "The Obedience of the Son in the Theology of Karl Barth and Thomas F. Torrance," *Scottish Journal of Theology* 67, no. 1 (2014): 50–69. He feels Barth "conceptually introduces a hierarchy into the divine being," "blurs the distinctions between processions and missions," and "seems to confuse the order of the inner trinitarian relations with the being of the persons of the Trinity" (61, 64). (I address the latter two concerns, which I think express misunderstanding of what Barth is doing, in the note below.) Molnar rightly observes that "*perichoresis* . . . is virtually missing at this point in Barth's analysis," viz. in §59 (see "Obedience of the Son," 64).

[121]   See, for example, Elizabeth Frykberg, *Karl Barth's Theological Anthropology: An Analogical Critique regarding Gender Relations* (Princeton: Princeton Theological Seminary, 1993); Timothy Gorringe, *Karl Barth: Against Hegemony* (Oxford: Oxford University Press, 1999), 200–207; Paul Fiddes, "The Status of Woman in the Thought of Karl Barth," in *After Eve*, ed. Janet M. Soskice (London: Collins Marshall Pickering, 1990), 138–53; and Alexander J. McKelway, "Perichoretic Possibilities in Barth's Doctrine of Male and Female," *Princeton Seminary Bulletin* 7, no. 3 (1986): 231–43, and see esp. 290.

the doctrine of election (*CD* II/2), Barth gives limited attention to the immanent Trinity, and his early definitions of "appropriations" and "perichoretic unity," borrowed from Aquinas, are incompatible with "divine obedience" attributed exclusively to the Son in IV/1.[122] So a Trinitarian approach may not be as effective for redressing the hierarchical binitarianism and subordinationism of Barth's later Christology, at least not on his own terms.[123] However, there are several other ways in which we might query Barth and qualify his later grounding of election and reconciliation in the slavery he attributes to the Son. Without unpacking all of the attendant ontological implications here, the following set of observations helps us set the Trinitarian ramifications of Barth's retelling of the Parable of the Prodigal Son in critical dialogue with that of Julian.

First, the content Barth draws from his relational analogies runs counter to his presiding assertion about divine power and love. While he tends toward a lively oscillation between poles such as power and weakness, freedom and

[122] The eternal obedience of the Son appears to be a case in which *opera trinitatis ad extra non sunt indivisa* (the external works of the Trinity are *not* indivisible) (IV/1, 195). Christ's obedience, as Barth speaks of it and as an essential feature of incarnation, cannot be appropriated to one person as that which is "common to all." This is because it is grounded in election, as a temporal kenosis that corresponds to that primal kenosis. Election is the beginning of God's *opera ad extra*. But, Jüngel points out, "as the beginning of all the ways and works God's election of grace is not only an *opus Dei ad extra* [external work of God] or, more precisely, an *opus Dei ad extra externum* [external work of God directed outwards]; it is at the same time an *opus Dei ad extra internum* [external work of God directed inwards]" (*God's Being Is in Becoming*, 83–84). It is a decision that "affects God." In this case, we must see election as overlapping with divine processions. If obedience belongs to the mission of Jesus Christ, it can only be specially appropriated to him as what is *not* common to the other persons of the Trinity if it becomes a characteristic of a divine relation (rather than essence)—that is, if it is regarded as a feature of the Son's procession from the Father. Barth thus appears to retain some classical rules of Trinitarian thought while disregarding others. On his own terms, there is no reason to accept the tools of the tradition unless they cohere with the biblical narrative. The question, then, can only be whether those he continues to employ—namely (1) the grounding of distinction between persons in relations (i.e., through processions) (Aquinas) and (2) the movement from missions "back" to processions (Augustine)—are "in accordance with the biblical testimony" (II/2, 18). If not, what justifies Barth's recourse to processions (without giving the doctrine the same overhaul he gives everything else)? What processions and the *theologoumenon* of *Gehorsam* have in common is sequential hierarchy. This seems revealing.

[123] Of course, Barth openly rejects ancient versions of subordinationism as a graduation of divinity (e.g., IV/1, 196). I am using the term descriptively to indicate (1) the type of "subordination" that he says "belongs to the inner life of God" in the Son (201) and (2) his hyper-focus on the Father-Son dyad (e.g., "God is God in these two modes of being"; 203).

submission, divinity and humanity, lordship and servanthood, and so on, this flattens out when he extends these concepts to the human analogues fathers/sons and husbands/wives.[124] This irreversibility is at odds with the predominant pattern of his mature writings, in which we find a carefully dialectical presentation of God's freedom in self-giving. Barth characteristically resists opposing or fixing terms related to super- and sub-ordinance in the divine economy, inverting them in surprising ways. Incarnation and crucifixion, for example, are interpreted as the very power of God, as capacity rather than a lack, diminution, or stoical resignation (e.g., IV/3.1, 180, 196–97). Similarly, Barth insists on an exchange or reversal in grace, where God (primary) is made low in order that humans (secondary) are made high, assigning exaltation to Christ's humanity and humiliation to his divinity. While human sanctification involves discipleship or "conformity" as a proper creaturely mode of correspondence to God (e.g., IV/2, 93), the "overlordship" of God is best understood as the grounding and confirmation of human freedom, rather than what Barth sometimes describes in terms of subjection or subjugation (e.g., III/3, 146; IV/2, 578–79).[125] Appealing to New Testament passages concerning the poverty of God (1 Cor 1:25; 2 Cor 8:9), Barth speaks of the "transvaluation of all values" in Christ's preference for the poor, the weak, the sinner (IV/2, 169). The one who is rich (God) becomes poor (human). So were we to draw an analogy to divine/human relations, and by extension the intratrinitarian Father/Son dynamic, from the gendered familial terms Barth employs, according to his own logic, the downwardness or humiliation (poverty, kenosis, obedience) would belong to father/husband and upwardness or exaltation to the child/wife.[126] It is inconsistent, then, for the tension between

---

[124] If one were to accept the biblical metaphor in which male/female relations in some way mirror divine/human relations, as Barth points out "even Paul does," we would want to remind Barth that "even Paul" gets that, in the scenario of mutual submission described in Eph 5, the heavier burden of "laying down his life" falls to the man/Jesus/God rather than to the woman/church/humanity. "He" leads, yes—but the way to death. As problematic as the Christianized household codes are, Paul's social analogy retains a strongly tensive relationship between lordship and servanthood.

[125] Barth does speak of the "compulsion" of Grace. But never a "mere compulsion." Never an abstracted structure of subjection, an end in itself. The life-giving "compulsion" of Grace is a means for combating the "hellish compulsion" of sin and death and establishes the human, grants genuine freedom, which is so much more than the freedom of "self-deciding." See IV/4, 578–79.

[126] In other words, we would have what Rosemary Radford Reuther calls "the kenosis of *patriarchy*." See Ruether, *Sexism and Godtalk: Toward a Feminist Theology* (Boston: Beacon, 1993), 137 (emphasis added). That Barth does not follow his

these terms to slacken and for polar reversals in power and need or wealth and poverty to stall out. Yet this is what happens when the "lowliness" of God is strongly localized in one Trinitarian person and linked up with unexamined hierarchical human models.

Second, insofar as Jesus Christ does in fact "subject himself," it is a moment on the way, a means to an end. Humiliation is fundamentally in the service of claiming his rightful "inheritance," his "crown"—humankind—ever with a view to being "a King who draws [others] after him to share his destiny" (IV/2, 24).[127] *Gehorsam* appears disconnected from its concrete manifestation and goal in the economy of salvation when Barth makes it a structure of the divine life itself, an eternal dynamic between Father and Son apart from its salvific orientation.[128] This exposes a "lapse" in Barth's "concentration." According to McCormack, it is incongruous with Barth's "mature doctrine of election" that he "continued to make statements which created the space for an independent doctrine of the Trinity, a triune being of God which was seen as independent of the covenant of grace."[129] While there is much disagreement over how Barth relates the immanent Trinity and the economic Trinity and to what extent he collapses missions and processions, what is clear is that the way Barth typically organizes election and reconciliation is, at times, in tension with his reasoning in §59.1. From a rather different side of the debate, Paul Molnar registers this complication, observing that sometimes Barth asserts "simply that the Son fulfills his subordination and the Father his superiority, without clearly and consistently stating that what is *fulfilled* is God's salvific purpose and activity

---

own logic in this direction is indicative of the extent to which his social imagination interferes with the radical truth he himself uncovers.

[127] This "so that," this inherent purpose and telos, is pivotal in nearly all of the verses to which Barth appeals (2 Cor 10:1; 11:7; Phil 2:6f.; 4:2; Eph 4:9; etc.).

[128] There is a wonderful passage where Barth offers a well-ordered understanding of obedience (see IV/1, 207–8). Here he describes Jesus' earthly obedience as a manifestation of the love and power of God and as a model for the human relationship to God. At times he seems to clearly apportion obedience to Jesus' humanity here, saying, "He shows Himself the One He is by the obedience which He renders *as* man" (208, emphasis added). But he goes on to say, "In His mode of being as the Son He fulfils the divine subordination, just as the Father in His mode of being as the Father fulfils the divine superiority."

[129] McCormack, "Grace and Being," 193. McCormack makes this point on the way to his argument that "the words of God *ad intra* (the trinitarian processions) find their ground in the *first* of the works of God *ad extra* (viz., election)" (194). However, it is not necessary to conclude that God's triunity arises from the divine decision to appreciate the "inconsistency" he observes in Barth's thinking (see, for example, IV/1).

for us.[130] From either angle, the concept of "fulfillment" (*Vollzug*) is vital. "Reconciliation is the *fulfillment* of the covenant between God and humanity," as Neder puts it.[131] On those occasions where Barth speaks of divine obedience disconnected from its economic reference, when he slips into "free-floating talk of the 'eternal Son,'" he loses the proper teleological ordering of covenantal election and reconciliation.[132] As Barth himself summarizes the christological hymn using the language of 2 Corinthians 11:7, "I abase myself that ye might be exalted" (189). There is no divine "lowliness" for its own sake; it is essentially oriented to the "so that."

To claim economic subjection is taken up into the triune life in the identity of the Son is one thing; making his being "a slave of God" the ground for the unfolding of the salvation drama is quite another. T. F. Torrance argues, "There are . . . elements in the incarnate economy such as the time pattern of human life in this world which we may not read back into the eternal Life of God."[133] This "not reading back" of everything does not have to entail any disparity between God's being *in se* and God's action *pro nobis*. On the contrary, it only means we are preserving the distinction between fulfillment or consequence and its basis or ground. Their "correspondence" (*Entsprechung*) (IV/1, 203) does not undermine their ordering. It may be argued that Barth conflates the two because of his radical wedding of immanence to economy, in order to maintain that "God's essence and work are not twofold but one" (I/1, 372).

---

[130] Molnar, "Obedience of the Son," 63 (emphasis added). I share Molnar's observation, although not the basis for his concern. He worries that this "implies a need on the part of God for fulfillment" and threatens God's freedom. In other words, he thinks Barth is being metaphysically imprecise, but not maintaining enough distance between the immanent Trinity and economic Trinity. By contrast, I think the problem is that dissociating from direct reference to the *pro nobis* is abstraction and speculation. Barth suddenly talks as if there is a "before" or "above" reconciliation, which he otherwise avoids doing. That is why McCormack considers such statements a "lapse" into substantialist or non-actualist ways of thinking.

[131] Neder, *Participation in Christ*, 42 (emphasis added). "Election and obedience are related to one another as ground and consequence." Neder says this of the election and obedience of humans in Christ; however, as analogous, the same can be said with regard to Jesus Christ (18).

[132] McCormack, "Obedience and Grace," in *Orthodox and Modern*, 194.

[133] Thomas F. Torrance, *The Christian Doctrine of God, One Being Three Persons* (London: T&T Clark, 2001), 109. Even if one endorses a hierarchical view of the Trinity, there is a critical distinction to be drawn between the slavery to evil and nothingness that Jesus Christ undertakes in order to overcome it and his unchanging deference to "the will of the Father." Otherwise, Barth is left with the same problem that faced Calvin's account of election, the possibility of a divine Father who wills evil.

But from another vantage point, precisely the opposite appears to be the case: it begins to look like a retreat into abstraction about intratrinitarian preconditions.

Third, the eternality or divinity of the Son's subjection is an unnecessary claim in light of not only the teleological relation of election and reconciliation but also the nature of analogy and identity. There are two related issues here: drawing the wrong point of analogy and drawing it too closely. Although Barth qualifies the language of "son," indicating he does not imagine the "Father" is *a* father and the "Son" is *a* son, at times the meaning he invests in the titles is overliteralized, static, and even univocal.[134] He defines the Father as the "one who commands" and the Son as the "one who obeys." But, as we have seen, if he were in fact deriving the meaning of son from the biblical witness, say from Luke 15:11–32, the main accent would not be obedience construed as servility (being-under) but rather heirship (being-gifted).[135] In a biblical sense, and certainly in the paradigm of the parable, to say "son" is finally to say "heir," "gifted one"—*beloved*—not "slave," as the elder son sees himself, or "hired hand," as the younger son sees himself. In the language of Galatians, "God has sent the Spirit of his Son into our hearts, crying, 'Abba! Father!' So you are no longer a slave but a child, and if a child then also an heir" (Gal 4:6–7).[136] Reading sonship as a kind of subservience or slavery mistakes one of the strongest biblical points of dissimilarity between the divine Father/Son and human fathers/sons for the primary point of similarity.[137]

Compounding this problem, Barth seems to forget that he is talking about one thing in terms that are only suggestive of another. The danger is perhaps not so much in the word "obedience" itself but in forgetting that the thing being talked about (divine self-giving) is distinct from the thing from which the terms are borrowed (subordination understood humanly)—a risk implicit in metaphorical language. In the case that we must speak of "obedience" in

[134] At least, Jesus Christ is not a son of "a father," though he is genuinely a son of a mother.

[135] See my rhetorical reading of Luke 15:11–32 in ch. 1 of this book, "Prodigal Reading."

[136] Barth portrays Christ not only as Servant but also as *Liberator* (IV/1–3, passim); however, his role in liberating humanity is still rooted in his own status as a slave of the Father. Ironically, then, the soteriological claim of liberation depends upon a primordial ontological enslavement, one that is never overcome. Slavery rather than liberation is situated at the heart of God, between the Father and Son. But could it not just as easily be otherwise—that (if one is to continue with the supposition of divine processions) the generation of the Son is described in terms of making space, granting freedom and otherness?

[137] See my analysis of the parable in ch. 1.

God—what can this mean?[138] Even if one posits a structural or relational analogue or antecedent for Jesus' human obedience in the second person of the Trinity—as Hans Urs von Balthasar goes on to do with the concept of *Urkenosis*—there is no reason the pretemporal and temporal terms should become identical.[139] In fact, it is more appropriate to maintain that the temporal obedience of the Son is antecedently rooted in something other than an eternalized version of the same—for correspondence implies differentiation. To be analogous or to be identified in a narrative sense is not, after all, to be identical in a univocal or analytic sense.[140] The "obedience *to the Father*" that we see in Gethsemane can be appropriated to the humanity of the Son in such a way that its intratrinitarian correlate is a self-election of "obedience *to death*" (Phil 2:8) rather than eternal subjection to the superior will of another.[141] Alternately, the analogue or antecedent of the Son's far

[138] One of the ontological considerations concerns what "obedience" can (and cannot) mean for a *divine* existence in distinction from a human existence, for the life of Jesus Christ as he "exists in the manner of God" rather than as he "exists in the manner of [human flesh]" (IV/3.1, 39). How does God participate in the obedience of the Son's incarnate life? How does God "experience" God's own voluntary descent to death? The logical difficulty the metaphor poses when attached to triunity suggests Barth is literalizing from a model of sons/fathers.

[139] Balthasar follows missions back to processions, without collapsing them. He grounds Christ's kenosis described in Phil 2 analogically in the eternal "event" of intra-Trinitarian processions of love. Reworking Aquinas, he plays up movement as a perfection of the divine life. See, for example, his works *Mysterium Paschale* and *Theo-Drama*.

[140] "Conformity," "correspondence," and "identity" are concepts clearly marked by a structure of analogy in Barth's thought—i.e., by similarity in the midst of dissimilarity. "Identity," here, is narratival and not logical. It is not at all $A = A$ but very much $A = not\ A$. A narratival identity is, by definition, not of things that are the same but of things that are different, bearing both similarity and dissimilarity. That being the case, there is no clear reason why "obedience" should become a matter of simple identity (understood analytically, $A = A$). Perhaps it could be argued that Barth deliberately uses the term nonmetaphorically on account of the identity between the Son and Jesus Christ, but this would run counter to his overt acknowledgment that even "son" is an insufficient analogical descriptor.

[141] In the christological hymn, the "obedience" attributed to Christ who was in the form of God but took on the form of the servant is obedience *to death* rather than *to the Father*. Barth, however, appears to conflate the two. A clear distinction could prevent both (1) a disconnect between the history of Jesus and the being of God and (2) the appearance of two divine wills. Insofar as he is here reflecting on antecedent Trinitarian conditions (and this may be proof that he should not do so), to speak of the Eternal Son subjecting his will to the Father introduces the

journey could simply be love, rather than subordination or slavery. To give oneself, to subordinate oneself—that is a legitimate capability and "consequence" of love that does not define or exhaust its own basis or "ground." It is a fulfillment (temporal) of love (eternal) that cannot be reduced to its manifestation. Or is there no reason we say "God is love" and not "God is obedience"?

Fourth, and closely related, there is the doctrinal problem of how we can meaningfully predicate subjection between God and God. Barth's comments on sons define obedience as subjection to the will of another, namely to that of a ruler or father (IV/1, 203). What can this mean intratrinitarianly in view of the unity of the divine will? Even if one radicalizes the identity between Jesus of Nazareth and the second person, as Barth seems to, he would not posit two *divine* wills.[142] While he affirms *dyothelitism*, that is a christological claim about the divine and human wills of Jesus Christ, not of the first and second members of the Trinity.[143] In submitting to the Father's will, the eternal Son, even conceived as the *logos incarnandus*, can be submitting only to his own singular divine will.[144] Often Barth rightly stresses the reflexivity of the Son's humiliation. It is *self*-ordination, *self*-election, *self*-determination,

appearance of two divine wills, which it seems Barth would otherwise deny. This will be addressed below.

[142] Throughout volume one of *Church Dogmatics*, Barth emphasizes that God is a single subject and worries about "Eastern" conceptions of the persons as three agents or centers of willing. But does Barth's later Trinitarian imagination betray a similar vision of the first and second persons? In the context of his rejection of the seventeenth-century notion of a "covenant of redemption," Barth asks, "Can we really think of the first and second persons of the triune Godhead as two divine Subjects and therefore as two legal Subjects who can have dealings and enter into obligations with one another? This is mythology, for which there is no place in a right understanding of the doctrine of the Trinity as the doctrine of the three modes of being of the one God" (IV/1, 65). Yet, this is precisely the sort of arrangement as Barth's description of the Son as "one who obeys" and the Father as "one who commands" (203).

[143] See IV/1, 163f., 194. *Dyothelitism* is the position that Jesus Christ has two wills (divine and human in concord) rather than one (just divine or just human). This gets tricky, because Jesus Christ *is* the second person of the Trinity. But Barth himself makes the distinction. He is not merely talking about the *human* will of Jesus Christ submitting to the eternal Father, but his *eternal* will as the Son.

[144] From the beginning of *Church Dogmatics*, Barth carefully avoids the modern understanding of the word "person" as "center of consciousness." Even here in IV/1, he refers back to his formulation in I/1:

self-humiliation, *self*-giving. However, this affirmation weakens considerably when the Son's obedience is rendered intratrinitarian. In II/2, the Son's election is described as self-election to election by the Father (to a human life and identity that entails subjection), but in IV/1 "obedience" supplants more reflexive terms and gives the appearance of an eternal ordering of plural wills within a static hierarchy of persons, something Barth consistently rejects. This is at odds with his account of the one divine subject of the Trinity, which he still maintains in IV/1, as in I/1, is one in "self-consciousness, cognition, volition, activity, effects, revelation and name" (IV/1, 205). "Obedience" conceived nonmetaphorically as the submission of one's own will to that of another is logically incompatible with the assertion of volitional oneness.

Finally, these considerations give rise to the question of which, for Barth, is more basic to the character of God—that the Son subjects his will to that of the Father or that from all eternity God elects not to be God without the human other? The parabolic retelling that governs Barth's account of reconciliation as well as the scriptural nexus through which Barth filters the story resist a reduction of love to servility.[145] In view of the parable, especially as it is overlain with the logic of the christological hymn, obedience is neither the origin nor the telos of the Son's

---

By Father, Son and Spirit we do not mean what is commonly suggested to us by the word "persons." This designation was accepted—not without opposition—on linguistic presuppositions which no longer obtain today. It was never intended to imply—at any rate in the main stream of theological tradition—that there are in God three different personalities, three self-existent individuals with their own special self-consciousness, cognition, volition, activity, effects, revelation and name. The one name of the one God is the threefold name of Father, Son and Holy Spirit. The one "personality" of God, the one active and speaking divine Ego, is Father, Son and Holy Spirit. Otherwise we should obviously have to speak of three gods. And this is what the early Church not only would not do, but in the conception of the doctrine of the Trinity which ultimately prevailed tried expressly to exclude, just as it did any idea of a division or inequality between Father, Son and Holy Spirit. Christian faith and the Christian confession has one Subject, not three. But He is the one God in self-repetition, in the repetition of His own and equal divine being, and therefore in three different modes of being—which the term "person" was always explained to mean. (IV/1, 204–5)

[145] Apparently Hans Frei would disagree. His argument supports Barth's understanding of obedience as more basic than loving-kindness: "In the pattern found in Isaiah and also in the gospel narrative, the focus of obedience is, of course, God. . . . There is no single clue—not even love—to unlock the character and deportment of Jesus in the Gospels. As the governing motif of Jesus' life, love is far more nearly an indirect than a direct focus of his behavior. His love is a function of his mission, but his mission is to enact the salvation of humanity in obedience to God. Love is subsidiary to that mission" (*Identity of Jesus Christ*, 83–84). However, it does not seem that Frei would, on this basis, "lapse" as Barth does into metaphysical talk (e.g., of processions).

trajectory but only the means or path (self-sacrifice) and nadir (slavery to death). The beginning is "towardness" (*Fügsamkeit*), yes, but the "towardness" and "movement" of God to humankind is love. The end is the raising up, the exaltation, of humankind in Christ, also love. But, in his teaching on divine obedience, Barth distills both to the towardness of Son to Father—and, in that sense, the direction of the Son toward the world appears to be subsumed in what happens within the Trinity in God's "self-positing" (IV/1, 209–10). What begins as a relentless focus on the revelation of God in Christ ends by tracing his earthly obedience back to a vestigial account of divine processions in which one who is primary, superior, and commanding posits one who is secondary, junior, and submissive.

There are surely other ways of forestalling Barth's conclusion, but these points suffice to suggest Jesus Christ's earthly subjection—which, according to Barth's central intertexts, is not simply to the Father but to sin and death as well—does not necessarily derive from and point back to a comparable relational subjugation within the Trinity. It is impossible and, moreover, undesirable to avoid metaphors such as "obedience" in theological language, but it is critical to get the analogical similarities and dissimilarities right and to avoid drawing the comparison too closely. Without undertaking the daunting task of reconstructing his entire doctrine of the Trinity in light of IV/1–2, Barth might still avert from the conclusion that there is a slavery primordial to the Son's relationship with the Father were he to (1) remain dialectical about power and position, theologically and ethically, (2) keep the teleological focus of Christ's earthly obedience in view, (3) resist overliteralizing from human analogues, (4) stress the reflexivity of the Son's obedience and his volitional unity with the Father, and (5) reduce the Son's assumption of servanthood to love, rather than vice versa.[146]

Further, if we stop short of the *theologoumenon* of the Son's eternal slavery, we see that this conclusion is in conflict with Barth's own methodological principle. Contrary to his assertion that if we do not uphold a divine subjection, we risk the appearance of a God behind God, it seems that Barth himself does not hold the line, moving beyond revelation in order to reflect on God *in se*. Over against the common theological preoccupation with God's abstract "personhood," Barth says, "Everything depends on the statement that God is the One who loves" (II/1, 296). Perhaps the same point needs to be made with respect to assertion of a pretemporal "ranking and ordering" in the Trinity. For all his criticism of Calvin's "speculative" teaching about a hidden or split divine will—his "fatal glancing aside at

---

[146]   For a reconstruction of Barth's doctrine of the Trinity based on IV/1, see McCormack, "Doctrine of the Trinity."

an election which takes place behind and above Christ in the hiddenness of God"—Barth's own teaching on *göttlichen Gehorsam* reflects a similar inclination (II/2, 17–18, 70).

However, there is a rich christological image in Barth's thought that, if kept front and center, could help deflect the temptation to look behind the claim that God is God's grace for a more basic precondition. Barth describes Jesus Christ as "Bearer" (e.g., I/2, 156; IV/2, 73, 106, 396; IV/3.1, 40, etc.). As Julian traces the Son's far journey to his divine motherhood, Barth describes his assumption of the form of the servant as a kind of "enburdenment."[147] Kenosis is construed as a "capacity," a power and potentiality, the ability to be for, to be more than oneself, to carry, to bear up and bear away.[148] Barth imagines incarnation not just as a putting-on but as an enclosing, containing, or holding.[149] Like Julian, he interweaves metaphors of clothing and indwelling. He calls Christ's humanity "a clothing which [God] does not put off . . . his temple which he does not leave . . . the form which he does not lose" (IV/2, 100), and he see humankind "hidden and enclosed and laid up . . . in [Christ]" (IV/1, 92). Barth speaks of the incarnational condescension of Jesus Christ as the "readiness" of God to be known (II/2, §26). Julian's example similarly stresses the eagerness of the servant, the earnest leaping up to labor that lands him in the ditch of incarnation and death. The ready willingness of the Son (Phil 2) to traverse the land of lost human existence is mirrored in the urgency of the parabolic father to hold his child and celebrate (Luke 15:32). Jesus Christ in his self-giving is that expectancy, that heavy waiting, the enburdenment of God. We might keep this "ladenness" and glad "readiness" in view when we hear the phrase "divine obedience," so as to preserve its primordial connection with the overflowing joy that conceives the humanity of God, borne eternally in the Trinity, beyond which we must not go.

[147]   This is something Jones stresses in *Humanity of Christ* (43, 163, 209, 236).

[148]   Barth stops here in *Humanity of God*, where he addresses the downwardness of God without positing the Son's eternal subjection or subordination. He simply says, "How could God's deity exclude His humanity, since it is God's freedom for love and thus His capacity to be not only in the heights but also in the depths, not only great but also small, not only in and for Himself but also with another distinct from Him, and to offer Himself to him?" (49). So it is possible for Barth to claim that the "going out" of love is proper to God's being without resorting to explanations of sub- and super-ordination.

[149]   Among many examples, he says, "If we would know who God is . . . we must look only upon the name of Jesus Christ, and the existence and history of the people of God enclosed within Him" (II/2, 54). Barth, like Julian, interweaves the metaphors of clothing, enclosure, and indwelling.

5

Parabolic Theology

"Parable is the form of the language of Jesus which corresponds to the incarnation."[1]

—Gerhard Ebeling

"One can and must say Jesus is *the parable of God*."[2]

—Eberhard Jüngel

"God is *human*."[3]

—Karl Barth

To call divine love "prodigal" is to accentuate its extravagance, its openhanded gratuity. Augustine prays to God, "Prodigality [*effusio*] shows, as it were, the shadow [*umbra*] of liberality; but you are the most supremely rich bestower of all good things."[4] According to the golden mean of liberality or generosity, prodigality or wastefulness and miserliness or stinginess are polar vices of excess and

---

[1]   Gerhard Ebeling, *Evangelische Evangelienauslegung: Eine Untersuchung zu Luther's Hermeneutik*, 2nd ed. (Darmstadt: Wissenschaftliche Buchgesellschaft, 1962), 108. Barth says, "It is rare in life to be able to separate form and content," and this seems particularly true in the case of Christology. See Karl Barth, *Dogmatics in Outline*, trans. G. T. Thompson (New York: Harper & Row, 1959), 96. Cf. *CD* I/2, 493.

[2]   Eberhard Jüngel, *God as the Mystery of the World: On the Foundation of the Theology of the Crucified One in the Dispute between Theism and Atheism*, trans. Darrell Guder (Edinburgh: T&T Clark, 1983), 288–89.

[3]   Karl Barth, *The Humanity of God*, trans. John Newton Thomas and Thomas Wieser (Richmond, Va.: John Knox, 1960), 50–51.

[4]   Augustine, *Confessions* II.6.13. Chadwick translates it, "Prodigality presents itself under the shadow of generosity; but you are the rich bestower of good things." *Confessions*, trans. Henry Chadwick (Oxford: Oxford University Press, 2008), 31. Here Augustine interprets liberality and prodigality among a larger set of virtues and vices.

deficiency.[5] Liberality is one of the few virtues that tips away from the mean, ful-filled not through strict moderation but by favoring the good of the other even at one's own expense.[6] The parabolic father thus exemplifies perfect liberality over against the extremes of his children's mismanagement of what they have been given—grasping on the one side, squandering on the other. He figures the abundant grace of God. But the retellings of the parable we encounter in Julian and Barth stretch Aquinas' claim *ille est maxime liberalis.*[7] The Lord is *exces-sively* liberal—wasteful, compromised, burdened, and yet unblaming. Julian and Barth retain the double sense of "prodigal," as not only lavish or extravagant but also reckless or imprudent. God's giving does not preclude cost and dan-ger. "If I might suffer more, I wolde suffer more," Christ says to Julian (22.4–5). God grants the vagrant child what she requests and, when she loses it, gives it to her all over again. Nothing is held back from the child who stays at home either, even when she protests the magnanimity of God.[8] God gives—and keeps giving.[9] There is no regard for just deserts, for choice, service, or merit. One is reminded of the lines from *Babette's Feast*: "See! that which we have chosen is given us, and that which we have refused is, also and at the same time, granted us. Ay, that which we have rejected is poured upon us abundantly. For mercy and truth have met together, and righteousness and bliss have kissed one another!"[10] God is, by human accounting, a foolhardy steward. This is the divine economy, *God's* housekeeping. For, in Bernard's words, "His *very nature* is to be good, to

---

[5]   Holgate's analysis of the Parable of the Prodigal Son in terms of this Greco-Roman topos is illuminating (see ch. 2). The father figures the virtue of liberality (freehandedness), while the elder son represents the vice of miserliness (closehand-edness) and the younger son the vice of prodigality (overreaching). In view of this ethics, Barth unmistakably sets God on one side of the spectrum, reinforcing his point that the wisdom of God is foolishness to humans. God's grace is not perfectly or absolutely liberal, but, so far as we can see, it is overly liberal.

[6]   Aquinas says, "A generous [i.e., liberal] individual measures out more things for others than for himself" (*ST* II-II, q. 117, a. 1). He is following Aristotle, who says, "It is most definitely characteristic of a generous person to go to excess in giving, so that less is left for himself." See *Nicomachean Ethics*, trans. Joe Sachs (Indianapolis: Hackett, 2002), book 4, 1120b, 60. For Aristotle, wastefulness is self-destructive (1120a, 59).

[7]   Aquinas, *ST* Ia, q. 44, a. 4.

[8]   On Julian's and Barth's reading, there is no way to figure the elder son as the reprobate.

[9]   This is a central insight in Kathryn Tanner's theology—e.g., see her discussion of "God's kingdom of unconditional giving," in *Economy of Grace* (Minneapolis: For-tress, 2005), 65.

[10]   Isak Dinesen, *"Babette's Feast" and Other Anecdotes of Destiny* (New York: Vintage, 1988), 40. From General Lowenhielm's speech.

show mercy always and to spare."[11] In the "midperson" of the Trinity, "courteous homeliness" is unveiled as God's "kindness" or nature. Barth claims "grace is the very essence of the being of God"; God's "whole being . . . is simply grace" (II/1, 356, 358). "Grace is God," writes Julian (63.8).

This is the radical conclusion of Julian's and Barth's creative theological retellings of the Parable of the Prodigal Son. The generative intertextuality of their interpretations renders the parable on three levels, as the narrative of salvation, atonement, and election. It pushes back into the divine life, dramatizing God's primal "thirst" for the world. Julian's *exemplum* prefigures Barth's reading, and his exegesis sheds light on the sophisticated systematic claims embedded in hers. Both invite us to consider the allusive nexus of biblical images and narratives that produce such christological interpretation. This has been the focus of my engagement with them. Reading Julian and Barth together surely uncovers other points of contact as well, which have been left undeveloped but are worth noting. We might consider further their pre- and post-historical-critical scriptural reading practices, the origins and impact of gendered language and images for God, the relationship between narrative and concept in their theological methods, "unnature" as a vital third term in the interplay of nature and grace, divine judgment construed as restorative, the ordering of salvation before creation and the universalistic scope of Christ's recapitulation of Adamic humanity, the question of what the concept of processions can mean or where it can be located in view of the eternal identity of the Son with humankind, the ambiguity of the son/servant motif in Scripture and theology, and the doctrinal implications of conceiving divine love as eros (Julian) instead of agape (Barth). In conclusion, however, I want to draw out several threads that have been interwoven in the preceding chapters. The first set concerns the methodological and ethical implications of Julian's and Barth's christological renderings of the parable. The second set is related to parable as a form of theology.

Theology as "Theanthropology"

In offering the Parable of the Prodigal Son as the condensation of the whole of the gospel, Julian and Barth resist separating the thought of God from the thought of salvation, and therefore from the world, humanity, and sin. In view of her "wonderful example of a lorde that hath a servant," Julian explains how Christ's human life, being "knit" to him, forms a knot "so suttel . . . that it is

---

[11]   Bernard of Clairvaux, sermon 36 in *On the Song of Songs II*, vol. 3 of *The Works of Bernard of Clairvaux*, trans. Kilian Walsh, O.C.S.O. (Kalamazoo, Mich.: Cistercian, 1983), 179 (emphasis added).

oned into God" such that that humankind itself be "knit in this knot, and oned in this oning" (53.30). Julian construes the at-one-ment between God and humanity in Christ as one of dwelling together and indwelling one another, of being-at-home-with-and-in one another. A "suttel knot" is a "love knot"—a nuptial symbol—but it is also a paradox, puzzle, or mystery.[12] This elemental "oning" of humanity into God is an act of love that scandalizes thought. Theology attempts to get behind it to God alone and apart. However, as Barth says in *The Humanity of God*, theology can no longer be the "doctrine of God" only; it is always "theanthropology," the doctrine of God and humanity together.[13]

God cannot be thought alone or apart because Jesus is the primary *medium* of the revelation of God and, further, *is* himself the revelation of God. This first point is basic to both Julian's and Barth's readings of the parable. Second, the human can no longer be thought alone or apart from God because the humanity of the human is defined in this one who is also with God in the beginning. Third, both subjects are inextricably bound in that what Christ reveals is the *humanity of God*—or, in Julian's language, that God's kindness (essential nature) is kindness (kinship or fellowship with humankind). Of course, Julian and Barth make these points from within profoundly different ontological frameworks. Julian works with a Neoplatonic substantialist or essentialist ontology, Barth within a post-Hegelian actualist ontology. Julian seems to affirm something like an *analogia entis*, a substantial bond and likeness between God and humankind by virtue of creation—hence her free use of the language of kinship.[14] Incarnation only reinforces and elevates the creational bond. Barth would be wary of the kind of substantial union by virtue of creation that Julian describes and especially her appeal to the fecundity of the maternal body.[15] Yet he translates what in her theological milieu is spoken of as "mystical union" or "participation in God" in terms of "covenantal

---

[12]   Nicholas Watson and Jacqueline Jenkins, eds., *The Writings of Julian of Norwich: "A Vision Showed to a Devout Woman" and "A Revelation of Love"* (University Park: Pennsylvania State University Press, 2006), 294.

[13]   Barth, *Humanity of God*, 9.

[14]   At the same time, it could be argued that she does not make her analogy on the basis of creation strictly speaking since she clearly does not understand creation apart from the Son's own incarnation. In that sense, her account of the relationship between God and humanity is as utterly christological as Barth's.

[15]   On this point, see Faye Bodley-Dangelo, *Sexual Difference, Gender, and Agency in Karl Barth's "Church Dogmatics"* (London: T&T Clark, 2020), 76. Catherine Keller also critiques Barth's aversion to maternal imagery, viz. in his reading of the first chapters of Genesis, in *Face of the Deep: A Theology of Becoming* (New York: Routledge, 2003), 90–95.

fellowship."[16] Fellowship, being-at-home-with, is there "in the beginning" for Barth, as kindness and kinship are for Julian. Despite their different ontological resources, their resulting visions of the primordial divine-human relationship are richly resonant.

The thoroughgoingness of their commitment to theology as "theanthropology" is evident in that even in reflecting on the Trinity "before the creation of the world," they do not envision God without humanity. As Barth maintains, "At no level or time can we have to do with God without having also to do with this human" (IV/2, 33, rev.). For "God alone is God. But God is not alone." We must "proceed from the simple fact that in the revelation of God in Jesus Christ, God and [humanity] *meet*, and therefore are really *together*." In fact, "we have to use an even stronger expression than this, and speak of God being *one with* humanity."[17] In Jüngel's paraphrase of Barth, there is "no non-human God."[18] Thus the methodological premise of "theanthropology" helps protect the ontological claim—God and humankind are eternally "knit" together in Jesus Christ—and, concomitantly, its soteriological assurance: humans are "oned" into God in this "oning," "hidden with Christ in God" (Col 3:3). As Spearing says of Julian's image of the Son crowned with humanity before the Father, "At the very centre of Julian's vision is a God inseparable from man and woman: transcendent in some sense, yes, but unable to set aside the bodily kinship he has chosen with his creatures."[19] Trying to think God and humanity apart threatens the very fabric of grace and gives rise to such "dark

[16]   While Barth acknowledges that a "mystical vocabulary . . . can hardly be avoided," when it comes to our participation in the dying and rising of Christ (I/1, 222), he tends to mistake mysticism as having to do with "an indefinable and ultimately unknown divine somewhat, which stands over us" (*Dogmatics in Outline*, 89). For an extended treatment of this theme in Barth's thought, see Adam Neder, *Participation in Christ: An Entry into Karl Barth's "Church Dogmatics"* (Louisville, Ky.: Westminster John Knox, 2009). For an analysis of the christological basis of Barth's understanding of the *analogia*, see Kenneth Oakes, "The Question of Nature and Grace in Karl Barth: Humanity as Creature and as Covenant Partner," *Modern Theology* 23, no. 4 (2007): 598–616.

[17]   See Barth's fourth Gifford Lecture, "The Glory of God and the Glory of Man," in *The Knowledge of God and the Service of God according to the Teaching of the Reformation: Recalling the Scottish Confession of 1560*, trans. J. L. M. Haire and Ian Henderson, The Gifford Lectures (London: Hodder and Stoughton, 1938), 4.1–3.

[18]   John Thompson, *Christ in Perspective: Christological Perspectives in the Theology of Karl Barth* (Edinburgh: Saint Andrew Press, 1978), 102. Extending Barth's train of thought, Jüngel uses the phrase "keine Meschenlogiskeit Gottes," in *Unterwegs zur Sache: Theologische Bemerkungen* (Münich: Christian Kaiser, 1972), 384.

[19]   A. C. Spearing, introduction to *Revelations of Divine Love*, trans. Elizabeth Spearing (New York: Penguin, 1998), xxxi.

speculations" as are evident, for example, in the older Augustinian-Reformed variety of supralapsarian double predestination that Barth rejects. He attempts to follow through with Calvin's purported intention to bracket the question "What is God?" and focus on "what *sort*," as revealed through God's works.[20]

Theological conundrums naturally arise when speaking of God's love for humankind as basic, primal, or originary. We see this when Barth is pushed to assert the Son's eternal subordination and when his critics, distinguishing too sharply between the immanent and economic being of God, risk splitting the personhood of the Son. This is where Julian's rather different handling of kinship analogies may be instructive. While he traces the parabolic father/son relationship back to an abstracted master/slave dynamic within the divine life, her theological interpretation of the parable moves from the models lord/servant to father/son to mother/child in a way that keeps the divine-human relationship always in view. Even if, for Julian, the parable communicates something about intratrinitarian processions and relations, concentrating on the "motherhood" of God prevents her from at any point ducking behind the conclusion that "God never began to love humankind" (53.1). The divine name is not sheer being but "It I am *thine*."[21]

The decisive theological function of asserting divine motherhood, for Julian, is that it prevents us from reducing the reciprocal relationship between God and the world established and sealed in the eternal at-one-ment of Christ's humanity in the Trinity. Motherhood, as Julian presents it, is not simply the feminine counterpart to fatherhood. It is not as if she appeals to the image as a proto-feminist who merely wants to remind the world that women are, like men, *capax Dei*.[22] Calling God "Moder" conceptually supplements and expands what is meant by God's paternity. On the one hand, eternal motherhood contains much of what one would otherwise communicate via the familial language fatherhood: that God is origin and creator, sovereign provider,

---

[20]   Calvin, *Institutes* I.III.2 (emphasis added).

[21]   See Julian, *A Revelation* 26.4–8; 59.11–16; discussed in ch. 3, pp. 159–60.

[22]   Barth, of course, denies that all humans, not just women, are capable of imaging God on their own. He says the image of God "is not a quality of man. . . . It does not consist in anything that man is or does" (*CD* III/1, 184). Where Julian naturally articulates a more Catholic and ancient position on the relationship between nature and grace, Barth stresses the wholly-otherness of God and rejects any affinity, likeness, or capacity humans have with God by virtue of their creation. But, while Julian does seem to be suggesting we can speak cataphatically about God on the basis of female bodies and experiences, that is not the primary analogical point. What is more salient here is the way maternal imagery prevents a certain kind of theological abstraction.

sustainer and nurturer, and so on. On the other hand, the model of father is unable to convey for her the "beclosure" of God and humankind in incarnation and election, which is aptly captured in the anatomical analogy of a pregnant body. The point at which a maternal metaphor becomes incongruous only functions to strengthen its imaginal power. Julian says Christ is "oure very moder, in whome we be endlessly borne and *never shall come out of* him" (57.43). The analogical breakdown ensures our comprehension of the remarkable claim: humanity is born of and yet ever borne in Mother Christ, who is eternally "oned" (united) and "wonning" (dwelling) with her children.

In this image, the critical thing to see is not that Julian simply makes better use of gendered imagery and kinship analogies than Barth but that she deploys a model that is resistant to further theological distillation. Maternity is methodologically regulative. It better enables her to hold the line of God's self-revelation, or "theanthropology." Julian sees humanity endlessly knitted into the Trinity. Barth's theory of the eternal subordination of Son to Father—while indeed rooted in his incarnational understanding of election—seems to extend beyond the appearing of the divine *philanthropia* revealed in Christ. It becomes a speculative basis, a theorizing about what is manifest that distracts from and is only tangentially related to what is manifest. Juxtaposed with Julian's reduction of the parabolic father to divine motherhood, the trouble with Barth's fatherhood and sonship language is that it leads him back to a more primal structure of superordination and subordination that has less power to evoke the lovingkindness he otherwise asserts is God's very "essence." The content of his description of filial obedience raises the question of whether the point is really that "God is human" or that the second member of the Trinity is subject to the first. It is worth reiterating Soskice's insight that "the principal reason why the biblical writings are so dependent on gendered imagery . . . is not because its writers were so very interested in sex, or even hierarchy as subordination, but because they were interested in kinship."[23] By shifting fatherhood and sonship past an affirmation of kinship and love to an arrangement of wills, Barth risks losing the clarity and radicalness of his assertion in *The Humanity of God*: "The truth of *God* is loving-kindness towards [humans] . . . and nothing else."[24] The trajectory of Julian's metaphors keeps our imaginations on course here.

Notwithstanding the ontological pitfalls of eternal atonement, what Julian's and Barth's readings teach us is that "theanthropology" can at least serve as a methodological limit for theology. Their conviction that the God we are given

---

[23]   Janet Martin Soskice, *The Kindness of God: Metaphor, Gender, and Religious Language* (Oxford: Oxford University Press, 2007), 4.

[24]   Barth, *Humanity of God*, 51–52.

to know is never without this eternal bond with the world sets up two significant guardrails for theological reflection: namely, (1) it is a distraction to consider God strictly *in se* (even if one suspects there is such a thing), and (2) to be human is elementally to be seen by God in Christ as a beloved child. The first guardrail does not necessarily imply an apophatic move, although one could take that route. Rather, it only requires an intentional bracketing off, or a decentering, in dogmatics, of the question of who or what God is apart from the revelation of God's love for the world in Jesus Christ.[25] The second is embedded with an important ethical imperative.

Go and See Likewise

In the "two domes" motif animated through her example, Julian's concern with how God sees is bound up with the desire to learn to see herself and others as God does. She wishes to reeducate human vision with respect to itself, to help it see itself as God does, through the eyes of love and not rejection. This requires a thorough reimagining of fallen humanity before God. Her retelling of the Parable of the Prodigal Son in particular, as well as her subsequent reflection on the inclusive love of the Trinity, provides new images for meditation and self-knowledge: an earnest and injured servant viewed piteously by his lord, a frightened child climbing into her mother's lap. Julian says "oure good lorde Jhesu reformeth" human self-judgment "by mercy and grace thorow [through] vertu of his blessed passion" (45.7–8). This re-visioning is not optional, as she sees it. It is not simply unnecessary to see oneself judged guilty; it is no longer permissible.[26] This is what is "owed" in the debt of reconciliation, relinquishing the lens of sinful human judgment.

Julian advances her theology pastorally, reforming her reader's sense of self as she goes. She draws on common devotional and theological tropes and terms in order to reinvest them with different meanings, for example, by consistently defining words such as "righteousness," "judgment," and "justice" in

---

[25]   I think this includes a bracketing off many of the solutions we find to the problem of "how" God can become human "without changing," particularly those that involve speculating about a more original basis in God than the loving-kindness that has appeared in the savior (Titus 3:4).

[26]   In between plague outbreaks, Julian would have been familiar with the religious argument that the symptoms of sickness are an outward sign of sin and should be received as a deserved punishment. Against this sort of simplistic theodicy (in which God is justified through victim-blaming), Julian argues that visible suffering is *not* a sign of divine wrath and, further, that God does not vindicate Godself on humanity at all. See Denise Baker, *Julian of Norwich's Showings: From Vision to Book* (Princeton: Princeton University Press, 1994), 83f.

terms of mercy, goodness, and love. Using an accepted vocabulary, through repetition her text reconditions expectations so that these words once used to indicate one thing evoke something else in the reader's imagination. God's judgment becomes synonymous with grace, comfort, and healing. Included in the antidote to sin is the exclusion of any self-judgment that contradicts God's gracious judgment.[27] So at the heart of Julian's text there is more than a leap of faith over the logical gap between human sin and divine love. There is something given in addition to the hope of an eschatological resolution in a mysterious "great deed." Salvation, for Julian, is not all present blindness and eschatological delay. There is an imperative, something to receive and enact: a new vision of being human, one mediated by the "otherwise beholding" of God's providential, benevolent gaze. For Julian "to see spiritually" is "to see from within the body of Christ, as the locus of all there is in a place where all can be incorporated." It is only from this inclusive perspective that the human "is capable of seeing itself as Christ sees it," as it really is.[28] This is the work of meditation in the task of conforming to Christ. This is discipleship. Christ's "office of motherhood" invites what is owed—the "condition of childhood," which is trust in God's ready and laden embrace.

Barth's understanding of election and atonement similarly leads him to describe faith as not believing in one's own rejection.[29] This undertone can be obscured in his account of human vocation, which lays a heavier stress on obedience, service, and discipleship.[30] In a number of ways, Julian's and Barth's

[27] Julian implicates the church's theology in the perpetuation of sinful self-accusation.

[28] Kevin McGill, *Julian of Norwich: Mystic or Visionary?* (New York: Routledge, 2006), 89.

[29] Barth commends self-accusation at multiple points as the appropriate attitude of the human before God. While Barth offers a fuller picture of sin (as pride, sloth, and falsehood) than is common for pre-twenty-first-century (privileged, male) theologians, he is still fairly preoccupied with prideful human assertion (even in his discussion of sloth). This corresponds to his emphasis on human fault. Julian does not deny the reality of sin or human responsibility for it, but her tone is more pastoral. She assumes her audience practices self-accusation, perhaps even to an unhealthy degree—hence her attention to the fact that "beloved" is the first and last word of God toward the human. This is a difference of accent and one that may be explained by things like social situation, gendered experience, and prevailing theological attitudes at specific points in history.

[30] Throughout §74, Barth relies on the narrative of the Parable of the Prodigal Son, but this time not to describe the Son's gracious rewriting of human history. Instead, applying the story anthropologically, he commends the younger son's confession to the father ("I am not worthy") as proper to his fallenness as well as his humanity. This reading of the parable runs counter to the one I offered in ch. 1. It also poses a problem

conclusions are in tension.[31] However, there is an important point of consonance in their understandings of the atonement for the life of faith. As Barth
writes in his doctrine of election,

> Faith in the divine predestination as such and *per se* means faith in the non-
> rejection of [humanity], or disbelief in its rejection. [Humanity] is not reject-
> ed. In God's eternal purpose it is God Himself who is rejected in His Son. The
> self-giving of God consists, the giving and sending of His Son is fulfilled, in
> the fact that He [God] is rejected in order that we might not be. (II/2, 167)

This is the basis for any human response to God. God's definitive word to
humans is: "In Jesus Christ, thou, too, art not rejected—for He has borne thy
rejection—but elected" (322). While concepts like wrath, judgment, punishment, accusation, and so on figure much more prominently in Barth's rhetoric
and theology than in Julian's, at the same time, over against a certain caricature
of Reformed theology in which God is "everything" and humanity is "nothing," Barth insists that in Christ we have the glory of God *and* the glory of the
human.[32] Inasmuch as God sees all people in Christ on account of the atonement, he says, "We may, and should, understand ourselves as seen by God in
Him."[33] We must continue to affirm that "sin cannot and does not change our
fundamental nature as beings that are essentially loved."[34] That means believing the ultimate word of God's grace that there is now no condemnation for
those who are in Christ. There is no remainder of judgment.

Conformity to the will of God is conformity to God's "counter-perspective"
on human beings.[35] The ethical outworking of the atonement as being-

---

for Barth's own thinking about the divine establishment of human agency as well as
his understanding of humanity as cohumanity with Christ. For a criticism of Barth's
difficulty finally affirming the goodness of human action, even obedience, see Neder
(*Participation in Christ*, 86).

[31]   While Julian moves from the pairs lord/servant in the example to father/
son in God to mother/child to describe the relationship between God and humankind, Barth moves from father/son in the parable to a structure of lord/servant
within God as well as between God and humankind. These trajectories are telling.
Barth translates sonship into subjection while Julian renders the servant a beloved
child. There are multiple similarities in the ways they describe the appropriate
human response to the condescension of God, but their difference in emphasis has
consequences.

[32]   See Barth, "Glory of God and the Glory of Man," 4.1.

[33]   Barth, *Dogmatics in Outline*, 91.

[34]   Oakes, "Question of Nature," 611. See *CD* III/2, 319.

[35]   On the face of it, Barth's own "divine command" ethics (in *CD* III) shows little
material similarity with what I am saying here. I am only noting that, *formally*, his

(seen)-in-Christ requires reimagining oneself (and others) beheld by God as a beloved child, as the father in the parable sees his son, as a mother regards an injured child. It is on this basis that gratitude, openness, as well as a certain kind of service and obedience are appropriate human responses to God's lordship and "summons."[36] Julian's and Barth's texts appear intentionally crafted to effect this re-visioning, which draws attention to the way ethical formation is intrinsic to the writing and reading of theology. Julian's writing unfolds as a performative heuristic, enfolding its readers into another way of seeing themselves. This is a distinctive feature of the narrative form of *exempla* with which she works. The same can be said of Barth's sprawling theology. In both cases, narrativity is integral to the effectiveness of their recruitment of readers into a new theological vision of reality. Barth's use of theological narrative

> brings out the dimensions of wresting, of pulls and counter-pulls, quite well. It is a more originary literary form, remaining close to the rich texture, the *eros*, of human existence. It also combines, in varying degrees of energy, participation and distance in a manner quite appropriate again to Incarnation and redemption. As we follow along the path of the plot . . . we actually experience the temporal drama. We are drawn into it. . . . We participate. . . . But participation is not simply identity. Participation also presupposes distance and difference from the event and the characters. We must make a response, experience our own pulls and counter-pulls, decide to follow along or resist.[37]

The participatory or implicatory force of theological narrative subjects us to the drama laid out in a way that can fundamentally alter our posture and

---

assertion "the eternal will of God is humankind" (II/2, 167) bears ethical import and could be taken in the direction I am suggesting. As Barth's editors remark in the preface to II/2, "The chapter on the divine command follows naturally from that on election, for the predestinating will of God is necessarily His will for the object of His love. Here then, in his doctrine of God, Barth lays the foundation for a theological ethics covering the whole area of man's freedom and self-determination as one called to be a covenant-partner of God. In virtue of the election of grace, his existence is not left to itself, but adopted and assumed into the existence of God in Jesus Christ. A general ethics is impossible, because it attempts to ignore the election of grace. It can be attempted only in a sinful self-isolation from God" (II/2, vii). But in Julian's assessment, it is sin itself, or a sinful theology of sin, that causes us to image the divine-human relationship in terms of subjection or "bondage." *That* would be the "general ethics," one that has not perceived the particular quality of God's "deeming" in Christ.

36   The keyword "summons" pops up throughout *Church Dogmatics*, but see, for example, III/2.

37   William Thompson, *The Struggle for Theology's Soul: Contesting Scripture in Christology* (New York: Crossroad Herder, 1996), 90.

perspective.[38] We are led along at a distance and, as in the parables of Jesus, summoned to a lived response. Ricoeur tells us that to read is to traverse this distance, to "redo with the text a certain 'line' or 'course' (*parscours*) of meaning."[39] Far from rendering a contentless crisis moment then, the Parable of the Prodigal Son and these retellings of it depict with specificity and clarity who we are and pull us toward how we ought to be.

Parable as Narrative Icon

Parable is a narrative form that prompts the purgation and conversion of the gaze.[40] The phenomenological language of "bracketing" and "reduction," which pervades much contemporary parable scholarship, illuminates the dynamics of reading or hearing the parables. The metaphoricity of parable takes place between text and world (Ricoeur), between the thumbnail-of-a-story and its lived reception.[41] It belongs to parable that it makes *us* the bridge between expectation and fulfillment (Alter) and invites its hearers into a space where their prejudgments and habits may be "contravened" (Husserl). It integrates those before the text into its world, reversing the order of perception and exposing the reader or hearer. In this sense, parable functions like a *narrative icon*.

As discussed in chapter 1, inverting ordinary pictorial perspective, a painted icon protrudes on the world in an incisive way. Rather than drawing viewers into an enclosed spectacle (/\), the perspectival lines of an icon converge outside the plane on the viewer (\/).[42] The flat surface of the icon thus appears to take aim;

---

[38] See ch. 1 on how metaphor and parable implicate hearers.

[39] Paul Ricoeur, *The Rule of Metaphor: Multi-disciplinary Studies of the Creation of Meaning in Language*, trans. Robert Czerny, Kathleen McLaughlin, and John Costello, S.J. (London: Routledge & Kegan Paul, 1978), 150.

[40] This is not exclusively true of parable. Other narratives and visual forms can have the same effect. What is peculiar to parable is its density or compactness. To speak at all, it must say more than it is saying. Because of this, it is more clearly an instance of metaphorized narrative, or rather it explicitly asks to be metaphorized in the direction of the world. Again, by "metaphorized" here I only mean the narrative is made to speak of one thing in terms that are suggestive of another (Soskice). Far from belittling the (plain or "literal") import of the story, this is how the story grows.

[41] As I pointed out in ch. 1, this "lived reception" is a matter of the "spiritual meaning" of the text (de Lubac), which often gets dismissed as "allegorizing" (Funk et al.), but the impulse belongs to the text itself (Ricoeur).

[42] In linear perspective, the painting plane approximates the way the eye sees in nature such that looking at a painting is like looking out a window or, in portraiture, at the person. The emphasis is on creating three-dimensionality, in which contours round and space recedes. This understanding is clearly articulated in the first great modern treatise *On Painting* by Renaissance artist Leon Battista Alberti (1435). By contrast, the reverse perspective of icons feels remedial and unnatural,

it forms the point of a gaze, a gaze that issues as a counterjudgment and also call.[43] As before the icon the viewer is viewed, so before the parable the reader is read, questioned, constituted. This phenomenon is utterly common to the reading or viewing experience.[44] The Parable of the Prodigal Son provides a paradigmatic case in which the form of parable—its ability to generate a countergaze—corresponds neatly with the content of the parable—its narration of two economies of worth, value, or identity and their attendant perspectives. At the center of the story, we encounter the compassionate look of the father (v. 20) directed toward both sons, his hospitable insistence that they are "you are no longer a slave but a child, and if a child then also an heir" (Gal 4:7).

---

hence the primitivism of which icon writers are sometimes accused. However, the effect is deliberate, not a lack of skill. A story about the recontextualization of icons designed for worship in modern museums exemplifies this: "Two learned people were standing before some icons in a museum, making disparaging comments about their primitiveness and lack of perspective. An old Russian lady could not help overhearing and . . . asked if she could say something. . . . 'It is not we who judge icons,' she said, 'but icons which judge us.'" See Aidan Hart, *Beauty, Spirit, Matter: Icons in the Modern World* (Herefordshire, U.K.: Gracewing, 2014), 5.

[43] For a developed phenomenology of the icon, see the work of Jean-Luc Marion, for example, *God without Being*, trans. Thomas A. Carson (Chicago: University of Chicago Press, 1991), esp. ch. 1, "The Idol and the Icon"; *In Excess: Studies of Saturated Phenomena*, trans. Robyn Horner and Vincent Berraud (New York: Fordham University Press, 2002), esp. ch. 5, "The Icon or the Endless Hermeneutic"; and *The Crossing of the Visible*, trans. James K. A. Smith (Stanford: Stanford University Press, 2004). Marion notes that due to its inversion of pictorial perspective, the icon shows a gaze that "sees more than is seen" and thus "looks at, outside of the icon and in front of it," the one in prayer (*orant*) (*Crossing of the Visible*, 22).

[44] Alongside the examples from the phenomenology of parable given in the first chapter, consider the description of the "word of God" (the Hebrew Bible) in Heb 4:12, as "living and active, sharper than any two-edged sword, piercing until it divides soul from spirit, joints from marrow . . . able to judge the thoughts and intentions of the heart." The final lines of Rainer Maria Rilke's "Archaic Torso of Apollo" likewise come to mind: "For here there is no place / that does not see you. You must change your life." From *Ahead of All Parting: The Selected Poetry and Prose of Rainer Maria Rilke*, trans. Stephen Mitchell (New York: Modern Library, 1995). Tomas Tranströmer often alludes to such inversions of the gaze. In his poem "The Crossing-Place," he writes, "I get the idea that the street can see me," and in "Prelude," "Two truths draw nearer each other. One moves from inside, one moves from outside / and where they meet we have a chance to see ourselves. / He who notices what is happening cries despairingly: 'Stop! / Whatever you like, if only I avoid knowing myself.'" From *The Great Enigma: New Collected Poems*, trans. Robin Fulton (New York: New Directions, 2006), 144, 3. As Jean-Luc Marion says, selfhood consists "more originarily" in an "I am affected" than in an "I think." *Being Given: Toward a Phenomenology of Givenness*, trans. Jeffrey L. Kosky (Stanford: Stanford University Press, 2002), 250.

In this parable, the "natural attitude"—which I have identified as the sons' servile self-perception—is narrated only in order to be bracket and excluded, to clear space for the counterperception of God that emanates from the "seeing and having compassion" of the parabolic father. His gaze forms the inverted lines of perspective from storyteller to hearer. We do not judge the story; it judges us, and with the most gracious "dome" of "courtesy" and "homeliness." The debt we owe is to receive this.

Visualizing parable as a narrative icon helps shed light on Julian's and Barth's engagement with the passage as a performative reparabolizing of the biblical text. Reanimating it as "other-speaking," Julian and Barth make what is known speak anew. Recounting the story, they do not merely interpret the story's content but recreate its parenthesizing and focusing effect. Drawing us along as they undergo the parable's trajectory of meaning within the Gospel, they lead their readers back to the basic loving-kindness of God manifested "in, with, and under" this portrait of a lost child. The Parable of the Prodigal Son is not framed as a "parable of the kingdom" in Luke, but Julian and Barth proclaim Christ as "the kingdom in person" (IV/2, 184). The kingdom of heaven is like a lord, a father, a mother, who seeks "to all the ends of the earth," and saves. The parable is "about" God's grace, yes, but again—*grace is not a thing*.[45] *God is God's grace*.[46]

Parable as Christology: Toward a "Parabolic Theology"

The christological interpretations of the Parable of the Prodigal Son under consideration are not simply readings of a parable; they offer Christologies in the mode of parable, constituting what we might call "parabolic theology." Julian's and Barth's retellings encourage us to examine the function of parable as a theological genre. The prominent constructive role parable plays in their theologies suggests that it is a fitting and perhaps irreducible form for communicating the meaning of Jesus Christ.[47] This seems to be so for at least several reasons.

First, it is well-suited to the "storied" nature of the *name*.[48] The essential narrativity of the subject matter elicits theology in the mode of retelling. While, in a certain sense, a narrative approach may leave matters muddier than do fine classical schema and definitions, rhetorically and conceptually,

---

[45]   Neder, *Participation in Christ*, 49.
[46]   See Julian (63.8) and Barth (II/1, 356, 358).
[47]   Again, parable, even a realistic narrative-parable, is distinguished from narrative per se in that it is inherently metaphorized or dynamized in the direction of significations beyond the text. In this sense, any narrative, and in fact any history, can become a parable.
[48]   See, for example, IV/1, 157–58.

it lends a liveliness to theology and enacts Barth's prescription that doctrine always be rooted in its historical reference. Focusing on the narratival confluence of christological affirmations in Barth's presentation of election and reconciliation, less attention was given to the usual soteriological language of "justification," "substitution," "judgment," "satisfaction," or his more conventional headings, such as "the divine verdict" and "the Judge Judged." Instead, a different set of correlates has been raised to the surface—"condescension," "movement toward," "direction," "overflowing," "going out," "compassion," "far journey," "self-giving," "taking the form of a servant," "becoming lost," "relation and attitude," "taking up," "at-oning," and so on. This is because what finally holds the various antitheses of Christology together for Barth is "not a concept but a name, not a system, but a narrative." Barth maintains,

> Whatever might be said over and above this Name could only be a form of broken or dialectical discourse. No system could possibly contain it. The Name . . . meant an end to metaphysical business as usual. It was an irruption of the new aeon into the old, and the old could not contain it. This Name was the event that could not be transcended, but transcended and embraced all things. The bearer of this Name was not determined by them, but they by him.[49]

The name is not determined by a general metaphysics. Avoiding any generic claim about the humanity and divinity of Christ, Barth is supremely concerned with *what kind of* God and *what kind of* human—"not that God is a person, but the particular person He is" (II/1, 296), that "God is the *reconciling* God" and that the human is a "*reconciled*" human (IV/1, 158). The character of both is only accessed through the concrete story or history (*Geschichte*) of reconciliation. Given the subject matter, "historical thinking" is "the fitting mode of description."[50] Barth commences §59 with the dramatic assertion, "The atonement is history [*Geschichte*]. To know it, we must know it as such. To think it, we must think of it as such. *To speak of it, we must tell it as history*. To try to grasp it as supra-historical or non-historical truth is not to grasp it all." This is because, "to say the atonement is to say Jesus Christ. To speak of it is to speak of *His* history. . . . For *He is the history* of God with [humankind] and the history of [humankind] with God" (157–58).[51] Barth clearly trends away from the metaphysical language "two natures in one person" toward something more

---

[49]   George Hunsinger, introduction to *Thy Word Is Truth: Barth on Scripture*, ed. George Hunsinger (Grand Rapids: Eerdmans, 2012), xviii.

[50]   Neder, *Participation in Christ*, 61.

[51]   Emphasis added.

like "two (hi)stories in one name."[52] And that is precisely what he offers in his "imaginative reconstruction of Christology upon the scaffold of the Prodigal Son narrative."[53] The "narrative commitment" attending the "absolute priority" Barth places on "Jesus' existence" has long drawn attention to the conceptual irreducibility of categories such as story, history, and, of course, what has come to be known as "narrative identity."[54] The person and work of Christ are to be thought of not as abstract "things" but as concrete enacted identities: Adam,

---

[52]   Barth speaks of Jesus Christ as the twofold history of God with humanity and humanity with God (IV/1, 158). See Paul Dafydd Jones, *The Humanity of Christ: Christology in Karl Barth's "Church Dogmatics"* (London: T&T Clark, 2008), 66; and Neder, *Participation in Christ*, 34. Although Barth's ontology is thoroughly actualized, he still retains the basic pattern of Chalcedonian Christology. This, too, is a much-debated aspect of his theology. Some scholars believe Barth's Christology remains thoroughly Chalcedonian. See George Hunsinger, "Karl Barth's Christology: Its Basic Chalcedonian Character," in *The Cambridge Companion to Karl Barth*, ed. John Webster (Cambridge: Cambridge University Press, 2000), 127–42. However, a basic assumption of my reading is that, as Jones argues, Barth "effectively discards the language of 'nature' in his 'mature' Christology" (*Humanity of Christ*, 28). Following Sarah Coakley, I use the word "pattern" here to signal not *physis* but the tensive relationship established in the twofold history of Jesus Christ by the four Chalcedonian adjectives *inconfuse, immutabiliter, inseperabiliter, indivise* (unconfused, unchanged, inseparable, indivisible). These do not drop out even in view of the strong "identity" Barth draws between Jesus Christ and the second member of the Trinity. For a compelling reassessment of Chalcedon as "horizon," "boundary," or "pattern," see Coakley, "What Does Chalcedon Solve and What Does It Not? Some Reflections on the Status and Meaning of the Chalcedonian View," in *The Incarnation: An Interdisciplinary Symposium on the Incarnation of the Son of God*, ed. Stephen T. Davis, Daniel Kendall, S.J., and Gerald O'Collins, S.J. (Oxford: Oxford University Press, 2002), 160.

[53]   Lewis, *Between Cross and Resurrection*, 192.

[54]   Sarah Coakley uses the phrase "narrative commitment" in "*Kenōsis* and Subversion: On the Repression of 'Vulnerability' in Christian Feminist Writing" (in *Powers and Submissions: Spirituality, Philosophy and Gender* [Malden, Mass.: Blackwell, 2002], 3–39). Robert Jenson addresses the "absolute priority" of narrative in Barth's theological method in *God after God: The God of the Past and the God of the Future Seen in the Work of Karl Barth* (New York: Bobbs-Merrill, 1969), 72. On "narrative identity," see Hans Frei, *The Identity of Jesus Christ: The Hermeneutical Bases of Dogmatic Theology* (Eugene, Ore.: Wipf & Stock, 2013), 51f., 95f.; and Paul Ricoeur, "Interpretive Narrative," in *Figuring the Sacred: Religion, Narrative and Imagination* (Philadelphia: Fortress, 1995), 185. Frei and Ricoeur differ in many respects. However, they both maintain that a personal character or identity must be narrated. When Ricoeur speaks of "narrative identity," he means: "To answer the question 'Who?' . . . is to tell the story of a life." Ricoeur, *Time and Narrative*, vol. 3, trans. Kathleen Blamey and David Pellauer (Chicago: University of Chicago Press, 1990), 246. Similarly Frei ties "identity description" to the "narrative account" of an individual's life (*Identity of Jesus Christ*, 58).

Israel, the Suffering Servant, the lost son, fallen humanity. They are all retold in him. Barth's account of the person and work of Christ is an expository retelling of the biblical narratives, all of which are Gospel, all of which echo and evoke the governing narration of his Name.

However, second, it is notably a parable—and not simply historicity or narrativity per se—that helps Julian and Barth to make a range of complex christological claims and coordinate multiple scriptural predicates. This is not incidental. Parable allows us to speak of two things at once and as one. This is extremely advantageous when it comes to narrating something like the hypostatic union, which both Julian and Barth apparently intuit without feeling the need to explain as much. The form of parable frees us from having to speak out of both sides of our mouths at once, something that seemed to trouble Barth earlier in *Church Dogmatics*, where he says,

> It is impossible to listen at one and the same time to the two statements that Jesus of Nazareth is the Son of God and that the Son of God is Jesus of Nazareth. One hears either the one or the other or one hears nothing. When the one is heard, the other can be heard only indirectly, in faith. (I/1, 180)

Barth's later use of the parable form constitutes a methodological discovery that lets him, at least partially, overcome the "onesidedness" of theological propositions he describes here (181). This is not just a methodological point. Parable facilitates a bifocality befitting the content as it capacitates the narration of multiple histories, identities, and realities in one *concretum*. Retelling the person and work of Jesus Christ through a parabolic or metaphorized story—and not just any story, but one told by Jesus, embedded in the encompassing Gospel narrative, reverberating within his life—enables Barth to retain the logic or pattern of Chalcedon while minimizing the language of *physis* and maximizing a sense of the eventfulness of divine and human cooperation in Jesus Christ.

Third, as an inherently excessive or productive form of speech, parable is uniquely capable of narrating the "how much more" of grace that is the centerpiece of the Gospel and its retelling in the Parable of the Prodigal Son. The comparison (*parabola*) made in a narrative-parable involves a substitution or exchange (*metaphora*)—but one that is unavoidably catachrestic rather than synonymous or proportionate. Parable, as metaphorized narrative, is not simply a matter of comparison, nor is it ever strictly substitutable for so-called "words proper" or propositions.[55] As Ricoeur, Jüngel, and others are quick to point out,

[55] Ricoeur speaks of parable as "metaphorized narrative." Jüngel means approximately the same thing when he (somewhat less precisely) calls parable "an extended metaphor" and metaphor "an abbreviated parable." Jüngel thinks the only difference

there is an aporia or "misappropriation" at the heart of metaphorical predication, and this is not a deficiency but precisely that which empowers language
to articulate "new dimensions of reality," more than was previously actual.[56] For
Jüngel, this is what grants linguistic and epistemological, if not ontological, priority to the category "possibility."[57] That grace (content) and parable (form) go
hand in hand is signaled in the way Julian and Barth each coordinate the excess
of the lost son's identity with Romans 5:20 and the beneficial and productive
asymmetry of the "exchange" of grace.[58] As the "much more" of the meaning of
the parables invites inquiry, so too the prodigality of the divine disproportion
between transgression and grace enfolds us through wonder.

Fourth, it is specifically its "analogy-structure" that helps parable articulate the similarity-in-the-midst-of-dissimilarity of the Word-made-flesh.
Parable corresponds to "the certainty of a God who is human in his divinity."[59] This is closely related to but not identical with the point about parable narrating the twofoldness of Christ's being and history. Perceiving that
Barth's later concern about the *anologia entis* is that it does "not do justice
to the difference" between God and the world precisely because it overlooks
the *nearness* of God, Jüngel inverts the analogical rule. A "greater dissimilarity in so great a likeness" is rooted in the theory that "the divinity of God

---

is that "a parable narrates while metaphor coalesces the narrative in a single word"
(or name). But a "narrative structure is also immanent in the metaphor," if we
understand metaphor as "the epiphora [transfer] according to analogy" (*Figuring
the Sacred*, 289–90). This may shed light on Barth's emphasis on the "name" of Jesus
and its intelligibility only through narration.

[56]   To reiterate the findings of the first chapter on this point, Soskice disagrees with
the assumption that metaphors are primarily a mode of comparison or redescription
using two known referents. She asserts instead, "The interesting thing about metaphor,
or at least about some metaphors, is that they are used . . . to disclose for the first time."
Janet Martin Soskice, *Metaphor and Religious Language* (Oxford: Oxford University
Press, 2002), 89. Metaphor not only communicates what "words proper" (Hobbes)
cannot but also produces new referents.

[57]   There is much more to say about the relationship between metaphor and "the
new" for theological purposes. See, for example, Eberhard Jüngel's excursus on analogy, metaphor, and parable in *God as the Mystery of the World*, 281f.

[58]   Julian, 29.10–13; Barth, IV/1, 68, 82. Ricoeur and Jüngel both make this theological link with the form of parable.

[59]   Jüngel understands metaphor (including parable) as analogy by *epiphora* or
transfer. But metaphor is not, as Soskice points out, exactly the same as the "middle-
way" of analogy. The primary difference, as she sees it, is that analogy can be a
"literal" form of speech and typically "stretches" usage between known quantities,
whereas metaphor as "figurative" speech based on a "model" establishes new uses
that have the power to create new referents (Soskice, *Metaphor and Religious Language*, 66). Jüngel, *God as the Mystery of the World*, 289, 280.

excludes humanity," which Barth rejects.[60] On the basis of the atonement, he asserts instead "a still *greater similarity* in the midst of a great dissimilarity." The generative identity-in-difference of inverted analogical language intimately fits the actuality of God's greater nearness to the human other in Jesus Christ.[61] While Julian does not present this claim hermeneutically, it is consonant with the tensive images that emerge organically in her work, the way she occasionally loses sight of any difference between God and the "soul," and her motif of "wonning"/"oning" or dwelling-in-unity, where being-with or being-inside is predicated upon irreducible difference. The transcendent immanence of the divine is imaged as the "courteous homeliness," the high lowliness or gentle condescension, of a mother. Perhaps this is why she predicates motherhood of God by way of supereminence; the very power of the distinction is the capacity to bear another.

It might be inferred from these first points that parable is merely a linguistic form that is conveniently applicable to the content of incarnation and atonement. However, a final reason that parable is appropriate for christological discourse is that "one can and must say Jesus is *the parable* [*Gleichnis*] *of God.*"[62] The coherence of referring to Jesus as "a parable" has been called into question.[63] But two interrelated points bring definition to the sense in which Jesus may rightly be understood as "the parable of God."

[60]   Jüngel, *God as the Mystery of the World*, 280. On Barth and the *analogia entis*, see ch. 5, p. 98, n. 21.

[61]   For Barth as well as Jüngel, the identity between God and the human in Christ does not obliterate but preserves difference. Jüngel writes, "Identity in the sense of the removal of every difference knows nothing of nearness. . . . Identity as the ending of distance without nearness is the establishment of absolute distance" (*God as the Mystery of the World*, 288). The "identity" they (and I) have in mind is, again, narratival, not analytic.

[62]   Jüngel, *God as the Mystery of the World*, 288–89. As Jüngel says here, "The *son* is the *personal parable of the father.*"

[63]   While I agree with Soskice's understanding of metaphor and her critique of simply extending it to parable, I think there is a way around the assertion that calling Jesus the "parable of God" is incoherent (see Soskice, *Metaphor and Religious Language*, 56). She rules this possibility out on the premise that metaphors and parables are linguistic realities. Soskice argues that it is a category mistake to refer to a nonverbal reality, such as an image or person, as "a parable." However, it is worth noting that the genre of "parable" could function as a model and thus yield metaphorical claims about a person. (After all, even metaphors can be used metaphorically—by speaking of things as though they have those qualities otherwise usually restricted to linguistic instances.) But, more importantly, as "the Word of God," Jesus Christ is in fact regarded as a speech act, an event of communication. That is precisely the point for Jüngel: the person of Jesus Christ is the *verbum dei*. So, on that basis, even a strictly linguistic definition of metaphor and parable may be applied to him. As the

The phrase draws attention to (1) the way *a life* itself can become a kind of "other-speaking" (see chapter 1): a life, a history, a person can become or produce a "text" in which one thing is articulated in ways that are suggestive—and even reformative—of something else. Of course, this means that, against the common historical-critical division between the speech and life of Jesus, we must understand parable theologically not only in terms of a genre of fictional storytelling but also in terms of a life lived. There is no clear line between story and life. This is not simply because of the basic narrativity of temporal existence and the structure that is brought to a life in its retelling. It is also because life is craft; it involves a measure of intentional construction and authorship.[64] One may parabolize one's own life—symbolically, as did the Hebrew prophets, or definitively and ontologically, as God does in Christ.[65] For this reason, Ricoeur is absolutely right to reject the critical separation between Jesus' speech—from which the parables are taken as the most "authentic" tradition—and his life—which is analogously crafted as a story, a retelling, a kind of "other-speaking."[66] Jesus "curates" or "writes" himself, offering his very life as an iconic reimaging and textual retelling. In himself, he represents and retells a certain story—of the identity of the people of God—by way of another medium—his own being and action. In this lived retelling, the same dynamic is at work on another level. As God's "self-interpretation" (Barth), Jesus is God's speaking otherwise about Godself, God's "commandeering" of a wholly other (human) medium to communicate the divine reality.[67] He is the *verbum dei*—in and as an alien form.

To speak of *Jesus* as "a parable" is also (2) a way of articulating the ontologically irreducible *doubleness* of his existence. Jesus Christ is the "twofold

---

Word, he is God's self-interpretation, God's story about Godself. And it happens to be a twofold story—which is to say, fundamentally parabolic.

[64]   See, for example, Alasdair MacIntyre on the narrative of a life and "co-authorship," in *After Virtue* (Notre Dame, Ind.: University of Notre Dame Press, 2007), 213.

[65]   See *CD* IV/3.1 on the similarity and dissimilarity of Jesus and the prophets (and on the prophetic role of Israel as a whole).

[66]   Think, for example, of Jesus' encounter with the woman at the well. Is this "only" history? Is it not also a type-scene and thus a lived parable? Are the triple parables of lostness in Luke 15 not embedded in what must be seen as the parable of Jesus' prophetic and highly symbolic eating and drinking with sinners?

[67]   Eberhard Jüngel, *God's Being Is in Becoming: The Trinitarian Being of God in the Theology of Karl Barth; A Paraphrase*, trans. John Webster (London: T&T Clark, 2001), 26.

(hi)story" of God with humanity and humanity with God. The prevalence of these categories in Barth's theology—narrative, history, event, action, and so on—has long been recognized and developed in "narrative theology."[68] The "narrative identity" of Jesus Christ recounted in the Gospels is specifically marked by a certain twofoldness, by a paradoxically integrative movement in two directions at once. This is where the linearity of narrative per se breaks down. The "double movement" (*Doppelbewegung*) is unified in a name. A name must be narrated; that is how we answer the question, "Who?"[69] The form of parable enables us to narrate—simultaneously, not sequentially—complex identities enacted in time. Parable is thus an apt vehicle for Christology. It is, as Gerhard Ebeling says, "the form of the language" that "corresponds to the incarnation."[70] In short, it corresponds not only to what Christ is (divine and human) but also to what he does (atonement and reconciliation), to the whole sequence of action (crucifixion–resurrection) in which, Hans Frei says, he is "most of all himself."[71]

We might speak, then, not simply of "narrative theology" but more specifically of "parabolic theology." This is what I think we encounter in Julian's and Barth's rich and expansive theological retellings of the parable. In reenacting both the form and the content of the story, they keep clearly before us that Jesus' own history has an intrinsically parabolic character—the divine and human, thrown alongside one another, distinct yet inextricable. If narrative theology enables us to say, "Jesus is his story," parabolic theology stresses that

[68]   See, for example, Hans Frei, *The Eclipse of Biblical Narrative: A Study in Eighteenth and Nineteenth Century Hermeneutics* (New Haven: Yale University Press, 1975); David Ford, *Barth and God's Story: Biblical Narrative and the Theological Method of Karl Barth in the "Church Dogmatics"* (Frankfurt am Main: Peter Lang, 1981); George Hunsinger, "Beyond Literalism and Expressivism: Karl Barth's Hermeneutical Realism," *Modern Theology* 3 (1987): 209–23; David H. Kelsey, *The Uses of Scripture in Recent Theology* (Philadelphia: Fortress, 1975); Ronald F. Thiemann, *Revelation and Theology: The Gospel as Narrated Promise* (Notre Dame, Ind.: University of Notre Dame Press, 1985); Kathryn Tanner, "Theology and the Plain Sense," in *Scriptural Authority and Narrative Interpretation*, ed. Garrett Green (Philadelphia: Fortress, 1987), 59–78; and Stanley Hauerwas and L. Gregory Jones, eds., *Why Narrative? Readings in Narrative Theology* (Grand Rapids: Eerdmans, 1989).

[69]   Again, as Larry Bouchard says, "Narrative . . . is really an enlarged act of *naming* that answers the question, 'Who?'" (*Theater and Integrity: Emptying Selves in Drama, Ethics, and Religion* [Evanston, Ill.: Northwestern University Press, 2011], 32).

[70]   Ebeling, *Evangelische Evangelienauslegung*, 108. Cf. *CD* I/2, 493.

[71]   Frei, *Identity of Jesus Christ*, 2.

in Jesus' story he is himself *and* another; God is God *with* and *as* another; we are ourselves only through another.[72] So in contrast to the notion of authenticity upon which defenses of the absolute singularity of Jesus' identity depend (Frei), parable forces us to consider not the question of being oneself (*autos*) but of not quite being oneself, of clothing and identifying oneself otherwise, of being seen and known otherwise, of becoming another, of being more than oneself.[73] As Barth writes, it was not an "an inalienable necessity" for Jesus Christ "only to be God, and therefore only to be different from the creature. . . . He was not committed to any such 'only.' In addition . . . he had this other possibility . . . in taking it upon Himself to be Himself in a way quite other" (IV/1, 180). Correspondingly, humanity "comes to itself" outside of itself, when reperformed aright in and by this other's twofold story. The lost child is found in "our savioure . . . oure very moder, in whome we be endlessly borne and never shall come out" (57.40–43).

Jesus' own parabolic speech is derivative of and must be understood from his being as the self-communication of God.[74] In Julian's language, "to se this

---

[72]   Hans Frei, *Theology and Narrative: Selected Essays*, ed. George Hunsinger and William C. Placher (Oxford: Oxford University Press, 1993), 42.

[73]   I certainly do *not* wish to deny the claim about Jesus' singularity. I only point out here that parabolic theology might help us articulate something else, which is not included in the usual emphasis of narrative theology on unrepeatable personal identity. We have a paradox in the person of Christ, the unsubstitutable substitution.

[74]   The "*self*-revelation" of God can be seen as a peculiarly modern concept, traced to German Idealism and particularly Hegel. However, it is not as if it is the case that, prior to Hegel, there was no notion of God's revelation in Jesus Christ as *self*-disclosure and *self*-giving, as the presentation and communication of God's very being, will, heart, mind, and so on. The idea of self-revelation is found in Hilary of Poitiers (*On the Trinity* VII, 16) and Pseudo-Dionysius (*Divine Names* XIV). Bonaventure speaks of God manifesting Godself (*Sentences* 16.1.1), and, of course, contemplation of the beatific vision includes the idea (e.g., Aquinas, *De caritas* 13). Self-revelation may be inferred from Aquinas' claim that "it belongs to goodness to communicate itself" (hence the "fittingness" of the incarnation) (*ST* III, q. 1, art. 1). Calvin considers all revelation self-revelation or self-disclosure (e.g., *Institutes* I.V.1). Admittedly, "the revelation of God in Christ" is more prevalent than the phrases like "self-revelation." But consider the logic of Julian's text—moving from the cross, to the Son's relationship to the Father, to intratrinitarian love. She states the hermeneutical principle: where we see Christ, we see Trinity. He does not simply lead away from himself, as if he were the medium for some other message. He *is* the message. He leads into God; and he is there in, with, and as God. God shows love and *is* the love that is shown. If revelation is not *self*-revelation, what is it? The revelation of God's saving decree/will (i.e., God's love)? But what is the connection between God and God's will or between God's will and its execution in Jesus Christ? Is God God's love? Does the *manifestation* of God's love in fact communicate that *God is love*? In

overpassing noblete," revealed in the servant's fall, "was my understanding led into God" (52.40–41). We find God where God "has sought us," Barth says. God "seeks us," the lost, "in His Word," by becoming "lost and found" (II/1, 11). Jesus' reality is fundamentally implicated in what he discloses. His life is to be read as told, as the story of God Godself, and in such a way the communication is indispensable to the communicated. This raises the question whether name, history, and parable may better correspond to the subject matter than metaphysical accounts of hypostatic union. Julian's example and Barth's exegesis point toward the same "pattern" of claims about *who* Christ is without abstracting or looking away from the integral complexity of his story.[75] The irreducibility of parable is not only fitting here, it consigns abstract or purely conceptual forms of theological reflection to an epexegetical rather than essential status.[76] As Barth says, classical categories are merely commentary on the Gospel condensed in the smallest narrative nutshell, "the Word became flesh," which is reiterated and amplified in the Parable of the Prodigal Son.[77]

Conclusion

To "do justice" to the parable, we must say all of this. To not leave it underinterpreted, we must receive from the journey of the wayward son more than any simple one-to-one comparison. His vital story has long been emblematic of "God's presence and gracious acts," and in a way that evokes "a whole tradition of experiences and of the literary tradition which records and interprets them." It warrants "study of gloss upon gloss" and inspires endless textual and lived refigurations.[78] The parable genuinely refers, though it is not done making meaning. It continues to elicit complex connections between narratives, metaphorizing itself by itself, by virtue of its evocative embeddedness within concentric stories. Its structure echoes the Genesis creation myths, Israel and the Suffering Servant, the christological hymn of Philippians, and Christ's

---

many "premodern" theologians, there is evidence of a strong identity (if not necessarily via the same philosophical apparatus) between subject and content. Even in Scripture, we have to reckon with the close relationship between the Word and the being of God.

[75]   Coakley, "What Does Chalcedon Solve," 160. For further discussion, see ch. 5, esp. p. 242, n. 52.

[76]   Pace G. W. F. Hegel's ultimately negative assessment of "representation" in religion, sublated on the way to a fully actualized and concretized "concept," in his *Lectures on the Philosophy of Religion*, vol. 3, *The Consummate Religions*, ed. Peter C. Hodgson (Berkeley: University of California Press, 1998).

[77]   See Barth on classical christological categories as mere commentary on the condensed narrative of John 1:14 (IV/2, 66; I/2, 132).

[78]   Soskice, *Metaphor and Religious Language*, 158–60.

radical recapitulation of Adamic humanity. It reverberates within many other biblical and historical narratives of *exitus* and *reditus*. Home as origin and telos of human mischief conjures the garden of Eden, the promised land, Zion, birth and life, real presence. The nadir of the pit summons the fall, the wilderness, exile, the grave, hell, the whole history of humanity wandering and perishing. A climactic reception figures the eschaton, that final homecoming, the wedding feast of the Lamb, a divine love that rushes forward in affectionate embrace and restorative welcome. These pivotal moments are intertextual emblems impressed on our imaginations, heuristics shaping interpretation and existence. This basic substrate of human drama, Julian and Barth tell us, has been taken up into the divine life in Christ, made holy, and returned to us "in, with, and under" a story he tells of a young man who took off, was brought low, and came home, raised up with astonishing rejoicing.

BIBLIOGRAPHY

Primary Sources, Karl Barth

Barth, Karl. *Christliche Dogmatik*. Münich: Chr. Kaiser, 1927.

———. *Dogmatics in Outline*. Translated by G. T. Thompson. New York: Harper & Row, 1959.

———. *The Epistle to the Romans*. Translated by Edwyn C. Hoskyns. London: Oxford University Press, 1968.

———. *The Humanity of God*. Translated by John Newton Thomas and Thomas Wieser. Richmond, Va.: John Knox, 1960.

———. *Die Kirchliche Dogmatik*. 4 vols. in 13 parts. Münich: C. Kaiser; Zürich: Theologischer Verlag, 1932–1967. ET: *Church Dogmatics*. Edited and translated by Geoffrey William Bromiley and Thomas F. Torrance. Edinburgh: T&T Clark, 1956–1975.

———. *The Knowledge of God and the Service of God according to the Teaching of the Reformation: Recalling the Scottish Confession of 1560*. Translated by J. L. M. Haire and Ian Henderson. The Gifford Lectures. London: Hodder and Stoughton, 1938.

———. *The Word of God and the Word of Man*. Translated by Douglas Horton. New York: Harper, 1957.

Primary Sources, Julian of Norwich

Baker, Denise, trans. *The Showings of Julian of Norwich*. New York: W. W. Norton, 2005.

Colledge, Edmund, and James Walsh, S.J., eds. *A Book of Showings to the Anchoress Julian of Norwich*. 2 vols. Toronto: Pontifical Institute of Medieval Studies, 1978.

———, eds. and trans. *Julian of Norwich: Showings*. New York: Paulist, 1978.

Spearing, Elizabeth, trans. *Revelations of Divine Love*. New York: Penguin, 1998.

Watson, Nicholas, and Jacqueline Jenkins, eds. *The Writings of Julian of Norwich: "A Vision Showed to a Devout Woman" and "A Revelation of Love."* University Park: Pennsylvania State University Press, 2006.

Secondary Sources

Aers, David. "The Humanity of Christ: Reflections on Julian of Norwich's *Revelation of Love*." In *The Powers of the Holy: Religion, Politics, and Gender in Late Medieval English Culture*, edited by David Aers and Lynn Staley, 77–106. University Park: Pennsylvania State University Press, 1996.

Ahlgren, Gillian T. W. "Julian of Norwich's Theology of *Eros*." *Spiritus: A Journal of Christian Spirituality* 5, no. 1 (2005): 37–53.

Almeida, Ivan. *L'Opérativité sémantique des récits paraboles: Sémiotique narrative et textuelle; Herméneutique du discours religieux*. Louvain: Peeters, 1978.

Alter, Robert. *The Art of Biblical Narrative*. New York: Basic Books, 1981.

Ambrose of Milan. *Expositionis Lucam VII*. Patrologia Latina 15. Edited by Jacques-Paul Migne. Paris: Migne, 1844–1855.

Anselm of Canterbury. *Opera omnia*. 6 vols. Edited by Franciscus Salesius Schmitt, O.S.B. Edinburgh: Thomas Nelson and Sons, 1936–1961.

Aquinas, Thomas. *Summa Theologiae*. 61 vols. Cambridge: Cambridge University Press, 2006.

Aristotle. *Nicomachean Ethics*. Translated by Joe Sachs. Indianapolis: Hackett, 2002.

———. *On Rhetoric: A Theory of Civic Discourse*. Translated by George A. Kennedy. Oxford: Oxford University Press, 2006.

———. *Poetics*. Translated by Malcolm Heath. New York: Penguin, 1997.

———. *Physics*. Translated by David Bostock and Robin Waterfield. Oxford: Oxford University Press, 2008.

Auerbach, Erich. *Mimesis: The Representation of Reality in Western Literature*. Translated by William R. Trask. Princeton: Princeton University Press, 1953.

———. "Figura." In *Scenes from the Drama of European Literature*. Translated by Ralph Mannheim. Minneapolis: University of Minnesota Press, 1984.

Augustine of Hippo. *Confessions*. Translated by Henry Chadwick. Oxford: Oxford University Press, 2008.

———. *Contra adversarium legis et prophetarum*. Corpus Christianorum, Series Latina 49. Edited by K. D. Daur. Belgium: Brepols, 1985.

———. *Oeuvres de Saint Augustin*. Vol. 11. Paris: Desclée de Brouwer, 1949. ET: *The First Catechetical Instruction IV.8*. Translated by Joseph P. Christopher. Westminster, Md.: Newman Press, 1962.

———. *On Christian Doctrine*. Translated by D. W. Robertson Jr. Upper Saddle River, N.J.: Prentice Hall, 1997.

———. *Quaestionum evangeliorum II*. Patrologia Latina 35. Edited by Jacques-Paul Migne. Paris: Migne, 1844–1855.

———. *The Trinity*. Translated by Edmund Hill, O.P. New York: New City Press, 2007.

Baker, Denise. *Julian of Norwich's Showings: From Vision to Book*. Princeton: Princeton University Press, 1994.

Baker, Denise, and Sarah Salih. Introduction to *Julian of Norwich's Legacy: Medieval Mysticism and Post-Medieval Reception*, edited by Denise Baker and Sarah Salih, 1–12. New York: Palgrave Macmillan, 2009.

Balthasar, Hans Urs von. *Mysterium Paschale*. Translated by Aidan Nichols, O.P. San Francisco: Ignatius, 1990.

———. *Theo-Drama: Theological Dramatic Theory*. Vol. 5, *The Last Act*. Translated by Graham Harrison. San Francisco: Ignatius, 1998.

Barthes, Roland. "An Introduction to the Structural Analysis of Narrative." *New Literary History* 6, no. 2 (1975): 237–72.

Beardsley, Monroe. *Aesthetics: Problems in the Philosophy of Criticism*. New York: Harcourt, Brace, 1958.

Bernard of Clairvaux. *On the Song of Songs II*. Vol. 3 of *The Works of Bernard of Clairvaux*. Translated by Kilian Walsh, O.C.S.O. Kalamazoo, Mich.: Cistercian, 1983.

———. "The Story of the King's Son." In *"The Parables" & "The Sentences,"* translated by Michael Casey, O.C.S.O., and Francis Swietek. Cistercian Father's Series 55. Kalamazoo, Mich.: Cistercian, 2000.

Betz, John R. "Beyond the Sublime: The Aesthetics of the *Analogy of Being*." 2 parts. *Modern Theology* 21, no. 3 (2005): 367–411; and 22, no. 1 (2006): 1–50.

Biddick, Kathleen. *The Typological Imaginary: Circumcision, Technology, History*. Philadelphia: University of Pennsylvania Press, 2003.

Black, Max. *In Models and Metaphors: Studies in Language and Philosophy*. Ithaca, N.Y.: Cornell University Press, 1962.

Bodley-Dangelo, Faye. *Sexual Difference, Gender, and Agency in Karl Barth's "Church Dogmatics."* London: T&T Clark, 2020.

Bonaventure of Bagnoregio. *Commentarius in evangelium Lucae*. In *Opera omnia*, vol. 7. Florence: Ad Claras Aquas, 1895. ET: *St. Bonaventure's Commentary on the Gospel of Luke*, edited by Robert Karris, 3 vols. St. Bonaventure, N.Y.: St. Franciscan Institute Publications, 2001–2004.

Bornkamm, Günther. *Jesus of Nazareth*. New York: Harper & Brothers, 1960.

Bouchard, Larry. *Theater and Integrity: Emptying Selves in Drama, Ethics, and Religion*. Evanston, Ill.: Northwestern University Press, 2011.

Boyarin, Daniel. *Intertextuality and the Reading of Midrash*. Bloomington: Indiana University Press, 1990.

Boyd, Richard. "Metaphor and Theory Change: What Is 'Metaphor' a Metaphor For?" In *Metaphor and Thought*, 2nd ed., edited by Andrew Ortony, 481–532. Cambridge: Cambridge University Press, 1993.

Brown, Colin. "Parable of the Rebellious Son(s)." *Scottish Journal of Theology* 51, no. 4 (1998): 391–405.

Brown, Frank Burch. *Transfiguration: Poetic Metaphor and the Languages of Religious Belief*. Chapel Hill: University of North Carolina Press, 1983.

Bruun, Mette B. *Parables: Bernard of Clairvaux's Mapping of Spiritual Topography*. Brill's Studies in Intellectual History 148. Leiden: Brill, 2007.

Bultmann, Rudolf. *History of the Synoptic Tradition*. Translated by John Marsh. Peabody, Mass.: Hendrickson, 1963.

Burnett, Richard. *Karl Barth's Theological Exegesis: The Hermeneutical Principles of the Römerbrief Period*. Tübingen: Mohr [Siebeck], 2001.

Busch, Eberhard. *Karl Barth: His Life from Letters and Autobiographical Texts*. Translated by John Bowden. Philadelphia: Fortress, 1976.

Bynum, Caroline Walker. *Fragmentation and Redemption: Essays on Gender and the Human Body in Medieval Religion*. New York: Zone Books, 1991.

———. *Jesus as Mother*. Berkeley: University of California Press, 1982.

Calvin, John. *Commentary on a Harmony of the Evangelists, Matthew, Mark, and Luke*. Vol. 1, in vol. 16 of *Calvin's Commentaries*. Grand Rapids: Baker, 2003.

———. *Institutes of Christian Religion*. 2 vols. Edited by John T. McNeill. Translated by Ford Lewis Battles. Louisville, Ky.: Westminster John Knox, 2006.

Camille, Michael. "Seeing and Reading: Some Visual Implications of Medieval Literacy and Illiteracy." *Art History* 8, no. 1 (1985): 26–49.

Campbell, Cynthia. "Imago Dei Reconsidered: Male and Female Together." *Journal for Preachers* 4, no. 2 (1981): 9–14.

Cassian, John. *Collationes*. Patrologia Latina 49. Edited by Jacques-Paul Migne. Paris: Migne, 1844–1855.

Chadwick, Henry. *Early Christian Thought and the Classical Tradition: Studies in Justin, Clement, and Origen*. Oxford: Oxford University Press, 1966.

Childs, Brevard. *Biblical Theology of the Old and New Testaments: Theological Reflection on the Christian Bible*. Minneapolis: Fortress, 1993.

Claudel, Paul. "L'Ecriture sainte." *La Vie intellectuelle*, May 1948.

Coakley, Sarah. "Introduction—Gender, Trinitarian Analogies, and the Pedagogy of *The Song*." In *Re-thinking Gregory of Nyssa*, 1–14. Oxford: Blackwell, 2003.

———. *Powers and Submissions: Spirituality, Philosophy and Gender*. Malden, Mass.: Blackwell, 2002.

———. "What Does Chalcedon Solve and What Does It Not? Some Reflections on the Status and Meaning of the Chalcedonian View." In *The Incarnation: An Interdisciplinary Symposium on the Incarnation of the Son of God*, edited by Stephen T. Davis, Daniel Kendall, S.J., and Gerald O'Collins, S.J., 143–63. Oxford: Oxford University Press, 2002.

Cohen, Jean. *Structure du langue poétique*. Paris: Flammarion, 2009.

Colledge, Edmund. *The Medieval Mystics of England*. New York: Charles Scribner's Sons, 1961.

Colledge, Edmund, and James Walsh, S.J. "Editing Julian of Norwich's *Revelations*: A Progress Report." *Medieval Studies* 38 (1976): 404–27.

Cousins, Ewert. "Francis of Assisi: Christian Mysticism at the Crossroads." In *Mysticism and Religious Traditions*, edited by Steven T. Katz, 163–90. Oxford: Oxford University Press, 1983.

Cox, Kendall. "The Parable of God: Karl Barth's Christological Interpretation of Luke 15:11–32." *Journal of Reformed Theology* 13 (2019): 215–37.

———. "Parabolic Retelling and Christological Discourse: Julian of Norwich and Karl Barth on the Parable of the Lost Son." In *Reading the Gospels with Karl Barth*, edited by Daniel L. Migliore. Grand Rapids: Eerdmans, 2017.

Craig, Hardin. "Morality Plays and Elizabethan Drama." *Shakespeare Quarterly* 1, no. 2 (1950): 64–72.

Crawford, Robert G. "A Parable of the Atonement." *The Evangelical Quarterly* 50, no. 1 (1978): 2–7.

Crossan, John Dominic. *Cliffs of Fall: Paradox and Polyvalence in the Parables of Jesus*. New York: Seabury, 1980.

———. *The Dark Interval: Towards a Theology of Story*. Salem, Ore.: Polebridge, 1994.

———. *In Parables: The Challenge of the Historical Jesus*. New York: Harper & Row, 1973.

———. *Raid on the Articulate: Comic Eschatology in Jesus and Borges*. New York: Harper & Row, 1976.

Cunningham, Mary Kathleen. *What Is Theological Exegesis? Interpretation and Use of Scripture in Barth's Doctrine of Election*. Harrisburg, Pa.: Trinity Press International, 1995.

Danermark, Berth, Mats Ekström, Lisselotte Jakobsen, and Jan Ch. Karlsson. *Explaining Society: Critical Realism in the Social Sciences*. New York: Routledge, 2006.

Davidson, Donald. "What Metaphors Mean." In *On Metaphor*, edited by Sheldon Sacks, 29–48. Chicago: University of Chicago Press, 1979.

Davies, Oliver. "Transformational Processes in the Work of Julian of Norwich and Mechtild of Magdeburg." In *The Medieval Mystical Tradition in England*, 39–52. Cambridge: D. S. Brewer, 1992.

Dawson, John David. *Christian Figural Reading and the Fashioning of Identity*. Berkeley: University of California Press, 2002.

de Lubac, Henri. *Medieval Exegesis: The Four Senses of Scripture*. Vol. 2. Translated by Mark Sebanc. Grand Rapids: Eerdmans, 2000.

———. *Scripture in the Tradition*. Translated by Luke O'Neill. New York: Crossroad, 2000.

Derrett, J. Duncan M. *Law in the New Testament*. Eugene, Ore.: Wipf & Stock, 2005.

———. "The Parable of the Prodigal Son: Patristic Allegories and Jewish Midrashim." *Studia Patristica* 10 (1970): 219–24.

Derrida, Jacques. "La mythologie blanche." *Poetique* 5 (1971): 1–52.

———. *Of Grammatology*. Translated by Gayatri Chakravorty Spivak. Baltimore: Johns Hopkins University Press, 1976.

———. "The *Retrait* of Metaphor." In *Psyche: Inventions of the Other*, vol. 1, edited by Peggy Kamuf and Elizabeth G. Rottenberg, 48–80. Stanford: Stanford University Press, 1998.

———. "Structure, Sign, and Play in the Discourse of the Human Sciences." In *Writing and Difference*, translated by Alan Bass, 278–93. Chicago: University of Chicago Press, 1978.

———. "White Mythology: Metaphor in the Text of Philosophy." *New Literary History* 6, no. 1 (1974): 5–74.

Dilthey, Wilhelm. *Dilthey: Selected Writings*. Edited by H. P. Rickman. Cambridge: Cambridge University Press, 1986.

Dinesen, Isak. *"Babette's Feast" and Other Anecdotes of Destiny*. New York: Vintage, 1988.

Denys the Carthusian. *Opera omnia*. 42 vols. Tournai: Pratis, 1896–1935.

Dodd, Charles. *The Parables of the Kingdom*. New York: Scribner, 1961.

Donahue, John, S.J. *The Gospel in Narrative: Metaphor, Narrative, and Theology in the Synoptic Gospels*. Philadelphia: Fortress, 1988.

Douglas, Mary. *Purity and Danger: An Analysis of Concepts of Pollution and Taboo*. New York: Routledge, 2002.

Dutton, Elisabeth. *Julian of Norwich: The Influence of Late-Medieval Devotional Compilations*. Cambridge: D. S. Brewer, 2008.

Ebeling, Gerhard. *Evangelische Evangelienauslegung: Eine Untersuchung zu Luther's Hermeneutik*. 2nd ed. Darmstadt: Wissenschaftliche Buchgesellschaft, 1962.

———. *Wort und Glaube*. Tübingen: Mohr [Siebeck], 1975. ET: *Word and Faith*. Translated by James Leitch. Philadelphia: Fortress, 1963.

Fiddes, Paul. "The Status of Woman in the Thought of Karl Barth." In *After Eve*, edited by Janet M. Soskice, 138–53. London: Collins Marshall Pickering, 1990.

Fiebig, Paul. *The Parables of Jesus in Light of the Rabbinic Parables of the New Testament Period*. Tübingen: Mohr, 1912.

Fleischer, Roland E., and Susan C. Scott, eds. *Rembrandts, Rubens, and the Art of Their Time: Recent Perspectives*. University Park: Pennsylvania State University Press, 1997.

Ford, David. *Barth and God's Story: Biblical Narrative and the Theological Method of Karl Barth in the "Church Dogmatics."* Frankfurt am Main: Peter Lang, 1981.

———. "Narrative in Theology." *British Journal of Religious Education* 4, no. 3 (1982): 115–19.

Frei, Hans. *The Eclipse of Biblical Narrative: A Study in Eighteenth and Nineteenth Century Hermeneutics*. New Haven: Yale University Press, 1975.

———. *The Identity of Jesus Christ: The Hermeneutical Bases of Dogmatic Theology*. Eugene, Ore.: Wipf & Stock, 2013.

———. *Theology and Narrative: Selected Essays*. Edited by George Hunsinger and William C. Placher. Oxford: Oxford University Press, 1993.

Frye, Northrop. *Anatomy of Criticism*. Princeton: Princeton University Press, 1957.

Frykberg, Elizabeth. *Karl Barth's Theological Anthropology: An Analogical Critique regarding Gender Relations*. Studies in Reformed Theology and History 1, no. 3, Summer 1993. Princeton: Princeton Theological Seminary, 1993.

Fuchs, Ernst. *Marburger Hermeneutik*. Tübingen: Mohr [Siebeck], 1968.

————. "The New Testament and the Hermeneutical Problem." In vol. 2 of *The New Hermeneutic*, edited by James M. Robinson and John B. Cobb Jr., 111–46. New York: Harper & Row, 1964.

Funk, Robert. *Language, Hermeneutic, and the Word of God: The Problem of Language in the New Testament and Contemporary Theology.* New York: Harper & Row, 1966. See esp. "The Parable as Metaphor."

————. "The Old Testament in Parable: A Study of Luke 10:25–37." *Encounter* 26 (1965): 251–67.

————. *Parables and Presence: Forms of the New Testament Tradition.* Philadelphia: Fortress, 1982.

————. "Sauntering through the Parables." In *Funk on Parables: Collected Essays*, edited by Bernard Brandon Scott, 93–142. Santa Rosa, Calif.: Polebridge, 2006.

————. "Saying and Seeing: Phenomenology of Language and the New Testament." *Journal of Bible and Religion* 34 (1966): 197–213.

Genette, Gérard. *Narrative Discourse: An Essay in Method.* Ithaca, N.Y.: Cornell University Press, 1983.

Gignilliat, Mark. *Karl Barth and the Fifth Gospel: Barth's Theological Exegesis of Isaiah.* New York: Fordham, 2009.

Gilby, Thomas. "The Senses of Scripture." Appendix 12 in *Summa Theologiae*, vol. 1 (Ia. I), edited by Thomas Gilby. Cambridge: Cambridge University Press, 2006.

Goebel, Hans Theodor. "Trinitätslehre und Erwählungslehre bei Karl Barth: Eine Problemanzeige." In *Wahrheit und Versöhnung: Theologische und Philosophische Beiträge zur Gotteslehre*, edited by Dietrich Korsch and Harmut Ruddies, 147–66. Gütersloh: Gütersloher Verlagshaus Gerg Mohn, 1989.

Gollwitzer, Helmut. *Die Freude Gottes: Einführung in das Lukasevangelium.* Vol. 2. Studienreihe der Jungen Gemeinde, Heft 27–29. Berlin: Burckhardthaus-Verlag, 1941.

Goodman, Nelson. *Languages of Art.* Indianapolis: Hackett, 1976.

Gorringe, Timothy. *Karl Barth: Against Hegemony.* Oxford: Oxford University Press, 1999.

Grant, Jacquelyn. *White Women's Christ and Black Women's Jesus: Feminist Christology and Womanist Response.* Atlanta: Scholars Press, 1989.

Gravett, Emily Olmstead. *The Literary Phenomenon of Narrative Biblical Retellings.* PhD diss., University of Virginia, 2013.

Gray, Richard T. *A Franz Kafka Encyclopedia.* Westport, Conn.: Greenwood, 2005.

Green, Clifford. "Karl Barth's Treatment of the Man-Woman Relationship: Issues for Theological Method." In *Reflections on Bonhoeffer*, edited by Geoffrey B. Kelly and C. John Weborg, 228–37. Chicago: Covenant, 1999.

————. "Liberation Theology? Karl Barth on Women and Men." *Union Theological Seminary Quarterly* 29 (1974): 228–29.

Greene-McCreight, Kathryn. *Ad Litteram: How Augustine, Calvin and Barth Read the "Plain Sense" of Genesis 1–3.* New York: Lang, 1999.

———. "'The Type of the One to Come': Leviticus 14 and 16 in Barth's *Church Dogmatics*." In *Thy Word Is Truth: Barth on Scripture*, edited by George Hunsinger, 67–85. Grand Rapids: Eerdmans, 2012.

Habermas, Jürgen. "Hermeneutics and the Social Sciences." In *The Hermeneutics Reader: Texts of the German Tradition from the Enlightenment to the Present*, edited by Kurt Mueller-Vollmer, 293–319. New York: Continuum, 2002.

Hamburger, Jeffrey. *The Visual and the Visionary: Art and Female Spirituality in Late Medieval Germany*. Princeton: Princeton University Press, 1998.

Harnack, Adolf von. *What Is Christianity?* Translated by Thomas Bailey Saunders. Eastford, Calif.: Martino Fine Books, 2011.

Hart, Aidan. *Beauty, Spirit, Matter: Icons in the Modern World*. Herefordshire, U.K.: Gracewing, 2014.

Hart, Kevin. "The Christian Reduction." Response paper presented at "The Promise of Phenomenology and Scripture" panel at the American Academy of Religion annual meeting, Montreal, November 2009.

———. *Kingdoms of God*. Bloomington: Indiana University Press, 2014. See esp. "The Manifestation of the Father" (115–38) and "Phenomenology of the Christ" (139–58).

Hauerwas, Stanley, and L. Gregory Jones, eds. *Why Narrative? Readings in Narrative Theology*. Grand Rapids: Eerdmans, 1989.

Hays, Richard B. "Christ Died for the Ungodly: Narrative Soteriology in Paul." *Horizons in Biblical Theology* 26, no. 2 (2004): 48–68.

Hector, Kevin. "God's Triunity and Self-Determination: A Conversation with Karl Barth, Bruce McCormack and Paul Molnar." *International Journal of Systematic Theology* 7, no. 3 (2005): 246–61.

Hegel, G. W. F. *Lectures on the Philosophy of Religion*. Vol. 3, *The Consummate Religions*, edited by Peter C. Hodgson. Berkeley: University of California Press, 1998.

Heidegger, Martin. *Four Seminars: Le Thor 1966, 1968, 1969, Zähringen 1973*. Translated by Andrew Mitchell and Francois Raffoul. Bloomington: Indiana University Press, 2003.

———. "Phenomenological Interpretations with Respect to Aristotle." In *Becoming Heidegger: On the Trail of His Early Occasional Writings, 1910–1927*, edited by Theodore Kisiel and Thomas Sheehan, 155–84. Evanston, Ill.: Northwestern University Press, 2007.

Hesse, Mary. *Models and Analogies in Science*. Notre Dame, Ind.: University of Notre Dame Press, 1966.

———. *The Structure of Scientific Inference*. Berkeley: University of California Press, 1974.

Hide, Kerri. *Gifted Origins to Grace Fulfillment: The Soteriology of Julian of Norwich*. Collegeville, Minn.: Liturgical, 2001.

Hilton, Walter. *The Scale of Perfection*. Translated by John P. H. Clark and Rosemary Dorward. New York: Paulist, 1988.

Holgate, David. *Prodigality, Liberality, and Meanness in the Parable of the Prodigal Son*. Sheffield, U.K.: Sheffield Academic Press, 1999.

Hultgren, Arland A. *The Parables of Jesus: A Commentary*. Grand Rapids: Eerdmans, 2000.

Hunsinger, George. "Beyond Literalism and Expressivism: Karl Barth's Hermeneutical Realism." *Modern Theology* 3 (1987): 209–23.

———. *Disruptive Grace: Studies in the Theology of Karl Barth*. Grand Rapids: Eerdmans, 2000.

———. "Election and the Trinity: Twenty-Five Theses on the Theology of Karl Barth." *Modern Theology* 24, no. 2 (2008): 179–98.

———. *How to Read Karl Barth: The Shape of His Theology*. New York: Oxford University Press, 1991.

———. Introduction to *Thy Word Is Truth: Barth on Scripture*, edited by George Hunsinger, xi–xxi. Grand Rapids: Eerdmans, 2012.

———. "Karl Barth's Christology: Its Basic Chalcedonian Character." In *The Cambridge Companion to Karl Barth*, edited by John Webster, 127–42. Cambridge: Cambridge University Press, 2000.

———. "Postcritical Interpretation: Rudolf Smend on Karl Barth." In *Thy Word Is Truth: Barth on Scripture*, edited by George Hunsinger, 29–48. Grand Rapids: Eerdmans, 2012.

Hunsinger, George, and William C. Placher. *Theology and Narrative: Selected Essays*. New York: Oxford University Press, 1993.

Hunt, Anne. *The Trinity: Insights from the Mystics*. Collegeville, Minn.: Liturgical, 2010.

Husserl, Edmund. *Ideas Pertaining to a Pure Phenomenology and to a Phenomenological Philosophy: First Book; A General Introduction to a Pure Phenomenology*. Translated by Fred Kersten. Dordrecht, Netherlands: Kluwer, 1998.

———. "Phenomenology as Transcendental Philosophy." In *The Essential Husserl: Basic Writings*, edited by Donn Welton, 60–85. Bloomington: Indiana University Press, 1999.

James, William. *The Varieties of Religious Experience: A Study in Human Nature*. London: Longmans, Green, 1902.

Janicaud, Dominique. *Phenomenology and the "Theological Turn": The French Debate*. Translated by Bernard G. Prusak. New York: Fordham University Press, 2000.

Jantzen, Grace. *Julian of Norwich: Mystic and Theologian*. New York: Paulist, 2000.

———. "Mysticism and Experience." *Religious Studies* 25 (1989): 295–315.

Jenson, Robert. *God after God: The God of the Past and the God of the Future Seen in the Work of Karl Barth*. New York: Bobbs-Merrill, 1969.

Jeremias, Joachim. *The Parables of Jesus*. New York: Charles Scribner's Sons, 1963.

John of Damascus. "Concerning What Is Affirmed about God." In *The Orthodox Faith IX*. Vol. 9 of *Nicene and Post-Nicene Fathers*, 2nd series, translated by Philip Schaff. Edinburgh: T&T Clark, 2004.

Johnson, Keith L. "Reconsidering Barth's Rejection of Przywara's *Analogia Entis*." *Modern Theology* 26, no. 4 (2010): 632–50.

Jones, Paul Dafydd. "The Heart of the Matter: Karl Barth's Christological Exegesis." In *Thy Word Is Truth: Barth on Scripture*, edited by George Hunsinger, 173–95. Grand Rapids: Eerdmans, 2012.

———. *The Humanity of Christ: Christology in Karl Barth's "Church Dogmatics."* London: T&T Clark, 2008.

———. "Karl Barth on Gethsemane." *International Journal of Systematic Theology* 9, no. 2 (2007): 148–71.

Jones, Serene. *Feminist Theory and Christian Theology: Cartographies of Grace.* Minneapolis: Fortress, 2000.

Jülicher, Adolf. *Die Gleichnisreden Jesu.* 2 vols. Tübingen: Mohr [Siebeck], 1888–1899. ET: *The Parables of Jesus.* Translated by S. H. Hooke. London: SCM Press, 1972.

Jüngel, Eberhard. *God as the Mystery of the World: On the Foundation of the Theology of the Crucified One in the Dispute between Theism and Atheism.* Translated by Darrell Guder. Edinburgh: T&T Clark, 1983.

———. *God's Being Is in Becoming: The Trinitarian Being of God in the Theology of Karl Barth; A Paraphrase.* Translated by John Webster. London: T&T Clark, 2001.

———. *Karl Barth: A Theological Legacy.* Translated by Garrett E. Paul. Philadelphia: Westminster, 1986.

———. *Paulus und Jesus.* Tübingen: Mohr [Siebeck], 1962.

———. *Unterwegs zur Sache: Theologische Bemerkungen.* Münich: Christian Kaiser, 1972.

Kafka, Franz. "On Parables." In *The Complete Stories.* New York: Schocken, 1971.

Keller, Catherine. *Face of the Deep: A Theology of Becoming.* New York: Routledge, 2003.

Keller, Timothy. *The Prodigal God: Recovering the Heart of the Christian Faith.* New York: Penguin, 2008.

Kelsey, David H. *The Uses of Scripture in Recent Theology.* Philadelphia: Fortress, 1975.

Kempe, Margery. *The Book of Margery Kempe.* Translated by B. A. Windeatt. Harmondsworth, U.K.: Penguin, 1985.

Kissinger, Warren. *The Parables of Jesus: A History of Interpretation and Bibliography.* Metuchen, N.J.: Scarecrow, 1979.

Koester, Helmut. "σπλάγχνον." In vol. 7 of *Theological Dictionary of the New Testament*, 553–55. Grand Rapids: Eerdmans, 1995.

Kurath, Hans, Sherman McAllister Kuhn, and Robert E. Lewis, eds. *The Middle English Dictionary.* Ann Arbor: University of Michigan Press, 1954.

Lasko, Peter, and Nigel J. Morgan, eds. *Medieval Art in East Anglia 1300–1520.* Norwich, U.K.: Jarrold and Sons, 1973.

Lewis, Alan. *Between Cross and Resurrection: A Theology of Holy Saturday.* Grand Rapids: Eerdmans, 2003.

Lewis, C. S. "Bluspels and Flalansferes: A Semantic Nightmare." In *The Importance of Language*, edited by Max Black, 36–50. Englewood Cliffs, N.J.: Prentice Hall, 1963.

Lindbeck, George. "Barth and Textuality." *Theology Today* 43, no. 3 (1986): 361–76.

Lindemann, Walter. *Karl Barth und die Kritische Schriftauslegung.* Hamburg-Bergstedt: Herbert Reich Evangelischer Verlag, 1973.

Linnemann, Eta. *Parables of Jesus: Introduction and Exposition*. London: SPCK, 1966.

Locke, John. *Essay concerning Human Understanding*. London: William Tegg, 1849.

Lombard, Peter. *In Epistolam ad Romanos 8*. Patrologia Latina 191. Edited by Jacques-Paul Migne. Paris: Migne, 1844–1855.

Luther, Martin. *Commentary on Galatians*. Translated by Erasmus Middleton. Grand Rapids: Kregel Classics, 1979.

MacIntyre, Alasdair. *After Virtue*. Notre Dame, Ind.: University of Notre Dame Press, 2007.

Marion, Jean-Luc. *Being Given: Toward a Phenomenology of Givenness*. Translated by Jeffrey L. Kosky. Stanford: Stanford University Press, 2002.

———. *The Crossing of the Visible*. Translated by James K. A. Smith. Stanford: Stanford University Press, 2004.

———. *God without Being*. Translated by Thomas A. Carson. Chicago: University of Chicago Press, 1991.

———. *In Excess: Studies of Saturated Phenomena*. Translated by Robyn Horner and Vincent Berraud. New York: Fordham University Press, 2002.

———. *In the Self's Place: The Approach of Saint Augustine*. Translated by Jeffrey Kosky. Stanford: Stanford University Press, 2012.

Mathewes, Charles T. "Augustinian Anthropology: *Interior intimo meo*." *Journal of Religious Ethics* 27, no. 2 (1999): 195–221.

Maury, Pierre. *Erwählung und Glaube*. Theologische Studien 8. Zurich: EVZ, 1940.

McAfee Brown, Robert. "Scripture and Tradition in the Theology of Karl Barth." In *Thy Word Is Truth: Barth on Scripture*, edited by George Hunsinger, 3–19. Grand Rapids: Eerdmans, 2012.

McCormack, Bruce L. "The Doctrine of the Trinity after Barth: An Attempt to Reconstruct Barth's Doctrine in Light of His Later Christology." In *Trinitarian Theology after Barth*, edited by Myk Habets and Phillip Tolliday, 87–118. Eugene, Oreg.: Pickwick, 2021.

———. "Grace and Being: The Role of God's Gracious Election in Karl Barth's Theological Ontology." In *The Cambridge Companion to Karl Barth*, edited by John Webster. Cambridge: Cambridge University Press, 2000.

———. *Karl Barth's Critically Realistic Dialectical Theology: Its Genesis and Development 1909–1936*. New York: Oxford University Press, 1995.

———. *Orthodox and Modern: Studies in the Theology of Karl Barth*. Grand Rapids: Baker, 2008.

McEntire, Sandra J. "The Likeness of God and the Restoration of Humanity in Julian of Norwich's *Showings*." In *Julian of Norwich: A Book of Essays*, edited by Sandra J. McEntire, 3–33. New York: Garland, 1998.

McFague, Sallie. *Speaking in Parables: A Study in Metaphor and Theology*. Philadelphia: Fortress, 1975.

McGill, Kevin. *Julian of Norwich: Mystic or Visionary?* New York: Routledge, 2006.

McGinn, Bernard. *The Presence of God: A History of Western Christian Mysticism*. Vol. 1 of *The Foundations of Mysticism*. New York: Crossroad, 1991.

McGlasson, Paul. *Jesus and Judas: Biblical Exegesis in Barth.* American Academy of Religion Series. Atlanta: Scholars Press, 1991.

McKelway, Alexander J. "Perichoretic Possibilities in Barth's Doctrine of Male and Female." *Princeton Seminary Bulletin* 7, no. 3 (1986): 231–43.

Menken, Maarten J. J. "The Position of σπλαγχνίζεσθαι and σπλάγχνα in the Gospel of Luke." *Novum Testamentum* 30, no. 2 (1988): 107–14.

Merleau-Ponty, Maurice. *Le visible et l'invisible.* Edited by Claude Lefort. Paris: Gallimard, 1964. ET: *The Visible and the Invisible.* Translated by Alphonso Lingis. Evanston, Ill.: Northwestern University Press, 1968.

———. *Signs.* Translated by R. C. McCleary. Evanston, Ill.: Northwestern University Press, 1964.

Merton, Thomas. "The English Mystics." In *Mystics and Zen Masters,* 128–53. New York: Dell, 1961.

Migliore, Daniel L. "Commanding Grace: Karl Barth's Theological Ethics." In *Commanding Grace: Studies in Barth's Theological Ethics,* edited by Daniel L. Migliore. Grand Rapids: Eerdmans, 2010.

Mikkelsen, Hans Vium. *Reconciled Humanity: Karl Barth in Dialogue.* Grand Rapids: Eerdmans, 2010.

Molnar, Paul. *Divine Freedom and the Doctrine of the Immanent Trinity.* London: T&T Clark, 2002.

———. "The Obedience of the Son in the Theology of Karl Barth and Thomas F. Torrance." *Scottish Journal of Theology* 67, no. 1 (2014): 50–69.

———. "The Trinity, Election, and God's Ontological Freedom: A Response to Kevin Hector." *International Journal of Systematic Theology* 8, no. 3 (2006): 294–306.

Moltmann, Jürgen. "The Motherly Father: Is Trinitarian Patripassionism Replacing Theological Patriarchalism?" In *God as Father?* edited by Johannes-Baptist Metz and Edward Schillebeeckx, 51–56. Concilium 143. Edinburgh: T&T Clark, 1981.

Mowry, Lucetta. "Parable." In *The Interpreter's Dictionary of the Bible,* vol. 3, 649–55. Nashville, Tenn.: Abingdon, 1962.

Neusner, Jacob. "Types and Forms in Ancient Jewish Literature: Some Comparisons." *History of Religions* 11, no. 4 (1972): 354–90.

Neder, Adam. *Participation in Christ: An Entry into Karl Barth's "Church Dogmatics."* Louisville, Ky.: Westminster John Knox, 2009.

Nicholas of Lyra. *Postilla in Cantia Canticorum.* Patrologia Latina 113. Edited by Jacques-Paul Migne. Paris: Migne, 1844–1855.

Nietzsche, Friedrich. "Rhétorique et Langage." Translated by P. Lacoue-Labarthe and Jean-Luc Nancy. *Poétique* 5, Éditions du Seuil (1971): 99–142.

Nimmo, Paul. "Election and Evangelical Thinking." In *New Perspectives in Evangelical Theology: Engaging with God, Scripture, and the World,* edited by Tom Greggs. London: Routledge, 2010.

Nouwen, Henri. *The Return of the Prodigal Son: A Story of Homecoming.* New York: Doubleday, 1992.

Nuth, Joan. "Two Medieval Soteriologies: Anselm of Canterbury and Julian of Norwich." *Theological Studies* 53 (1992): 611–45.

————. *Wisdom's Daughter: The Theology of Julian of Norwich*. New York: Crossroad, 1991.

Nygren, Anders. *Agape and Eros*. Philadelphia: Westminster, 1953.

Oakes, Kenneth. "The Question of Nature and Grace in Karl Barth: Humanity as Creature and as Covenant Partner." *Modern Theology* 23, no. 4 (2007): 598–616.

Ocker, Christopher. "Scholastic Interpretation of the Bible." In *The Medieval through the Reformation Periods*, 254–79. Vol. 2 of *A History of Biblical Interpretation*, edited by Alan J. Hauser and Duane F. Watson. Grand Rapids: Eerdmans, 2009.

O'Connor, Flannery. "The Fiction Writer and His Country." In *Mystery and Manners: Occasional Prose*. New York: Farrar, Strauss, and Giroux, 1970.

Ong, Walter. *Orality and Literacy: The Technologizing of the Word*. London: Routledge, 1982.

Origen. *Origenes. Origenes Werke*. Vol. 10.1–2. Edited by Erich Klostermann. Leipzig: Hinrichs, 1935–1937.

Perrin, Norman. "Historical Criticism, Literary Criticism, and Hermeneutics: The Interpretation of the Parables of Jesus and the Gospel of Mark Today." *Journal of Religion* 52 (1972): 361–75.

————. *Jesus and the Language of the Kingdom: Symbol and Metaphor in New Testament Interpretation*. Philadelphia: Fortress, 1976.

————. *Rediscovering the Teaching of Jesus*. New York: Harper & Row, 1967.

————. *What Is Redaction Criticism?* Philadelphia: Fortress, 1969.

Peterson, Eugene. *Tell It Slant: A Conversation on the Language of Jesus in His Stories and Prayers*. Grand Rapids: Eerdmans, 2008.

Pitkin, Barbara. "John Calvin and the Interpretation of the Bible." In *The Medieval through the Reformation Periods*, 341–71. Vol. 2 of *A History of Biblical Interpretation*, edited by Alan J. Hauser and Duane F. Watson. Grand Rapids: Eerdmans, 2009.

Putnam, Hilary. "Lecture III." In *Meaning and the Moral Sciences*, 34–45. London: Routledge, 1978.

Richards, I. A. *The Philosophy of Rhetoric*. Oxford: Oxford University Press, 1936.

Riesenfeld, Harald. "The Parables in the Synoptic and the Johannine Traditions." *Svensk Exegetisck Årsbok* 25 (1960): 37–61.

Rilke, Rainer Maria. *Ahead of All Parting: The Selected Poetry and Prose of Rainer Maria Rilke*. Translated by Stephen Mitchell. New York: Modern Library, 1995.

Ricoeur, Paul. "Biblical Hermeneutics." *Semeia* 4 (1975): 29–148.

————. "Fatherhood: From Phantasm to Symbol." In *The Conflict of Interpretations: Essays in Hermeneutics*, translated by Don Ihde, 468–97. Evanston, Ill.: Northwestern University Press, 1974.

————. *Figuring the Sacred: Religion, Narrative and Imagination*. Philadelphia: Fortress, 1995.

————. *Interpretation Theory: Discourse and the Surplus of Meaning*. Fort Worth: Texas Christian University Press, 1976.

————. *The Rule of Metaphor: Multi-disciplinary Studies of the Creation of Meaning in Language*. Translated by Robert Czerny, Kathleen McLaughlin, and John Costello, S.J. London: Routledge & Kegan Paul, 1978.

———. *The Symbolism of Evil*. New York: Harper & Row, 1969.

———. *Time and Narrative*. Vol. 3. Translated by Kathleen Blamey and David Pellauer. Chicago: University of Chicago Press, 1990.

Robbins, Jill. *Prodigal Son / Elder Brother: Interpretation and Alterity in Augustine, Petrarch, Kafka, Levinas*. Chicago: University of Chicago Press, 1991.

Robinson, James M., and John B. Cobb Jr., eds. *The New Hermeneutic*. 2 vols. New York: Harper & Row, 1963–1964.

Robinson, Marilynne. "Further Thoughts on a Prodigal Son Who Cannot Come Home, on Loneliness and Grace: An Interview with Marilynne Robinson." By Rebecca Painter. *Christianity and Literature* 58, no. 3 (2009): 487–89.

Rogers, Eugene F., Jr. *Sexuality and the Christian Body: Their Way into the Triune God*. Oxford: Blackwell, 1999.

Ruether, Rosemary Radford. "The Female Nature of God: A Problem in Contemporary Religious Life." In *God as Father?* edited by Johannes-Baptist Metz and Edward Schillebeeckx, 61–66. Concilium 143. Edinburgh: T&T Clark, 1981.

———. *Sexism and Godtalk: Toward a Feminist Theology*. Boston: Beacon, 1993.

Sanders, E. P. *Jesus and Judaism*. Philadelphia: Fortress, 1985.

Savage, Anne, and Nicholas Watson. *Anchoritic Spirituality: "Ancrene Wisse" and Associated Works*. New York: Paulist, 1991.

Scanlon, Larry. *Narrative, Authority, and Power: The Medieval Exemplum and the Chaucerian Tradition*. Cambridge: Cambridge University Press, 2007.

Schweizer, Eduard. *The Good News according to Luke*. Translated by David E. Green. Atlanta: John Knox, 1984.

Scott, Bernard B. *Hear Then the Parable: A Commentary on the Parables of Jesus*. Minneapolis: Fortress, 1989.

Simmons, T. F., ed. *The Lay Folks Mass Book: The Manner of Hearing Mass, with Rubrics and Devotions for the People, in Four Texts, and Offices in English according to the Use of York, from Manuscripts of the Xth to the XVth Century*. London: N. Trubner, 1879.

Smend, Rudolf. "Nachkritische Schriftauslegung." In *Parrhesia: Karl Barth zum 80. Geburtstag am 10. Mai 1966*, edited by Eberhard Busch, Jürgen Fangmeier, and Maz Geiger, 215–37. Zurich: EVA, 1966.

Sokolowski, Robert. *Introduction to Phenomenology*. Cambridge: Cambridge University Press, 2000.

Sonderegger, Katherine. "Barth and Feminism." In *The Cambridge Companion to Karl Barth*, edited by John Webster, 258–72. Cambridge: Cambridge University Press, 2000.

Soskice, Janet Martin. *The Kindness of God: Metaphor, Gender, and Religious Language*. Oxford: Oxford University Press, 2007.

———. *Metaphor and Religious Language*. Oxford: Clarendon, 1987; Oxford University Press, 2002.

Spearing, A. C. Introduction to *Revelations of Divine Love*, translated by Elizabeth Spearing, vii–xxxiii. New York: Penguin, 1998.

———. "The Subtext of *Patience*: God as Mother and the Whale's Belly." *Journal of Medieval and Early Modern Studies* 29, no. 2 (1999): 293–323.

Springs, Jason. "Following at a Distance (Again): Gender, Equality, and Freedom in Karl Barth's Theological Anthropology." *Modern Theology* 28, no. 3 (2012): 446–77.

Staley, Lynn. "Julian of Norwich and the Later Fourteenth-Century Crisis of Authority." In *The Powers of the Holy: Religion, Politics, and Gender in Late Medieval English Culture*, edited by David Aers and Lynn Staley, 107–78. University Park: Pennsylvania State University Press, 1996.

Stein, Robert. *The Method and Message of Jesus' Teaching*. Louisville, Ky.: Westminster John Knox, 1994.

Stephenson, Lisa P. "Directed, Ordered, and Related: The Male and Female Interpersonal Relation in Karl Barth's *Church Dogmatics*." *Scottish Journal of Theology* 61, no. 4 (2008): 435–49.

Stern, David. "Jesus' Parables from the Perspective of Rabbinic Literature: The Example of the Wicked Husbandmen." In *Parable and Story in Judaism and Christianity*, edited by Clemens Thoma and Michael Wyschodgrod, 42–80. New York: Paulist, 1989.

Tannehill, Robert. *Sword of His Mouth*. Philadelphia: Fortress, 1975.

Tanner, Kathryn. *Economy of Grace*. Minneapolis: Fortress, 2005.

———. "Theology and the Plain Sense." In *Scriptural Authority and Narrative Interpretation*, edited by Garrett Green, 59–78. Philadelphia: Fortress, 1987.

Taylor, Barbara Brown. "The Parable of the Prodigal Son." Lenten Noon Day Preaching Series. Calvary Episcopal Church, Memphis, Tenn., March 5, 1999.

Tertullian. *Liber de Pudicitia VIII–IX*. Patrologia Latina 2. Edited by Jacques-Paul Migne. Paris: Migne, 1844–1855.

Thielicke, Helmut. *Das Bilderbuch Gottes: Reden über die Gleichnisse Jesu*. Stuttgart: Quell-Verlag, 1957.

Thiemann, Ronald F. *Revelation and Theology: The Gospel as Narrated Promise*. Notre Dame, Ind.: University of Notre Dame Press, 1985.

Thompson, John. *Christ in Perspective: Christological Perspectives in the Theology of Karl Barth*. Edinburgh: Saint Andrew Press, 1978.

Thompson, William. *Struggle for Theology's Soul: Contesting Scripture in Christology*. New York: Crossroad Herder, 1996.

Tissot, Yves. "Patristic Allegories of the Lukan Parable of the Two Sons." In *Exegesis: Problems of Method and Exercises in Reading*, edited by François Bovon and Grégoire Rouiller, translated by Donald G. Miller, 362–409. Pittsburgh: Pickwick, 1978.

Torrance, Thomas F. *The Christian Doctrine of God, One Being Three Persons*. London: T&T Clark, 2001.

Tranströmer, Tomas. *The Great Enigma: New Collected Poems*. Translated by Robin Fulton. New York: New Directions, 2006.

Tseng, Shao Kai. *Karl Barth's Infralapsarian Theology: Origins and Development 1920–1953*. Downers Grove, Ill.: IVP Academic, 2016.

Turner, Denys. *Julian of Norwich, Theologian*. New Haven: Yale University Press, 2011.

Uggla, Bengt Kristensson. *Kommunikation på bristningsgränsen*. Stockholm: Symposion, 1994.

Vendler, Helen. *Dickinson: Selected Poems and Commentaries*. Cambridge, Mass.: Harvard University Press, 2008.

Via, Dan O. *The Parables: Their Literary and Existential Dimension*. Philadelphia: Fortress, 1967.

Wakefield, Gordon S. "Anglican Spirituality." In *Post-Reformation and Modern*, vol. 3 of *Christian Spirituality*, edited by Louis Dupre and Don E. Saliers. New York: Crossroads, 1996.

Walsh, James, S.J. *The Revelations of Divine Love of Julian of Norwich*. London: Burns & Oakes, 1961.

Watson, Francis. "The Bible." In *The Cambridge Companion to Karl Barth*, edited by John Webster, 57–71. Cambridge: Cambridge University Press, 2000.

Watson, Nicholas. "The Middle English Mystics." In *The Cambridge History of Middle English Literature*, edited by David Wallace, 536–65. Cambridge: Cambridge University Press, 1999.

Webster, John. "Translator's Introduction." In *God's Being Is in Becoming: The Trinitarian Being of God in the Theology of Karl Barth; A Paraphrase*, by Eberhard Jüngel. London: T&T Clark, 2001.

Wellhausen, Julius. *Das Evangelium Lucae*. Berlin: G. Reimer, 1904.

Wheelwright, Philip. *The Burning Fountain: A Study in the Language of Symbolism*. Bloomington: Indiana University Press, 1968.

Wilder, Amos. *The Language of the Gospel: Early Christian Rhetoric*. New York: Harper & Row, 1964.

Wiles, M. F. "Early Exegesis of the Parables." *Scottish Journal of Theology* 11, no. 3 (1958): 287–301.

Wilkins, Eliza Gregory. *"Know Thyself" in Greek and Latin Literature*. Diss., University of Chicago Libraries, 1917.

William of St. Thierry. *The Golden Epistle: A Letter to the Brethren at Mon Dieu*. Translated by Theodore Berkeley, O.C.S.O. Vol. 4 of *The Words of William of St. Thierry*. Spencer, Mass.: Cistercian, 1971.

Windeatt, B. A. "Julian's Second Thoughts: The Long Text Tradition." In *A Companion to Julian of Norwich*, edited by Liz Herbert McAvoy, 101–15. Cambridge: D. S. Brewer, 2008.

Wright, N. T. *Jesus and the Victory of God*. Minneapolis: Fortress, 1996.

Wyatt, David. *Prodigal Sons: A Study in Authorship and Authority*. Baltimore: Johns Hopkins University Press, 1980.

Young, Brad. *The Parables: Jewish Tradition and Christian Interpretation*. Peabody, Mass.: Hendrickson, 1998.

Young, Francis. "Allegory and the Ethics of Reading." In *The Open Text: New Directions for Biblical Studies?* edited by Francis Watson, 103–20. London: SCM Press, 1993.

INDEX